DATE DUE

16.95

Ewa 12/90

RUSSELL

The Arguments of
the Philosophers

EDITOR: TED HONDERICH
Reader in Philosophy, University College London

The group of books of which this is one will include an
essentially analytic and critical account of each of the
considerable number of the great and the influential
philosophers. Each book will provide an ordered
exposition and an examination of the contentions and
doctrines of the philosopher in question. The group of
books taken together will comprise a contemporary
assessment and history of the entire course of
philosophical thought.

RUSSELL

R. M. Sainsbury

Department of Philosophy
Bedford College
University of London

Routledge & Kegan Paul
London, Boston and Henley

First published in 1979
by Routledge & Kegan Paul Ltd
39 Store Street, London WC1E 7DD,
Broadway House, Newtown Road,
Henley-on-Thames, Oxon RG9 1EN and
9 Park Street, Boston, Mass. 02108, USA
Set in 11 on 12 pt Baskerville
and printed and bound in Great Britain by
The Camelot Press Ltd, Southampton

British Library Cataloguing in Publication Data

Sainsbury, R. M.

Russell — (The arguments of the philosophers)
1 Russell, Bertrand, Earl Russell
I Title   II Series
192   B1649.R94   79-40367

ISBN 0 7100 0155 X

I heard the beat of the centaur's hoofs over the hard turf
As his dry and passionate talk devoured the afternoon.
'He is a charming man' – 'But after all what did he mean?' –
'His pointed ears. . . . He must be unbalanced.' –
'There was something he said that I might have challenged.'

T. S. Eliot: *Mr Apollinax* – a poem about Bertrand Russell

Errata : RUSSELL

xi	The dot should be square, not oblong, and much smaller: ▫.
xii	8 lines up: for the last 'α' read 'β'.
80	note 2: for '⊡' read '▫' and for '▫' read '⊡' throughout.
144	note 2: for 'section 4' read 'section 3'.
159	8 lines up: for 'on' read 'in'.
241	15 lines up: for "Russell'a" read "Russell's".
291	line 4: for 'φ' read 'ϕ'.
296	first displayed formula: delete second occurrence of '!'.
325	top of page: the occurrences of 'namable' should read 'nameable'.

Contents

CONTENTS

Preface

Understanding a philosophical doctrine stands close to seeing its strengths and weaknesses, how best it could be defended and how best attacked. I have tried, therefore, not merely to state Russell's philosophical doctrines, but also to appraise them: to determine, if possible, whether they are true, or at least what arguments tell in their favour, and what tell against them. Sometimes I have had to be content with less: the mere statement of an alternative to Russell's position. But even this may, I hope, promote understanding of Russell, for in showing what an upholder of a doctrine must refute, you make plainer the ground the doctrine occupies.

My concern is Russell's philosophy, not Russell. Thus, setting aside one or two remarks in the Introduction (which should be read only by those quite unacquainted with Russell's life), the sources and origins of Russell's doctrines and the doctrinal influences to which he was subject are of no concern, unless they affect our understanding or assessment of Russell's philosophy.

Understanding this philosophy is not impeded by the inaccessibility of his works. I have drawn only on his published writings, though there is unpublished material in the archives of McMaster University. Our understanding is, however, impeded by three things. One is the difficulty of the subject-matter, philosophy; but, of course, this is nothing special to Russell's philosophy. Another is the large number of different attacks he made at different times on the same problems. It may be useful to draw some of these together. The third is Russell's style. It is much vaunted for clarity, but this clarity is, in his technical philosophy, superficial, a matter of short words and short sentences rather than the delivery of a clear message. He makes the distinction himself:

> My mother-in-law, a famous and forceful religious leader, assured
> me that philosophy is only difficult because of the long words that it

uses. I confronted her with the following sentence from notes I had made that day: 'What *is* means is and therefore differs from *is*, for "*is* is" would be nonsense'. It cannot be said that it is long words that make this sentence difficult (*MPD* 63).

I have often found it hard to see what Russell means and how his doctrines are logically related. If my reader finds this task easier as a result of reading this book, it will have been worth writing.

I have confined myself to Russell's philosophy in the narrowest sense. Thus I have, without qualms, ignored his social and political writings at one extreme, and his mathematical ones at the other. Even within these limits, I have not been able to give a comprehensive treatment. I have left aside his work in moral philosophy, on the grounds that, in both its main phases, it is too derivative to justify a discussion of it, at the expense of dealing more fully with topics to which his contribution was more original: the first phase, represented by the admirable 'The Elements of Ethics' in *Philosophical Essays*, is, as Russell acknowledges, deeply indebted to Moore's *Principia Ethica*; the second phase, represented by *Human Society in Ethics and Politics*, is close to Hume's, with a dash of emotivism. Although I have not attempted to discuss any of Russell's work which lies clearly within mathematics, I have considered the philosophical aspects of his logicist programme, and in particular the philosophical rationale for his attempt to deal with the contradictions which, as he discovered, beset logic and semantics. There remain genuinely philosophical topics for which I have, with regret, not found space: for example, Russell's various theories of memory, and his account of desire and other psychological states in *The Analysis of Mind*.

Several people have read drafts of this book in part or whole, and I am very grateful for the large number of helpful comments I have received. I would like to mention in particular: J. C. B. Gosling, Christopher Kirwan, Colin Phillips and Michael Woods. I would also like to ˙thank Daniel Isaacson for discussing with me Russell's ramified theory of types. My greatest debt is to Martin Davies who provided me with a large number of extremely helpful comments on drafts of the greater part of the book, and I have also learnt much from several conversations with him.

Finally, I have two debts of a more institutional nature: to the Principal and Fellows of Brasenose College, Oxford, for electing me to a Radcliffe Lecturership from 1973–5, and thereby providing me with a stimulating environment in which to begin work on the book; and to the Chairman and other members of the Philosophy Department at the University of Essex, whose generosity and encouragement have been of great help in the completion of the writing.

Note on Symbolism

symbol used in this book	Russell's symbol in *PM*	approximate meaning
~	~	'not'. '~p' is true iff 'p' is false.
&	▬	'and'. 'p & q' is true iff both 'p' and 'q' are true. Russell also used '▬' as a scope-indicating device in place of parentheses.
v	v	'or'. 'p v q' is true iff 'p' is true or 'q' is true.
→	⊃	'if ... then——'. '$p \rightarrow q$' is true iff 'p' is false or 'q' is true.
↔	≡	'iff'. '$p \leftrightarrow q$' is true iff 'p' and 'q' have the same truth-value.
$(\forall x)$ ...	(x) ...	'all'. '$(\forall x)Fx$' is true iff everything is an F. E.g., '$(\forall x)$ (man $x \rightarrow$ mortal x)' is true iff 'man $x \rightarrow$ mortal x' is true of everything; i.e. iff everything is such that either it is not a man or it is mortal.
$(\exists x)$ ...	$(\exists x)$ ...	'some'. '$(\exists x)Fx$' is true iff at least one thing is an F. E.g., '$(\exists x)$ (man x & happy x)' is true iff 'man x & happy x' is true of something; i.e. iff something is both a man and happy.
$(\imath x)$ ...	$(\imath x)$	'the' (in the singular). See Chapter IV.

xi

symbol used in this book	Russell's symbol in *PM*	approximate meaning
$F\hat{x}$	$\varphi\hat{x}$	'the property of being F'. Russell uses the Greek letters 'φ', 'ψ' and 'χ' both as variables and schemata. I normally use these Greek letters as variables, and 'F', 'G' and 'H' as schemata.
$=$	$=$	'is the same as'. Thus, e.g., 'Tully $=$ Cicero' is true, for Tully is the same person as Cicero.
$\neq$	$\neq$	'is not the same as'. Thus 'Hume $\neq$ Kant' is true, for they were not the same person.
$\{\hat{x}(Fx)\}$	$\{\hat{x}(\varphi x)\}$	'the class of things that are F (φ)'. 'Has five members $\{\hat{x}(Fx)\}$' is true iff the class consisting of all and only the things that are F has five members; i.e. iff there are five Fs.
$\in$	$\in$	'is a member of'. 'Socrates $\in$ $\{\hat{x}(\text{man } x)\}$' is true iff Socrates is a member of the class of men.
$\notin$	$\notin$	'is not a member of'.
$\wedge$	$\wedge$	'the empty set', i.e. the set having no members. E.g., '$\{\hat{x}(\text{man } x \ \& \ \text{over-twenty-feet-tall } x)\} = \wedge$' is true, for there are no men over twenty feet tall. Classes are identical iff they have exactly the same members.
$\alpha \cup \beta$	$\alpha \cup \beta$	$\alpha \cup \beta = \{\hat{x}(x\in\alpha \text{ v } x\in\alpha)\}$
$\alpha \cap \beta$	$\alpha \cap \beta$	$\alpha \cap \beta = \{\hat{x}(x\in\alpha \ \& \ x\in\beta)\}$
$\alpha - \beta$	$\alpha - \beta$	$\alpha - \beta = \{\hat{x}(x\in\alpha \ \& \ x\notin\beta)\}$

I use 'class' and 'set' interchangeably. (These terms are used in axiomatic set theory to mark a sharp distinction.)

I use '$\vdash$' as an abbreviation for 'yields (by a proof)'. Russell also uses this sign (roughly to abbreviate 'the following is a theorem:'), which derives from Frege. I do not discuss Russell's usage.

Acknowledgments

The authors and publishers would like to thank the following for permission to reproduce copyright material: George Allen & Unwin Ltd, for numerous extracts from their editions of the works of Bertrand Russell; Cambridge University Press for extracts taken from their edition of Russell's *Principia Mathematica*; Faber & Faber Ltd, London and Harcourt Brace Jovanovich, Inc., New York, for lines from T. S. Eliot's 'Mr Appolinax' from his *Collected Poems 1909–1962*.

Abbreviations

I

Introduction:
Biographical Sketch

Russell's interest in philosophical problems began early. In his *Autobiography* (*A*) he recounts how, at the age of eleven (and thus in 1883 or 1884) his brother introduced him to Euclid: 'This was one of the great events of my life, as dazzling as first love' (*A* I 36). The future author of *The Principles of Mathematics* (*PofM*) demanded to know what grounds there were for accepting Euclid's axioms, and received the unsatisfying reply, 'If you don't accept them, we cannot go on.' 'The doubt as to the premises of mathematics which I felt at that moment remained with me, and determined the course of my subsequent work' (*A* I 36). He even claims that only his desire to know more mathematics prevented him from committing suicide while a schoolboy (*A* I 43); but it is possible that this retrospective explanation of his survival is unduly romantic (cf. *A* I 55, where he attributes it to concern for his people).

At about the age of fifteen his passionate interest in religion led him to consider a number of philosophical problems: freewill, materialism, the existence of God. These early meditations he recorded in a diary, from which interesting excerpts have been reprinted (*A* I 47–55; *My Philosophical Development* (*MPD*) 28–34). He kept the diary and its opinions secret, for fear of provoking the disapproval or ridicule of the relatives with whom he lived as a child.

Russell went up to Cambridge in 1890 as a scholar of Trinity College to read for a degree in mathematics. After a rather unhappy and lonely childhood 'Cambridge opened up to me a new world of infinite delight' (Schilpp 8). It was there that he first came across professional philosophers other than Mill, whom he had read shortly before going up. Whitehead, with whom Russell was to collaborate on *Principia Mathematica* (*PM*), was a Fellow and Lecturer at Trinity, and took an interest in Russell from the start, though it was some time before they became close friends. In his undergraduate years, the main philosophical influence upon Russell was that of McTaggart, a Hegelian who became a Fellow of Trinity in 1891 and was only half a dozen years Russell's senior. The mathematician James Ward and the philosopher and psychologist G. F. Stout had most to do with teaching Russell as an undergraduate (*MPD* 38). Ward was a Kantian, and from him, probably in about 1896, Russell received a copy of Frege's *Begriffsschrift*. Ward had not read it and had not supposed it to be of any value (*A* I 68). Russell himself claims not to have understood it until he had made some of its discoveries for himself some years later (*A* I 68). G. F. Stout was a Hegelian, who had a high opinion of Bradley's *Appearance and Reality* when it came out in 1893.

The prevailing atmosphere was thus Hegelian and idealist, and it is not surprising that Russell himself for a time accepted this sort of philosophy. He took his Mathematics Tripos in 1893 and was placed seventh Wrangler, and he stayed up for a further year to take the Moral Sciences Tripos in 1894, in which he was awarded a First with Distinction. It was during this year that he first occupied himself entirely with philosophy, and decided to devote his life to it (*The Philosophy of Bertrand Russell*, Schilpp 11).

An example of Russell's Hegelian philosophizings is the article 'On the Relations of Number and Quantity' which was published in 1896. Writing of it in 1959 he says:

> Although Couturat described this article as 'ce petit chef d'œuvre de dialectique subtile', it seems to me now nothing but unmitigated rubbish (*MPD* 41).

In 1895 Russell was elected to a Fellowship at Trinity, having submitted a dissertation on the foundations of geometry. This formed the basis of his *An Essay on the Foundations of Geometry*, which came out in 1897. After his election to the Fellowship, which carried no requirements of teaching or residence, he went to Berlin with his first wife, Alys Pearsall Smith, where, according to his later self, he planned

> to write a series of books in the philosophy of the sciences,
> growing gradually more concrete as I passed from mathematics to
> biology; I thought I would also write a series of books on social and
> political questions, growing gradually more abstract. At last I
> would achieve a Hegelian synthesis in an encyclopaedic work
> dealing equally with theory and practice. The scheme was inspired
> by Hegel . . . (Schilpp 11).

The first fruit of the scheme was *German Social Democracy* (1896). Despite the fact that not long afterwards Russell began 'to emerge

2

from the bath of German idealism in which [he] had been plunged by McTaggart and Stout' (*A* I 134), and thus to reject the notion of a Hegelian synthesis, his lifetime's work was to be scarcely less wide-ranging than he had hoped in his Hegelian scheme.

One of Russell's slightly younger contemporaries at Cambridge was G. E. Moore, of whose excellence Russell first became aware at meetings of The Society (*A* I 73), a group of dons and undergraduates who met to read and discuss papers on a wide variety of subjects. Russell attributes to Moore's influence his gradual emergence from the idealist bath (*A* I 134), but there already seems to have been a difference of emphasis in their interests. In these early days Russell was most interested in the monism which was associated with the sort of idealism then in vogue. According to Russell, this monism flowed from the erroneous belief that all propositions are of subject-predicate form, and he first attacked this belief in his *A Critical Exposition of the Philosophy of Leibniz* (*Leibniz* 1900). Moore, by contrast, though he certainly considered this issue, and, in his 'External and Internal Relations' arguably provides a clearer and more incisive criticism of the basis of monism than Russell ever achieved, none the less was in the early days more interested in the question of the relationship between experience and reality.

Russell speaks of his emergence from idealism as 'an intense excitement' (*A* I 135). Shortly afterwards occurred an event no less exciting, and which was to be a decisive turning point. This was the International Congress of Philosophy of July 1900, at which he met the Italian logician and mathematician Giuseppe Peano. After this point the main lines of Russell's philosophical interests are set, and it is only from this point that I offer any detailed discussion of his philosophy in this book.

Peano seemed to have done for arithmetic what Euclid had done for geometry: Peano's five axioms appeared to suffice for proving all arithmetical truths, and these axioms involve a small number of apparently non-logical notions, 'number', 'o' and 'successor'. Russell had for years been trying to analyse the fundamental notions of mathematics, and now he found his task greatly aided by Peano's work, both in virtue of Peano's reduction of the necessary arithmetical concepts, and in virtue of his notation which 'extended the region of mathematical precision backwards towards regions which had been given over to philosophical vagueness' (Schilpp 12).

On returning from the Congress Russell set to work to master Peano's notation and results, and to use them for his own purposes.

The time was one of intellectual intoxication. My sensations resembled those one has after climbing a mountain in a mist, when, on reaching the summit, the mist suddenly clears, and the country becomes visible for forty miles in every direction. . . . Suddenly, in the space of a few weeks, I discovered what appeared to be definitive answers to the problems which had baffled me for years (*A* I 145).

By the end of 1900 Russell had finished a draft of the work which embodied these results, *The Principles of Mathematics* (*PofM*).

The sense of triumph which Russell felt at the end of the nineteenth century did not survive far into the twentieth. For one thing he 'suddenly' realized that he no longer loved his wife, and this realization was followed by a period of great emotional unhappiness (*A* I 147ff.). For another thing, in the course of thinking about Cantor's work he discovered the contradiction now generally known as Russell's paradox. Although the contradiction infected his proposals in *PofM*, he none the less published that book without offering any finished solution to the difficulty, for he had soon realized that finding an adequate solution would be a lengthy task. In the end, he proposed the ramified theory of types, the first version of which appeared in 1908 in an article entitled 'Mathematical Logic as Based on the Theory of Types' (*ML*). It was developed and embodied in *PM* which Russell wrote in collaboration with Whitehead. This came out in 1910–13 (vol. I in 1910, vol. II in 1912, vol. III in 1913) and is generally reckoned to constitute Russell's most important contribution to logic, mathematics and the philosophy of mathematics.

Although Russell's main efforts in the first decade of the century were devoted to *PM* and associated topics, it is also notable for the first publication of his famous theory of descriptions in the article 'On Denoting' (*OD*, 1905). In *PofM* he had with some reservations held the view that each significant unit of language must correspond to some element of reality. The theory of descriptions showed that phrases like 'the golden mountain' are not, in that sense, significant units, but contribute in a different way to the meaning of sentences in which they occur. The theory of descriptions purports to show how such phrases can be 'analysed', in such a way that what, in the analysis, corresponds to the descriptive phrase, cannot be thought of as a 'significant unit'.

The doctrine is bound up with Russell's views about what exists, or more precisely with his views about what the meaningfulness of language forces us to admit exists. According to the theory of descriptions, the meaningfulness of 'the golden mountain' does not require the existence of the golden mountain. However, the Austrian philosopher Meinong was led by various considerations to hold that

4

there are such things as the golden mountain (though he admitted that they are non-existent) and many of Russell's views on this topic were developed as a criticism of Meinong. His main discussions of Meinong, essays of 1904, 1905 and 1907, are reprinted in Douglas Lackey's collection of essays by Russell, *Essays in Analysis* (*EA*).

The period from 1900 to 1910 was the most intellectually fertile phase of Russell's life. It began with the writing of the substantial *PofM* and ended with the completion of his contribution to the massive *PM*. In addition there are a dozen or so articles of considerable originality and importance: not only *OD* and *ML* already mentioned, but also a number of essays on logic and mathematics (see essays 7 to 14 in *EA*), and on truth and idealism (see essays 4 to 7 in *Philosophical Essays* (*PE*)). At the end of it, and in particular on account of *PM*, Russell felt intellectually weakened:

> my intellect never quite recovered from the strain. I have been ever since definitely less capable of dealing with difficult abstractions than I was before. This is part, though by no means the whole, of the reason for the change in the nature of my work (*A* I 153).

The change he refers to is his turning away from mathematics and the philosophy of mathematics and his increased interest in both active politics and political theory. He had in 1907 stood unsuccessfully for Parliament, as candidate for the National Union of Women's Suffrage Societies for Wimbledon. In 1910 he considered politics as a career, and tried to become adopted as Liberal candidate for Bedford. The local association, however, rejected him on the grounds of his confessed atheism. In the *Autobiography*, Russell says he looked upon the rejection as a lucky escape, since it enabled him to accept a Lecturership at Trinity College, Cambridge, which 'was much more attractive to me than politics' (*A* I 201).

In 1912 Russell published a short book called *The Problems of Philosophy* (*PP*), which gives a brief and usually lucid account of his philosophical views at that time. On the question of our knowledge of the external world he argues that our common-sense beliefs are justified by the fact that they explain the course of our experience. An important concern is with the distinction between knowledge by acquaintance and knowledge by description, which arises out of the theory of descriptions (though it does not entail this theory). You may know that the best man will win the fight without knowing who the best man is. In this case, Russell says, you have purely descriptive knowledge of who will win the fight and not knowledge by acquaintance (even if, in fact, you are acquainted with both contestants).

Not long afterwards, Russell adopted a very different account of the external world, which exemplifies his application to empirical material of the method of 'logical construction' that had proved so fruitful in mathematics. Russell had defined integers as classes of classes, and had accepted from his predecessors the definition of rationals as classes of integers and reals as classes of rationals. Classes in their turn were defined as certain kinds of property or 'propositional function', and these thus become the ultimate building blocks out of which first classes, then integers, then rationals, then reals were constructed by logical techniques. In 'The Relation of Sense-Data to Physics' (*RSP*, 1914) he applied this sort of technique to physical objects and physical space. The result is that physical objects are identified with complicated classes, whose constituents are sense-data. The same theory is propounded in *Our Knowledge of the External World* (*OKEW*), which contains the Lowell lectures that Russell delivered in Harvard in 1914. The theory has Russell's characteristic dash and originality, but the statement of it is rather sketchy.

Russell had been an imperialist during the Boer War, but an almost mystical experience in 1901, vividly described in the *Autobiography* (I 146), led to his conversion to pacifism, and in general to a certain loosening of the emotional side of his nature. As is plain from the letters he wrote to his first wife when she was his fiancée (*A* I 95–108), the youthful Russell could be self-important and priggish to a repulsive degree. In later life he seems completely to have overcome these characteristics, and one of the turning points is the moment just referrred to, when he was led to reject his anti-Boer imperialism. (Another favourable influence seems to have been Ottoline Morrell's teasing: see *A* I 205.) This is the origin of the pacifism which he displayed during the first world war, and which eventually led to his imprisonment.

The outbreak of the war was a great emotional shock to him, heightened by the enthusiasm for war he discovered in some of his friends, like Whitehead and Gilbert Murray. Much of his time during the war was devoted to writing about it, and the two most significant publications are *Principles of Social Reconstruction* (1916) and *Roads to Freedom* (1918).

His pacifist attitude led to his removal in 1915 from his Lecturership at Trinity (see G. H. Hardy's *Bertrand Russell and Trinity*), and to his imprisonment for six months in 1918 for having written that the US Army was accustomed to intimidating strikers. While in prison he wrote the splendid *Introduction to Mathematical Philosophy* (*IMP*), which sets out in a lucid and non-technical way the main ideas of *PM*.

Earlier that year, before his imprisonment, he gave a series of lectures entitled 'The Philosophy of Logical Atomism' (*PLA*). This contains a statement of his famous doctrine of logical atomism, an exhilarating amalgam of views involving epistemology, metaphysics and the philosophy of language. Despite the superficial inconsistencies, and the large number of loose ends, this is one of the most enjoyable of Russell's philosophical writings. The 'strain' of the first decade of the century, and of the writing of *PM* in particular, seems to have inflicted no permanent damage on Russell's ability to contribute to general philosophy.

After the war, the proportion of Russell's philosophical works relative to the rest of his literary output fell markedly, though his philosophical publications are more numerous than those of many professional philosophers who do nothing else. He married Dora Black in 1921 and his first child was born in that year. He had given away most of his money and now parenthood made it imperative to earn some (*A* II 151). The result was that 'Most of my work during these years [1921 to the mid-1930s] was popular, and was done in order to make money' (*A* II 152). For the same purpose he undertook several lecture tours in America. He prospered financially with his writing and lecturing, which was fortunate, since the school he founded in 1927 with his second wife, aiming to provide a less authoritarian education than was then generally available, made large losses. The best known of these popular books are *Marriage and Morals* (1929) and *The Conquest of Happiness* (1930). In their day they were thought scandalous. The liberal attitude to sex and marriage which both advocate (especially the former), and which was the cause of the scandal, is now the conventional morality, and this fact is a tribute to the success of the ideas Russell championed.

The Analysis of Mind (1921) is, in my opinion, one of his most interesting post-war philosophy books. The main theme is the attempt to defend a version of philosophical behaviourism, and the overall position is that of 'neutral monism', which Russell accepted, after many hesitations, in about 1919. According to this doctrine, there is no radical distinction between mind and matter, since both are constructions out of the same neutral stuff. Behaviourism was seen as strengthening this position, since, if correct, it would show that psychological concepts can be reduced to non-psychological ones.

The other main philosophical works in this period were the Introduction to the second edition of *PM* (*PM*$_2$), in which some substantial changes in the foundations of the system were proposed, principally in order to avoid the axiom of reducibility, with which Russell had long been dissatisfied; and *The Analysis of Matter* (*Matter*, 1927), in which Russell started to move away from the view that physical objects are logical constructions towards the position, reminiscent of *PP*, that they are the largely unknown causes of experience.

In 1936 Russell married Patricia Spence, and two years later went with her to America to take up an appointment as Visiting Professor at the University of Chicago, where he lectured on words and facts under a title he thought would impress an American audience: 'The Correlation between Oral and Somatic Motor Habits' (*A* II 217). In the following year he took up a similar appointment at the University of California at Los Angeles, and in 1939 he was invited to become Professor at the College of the City of New York. However, there was an outcry against the appointment, on the grounds of Russell's alleged immorality in his writing and his private life, and this ended in a suit brought against the Municipality of New York which resulted in Russell's appointment being revoked. He faced financial difficulties, but was saved by an appointment to the Barnes Foundation, a private Foundation mainly devoted to the teaching of history. It was in his lectures there that Russell began the historical work that was to become his best-known philosophical book, *A History of Western Philosophy* (1945), and also a major source of income. It is possible that the idea of writing such a book sprang from the need to give a historical twist to the lectures at the Barnes Foundation. His appointment lasted only two years, rather than the promised five, but Russell sued for wrongful dismissal and eventually received financial compensation.

In 1940 he gave the William James lectures at Harvard, and the material was published in the same year under the title *An Inquiry into Meaning and Truth* (*IMT*). There are many fresh and original ideas in this book, for example concerning what Russell called 'egocentric particulars': words like 'this' and 'I', whose reference depends on the context of their utterance. The overall organization, however, is rather loose, and sometimes the same topic seems to be treated in different ways on different occasions.

Russell returned to Trinity College, Cambridge, as a Fellow in 1944. While he was there he wrote his last major philosophical book, *Human Knowledge: Its Scope and Limits* (*HK*, 1948). This is notable for containing his only extended treatment of the problem of induction, a problem vital for knowledge yet one which in previous writings he had barely discussed, apart from the short but admirable chapter in *PP*.

Shortly after the second world war, Russell reached what he called 'the apogee of [his] respectability' (*A* III 31). In 1949 he was awarded the Order of Merit and elected to an Honorary Fellowship of the

British Academy, and in 1950 he was awarded the Nobel Prize for literature. His marriage with Patricia Spence had by then broken up, and he married Edith Finch in 1952. He wrote two polemical books on the dangers of nuclear war, *Common Sense and Nuclear Warfare* (1959) and *Has Man a Future?* (1961), and became President of the Campaign for Nuclear Disarmament in 1958. He was instrumental in instituting the Pugwash Conferences, at which distinguished scientists from many countries meet to discuss international problems, and the first of these was held in 1956. In 1962 he became President of the British Who Killed Kennedy Committee, in 1964 he established the Bertrand Russell Peace Foundation, and in 1967 he set up an International War Crimes Tribunal which, together with his book *War Crimes in Vietnam*, condemned the policy of the United States. He died in 1970.

The bibliography of Russell's writings given in Schilpp has 438 entries for the years 1895–1951. Even allowing for the repetition of material (for example, both an article and the book in which it is reprinted are included as separate entries), this is an amazing output. Even if we narrow the field to his purely philosophical works, he is still among the most prolific philosophers there have ever been. Moreover, he ranges widely, from the most abstruse aspects of the philosophy of logic to the most practical aspects of political and social philosophy.

Was Russell a great philosopher? The question has two parts, of which the first is: Was his philosophy great? Concerning this part of the question, I invite the reader to form, revise or confirm his own opinion on the basis of the account of Russell's philosophy that I give in the following chapters, bearing in mind that I have been able to discuss only the main themes. The second part of the question is: to what extent is Russell's philosophy his own, and to what extent did he borrow his ideas from others? This second part has to be answered, for one who presents a great philosophy that is wholly derived from others is not a great philosopher.

A rough answer to this second part is easy enough: there can be little dispute that Russell was an immensely original philosopher, and that he left his distinctive mark even on ideas first acquired from others. Still, one may want a more detailed answer. How much of his logicism is owed to Frege? How much of his atomism to Wittgenstein? How much of his theory of knowledge to Hume and, more generally, to the British empiricist tradition?

These questions are historical and of no essential *philosophical* significance. They require, therefore, no prominent position in what is essentially a philosophy book. I say this in justification of the very scanty answer I now proceed to offer, which consists mostly in stating the well-known historical facts, and these do not decide the present delicate questions of influence.

In his book on Frege, Dummett describes the discovery of the notation of quantifiers and variables for the expression of generality as the solution of 'the problem which had foiled the most penetrating minds that had given their attention to the subject' and 'on the resolution of which a vast further area of progress depended' (8–9). Frege published this discovery in his *Begriffsschrift* of 1879. We have seen that Russell possesssed a copy of this in about 1896. In *PofM* (Appendix A) Russell discusses some of Frege's writings, including this one, in some detail. The natural conclusion, therefore, is that Russell can get no credit for the idea of quantifiers and variables, and indeed the authors of *PM* acknowledge that 'In all questions of logical analysis, our chief debt is to Frege' (*viii*).

There is, however, some evidence against this straightforward judgment. For one thing, Russell claimed to have independently discovered most of what the *Begriffsschrift* contained (*A* I 68). For another, one can show that Russell was capable of reading Frege without understanding him. An example is Russell's discussion of 'all' and 'any' in *ML* (64–9). He acknowledges a debt to Frege, but it is unlikely that Frege would have welcomed the acknowledgment, for Russell presents a savagely garbled and confused version of an entirely lucid Fregean distinction. So even though Russell read Frege's account of quantification, it cannot be assumed that he derived his own from his reading.

A third piece of evidence is this: Russell's own first systematic exposition of the idea of quantifier and variable, in *OD*, is clumsy and, though perhaps not confused, certainly not elegant. Frege's account, for example in the *Begriffsschrift*, is superior. Moreover Russell, though normally generous or over-generous in the acknowledgment of intellectual debts, does not, in *OD*, mention Frege as a source of the idea of quantification. Perhaps, then, Russell really did coax the idea out of himself, rather than out of Frege.

On balance, however, it would be rash to attribute independent discovery to Russell. Reading Frege may have affected him in ways of which he was barely conscious, and in the course of which ideas became radically transformed. In this sort of speculation, we rather quickly reach the point at which what is and what is not a man's own becomes a distinction with which we can no longer operate.

As a final note on quantification, I mention the rather curious fact that in 'Whitehead and *Principia Mathematica*' Russell says: 'Whitehead contributed the treatment of apparent variables and the notation $(x).\varphi x$' (137). The fact is curious because Russell, normally so scrupulous, had previously published the treatment and the notation in *ML* without any acknowledgment to Whitehead. The moral is that even the statements of honest participants do not settle questions of influence.

The question of the originality of Russell's definition of number is scarcely more tractable. Frege has historical priority with his *Grundlagen* (1884). Russell claims that his discovery of the definition in 1900 was independent (*IMP* 11). It would, however, be desirable to know rather more about the composition of *PofM* since the Appendix A is obviously written in the light of a reading of Frege careful enough to have extracted the definition. Perhaps one day someone will think it worth while to investigate the Russell archives at McMaster University with a view to settling this question. (The investigation would be an utter waste of time from the point of view of the advancement of philosophy.)

As *PM* is generally thought to be one of Russell's greatest achievements, the reader may wish to know how much of it is due to Russell and how much to Whitehead. The wish must, I fear, remain largely unsatisfied. I have already mentioned the account Russell himself gives, and its overall conclusion is that, for most parts of the book, authorship can not be attributed to a single man (138). On the other hand, many of the fundamental ideas appeared earlier under Russell's name, without acknowledgment to Whitehead (as in *ML*; 'The Theory of Logical Types', which came out after *PM* in 1910, is under Russell's name alone and contains verbatim extracts from *PM*). Once again, the archives may yield a more detailed answer, but in the present state of knowledge it seems reasonable to pin on Russell anything in *PM* which is more or less the same as anything he published under his sole name, though this certainly does not exhaust his contribution.

In the preface to the first published version of *PLA* Russell claims that the lectures 'are very largely concerned with explaining certain ideas which I learnt from my friend and former pupil Ludwig Wittgenstein' (*PLA* 177). However, it is not at all easy to see which ideas these are. Russell's theories of names and descriptions, his view that existence is not a predicate, his principle of acquaintance: all these are found not only in *PLA* but also in earlier writings, like *OD*, *PM*, 'Knowledge by Acquaintance and Knowledge by Description' (*KAKD*), and *PP*, produced before he had met Wittgenstein, or at any rate, before there is any reason to think that Wittgenstein was a philosophical influence.[1] The talk of facts does indeed first occur only after Russell had met Wittgenstein. But much of what is involved here

---

[1] Russell dates the beginning of Wittgenstein's influence at 1914 (see *MPD* 112). Ayer implies that the two men met in 1912 (*Russell* 24).

is the logical form of propositions, and this idea, together with that of the possible divergence, in ordinary language, of logical and grammatical form, can be traced back to *OD*. (Wittgenstein attributes it to Russell in the *Tractatus* 4.0031.) It is quite likely that it was Wittgenstein who showed Russell the inadequacy of his *PP* theory of belief, an inadequacy Russell acknowledges in *PLA*, but this is not of fundamental importance. The overall point about Wittgenstein and logical atomism can be put like this: had Wittgenstein never existed, there would be nothing inexplicable about Russell's work being much as it in fact was.

On a different issue, Wittgenstein had a definite and more direct influence. Russell's introduction to PM_2, written in about 1923, was in part a direct response to Wittgenstein's criticisms, and it develops Wittgenstein's extensionalist thesis.

The influence of Hume and the British tradition of empiricism is evident in Russell's work, and it has been traced in detail by David Pears (*Russell*). An unkind, and rather exaggerated, view of Russell's epistemology is that it is Hume's in set-theoretic dress (compare Hume's 'fictions' with Russell's 'logical fictions' or 'logical constructions'). At least this much must be conceded: to a large extent Russell took over from the tradition the idea that empirical knowledge has its foundations in sensory experience, whereas philosophers today would regard this as a highly controversial position, requiring elaborate defence.

Other influences are, in mathematics, the works of Dedekind, Cantor and Peano, whose results Russell used and acknowledged, and, in general philosophy, G. E. Moore. We have already seen that Russell thought that he emerged more quickly from his idealist bath than he would have done without Moore's influence, and it is known that they spent a great deal of time discussing philosophy, especially in the last years of the last century. What owes most to Moore's published work is Russell's 1908 essay, 'The Elements of Ethics' (*PE*). For the rest, there is probably nothing more interesting to say than that each learnt a great deal from the other.

II

Meaning

Russell's logical atomism is a complex fusion of doctrines concerning the nature of language, of knowledge and of the world. Two vital elements concern meaning. One of these, which I call Russell's realist theory of meaning, is that the meaning of an expression is an entity: the entity for which the expression stands. The other, which I call Russell's principle of acquaintance, is that understanding the meaning of an expression involves acquaintance with that entity which is its meaning. These two doctrines form the main themes of this chapter, and I aim also to locate them within the overall position that Russell referred to as logical atomism.

Both the realist theory of meaning and the principle of acquaintance concern meaning: the one, its nature; the other, its epistemology. On the face of it, they complement each other perfectly. The first might, for example, facilitate an account of the way in which the meaning of a complete sentence depends systematically upon the meanings of the words that compose it; or of what makes the difference between significant words and mere noises, and how this difference can be extended to sequences of words. But it is plausible to maintain that meaning, as it bears on such problems as these, must in the end be connected with, and constrained by, the notion of understanding, of what it is to know or grasp an expression's meaning. The reason is that no more can justifiably be said about meaning than what is required to give an account of what it is for someone to speak and understand a language: the meaning of an expression does not exceed what is known in virtue of understanding it. This link with understanding appears to be guaranteed by the principle of acquaintance.

The main link with logical atomism is this: the atoms are the entities which, according to the realist theory, are meanings. The doctrine is that only these are 'genuine entities': everything else is a 'fiction' or 'construction'. The essence of the contrast is that the meaningfulness of language requires atoms to exist, but does not require other things to exist. There may be other things, and we may meaningfully assert that there are, but their existence is not required for language to be meaningful, and so it will not be shown by 'analysis'. The realist theory, unaided, will not yield this contrast, as I shall shortly show. Hence the need for some further doctrine, and in particular the principle of acquaintance. To complete the picture, we in addition need to be told the nature of the atoms, and how they can be grouped into 'molecules'.

Since the two doctrines with which I shall be concerned in this chapter are doctrines about meaning, one might be tempted to regard them as part of Russell's 'philosophy of language'. For the most part, I shall yield to this temptation, but doing so is not without danger, and requires justification. The reason is that Russell introduces the notion of a 'logically perfect' or 'ideal' language, and it is unclear to what extent his doctrines about meaning apply, or are intended to apply, to arbitrary languages, and to what extent they apply, or are intended to apply, only to the special case of a logically perfect language. If the intended application is of this last, restricted, sort, then the doctrines may not be intended to say anything about the nature of language in general, and cannot, therefore, be criticized for failing to do so.

For the most part, I shall adopt the working hypothesis that the intended application is of the wider and more ambitious sort. In short, I shall read his doctrines concerning meaning as part of a philosophy of language. This interpretation is supported by his claim, made in his Introduction to Wittgenstein's *Tractatus*, that

> the whole function of language is to have meaning, and it only
> fulfils this function as it approaches the ideal language which we
> postulate (x).

The idea seems to be that the truth of the doctrines is plainer when we consider a perfect language, though they are no less true of any language, even if less plainly true, provided the language really works.

You may say: Russell was not out to describe language but to change it. However, if the changes are to constitute a way of presenting a philosophy of language, they must be read as changes which make the accidents of language more plainly reflect its essence. They must be seen as superficial and notational, or, at most, as simplifications or idealizations, aimed to clear away some of the cluttering and inessential features of our actual languages in order to

14

lay bare their fundamental features. Failing this, the idea of a perfect language risks becoming nothing more than a waste bin for prejudices which have not survived confrontation with linguistic reality.

For Russell, the logical form of a sentence in ordinary language is its translation into the perfect language. The point of the last paragraph can thus be re-expressed: if doctrines about meaning in a perfect language are to constitute a philosophy of language, a sentence's logical form must preserve the essential features of its meaning.

There are two aspects to the perfection possessed by the perfect language. Russell calls them perfection in syntax and perfection in vocabulary. The perfect syntax is that of *PM*, in which the following constructions are permitted: atomic sentences and their truth-functional combinations, quantification of every finite order, applied to any of the foregoing constructions, and a term-forming operation called circumflexion, applied to open sentences. Further details are given in my 'Note on Symbolism' and in Chapter V. For the moment, it will do no harm to assume, what is literally false, that the perfect syntax is that of the classical predicate calculus with identity. As for the perfect vocabulary, the constraints vary with the different stages in the development of Russell's philosophy. In *PLA* (197–8) they are given as follows:

> In a logically perfect language, there will be one word and no more for every simple object, and everything that is not simple will be expressed by a combination of words, by a combination derived, of course, from the words for the simple things that enter in, one word for each simple component.

This somewhat obscure condition will be discussed at length during the course of this chapter, and so will Russell's reasons for subsequently abandoning it.

1   The realist theory of meaning

To the mind purged of philosophical preconceptions this theory has considerable initial appeal. The simplest thought is this: in using language, we talk *about* the world, so our words must somehow be tied to the world. Were there no such tie, they would be empty noises, signifying nothing. Words are symbols, and symbols are significant precisely in virtue of symbolizing something. 'The ordinary use of words is as a means of getting through to things' (*PLA* 246). *What* they symbolize, *what* they get through to: *that* is their meaning.

We might think of the most primitive species of communication as that which succeeds when the hearer's attention is drawn to some feature of the current scene: a hunter silently points out some half-concealed prey, or shouts to warn his companion of the presence of an enemy. In more sophisticated communication, the thought continues, the reality is not always before the eye. By using words, we bring it before the mind, but only in virtue of the fact that words go proxy for reality in a systematic way: to each word its slice of world. The words are like dabs of paint, the sentence like a picture. The picture as a whole can depict, correctly or incorrectly, only if each dab corresponds to some thing, or some kind of thing, in the world. Wittgenstein, in the *Tractatus*, made much of the analogy between picturing and meaning, but the general idea was present in Russell long before he met Wittgenstein. Of course, its ancestry can be traced back much further: to Hume, for example.

Russell's earliest and most explicit statement of the most extreme form of realist theory is in *PofM*: '*Words* all have meaning, in the simple sense that they are symbols which stand for something other than themselves' (*PofM* 47). This shows that Russell requires a correlation of each meaningful word with some entity. This is not to say that this entity is to be identified with the meaning of the word, as realism, as I have stated it, requires. For the moment, I shall make little of the difference between the doctrine that every word, in virtue of being meaningful, must be correlated with some entity, and the doctrine that the meaning of each meaningful word is some entity. However, Russell does in fact by implication hold the latter doctrine in *PofM*. For he says:

> The correctness of our philosophical analysis of a proposition may therefore be usefully checked by the exercise of assigning the meaning of each word in the sentence expressing the proposition (42).

An example of such a check is his assignment of A, difference, and B, respectively, to the words in 'A differs from B', on the hypothesis that 'differs' indicates difference. Since 'indicates' is a variant of 'stands for', the example amounts, in the presence of what has already been quoted, to the identification of a word's meaning with what it stands for. That the meaning of a word is an entity, rather than the fact of being correlated with an entity, is a view which Russell explicitly states in other writings (e.g., *IMP* 174) and, late in life, he attributed it to his earlier self. He had once believed, he writes in *MPD* (63), that 'if a word means something, there must be some thing that it means'.

The general word in *PofM* for what a word stands for, or indicates, is 'term'.

Among terms, it is possible to distinguish two kinds, which I call respectively *things* and *concepts*. The former are the terms indicated by proper names, the latter those indicated by all other words (44).

So every word indicates a term, and terms are 'in the world', are a part of reality. '. . . every term has being, i.e. *is* in some sense' (43). Admittedly, one needs to have an expansive conception of reality:

A man, a moment, a number, a class, a relation, a chimaera, or anything else that can be mentioned, is sure to be a term (43).

Points, instants, bits of matter, particular states of mind, and particular existents generally, are things in the above sense, and so are many terms which do not exist, for example, the points in a non-Euclidean space and the pseudo-existents of a novel (45).

Existence is to be regarded as a species of being: everything has being, but some things do not exist.

Russell's reason for abandoning the extreme form of realism adopted in *PofM* was that it was needlessly ontologically extravagant. The theory of descriptions offered a release from the supposed need for non-existent beings. However, I wish to focus on two more internal difficulties with the extreme version of the theory, difficulties to which Russell himself draws attention in *PofM*. One concerns the analysis of 'denoting phrases'. The other is the problem of the 'unity of the proposition'. Both these difficulties show that Russell did not suppose that once one has associated each word in a sentence with the term it indicates, one has said everything there is to be said about the sentence's meaning. In other words, the realist theory is thought to suggest only part of what a theory of meaning for a language must provide.

Proper names, adjectives, verbs and common nouns are said to 'indicate' the terms which are their meanings. But common nouns can enter into phrases which have an important further property, distinct from indicating: such phrases 'denote' (*PofM* 47). For example, taking the common noun 'man', one can form a denoting phrase by prefixing it with 'all', 'every', 'any', 'a', 'some' or 'the'. Denoting is unlike indicating for this reason: a proposition is *about* what the indicating expressions indicate, but is not *about* what the predicates in denoting phrases indicate. 'If I say "I met a man", the proposition is not about *a man*' (*PofM* 53). It is, of course, true that if I assert that I met a man, it does not follow that there is a man whom I thereby assert to have been met by me. But this is not Russell's point. He uses italicization to form expressions which apply to concepts. Thus his point here is that the proposition that I met a man is not about the concept: *a man*. By contrast, the proposition '*A* differs from

17

B' is about the concept of difference (among other things). Russell is drawing attention to the fact that denoting phrases, though they may occupy the same place in a sentence as does a proper name or a verbal noun (like 'killing') or an abstract singular expression (like 'humanity'), do not have the same semantic role. How, then, do denoting phrases function? After some discussion, Russell concludes that there is a single relation of denoting that holds between a denoting phrase and something in the world, and that what distinguishes the different kinds of denoting phrase are the different kinds of object to which they are related. 'The' is treated separately, but of the other phrases he concludes:

> There is, then, a definite something, different in each of the five cases, which must, in a sense, be an object, but is characterized as a set of terms combined in a certain way, which something is denoted by *all men, every man, any man, a man* or *some man*; and it is with this very paradoxical object that propositions are concerned in which the corresponding concept is used as denoting (*PofM* 62).

In other words, the common noun 'man' fixes the 'set of terms', the same set for each different denoting phrase into which 'man' enters, and the difference in meaning between the phrases is explained by the different objects into which the terms are combined.

The explanation is at its least successful, and the 'object' concerned all the more 'paradoxical', when the common noun fixes the 'set of terms' as the null set. For example, it is hard to see how one could explain the difference between 'all unicorns' and 'a unicorn' in terms of the first 'combining' unicorns in a way that the second does not, for there are no unicorns for either to combine. However, Russell tries to use the idea of combination to explain certain features of the interaction of the different denoting phrases. For example, 'An a is less than any b' differs in meaning from 'Some a is less than any b', and he suggests that the difference can be brought out by these paraphrases: 'Whatever b we take, there is an a which is less than it', and 'There is an a which is less than all the b's' (*PofM* 60). One might seem to detect, in such an explanation, an exploitation of the notion of difference of scope of 'a' relative to 'any'. But though no doubt such an explanation is available, there is no sign that Russell exploited it in any conscious fashion. Rather, for finite cases, he claims to show how the difference can be explained in terms of different denoted objects:

> *An a denotes a_1 or a_2 or . . . or denotes a_n, where *or* has the meaning that no one in particular must be taken, just as in *all a's* we must not take any one in particular. . . . Some a denotes a_1 or denotes a_2 or*

. . . denotes a_n, where it is not irrelevant which is taken, but on the contrary some one particular a must be taken (*PofM* 59).

These explanations, however, seem to me opaque.

Why this urge to attempt to explain meaning in terms of entities? We have seen that Russell applies the realist theory to single words, but he is evidently still to some extent influenced by it when he comes to consider denoting phrases, and he thus tends to look to objects. But why not associate 'man' with a single object, and each of 'all', 'every', 'any', 'a' and 'some' with a different object? Why, in other words, suppose that an object has to be found in terms of which the meaning of a phrase like 'all men' is to be explained? Russell has an explicit argument against treating 'all' and 'man' separately:

> If u be a class-concept, is the concept 'all u's' analyzable into two constituents, *all* and u, or is it a new concept, defined by a certain relation to u, and no more complex than u itself? . . . The word *all* has certainly some definite meaning, but it seems highly doubtful whether it means more than the indication of a relation. 'All men' and 'all numbers' have in common the fact that they both have a certain relation to a class-concept, namely to *man* and *number* respectively. But it is very difficult to isolate any further element of *all-ness* which both share. . . . It would seem, then, that 'all u's' is not validly analyzable into *all* and u, and that language, in this case as in some others, is a misleading guide (*PofM* 72–3).

The conclusion is highly implausible, for it seems to involve denying that 'all' is a semantic constituent of 'all us'. The argument seems to be that there is no plausible candidate for the entity which is the meaning of 'all', and hence analysis must apply to complete denoting phrases in which the word occurs, rather than to the word by itself. The implicit premise, if this interpretation is correct, is the implausible one that if there is no suitable entity, nothing can be said about the meaning of the word itself.

Whether or not a suitable entity can be found to be the meaning of 'all' depends on certain assumptions about the nature of a theory of meaning. One might say that the meaning of 'all' is a certain function, f, specified as follows: its arguments are functions, $g_1, g_2, \ldots$, from things to propositions, and its values are propositions, and $f(g_i)$ is true iff for every object x, $g_i(x)$ is true. There is plenty of scope for variations of detail in pursuance of a policy along the suggested lines. Why, then, did Russell hold that there was no suitable entity for the meaning of 'all'? The answer must be somewhat speculative, since Russell's assumptions concerning the nature of a theory of meaning are deeply buried, and unargued. Perhaps he was already under the spell of the principle of acquaintance, and subconsciously supposed that f would not be the kind of entity with which one could be acquainted. Or perhaps he felt that any suitable entity would be one which a proposition, expressed by a sentence containing 'all', is *about*, whereas the proposition that all men are mortal is certainly not about f. Or perhaps he felt that a suitable entity would be one which speakers who use the expression intend to pick out, yet users of 'all' do not intend to pick out f. These suggestions are, of course, not mutually exclusive.

This treatment of 'all', which is paralleled by the treatment of 'and' (72) and 'every', 'any', 'some', 'a' and 'the' (73), is already a partial retraction of the realist theory, for these words turn out not to have entities as their meanings. Later, Russell is to make this fully explicit: the realist theory is not to apply to the logical constants. Nor is it to apply to denoting phrases. The reason is that he explicitly abandons the dubious premise on which the argument just quoted relies, for he comes to hold that something can be said about the meanings of words whose meanings are not entities: they 'are not assumed to have any meaning in isolation, but a meaning is assigned to every proposition in which they occur' (*OD* 42). The result is that 'all' and 'u', in the phrase 'all u's', will be analysed separately in one sense, and in no sense will that phrase be treated as a single unit from the point of view of its meaning. The words in the phrase will be separately analysed in that 'u' will be assigned an entity as its meaning, and for 'all' a general rule will be given which determines the meaning of arbitrary sentences in which it occurs.

I turn now to the difficulty about the 'unity of the proposition'. As we have seen, Russell divides terms into two sorts, things and concepts, or, in his later terminology, particulars and universals. (For the sake of continuity with later discussions, it will be convenient to replace 'terms', in the *PofM* sense of the particulars and universals that are the meanings of words, by 'meaning-relata'. I shall use 'term' of expressions.) Concepts or universals are abstract objects, not perceptible by the senses, having no place in space or time, and neither suffering nor producing change: for example, justice, humanity, redness, triangularity. Particulars (things) partake of or instantiate universals, according to the following rule: where 'm' is a proper name of a particular, 'F' an adjective, common noun, or intransitive verb, and 'F-ness' the corresponding abstract singular expression, m instantiates F-ness iff m is F (or: is an F, or Fs). Russell argues, on grounds that we shall shortly examine, that F-ness is indicated both by 'F' as it occurs predicatively, and also by the corresponding abstract singular expression 'F-ness'.

The fact is, as we shall see, that *human* and *humanity* denote precisely the same concept (*PofM* 42).

(The use of 'denotes' seems to be a slip, since its official use makes it possible only for denoting phrases to denote.) The problem of how, in this case, to characterize the difference between the semantic roles of expressions used predicatively and corresponding abstract singular expressions is one facet of the problem of 'the unity of the proposition'. However, Russell uses this phrase with respect to a distinct facet.

What emerges from the Russellian analysis of the proposition '*A* differs from *B*' is a list of meaning-relata: *A*, difference, and *B*.

> Yet these constituents, thus placed side by side, do not reconstitute the proposition. The difference which occurs in the proposition actually relates *A* and *B*, whereas the difference after analysis is a notion which has no connection with *A* and *B*. . . . A proposition, in fact, is essentially a unity, and when analysis has destroyed the unity, no enumeration of constituents will restore the proposition. The verb, when used as a verb, embodies the unity of the proposition, and is thus distinguishable from the verb considered as a term, though I do not know how to give a precise account of the nature of the distinction (*PofM* 49–50).

Here the problem presents itself thus: what distinguishes a sentence, which expresses a proposition, from a mere list, which does not? In its most general form, the question perhaps is: how do sentences manage to *say* anything (as opposed merely to naming various entities)?

It is worth noting in this early exposition of the problem what was to be a persistent temptation. In characterizing the predicative role of the verb 'differs from' Russell says that the relation of difference 'actually relates *A* and *B*'. Now it is obvious that a verb may occur predicatively in a false sentence, whereas if the relation of difference actually relates *A* and *B* the sentence '*A* differs from *B*' must be true. Thus Russell is tempted to characterize the predicative role as one which suffices for truth, and plainly this is absurd. The temptation is responsible for his saying, in *PofM*, that in a 'logical' sense 'only true propositions are asserted' (49, cf. 504), and for his holding that what is puzzling about belief is how there can be *false* belief (*PLA* 225), and for his holding that while there are no compelling arguments against there being such entities as true propositions, he cannot bring himself to believe that there are false ones (*PLA* 223). Obviously the temptation must be resisted. It seems to arise from the merely verbal fact that when one is trying to explain the difference between a list and a proposition one may say that in the proposition a relation really 'hooks on' to its terms in a way that it does not in a list, and then one might re-express this by saying that the relation really relates its terms, and finally be tempted to construe this in such a way that a relation cannot really relate its terms unless the terms are thus related.

How serious a problem for Russell's realist theory is that of the 'unity of the proposition' in its various aspects? One might think to overcome part of it, at least, by assigning different sorts of entities to expressions occurring predicatively and their counterparts as they occur substantivally: thus, for example, to assign an entity of one kind to 'human', as it occurs in 'Socrates is human', and an entity of another kind to 'humanity' as it occurs in 'Socrates instantiates humanity'. Against this proposal, Russell argues that we shall still have to refer to the entity assigned to the predicatively used expression, in order to assign it, and when we thus refer we do so by a substantival expression. For example, suppose we assign *e* to 'human' (used predicatively). Then whatever we use to refer to *e* ('*e*', perhaps) will be a substantival expression. Hence our attempt to differentiate the different roles which expressions can play by assigning different kinds of entities fails. This, I believe, is the gist of Russell's argument in the first part of page 46 of *PofM* (cf. §483). It is, in effect, an exploitation of one consequence of the attempt to differentiate roles by entities, a consequence of the attempt to which Frege draws attention in his famous remark 'the concept *horse* is not a concept' ('On Concept and Object', 46). Unlike Frege,[1] Russell is unwilling to accept this consequence, and hence rejects the attempt to mark difference of semantic role in terms of different kind of meaning-relatum.

However, this leaves Russell with the problem of how one does mark the difference of semantic role. The problem remains unresolved in *PofM*, but it is worth mentioning here a much later attempt to resolve it. In *PLA* (205–6) and *LA* (337–8) Russell makes two suggestions, which he treats as intimately connected. One is that in understanding a predicative expression you have to know the form of atomic proposition in which it occurs. Thus to understand 'red' (in its predicative use), 'you have to know what is the meaning of saying that anything is red' (*PLA* 205). The other, associated suggestion is that 'A relation can never occur except as a relation, never as a subject' (*PLA* 206). This is, in effect, to say that there is no non-predicative use to be explained and that abstract singular terms can be eliminated without loss. The idea seems to be that the first

---

[1] According to Dummett (*Frege* 211ff.) Frege later proposed a way of avoiding this consequence. It rests on regarding 'ζ is a concept' as a pseudo-predicate.

suggestion provides a proper account of the meaning of predicates, and the second shows how this also suffices for the meaning of their corresponding abstract singular terms, since sentences containing the latter can be reduced to sentences containing the former.

The second suggestion seems quite unmotivated. There is a casual reference to the theory of types, though, as I argue in Chapter VIII, the theory provides no support that I can discover for the suggestion. On the contrary, Russell's formal language of *PM* creates the impression that there is a clear and irreducible contrast between a predicate and a corresponding abstract singular term, for the formal language contains a circumflexion operator, which converts expressions of the former kind into expressions of the latter kind, and the two kinds of expression play, at least superficially, distinct semantic roles.

If we combine Russell's second suggestion with his position in *PofM* the result is patently unsatisfactory. For there he holds that while 'Socrates is human' and 'Socrates possesses humanity' are equivalent, they do not express the same proposition (*PofM* 54). Granting this, it is hard to see how it can be denied that the role of 'human' differs from that of 'humanity', from which it follows that there is a distinctive contribution to be explained, and thus that it is wrong to suggest that there is no non-predicative use. Then, even if sentences like 'Socrates possesses humanity' are in some respect needless, in virtue of our possession of sentences like 'Socrates is human', this fact, in the presence of the concession that the sentences express different propositions, fails to show that there is no call for a distinct account of the employment of the abstract singular term.

Perhaps Russell is wrong to say, in *PofM*, that 'Socrates is human' and 'Socrates possesses humanity' express different propositions. If we were engaged in the radical interpretation of an alien language, that is, roughly, in an attempt to interpret an alien language based on no prior knowledge of it, it might well be that there was nothing to force us to choose one rather than the other sentence as translation of some alien sentence. If so, then we would have a reason for regarding our two sentences as expressing the same proposition, and so we would not have the ground given in the last paragraph for rejecting Russell's second suggestion, the suggestion that there is no such thing as a distinctive semantic role played by abstract singular terms but not by their corresponding predicates.

However, there are sentences containing abstract singular terms of which there is no obvious translation into sentences not containing such terms, for example, 'Patience is a virtue'. It is no good merely to *state* that these are illegitimate. A proper working out of the second of Russell's suggestions would require him to *show* that every intelligible sentence containing an abstract singular term is a mere notational variant of one free of such terms; and this he cannot be said to have done.

Russell's first suggestion, however, is surely essentially correct, and it identifies a fundamental inadequacy in the policy of assigning entities as meanings. The inadequacy is that whatever the nature of the entities assigned to subsentential expressions, no specification of entity-assignments can amount to a specification of what a sentence means. The reason has already been mentioned: a sentence is not a mere list, yet if you know only, for each of the words in a sentence, what entity the word stands for, you know no more than if the sentence were a list. You have not grasped the extra feature which makes a sentence something other than a list. Thus no mere assigning of entities can capture what must be grasped in understanding a sentence, and so no mere assigning of entities can constitute a complete theory of meaning, even if it is an essential part of such a theory. Russell shows awareness of this point when he says that understanding 'red' (as a predicate) involves knowing what it is to *say* that something is red. One could know that 'rust' has rust as its meaning-relatum, and that 'red' (or 'is red') has redness as its meaning-relatum, without knowing enough to know what 'Rust is red' says. It is this lacuna that Russell intends to fill by his suggestion that we must also know 'what is the meaning of saying that anything is red'. We have to know how 'red' or 'is red' contributes to the meaning of arbitrary sentences in which it occurs, and since sentences are not mere lists, what we need to know is not exhausted by knowing what is the meaning-relatum of the expression.

In the case of the logical constants we have seen that Russell thought that there was no call for the assignment of a meaning-relatum, and that instead what was needed was a statement of how they contribute to the meaning of arbitrary sentences. This statement he hopes to effect, in *OD*, by formulations along the following lines:

C (everything) means '$C(x)$ is always true' (*OD* 42).

The idea is that 'C(everything)' is an arbitrary sentence containing 'everything', and its meaning is equated with that of '$C(x)$ is always true', where 'always true' is taken as an 'ultimate and indefinable' predicate, applying to propositional functions, and '$C(x)$' is such a function, that is, roughly, something resulting from the proposition that C(everything) by replacing 'everything' by a variable, 'x'.

There are criticisms of detail to be made of this approach (see Chapter VIII below), but for the moment a general point suffices. It is reasonable to stipulate that a theory of meaning will state something knowledge of which would suffice for understanding the language to which it relates. However, one can know translational facts, facts to the effect that one sentence means the same as another, without knowing the meaning of the sentences involved in these facts. One could know that 'C(everything)' means the same as '$C(x)$ is always true' without knowing what either of these sentences means. Hence a theory which states only translational facts cannot be a theory of meaning.[2] To this extent, Russell's formulations in *OD* are defective, but they could, perhaps, be remedied. For example, the case quoted might be modified to:

'C(everything)' means that $C(x)$ is always true.

(Whether formulations of this kind could ever give a satisfactorily systematic account, genuinely yielding a statement of the contribution of the meaning of 'everything' to every sentence in which it occurs, is a different question. The reader is referred to Davidson's 'Truth and Meaning' and to the collection of essays edited by G. Evans and J. McDowell, for further discussion of these issues.)

To summarize the problem of the 'unity of the proposition': it arises from Russell's temptation to attempt the impossible task of providing a complete account of an expression's meaning in terms of its meaning-relatum. He shows that he is aware that this task is, at least in the case of general terms (e.g., verbs and adjectives), impossible: he argues that the difference between an expression used predicatively and the same or cognate expression used substantivally cannot be marked by a difference in the kind of meaning-relatum; he admits that knowing the meaning-relatum of a general term does not add up to understanding it; and finally he admits that knowing the meaning-relata of the words of a sentence does not add up to knowing what the sentence says. All this is found as early as *PofM*. In his later writing, he points the way to remedying the omissions left by the assignment of meaning-relata: one must also state how the expression contributes to what is said by an arbitrary sentence in which it occurs. In his discussion of some of the logical constants in *OD* he makes it clear that at least in these cases stating this is stating enough: there is no need for a meaning-relatum.

Despite the acknowledged shortcoming of realism as a complete theory of meaning, and despite the claimed inapplicability of it to logical constants, none the less it yields, in *PofM*, a rich ontology. We have already seen that included among meaning-relata are a whole gamut of non-existent entities. However, precisely because of this richness we have not yet the makings of Russell's logical atomism. Atomism essentially involves a contrast between the metaphysical

[2] The point is made with particular clarity in the editorial introduction of Evans and McDowell, *Truth and Meaning*.

status of 'atoms' and that of 'molecules'. The former are 'genuine entities', the latter 'constructions' or 'logical fictions'. There is no room for such a contrast in the *PofM* theory. To arrive at the contrast, an essential condition is the principle of acquaintance. For consider demonstratives like 'this' and 'that'. The author of *PofM* would undoubtedly assign these a meaning-relatum, varying with the occasion of use, just as the author of *PLA* was later to do. But nothing in *PofM* limits what can be demonstrated. In *PLA*, by contrast, only sense-data can be demonstrated, and these are the only particular atoms, for they are the only particulars with which we are acquainted. Other particulars, like physical objects, are 'molecules': logical constructions out of the bricks of sense-data. This is how the principle of acquaintance serves to generate the characteristic metaphysics of atomism.

2   The principle of acquaintance

The principle of acquaintance is stated clearly and definitely as early as *OD* (56), but its most famous and fullest statement is in the essay 'Knowledge by Acquaintance and Knowledge by Description' (1911), and the corresponding chapter in *PP* (1912). Thereafter, Russell consistently adhered to some form of the principle, though there were changes of mind about its consequences and its relations to other doctrines.

In *PP* the principle is formulated as follows:

> *Every proposition which we can understand must be composed wholly of constituents with which we are acquainted* (32; cf. *HK* 521, *MPD* 169).

Here we must regard a proposition as something distinct from a sentence: as what a sentence means or expresses. The identity of a proposition is partly but not wholly determined by the meaning-relata of those words in the sentence which have meaning-relata. These meaning-relata Russell refers to as the 'constituents' of the proposition.[3]

It is easy to see why the series of meaning-relata does not add up to the proposition. Since the logical constants like 'not' do not have meaning-relata, the series of meaning-relata corresponding to 'Socrates is not wise' is the same as that corresponding to 'Socrates is wise', but the two sentences express different propositions.

[3] Although Russell says that there are constituents of propositions, it seems that by the time of *PP* he did not believe that there are propositions (*PP* 72). (Colin Phillips drew my attention to this point.) This is a verbal oddity but not an inconsistency: 'constituent of a proposition' can be regarded as unstructured, and equivalent to 'meaning-relatum'.

The principle of acquaintance presupposes the realist theory of meaning, for it is within this theory that the notion of a constituent or meaning-relatum is embedded. As we shall see, there is also a relation of dependence running in the opposite direction.

Russell does not think that we are acquainted with unicornity or with Pegasus. How, then, can he square the principle of acquaintance with the fact that we understand such propositions as that Pegasus was a flying horse or that unicorns have a single horn? He holds that there are only two ways in which one can come to grasp the meaning of singular terms ('Pegasus' might be supposed to be an example) and general terms (like 'unicorn'): one way involves acquaintance, the other involves a verbal definition or 'analysis'. The second method depends on the first, since the definition must be in terms whose meaning we grasp through acquaintance or whose meaning we know thanks to a definition whose meaning we know thanks to . . . acquaintance. We can understand propositions expressed by sentences like 'Pegasus was a flying horse' or 'Unicorns have a single horn' thanks to knowing definitions of 'Pegasus' and 'unicorn', definitions which in the end run back to words whose meaning we have learnt by acquaintance. Thus replacing the words in a sentence by words each of whose meaning is such that learning it involves acquaintance is part of what is involved in 'analysing' the sentence. When we end up with a fully analysed sentence, one all of whose words admit no further analysis, it is easy to read off the constituents of the proposition the original sentence expressed: they are the meaning-relata of the singular and general terms of the corresponding fully analysed sentence. So it would be a mistake to hold that the principle of acquaintance says that in order to grasp the meaning of a singular or general term you must be acquainted with its meaning-relatum. Rather, the principle says that this applies only to unanalysable singular or general terms. It is implied that there are, and indeed must be, unanalysable expressions in any language, or at least in any language that can be understood, and that all analysable singular and general terms can be defined thanks to the unanalysable ones (though of course the logical constants will be used in the definitions). This last condition may be summarized thus: the unanalysable expressions provide an adequate definitional base.

It is important to realize that the doctrine that the meaning of a singular or general term can be learnt only by a method involving acquaintance or else by a definition ultimately in terms learnt through acquaintance does not entail that there are any unanalysable expressions. All that is entailed is that there must be some expressions whose meaning is learnt through acquaintance, and this falls short of the claim that there are some expressions whose meaning must be so learnt. There might be, so to speak, more than one way in to a circle of interdefinable expressions. Let us suppose that one takes '. . . is parent of ——' as a primitive predicate, i.e. one of which there is no definition. Then no doubt one would be able to define '. . . is child of ——' as '—— is parent of . . .'. But if one had taken '. . . is child of——' as primitive one could have defined '. . . is parent of——' in terms of it. It might even be true that one *must* take either 'parent of' or 'child of' as primitive. But it does not follow that it holds either of 'parent of' or 'child of' that *it* must be taken as primitive, and so it certainly does not follow that either is an unanalysable expression, i.e., one whose meaning must be learnt through acquaintance.

However, Russell's principle of acquaintance commits him to the doctrine that there are unanalysable expressions. This commitment is found in the form of a general statement in one of his later works. In *IMT* he says that 'there must be object-words' (66) and that 'The meaning of an object-word can only be learnt by hearing it frequently pronounced in the presence of the object' (64). Being in the presence of the object involves being acquainted with it in some sense (though not, admittedly, in the sense he would earlier have insisted on). Hence object-words are, in effect, unanalysable expressions, and their existence is deemed necessary. (It is worth pointing out that there is some suggestion in *IMT* of a drawing back from the commitment: see, e.g., the original definition of 'object-word' on page 23. The relativization to persons on page 66 also threatens the commitment.)

In the earlier period, say at the time of *PP* or even as late as *PLA* or *LA*, one does not find a clear and general statement of the commitment, though it is manifest in examples:

> To understand a name you must be acquainted with the particular of which it is the name (*PLA* 205).

> You cannot understand the meaning of the word 'red' except through seeing red things (*PLA* 194).

Russell is in danger of being misunderstood: he does not mean that one can know the meaning of names like 'Aristotle' and 'de Gaulle' only through being acquainted with their bearers. The principle applies only to unanalysable names, or as Russell called them 'logically proper names', and he at this time held that most of what ordinarily pass as names are not logically proper names. This issue is taken up later, and especially in the next chapter.

Just as the remark about names must be understood as restricted to unanalysable ones, so one must not extend the remark about 'red' to analysable predicates like 'unicorn'.

One can explain why we do not find a perfectly clear and general formulation of the principle of acquaintance in *PLA*. In these lectures one can disentangle two quite different doctrines of logical atomism, which Russell confused. One doctrine is that the atoms are the meaning-relata of unanalysable expressions, and the other is that the atoms are simple objects. He is able to confuse these different doctrines, which he later distinguished, because, no doubt under the influence of Wittgenstein, he supposed that, necessarily, an expression is unanalysable iff it stands for a simple object. The result is that he is led into a deviant usage of 'simple' as applied to expressions. In the standard usage, an expression is simple iff its meaning is not determined by the meaning of its meaningful proper parts (if it has any). In Russell's deviant usage, a 'simple' expression is one which stands for a simple object. In virtue of the Wittgensteinian equivalence just noted, this makes every 'simple' expression unanalysable. (I shall use 'simple' only in the standard way.) Now it is trivial that, if there is to be a language, there must be simple expressions, for these are what compose any complex expression. But it is far from trivial that there must be 'simple' (i.e. unanalysable) expressions. Russell's deviant use of 'simple', I suggest, helps to blind him to the controversial nature of the principle of acquaintance, and hence makes him feel a general statement of the need for unanalysable expressions to be needless.

The relationship between unanalysable expressions and simple objects will be discussed in the next section. Now I must return to the principle of acquaintance, interpreted as the doctrine that there must be unanalysable expressions, and that these form an adequate definitional base. So far, this doctrine has retained a very general form, since nothing has been said about what constitutes acquaintance. This must now be remedied. I shall start by giving an account of some of Russell's views about the connection between acquaintance and knowledge; and then I shall say what are the sorts of object with which he thought we could be acquainted.

Russell distinguishes between knowledge by acquaintance and knowledge by description. (The distinction can be detected as early as *PofM* (63) but the main expositions are *KAKD*, and *PP* ch 5.) Explaining this contrast involves first explaining a different one: that between knowledge of things and knowledge of truths.

The schema 'A knows . . .' can be completed in two grammatically distinct ways: by a 'direct object' like 'London', or by a 'that'-clause like 'that London is the capital of England'. The first species of completion typically expresses knowledge of things, the second knowledge of truths. It will be convenient to distinguish two verbs, 'to thing-know' and 'to truth-know'. (In *PP* (23) Russell suggests that the distinction is already roughly marked in French and German, by the

contrasting pairs 'savoir' and 'connaître' and 'wissen' and 'kennen'.)
Thing-knowledge is extensional in a way that truth-knowledge is not.
If A thing-knows x, and $x=y$, it follows that A thing-knows y, whereas
if A truth-knows that x is F, and $x=y$, it does not follow that A truth-
knows that y is F. Knowledge by acquaintance is a species of thing-
knowledge (PP 25).

At first sight, there is another species of thing-knowledge:
knowledge by description (PP 25). Such knowledge is expressed by
filling the blank in the schema 'A thing-knows . . .' by a definite
description, i.e. a phrase of the form 'the so-and-so'. However,
Russell holds that 'A thing-knows the so-and-so' will be true only if A
truth-knows some proposition of the form 'a is the so-and-so', where
a is something with which he is acquainted (PP 29, $KAKD$ 156). Failing
this, A has 'merely descriptive' knowledge, which is a species of truth-
knowledge: what A knows is merely that the so-and-so exists, and this
is merely the truth-knowledge that there is exactly one thing with the
property so-and-so.

A proposition involved in a case of truth-knowledge may, if it is
expressed by a sentence containing a description, be understood, and
even known, without the person who believes it being acquainted
with the object the description describes. Thus one can understand
the proposition that the first Chancellor of the German Empire was
an astute diplomatist without being acquainted with Bismarck. In
other words, descriptions do not introduce constituents of
propositions. They have no meaning-relata. (The theory of
descriptions is discussed at greater length in Chapter IV.) Only
acquaintance 'brings the object itself before the mind' ($KAKD$ 166).
Thus all thing-knowledge involves acquaintance. When a proposition
is fully analysed, the only particular things with which one must be
acquainted to understand it will be the meaning-relata of the
unanalysable names.

The main contrast of the last paragraph deserves more emphasis. It
applies as much to belief as knowledge. A sentence of the form 'A
believes that the F is G' does not, at least on one reading, entail that A
has any belief concerning the F. For example (cf. PP 30–1), A may
believe that the most long-lived of men was more than eighty years
old at death, but there may at no time be an object in the world of
which it is true to say: this is the man concerning whom A believes he
was more than eighty years old at death. By contrast, where A judges
that *this* is red, there is an object, namely *this*, concerning which A
judges. ('This' is a Russellian example of an unanalysable name. See
Chapter III.) We can express the contrast as that between general
belief and singular belief, and it can be defined as follows. Let us call a
sentence which follows 'that' in a sentence which begins 'A believes

that . . .' the 'believed-sentence'. When a singular term, a name or a definite description or a demonstrative or demonstrative phrase, say '*t*', occurs in the believed-sentence, the belief is singular (with respect to the object denoted by '*t*') iff '*A* believes that . . . *t* . . .' entails '*A* believes, concerning *t*, that . . . it . . .'. The position occupied by '*t*' in a sentence of this latter kind is what Quine has called 'referentially transparent' (*Word and Object*, 144: he borrows the term 'transparent' from *PM* 665): '*A* believes, concerning *t*, that . . . it . . .', together with '*t*=*s*' entails '*A* believes, concerning *s*, that . . . it . . .'. It follows from Russell's account of acquaintance, and is emphasized by him as a separate issue (*PP* ch 12), that all singular beliefs concern objects with which we are acquainted.

Thus in general Russell's conception of acquaintance requires that only objects with which we are acquainted can be objects of singular knowledge or belief, or of any other singular propositional attitude. It remains to state what he thinks these objects are. In *PP* (28) he maintains that the only particulars with which we are acquainted are our sense-data, our particular mental states, and, possibly, our selves, and that the only universals with which we are acquainted are those having particular instances with which we are acquainted, and on the basis of which we abstract to the universal itself. His reasons for holding this position are given in Chapter VI.

The consequences of this construal of acquaintance for the extent of our linguistic understanding are dramatic. For one thing, it follows that most of our ordinary expressions are analysable. There can be no unanalysable names of physical objects like tables, for none of these is, Russell claims, a sense-datum. Nor, for exactly the same reason, can there be any unanalysable predicates holding only of physical objects. Hence every name of a physical object, and every predicate of physical objects, must be analysable in terms of names and predicates which hold of sense-data. Hence none of our ordinary names is unanalysable names of physical objects like tables, for none of these is, physical objects like men, towns, and places. Likewise, rather few of the most commonly used predicates are unanalysable, since most of them do not hold of sense-data. (Exceptions, or apparent exceptions, include words for sensory qualities: 'red', 'hot', 'sweet', etc.) Russell accepts this consequence of his construal of acquaintance, and offers two different methods of analysing physical object words. From *RSP* (1914) until approximately the early 1920s, he held that physical objects are sets, ultimately composed of sense-data, and that this fact gives rise to a corresponding phenomenalistic analysis of words for physical objects. Subsequently, with some hesitation in *Matter* but more boldly in *HK*, he reverted to the method he had, somewhat unexplicitly, adopted in *PP* and which I shall call the noumenalistic analysis: physical object expressions are to be defined using the pattern '. . . causes such-and-such sense-data'. Thus, for example, as a first, and in detail plainly inadequate attempt, 'London' might be defined as 'whatever causes oblong red moving sense-data and white-domed sense-data and river-with-lifting-bridge-like sense-data'; or, in suitable circumstances, 'whatever causes precisely the sense-data I am now having'. The possibility of such an account presupposes, from Russell's point of view, that 'causes' is either further analysable into expressions which hold of sense-data, or else itself holds of some (pairs of) sense-data.

It is worth stressing that although both phenomenalistic and noumenalistic patterns of analysis may with propriety be referred to as 'sense-datum analyses', the latter carries, or at least may with further precisification carry, ontological implications different from those of the former. If physical objects are sets of sense-data, they cannot exist unless sense-data do. By contrast, unless it is part of the essence of physical objects that they at some time cause some appropriate sense-data, they could have existed even if sense-data had not. One can take a step towards ensuring this possibility by making the pattern of noumenalistic definition 'whatever *in fact* causes such-and-such sense-data'.

I shall assume for convenience of exposition that the only available patterns of analysis, consistent with Russell's principle of acquaintance, are the two he himself explicitly considers, the phenomenalistic and the noumenalistic. In these terms, one can state a startling further apparent consequence of the principle of acquaintance as follows: each one of us, in learning the meaning of our non-sense-datum expressions, has used a phenomenalistic or a noumenalistic analysis. For example, we cannot have learnt what 'table' means by acquaintance with tables, for no table is a sense-datum, so we must have learnt an analysis or definition of 'table' in terms of sense-data.

This consequence is obviously historically false. No one ever told us in infancy a sense-datum analysis of 'table', nor do most of us think we could state one, yet we understand the word 'table'. How could Russell have advanced a theory with such an absurd consequence?

The absurdity of the consequence lends support to the suggestion that Russell did not assert, or at any rate did not need to assert, anything entailing it. The doctrine that there are unanalysable expressions and that these form an adequate definitional base does not entail that analysable expressions are learnt through *explicit* knowledge of their definitions in terms of unanalysable expressions. It only entails that any analysable expression's meaning *could* be grasped in this way. Perhaps this weaker point is all Russell needs to justify his optimism about the possibility of providing sense-datum analyses of all physical object words.

There is an interesting analogy here with Hume's position in the *Treatise*. He *said* that every simple idea derives from a corresponding impression (Bk I, Pt I, Sc 1), yet he himself provided a counter-example to this assertion: given a series of shades of blue, suitably ordered, but with one shade missing, one could form an idea of the missing shade without this idea originating in a corresponding impression, despite the fact that such an idea would be a simple one. None the less he calmly invites us to ignore the counter-example and stick to the assertion, which is destined to play an absolutely fundamental role. To explain this curious behaviour, one can point out that Hume needs, not the strong principle he states, but the weaker one that for every simple idea one could have a corresponding impression. The missing shade of blue is no counter-example to the weaker principle, and Hume treats it lightly, perhaps, in virtue of his subconscious realization that he did not need the strong principle it refutes. (I owe to John Foster the observation that Hume needs only the weaker principle.)

However the case may be with Hume, it would be a mistake to think that a weakening as substantial as this would be a correct interpretation of Russell. There are many passages which suggest that he holds that when one uses an analysable expression, its analysis is in one's mind. Thus in the discussion of our use of 'Bismarck', which must be an analysable name since we are not acquainted with Bismarck, Russell suggests that some description of Bismarck must be in our mind when we use the word (*PP* 30, *KAKD* 157; cf. *PLA* 201). The suggestion, in other words, is that it is not enough that some analysis be available, it is in addition necessary that we be *aware* of the analysis, in some sense sufficient to make the analysed believed-sentence a closer representation of our thought than the believed-sentence prior to analysis. Russell's general view seems to be that we must in some sense be aware of what it is that we believe and thus of the analyses of analysable expressions in sentences we would use to state our beliefs. This does not add up to the claim that this analytic knowledge must be what mediated our grasp of analysable expressions, but it exceeds the claim that it is possible for us to learn the meaning of analysable expressions through definitions ultimately resting on unanalysable ones. This last weak claim does not imply that we actually have any (conscious) knowledge of the analysis, whereas Russell's position is that, in some sense, we do. So even if Russell can avoid the falsehood that we have learnt analysable expressions through coming to know analysis-stating propositions, he cannot avoid the falsehood that we are in some sense aware of the analysis of those analysable expressions which we understand.

A distinct criticism of Russell's principle of acquaintance concerns another consequence: that every language, or at any rate every humanly learnable language, is such that all its physical object expressions are definable in terms of sense-data expressions. To attack Russell's principle from this direction would require one to show the falsehood of both phenomenalism and 'noumenalism' (the latter being the doctrine that, for every learnable language, its non-sense-data expressions permit noumenalistic analysis into sense-data expressions). This task is one that I shall not here undertake in any detail. However, I believe it can be accomplished, and I shall give some brief indications of methods.

Russell's own phenomenalistic analyses are based on viewing physical objects as sets of sets of . . . sense-data, and I shall mention two lines of argument that can be brought against this position. One is to consider Cartesian scepticism, which is founded on the proposition, of which I give some defence in Chapter VI, section 2, that it is logically possible that any kind of series of sense-data should exist, even if no physical objects do. The other is grounded in the suggestion, which I amplify in Chapter VII, section 5, that the concept of an enduring thing is not captured by the concept of any sort of set. The reason is, roughly, that a set has all its members essentially, whereas some enduring things have some of their properties accidentally.

A line of attack against noumenalistic analyses is this. Suppose that you are in fact in full view of an object, say a table. You might consider defining the predicate '. . . is a table' as '. . . causes my current sense-data'. However, this is unsatisfactory, since you will want to allow for there being other tables than the one causing your current sense-data. You might therefore consider the definition '. . . causes sense-data similar to my current sense-data'. But this is also unsatisfactory, since something other than a table, say your nervous system or the evil genius, may cause in you sense-data as similar as you like to your present sense-data. The latter objection applies if you instead try to give a purely qualitative, as opposed to demonstrative, account of the nature of the relevant sense-data. The best move for the defender of the possibility of noumenalistic analysis seems to be to suggest that the proper definition is: '. . . resembles the cause of my current sense-data'. (Resemblance is reflexive.) But resembles in what respect? Nothing else resembles the present table in causing your present sense-data, but a non-table, say the evil genius, may resemble it in causing exactly similar sense-data. One wishes, of course, to offer some non-sense-datum characterization of the kind of resemblance, but this the noumenalist cannot allow. I can envisage various further turns in the argument, but the critic of noumenalism can, I think, always find an objection of essentially the kind presented here.

As we have seen, Russell held that we can have singular beliefs only concerning objects with which we are acquainted. This runs counter to our strong intuition that we have singular beliefs, indeed singular knowledge, concerning physical objects. I would not want to suggest that our views about the nature of our singular beliefs are bound to be correct. But one whose philosophy entails that we are all mistaken about what singular beliefs we have owes us an explanation. (The atheist can offer an explanation – correct or incorrect – of why the theist mistakenly supposes he has singular beliefs concerning God.) Perhaps it will be said that we mistakenly think we have singular beliefs concerning physical objects because we easily make the mistake of thinking that we are acquainted with them, our inference to them from sense-data being so smooth and rapid. This suggestion presupposes that we in fact intuitively believe that the objects of singular belief extend no further than acquaintance. However, we do not intuitively believe this. Even in the relatively generous everyday use of 'acquaintance', we ordinarily believe that, for example, we are not acquainted with Aristotle, yet we also believe we have singular beliefs concerning him. Thus the proposed explanation fails.

A phenomenalist might offer a different account of wherein lies the error of our views concerning the nature of our singular beliefs. He might say that it is about their content that we err, not about their singularity. We take ourselves to have singular beliefs concerning mind-independent physical objects, but this is because we have not appreciated the difficulties that attend any such conception. The truth is, the suggestion continues, that these beliefs concern sets of sense-data, and not mind-independent entities.

It is worth emphasizing that this reply is not open to Russell, in his phenomenalist period. The reason is that the sets of sense-data which, on his view at that time, reconstruct physical objects, are not allowed to be objects of acquaintance. Indeed it is doubtful whether his view can consistently permit acquaintance with any set. But it certainly cannot permit acquaintance with whatever set corresponds, in the phenomenalistic reconstruction, to, for example, Troy. The reason is that, though sets are defined in terms of properties, and though some properties are objects of acquaintance, they are so only if they hold of some sense-data we have experienced. This last condition will certainly not be satisfied by whatever property has as its extension just the sense-data that go to constitute Troy. Thus a Russellian position requires the rejection of the view that a belief that seems to be one concerning Troy is really singular, but he offers no explanation of how we come to believe, mistakenly on his view, that some such beliefs *are* singular.

There are, therefore, two kinds of ground for doubting the correctness of Russell's principle of acquaintance. One is that it entails that every learnable language is phenomenalistic or noumenalistic, but there are reasons for doubting whether English has either property. The other is that, so long as we hold constant the relationship between the principle of acquaintance and singular belief, the principle entails that we are gravely, and apparently inexplicably, mistaken about what singular beliefs we have. I find these grounds for doubt decisive, and therefore I reject the principle. I cannot pretend that my brief remarks in this chapter constitute a *refutation* of the principle. However, I think that I have said enough to show that the principle is doubtful, and thus to show that it would in any case be well to adopt the following maxim in expounding and criticizing Russell's philosophy: wherever possible, attempt to defend Russell's doctrines independently of the principle of acquaintance. In what follows I go further than the maxim, for I rely on the falsehood of the principle. Anyone who thinks this goes too far is invited to reconstrue the offending passages merely as an application of the maxim just mentioned.

It may be felt that Russell's principle has its heart in the right place, but is distorted by his narrow view of what counts as acquaintance. Broaden what counts as an object of acquaintance, it may be said, and all the foregoing doubts will disappear. I have some sympathy with this suggestion, but before I discuss it I shall consider the relationship between Russell's principle and the realist theory of meaning.

We have already seen that we need something like the principle of acquaintance in order to generate the characteristic metaphysics of atomism. The reason is that if the realist theory applies to every word one has no room for the characteristic atomist contrast between 'genuine entities', that is atoms, and 'constructed entities' or 'logical fictions', as Russell calls them; molecules, so to speak. In the presence of the principle of acquaintance, however, the realist theory is restricted simply to unanalysable expressions. Hence we need not find a meaning-relatum for 'Pegasus' or 'unicorn'. Pegasus and unicornity turn out to be logical fictions. The only atoms are meaning-relata, and the only meaning-relata attach to unanalysable expressions. Hence the realist theory in its post-*PofM* form, restricted to unanalysable expressions, requires the principle of acquaintance, in terms of which unanalysability is characterized. Conversely, the principle of acquaintance requires the realist theory, for the entities with which acquaintance is required are meaning-relata, and the notion of a meaning-relatum has application only if the realist theory is at least partly true.

One might be tempted to suppose that there is a further, and more direct, connection running from the realist theory to the principle of acquaintance. If, as the realist theory in its rough form maintains, the meaning of a word 't' is the thing t, then, one might argue, it follows that knowing the meaning of 't' must be a matter of knowing t. But knowing t is a case of thing-knowledge, as the form of expression reveals, and, according to Russell, all thing-knowledge requires acquaintance with the relevant thing. Hence knowing the meaning of 't' requires acquaintance with t.

One reason for being suspicious of this argument is that it looks as if it could as well lead to the plainly false conclusion that acquaintance is sufficient for understanding. (A sentence in *PLA* makes acquaintance a sufficient condition – 'in order to understand a name for a particular, the only thing necessary is to be acquainted with that particular' (202) – but this must be regarded as a slip of the pen. Cf. the further requirement on page 205: 'To understand a name you must be acquainted with the particular of which it is a name, and you must know that it is the name of that particular.') That acquaintance is insufficient for understanding is shown by the fact that Russell was (surely rightly) happy to allow that non-language-using animals are acquainted with particulars. Even if only language-using animals can abstract, and thus be acquainted with universals, acquaintance with universals is none the less insufficient for understanding general terms. It is not the case that anyone who understands one language understands all languages, and for any non-pantoglot there will be universals with which he is acquainted but to which there correspond terms he does not understand.

The argument which attempts to extract the principle of acquaintance from the realist theory is valid only if it is correct to treat a sentence of the form 'A knows the meaning of "t"' as expressing a relation between a person and an entity, that is, as expressing thing-knowledge. Otherwise it is not legitimate to apply the identity 'the meaning of "t" $=t$'. But what had to be proved was precisely that knowing the meaning of 't' is thing-knowledge. Hence the argument is unconvincing. In any case, as we saw in the last paragraph, its conclusion is false. Knowing the meaning of a word is neither thing-knowledge nor need it be truth-knowledge. (*What* truth is it truth-knowledge of?) Rather, to know the meaning of a word is to possess a practical ability, the ability to use it correctly.

I turn now to the suggestion that Russell's principle of acquaintance can be so weakened as to make it true. The aim is to cling to the idea that understanding a name (predicate) requires what one might call 'epistemic contact' with the bearer of the name (respectively, with something in the extension of the predicate), while leaving open the possibility that the range of this relation is far more extensive than that of Russell's principle of acquaintance.

In more detail, I suggest we consider replacing Russell's principle of acquaintance by the *epistemic principle*: applied to names, this is that a man A can understand a name for an object, a, only if there is an epistemic causal chain running from some event in the history of a to some event in the history of A (cf. Evans, 'The Causal Theory of Names'); applied to predicates it is that a man A can understand an undefined predicate 'F' only if there is an epistemic causal chain running from an event in the history of some F to some event in the history of A.

I take the notion of a causal chain for granted, but that of an epistemic causal chain requires some elucidation. Consider the following pair of cases. In the normal case, you press the appropriate buttons on your pocket calculator in order to discover what the eighth power of two is, and the number 256 appears. You believe that $2^8 = 256$, this belief is true, justified, and counts as knowledge. Now imagine an unusual case in which, unbeknownst to you, the calculator has a fault in virtue of which it will always display the number 256 whatever buttons are pressed. Again, you insert the sum $2^8 = ?$, and the number 256 appears. As a result, you believe that $2^8 = 256$, your belief is true, justified (we can make belief in the accuracy of the calculator as justified as desired, since the fault may have developed only the second before you effected the computation), but it is not, I submit, a case of knowledge. The reason lies in the fact that the calculator is defective, and so in general lies in some feature of the causal chain leading to the formation of your belief. We shall say: it is not an *epistemic* causal chain. This illustrates the difference between epistemic and non-epistemic causal chains, though I do not know how to give a general characterization of the distinction. I presume that one must make room for the intuitive notion that we have epistemic contact with physical objects, even ones which, like Troy, ceased to exist long ago. A very long causal chain may none the less be epistemic.

Abstract objects, future objects, and Hume's missing shade of blue show that either the epistemic principle requires some modification, or that common-sense metaphysics must be radically revised (e.g., so as to eliminate objects lacking causal powers). But let us set aside problems of this nature, in order to determine whether the causal principle, modified if need be, could serve as a suitable replacement for Russell's principle of acquaintance.

The answer is that it could not, since it is incapable of producing the contrast, which Russell's principle of acquaintance yields, between 'atoms' (the objects of acquaintance) and 'molecules' (everything else). The reason is that Russell's candidates for being molecules, those things which cannot be named and cannot comprise the extension of an unanalysable predicate, include things which may none the less be connected to us by an epistemic causal chain. In general, what lies beyond acquaintance does not thereby lie beyond knowledge. Even if we are not acquainted with physical objects, we may still have knowledge of them, albeit 'inferential' knowledge. In saying this, I do not simply fly in the face of Russell's epistemology, for he too for the most part allows knowledge of things which lie beyond acquaintance.

This last point requires two qualifications. The first concerns Russell's notion of singular knowledge. Sometimes Russell allows that we can have knowledge concerning objects which one knows merely by description (see, e.g., *KAKD* 156), and if we follow this loose usage we can without qualms report Russell as allowing that we can have knowledge of things with which we are not, and cannot be, acquainted. However, a stricter usage can also be detected, according to which the objects of possible singular knowledge, and indeed of possible singular propositional attitudes in general, are precisely the objects of acquaintance. In this usage, we cannot properly report Russell as allowing knowledge *of* things which lie beyond acquaintance. However, there can be no separating a finished theory of singular propositional attitudes from a finished theory of names: an object can be named by a man iff it can be the object of some singular propositional attitude of his, so any necessary condition for understanding a name, like the epistemic principle, will have to be matched by an analogous necessary condition for having a singular propositional attitude concerning some object. Hence in weakening the principle of acquaintance to the epistemic principle we must also weaken the conditions for singular knowledge, allowing this, too, to extend beyond acquaintance. A thoroughgoing adoption of the epistemic principle must involve a wider view of the objects of singular knowledge, and so cannot reinstate Russell's vital distinction between 'atoms' and 'molecules'.

The second qualification is this: in Russell's phenomenalistic period he held that the entities which lie beyond acquaintance are classes, and classes have no causal powers. But so far from this offering hope of putting the epistemic principle to the same use as the principle of acquaintance, such abstract objects provide *prima facie* counter-examples to all causal theories in this area, including the epistemic principle.

I shall conclude with some remarks about privacy, a subject which raises questions closely connected with the foregoing. In *PLA* Russell writes, referring to a logically perfect language:

> as regards its vocabulary, [it] would be very largely private to one speaker. That is to say, all the names that it would use would be private to that speaker and could not enter into the language of another speaker (198).

Philosophers who have been influenced by Wittgenstein's so-called 'private language argument' would doubtless seize on this feature of Russell's principle of acquaintance, above all others, as a target for their criticism. A language, *L*, is private to a speaker, *A*, iff necessarily no one other than *A* can understand *L*. If Russell's perfect language is meant to reveal the essential features of language in general, and if it is a private language, and if, as Wittgenstein is said to have argued in *Philosophical Investigations*, there could be no such thing as a private language, things look black for Russell's philosophy of language.

The first point I shall make is that Russell's official position does not commit him to the privacy of the perfect language. However, the official position is untenable, and once it is corrected the commitment returns.

Officially, the privacy Russell has in mind is something contingent. It consists in the supposed fact that, contingently, no two people are acquainted with the same sense-datum:

> there is absolutely nothing that is seen by two minds
> simultaneously. When we say that two people see the same thing,
> we always find that, owing to difference of point of view, there are
> differences, however slight, between their immediate sensible
> objects. (I am here assuming the validity of testimony . . .) (*OKEW*
> 95; cf. *NA* 156).

Thus according to Russell's official position the most that could follow is that it is a contingent truth that no one understands another's language, and this does not conflict with the conclusion of the private language argument (as I have interpreted it).

However, 'sense-datum' is subject to a type/token confusion, and once this is clarified it will be seen that Russell's official position is untenable. When I look out of my window today I have a fresh token of the very type of sense-datum of which I had a distinct token yesterday. Since sense-datum tokens are individuated, in part, in terms of who experiences them, it is a necessary truth that no sense-datum token is experienced by two people. On the other hand, it is in fact true that tokens of the same sense-datum type are sensed by several people. If a sense-datum type had to be maximally detailed and include the whole content of the sensory field, so that two tokens of the same type would be indistinguishable, then we might have to think hard before coming up with a realistic example to prove the point for the visual case. (Perhaps two people in different but indistinguishable hotel rooms watching the same television programme provides a case.) However, Russell characterizes a sense-datum as 'such a part of the whole as might be singled out by attention' (*RSP* 109). Plainly there will be endless instances of people experiencing (different tokens of) the same (type of) sense-datum, by this standard.

The upshot is that Russell was wrong to hold that sense-data are, contingently, never co-experienced: for sense-data types are commonly co-experienced and, necessarily, sense-data tokens never are. In the presence of the principle of acquaintance, this leads at once to the possibility of private languages: one need only introduce a name for a sense-datum (token) which one has experienced.

Since we have already agreed to reject the principle of acquaintance, there seems little point in embarking on the lengthy investigation, embroiled in questions of Wittgensteinian exegesis, that would be required to determine the correctness or otherwise of the conclusion of the private language argument. Instead, I shall conclude this section by stressing that if the principle of acquaintance is replaced by the epistemic principle, we are not led to the possibility of a private language. The reason is, simply, that the fact that one does not experience another's sense-datum does not mean that there is not an epistemic causal chain running from it to oneself. When Russell, in the recent quotation from *OKEW*, allows that he relies on testimony in order to find out about the sense-data of others, his claim relies on there being such epistemic causal chains. This granted, the epistemic principle is consistent with the possibility of one's mastering another's names for his sense-data.

3 Simplicity

This section has two connected themes. One concerns the simplicity of expressions, and how the relationship between simple and complex expressions affects Russell's realist theory of meaning. The other theme, closely connected, concerns the simplicity of objects, and how Russell at one time thought that in a perfect language simple expressions would have simple objects as their meaning-relata.

An expression is complex iff its meaning is wholly determined by the meaning of its proper parts, in such a way that knowledge of the meaning of the parts, together with knowledge of modes of combination, suffices for knowledge of the meaning of the whole. An expression is simple iff it is not complex. For example, 'Russell' is a simple expression, for although it contains meaningful proper parts like 'sell', these do not determine its meaning. By contrast, a phrase like 'the most prolific philosopher of the century' is complex, for we can work out what it means if we know what the parts 'the', 'most', 'prolific', and so on, mean. Not every expression that is written as more than one word in English is complex, for example 'take in', in the sense of 'deceive'. Arguably, some expressions that are written as single words in English are complex: 'foresee' and 'handkerchief' are putative examples.

Russell stresses the importance of the distinction between simple and complex expressions to our understanding of language. We can understand complex expressions in virtue of our understanding of their simple proper parts. Thus:

> You can understand a proposition when you understand the words
> of which it is composed, even though you never heard the
> proposition before. That seems a very humble property, but it is a
> property that marks it as complex (*PLA* 193).

Complexity is what enables us to know the meaning of each of the infinitely many sentences of our language, on the strength of a merely finite amount of learning.[4] Thus:

> When you know the vocabulary, grammar, and syntax of a
> language, you can understand a proposition in that language even
> though you never heard it before (*PLA* 193).

We could imagine a realist theory of meaning in which the general feature of the relationship between simple and complex expressions is mirrored in the meaning-relata. Such a theory will assign meaning-relata to simple expressions in such a way that a meaning-relatum for any complex expression is determined. This mirrors the determination of the meaning of the complex by the meaning of its simple parts. A realist theory of this kind is found, for example, for a language rather like English, in M. J. Cresswell's book, *Logics and Languages*. Russell's realist theory, however, is not of this kind, and this raises an important difficulty.

Three factors conspire to lead Russell to deny that complex expressions have meaning-relata. They are: (*i*) his refusal to assign meaning-relata to the logical constants; (*ii*) the problem of vacuity; (*iii*) his distrust of propositions. Let us for the moment pretend that all complex expressions are either atomic sentences (i.e. sentences containing nothing save an n-ary predicate and n names) or else expressions containing an occurrence of a logical constant, and we shall see these factors at work. In *PLA* (197) Russell denies that the

4 This is spelled out in Davidson's 'Action and Reaction'.

logical constants 'such words as "or", "not", "if", "then"', have meaning-relata. Now compare the simple expression 'married' with the complex expression 'unmarried', and assume that 'un' is a logical constant. Within Russell's framework, the only candidate for being the meaning-relatum of 'unmarried' is the very entity, namely marriedness, which he would assign as meaning-relatum to 'married'. So if 'unmarried' has a meaning-relatum, it has the same meaning-relatum as 'married'. So if the meaning-relatum is to come at all close to the meaning, 'unmarried' has no meaning-relatum.

It may be objected at this point that Russell has already confessed, in his acknowledgment of the problem of the unity of the proposition, that the meaning-relatum of predicative expressions falls short of their meaning, yet this was not enough to destroy his realist theory. Why, then, should the present problem lead to the denial of meaning-relata to complexes containing logical constants? Why not just admit that here, too, the meaning-relatum falls short of the meaning?

The present case, however, is much more serious than the previous one. What was missing before, the ingredient whose absence allowed the problem of the unity of the proposition to arise, seemed to be some one feature which, if added to the assignments of meaning-relata, would yield everything that was desired. In the present case, however, there is no one ingredient that is missing, for there is no limit to the degree of complexity with which logical constants can occur in a complex expression. Russell is therefore surely right to conclude that if, in his form of realist theory, assignment of meaning-relata is to come close to specification of meaning, he must deny meaning-relata to expressions containing logical constants.

The meaning-relatum is intended to be what an expression 'stands for'. But what does a complex expression like 'the King of France in 1978' stand for? Nothing. So it cannot have a meaning-relatum, within Russell's framework. (It might have a meaning-relatum within a very different framework. For example, its meaning-relatum might be a certain function f from properties to propositions such that for any property F, $f(F)$ is true iff there is exactly one King of France in 1978 and he has F.) In short, complex expressions may be vacuous and so cannot have meaning-relata.

The fact that logical constants are not assigned meaning-relata already shows that Russell cannot satisfactorily assign meaning-relata to whole sentences. (For example, 'John is married' and 'John is not married' would have the same meaning-relatum, if any.) Nor are there any tempting new directions in which to look for meaning-relata. The meaning-relatum of a sentence cannot be a fact, or else false sentences, to which no fact corresponds, would have no meaning-relatum although they are meaningful, which is enough to show that the meaning-relatum is doing no work in furthering an account of sentence-meaning. Moreover, Russell felt that the meaning-relatum of a sentence could not be the proposition that it expresses, because of the rather ill-grounded doubt he felt, as mentioned on page 21 above, about the existence of false propositions.

Thus Russell cannot assign meaning-relata to complex expressions. So should the realist theory be that every simple expression, if it is not a logical constant, has a meaning-relatum? This is unsatisfactory, since (a) some simple expressions, like 'Pegasus', are vacuous, and (b) some simple expressions are synonymous with complex ones. For example, Russell thought that most of our ordinary proper names are synonymous with some description (within a given speaker's idiolect). Moreover it may well be that 'unicorn' is synonymous with 'creature like a horse except in having one horn'. Given the principle that if two expressions mean the same and one has a meaning-relatum, the other has that entity as its meaning-relatum, it follows that a simple expression which is synonymous with some complex expression cannot be assigned a meaning-relatum. We are thus at a loss even to *state* Russell's realist theory.

As mentioned in the last section, one remedy is to rely on the notion of unanalysability, characterized in terms of the principle of acquaintance, and this is what, in effect, Russell does. Then the claim will be that the realist theory applies just to unanalysable expressions, that is, ones whose meaning can be mastered only through acquaintance with what they stand for. (All such expressions will, of course, be simple.) Now in the last section I proposed to reject the principle of acquaintance, and it must accordingly be held that there are no unanalysable expressions. Hence, if we were to adopt the suggested way of restricting the realist theory, we would go too far: if there are no unanalysable expressions, there would be no expressions to which the realist theory, thus restricted, would apply.

Though Russell does indeed hold that the realist theory applies just to unanalysable expressions, he arrives at this position in two, not well distinguished, steps. The fundamental idea is that the realist theory should apply to indefinable expressions. But, in the presence of the principle of acquaintance, any such expression is unanalysable. If we expunge the principle of acquaintance, the notion of indefinability promises a way of stating the intended scope of the realist theory that does not rely on the principle of acquaintance.

Whether or not the promise is realized is a difficult matter. One must, I think, to make out the best case, suppose that indefinability is absolute: that is, an expression is indefinable only if there is a no language in which it can be defined. (For present purposes, we assume that a definition is a complex synonym of a simple expression.) As I shall argue in the next chapter, there is a good case for thinking both that names are indefinable and that something close to Russell's realist theory holds of them. However, Russell thought that the realist theory applied also to predicates, but it is rather unclear whether any of these is indefinable. A Russellian candidate would be 'red'. In *PLA* he argues that we can use words, for example 'the colour with greatest wavelength', to fix the reference of 'red', but not to give its meaning (194–5). (There is an important disparity of terminology: Russell uses 'define' to mean what I mean by 'fix the reference', and 'analyse' to mean what I mean by 'define'.) Suppose, however, that there were a language containing a predicate, '. . . is rellow', which is not defined in that language, and that the translation of this predicate into English is '. . . is (red or yellow)'. (It is said that different peoples divide up the spectrum of colours differently, so perhaps this is not a wholly unrealistic example.) It could be argued that the following is a definition of 'red', thus showing that it is not indefinable: '. . . is red' $=_{df}$ '. . . is (rellow and not yellow)'. Whether this definition is correct is a hard question to resolve, as are many questions critically involving the notion of synonymy. Against its correctness one might argue as follows. Two sentences, 'p' and 'q', are synonymous iff 'A asserted that p' and 'A asserted that q' are mutually entailing. It does not follow in general that if 'p' entails 'q', 'A asserted that p' entails 'A asserted that q'. For example, one might suggest, 'A asserted that this figure is a triangle' does not entail 'A asserted that the sum of the internal angles of this figure equals two right angles'. Likewise, the argument continues, 'A asserted that this is red' does not entail 'A asserted that this is rellow', but this *is* entailed by 'A asserted that this is (rellow and not yellow)'. The last claim might be supported by analogy with our intuition that 'A asserted that p and q' does entail 'A asserted that p'.

However, one can easily imagine disagreements concerning what sentences of the form 'A asserted that p' entail, so that this argument is not entirely satisfactory. In particular, it is hard to see how the argument, if sound, could allow that any definition (of a simple expression by a complex one) is correct. This seems implausible, although there may be something to be said for it. This piece of terrain is very far from firm, and we must therefore be content with a conclusion that is also not firm. It is this: Russell *may* be right in holding that there are indefinable predicates, but there is considerable room for doubt. There is, therefore, at least a risk that the notion of indefinability cannot be used to give the intended restriction of the application of the realist theory, for there is a risk that there are no indefinable predicates, despite the fact that the realist theory is intended to apply to some predicates.

The epistemic principle would, obviously, yield a suitable restriction, since it applies only to undefined predicates. (The restriction is intended to offer an escape from the implausibility of applying it to, e.g., empty predicates.) However, whether or not one can devise a suitable sense of 'undefined', in the light of which the principle will be non-vacuously true, is open to the doubts just raised. In particular, if, as I think is correct, one holds that common words like 'table' are undefined, the principle is implausible (for the first table-maker might have introduced a predicate for tables when there were none). On the other hand, if one counts 'table' as defined, then the principle leans towards vacuity, for by this low standard it will be hard to find undefined words.

In *PLA*, Russell linked the indefinability of expressions not only with their unanalysability, but also with the fact that they stand for simple objects, and it is this link that I shall explore in the remainder of this section. We have seen that Russell said that in a perfect language the simple expressions will stand for simple objects, and for every simple object there will be a simple expression which stands for it (*PLA* 197). As Russell makes no further use of the second half of this claim, I shall not discuss it, save to note that it implausibly presupposes that there are only finitely many simple objects. So the question is: what are simple objects, and why did Russell suppose that these are what the simple expressions of an ideal language would stand for?

The simple objects are the atoms of Russell's logical atomism. To see what they are, and how their nature is determined, is to see what Russell's metaphysics is, and how it is arrived at. I start with Russell's account in *PLA*, and later briefly indicate the main subsequent modifications.

> The reason that I call my doctrine *logical* atomism is because the atoms that I wish to arrive at as the sort of last residue in analysis are logical atoms and not physical atoms. Some of them will be what I call 'particulars' – such things as little patches of colour or sounds, momentary things – and some of them will be predicates or relations and so on (*PLA* 179).

This occurs early in the lectures, and if we take it seriously, as a complete account, our expository problems are over. Russell is saying that particular atoms are sense-data, universal atoms are properties and relations. He says this, one may surmise, on the grounds that these are the only objects of acquaintance. This gives rise to one

46

version of logical atomism, and an essentially phenomenalistic one: the genuine entities are sense-data and their properties and relations, and everything else is a 'logical fiction'. As the lectures progress, however, other strands of thought become apparent.

Consider, for example, the exchange after the second lecture:

> *Mr Carr:* You do not mean that in calling the thing complex, you have asserted that there really are simples?
>
> *Mr Russell:* No, I do not think that is *necessarily* implied (*PLA* 202).

Here, and earlier in the exchange, Russell makes it clear that he thinks it could be argued that there are no simples. Yet he shows that he thinks particulars are one kind of simple (200–1), and one can infer that he also thinks that there are simple properties and relations. Also as we have seen, he treats sense-data as particulars, and the simple properties and relations hold among sense-data. Hence, if there were one single unified doctrine, the arguability of the existence of simples would amount to the arguability of the existence of sense-data and their properties and relations. However, it is certain that Russell did not think that the existence of sense-data and their properties and relations was arguable. Hence there is not a single unified doctrine.

The same conclusion is to be drawn from other passages; for example:

> The whole question of what particulars you find in the real world is a purely empirical one which does not interest the logician as such (*PLA* 199).

It is not easy to see how this is to be squared with the earlier claim that on analysis you arrive at particulars, more especially sense-data, as the *logical* atoms (*PLA* 179, quoted above).

In order to retain clarity in sorting out the different strands of Russell's philosophy in *PLA*, it will be useful to introduce some abbreviations. Let us say that 'sense-data-atomism' is the doctrine that sense-data and their properties and relations are the entities required, by the realist theory, for the meaningfulness of language, and that everything else is a logical construction out of sense-data, in the sense of being a class whose ultimate constituents are sense-data. Sense-data-atomism is a phenomenalist metaphysics, and the argument for it would presumably depend, at least in part, upon the principle of acquaintance. (This would not by itself be sufficient since, as we have seen, the principle is consistent with a noumenalistic analysis which does not guarantee phenomenalism.)

Further, let us say that an object is 'simple' iff it has no proper parts, and 'p-simple' iff it has no perceptually distinguishable proper parts. (P-simplicity does not suffice for simplicity, but simplicity suffices for p-simplicity.) Further, let us say that 'Those objects which it is impossible to symbolize otherwise than by using simple symbols' (*PLA* 194) are 's-simple'. (Russell just says 'simple'.) Finally, let us say that two objects are 'independent' iff it is true of each that it could have existed, whether or not the other had.

When Russell recognizes that some people might argue that there are no simples, he is thinking either of simples or of s-simples. He is not thinking of sense-data.

It is plain from the remark quoted from *PLA* 194 that Russell believes that there are s-simples, and indeed it is possible that he thinks all simples are s-simples. Why should anyone believe this? At first sight it seems absurd, or else rather trivial. If 'symbolize' is being used in such a way that a description does not symbolize what it denotes, if, in other words, 'symbolize' is to be used only of the relation that a (logically proper) name has to its bearer, then it is rather trivially true that all simples are s-simples. The reason is that anything that can be named is an s-simple, including, for all that has been said, complexes. But now suppose that a description does 'symbolize' the object it denotes. Then it is hard to see how any object could be an s-simple. For however simple an object may be, it may still be uniquely related to some other object, and this can be used to generate a description which symbolizes it. Hence any object, it appears, can be symbolized by a complex expression and thus no object is s-simple. (Cf. Ayer, *Russell and Moore* 39.)

Russell may well have been led to believe in s-simples through an acceptance of the first horn of the dilemma just posed. In a perfect language, there would be no simple expressions with complex meaning-relata, for if an entity is complex it can be described. Hence every simple expression in a perfect language will have a simple meaning-relatum. No complex entity is the meaning-relatum of any perfect-language expression. So, given that an object is symbolized by being a meaning-relatum, it follows that simples can, in the perfect language, be symbolized only by simple symbols. This is s-simplicity, relativized to the perfect language: p-l-s-simplicity. Simples alone possess it, so it is not the trivial notion that it was when unrelativized.

Notice that this introduces a new notion into the idea of a perfect language. So far as vocabulary goes, a perfect language has the vocabulary that is left, once our ordinary vocabulary has been subjected to analysis. But suppose our ordinary vocabulary contained a name of a complex. Because Russell (rightly) thought that no (logically proper) name means the same as any description, the perfect language will contain no analysis of any name for a complex. Thus if in our imperfect language there are names of complexes, we shall not be able to translate a sentence containing these names into the logically perfect language. In this case, it is quite unclear what the perfect language would have to teach us about language in general.

It may be that Russell thought that one restriction on a perfect language is that it should have no needless expressions. (He attributes this view to himself in *MPD*, and he explicitly advocates a similar view in much of his later philosophy: see Chapter V below and, e.g., *HK* Pt IV, ch 2.) Names of complexes are needless, not because we can find complex *synonyms* for them, but because, for ordinary purposes, we can manage with complex non-synonyms. Once again, one might wonder what, in this case, is the interest of p-l-s-simplicity. But there is a more serious problem. If a needless expression is what it must be to generate the idea that there is no need for names of complexes, that is, an expression we can manage without provided that we are equipped with certain other expressions, it seems that all expressions are needless. All names are needless, since we surely could, at some cost of convenience, make do with descriptions. And every predicate is needless, in virtue of a generalization of an earlier point about 'red'. Even if 'red' cannot be *defined* in terms of 'rellow' and 'yellow' (any more than a logically proper name of a complex can be defined), we could certainly get by without 'red', provided we had 'rellow' and 'yellow'.

I have assumed that there *could* be logically proper names for complexes, even if they are to be dispensed with in a perfect language, but Russell denies this in *PLA*, and I now turn away from the doctrine that simples are s-simples in order to examine this denial. A particular, as we have seen, is one kind of simple, and he suggests, provisionally:

Proper names = words for particulars. Df (*PLA* 200).

Hence proper names can name only simples. Why should anyone hold this? One is tempted into a circle: if an object is complex, then it can be described, and the description could be used to define a name for it, if there were one. But as names cannot be defined, there cannot be names of complexes. However, in the presence of the doctrine that names cannot be defined, one is not entitled to the premise that names of complexes would be definable, and the doctrine, as I hope to show in the next chapter, can be established independently of whether the bearers of names are simple.

I can find no argument in Russell for the claim that the bearers of names cannot be complex, but this claim is also made by Wittgenstein, who quite likely persuaded Russell of it, so we should look to the *Tractatus* to see if there is any support for the claim.

'Object' is Wittgenstein's generic term for whatever is the bearer of a proper name (*Tractatus* 3.203) and he claims that 'Objects are simple' (2.02). In his book *Wittgenstein's Philosophy of Language* (68), J. Bogen has suggested that 2.021–2.0211–2.0212 provides an argument for this claim. The passage is as follows:

Objects make up the substance of the world. That is why they cannot be composite.

If the world had no substance, then whether a proposition had sense would depend on whether another proposition was true.

In that case, we could not sketch out any picture of the world (true or false).

I take it that the structure of the argument is this: in the first step one equates the simplicity of objects with the world having substance; in the second step, one shows that an absurdity results from the supposition that the world has no substance. One therefore concludes that an absurdity results from the supposition that objects, the bearers of names, are complex: so names cannot name complexes.

The second step, in more detail, might look like this: if names named complexes, whether or not the name was meaningful would depend on whether another proposition, one that stated that the complex in question existed, was true. (This interpretation of how Wittgenstein would have expanded the argument is supported by Bogen's quotation from a later work, *Philosophische Bemerkungen*, 'What I formerly called objects, simples, is just what I can refer to without fear that perhaps they don't exist' (Bogen 66).) But this consequence is, supposedly, absurd.

To refute the argument, it suffices to show that the consequence is not absurd, and this can be done as follows. Take any sentence '*s*' and abbreviate the sentence '"*s*" has sense' by '*p*'. The proposition expressed by '*p*' is not the same as the proposition expressed by '*s*'. Yet whether or not '*s*' has sense depends on whether another proposition (that expressed by '*p*') is true. Plainly, there is nothing absurd in this. It will hold for every sentence. Perhaps what Wittgenstein claims is that whether the proposition that '*s*' has sense is true should not depend on whether any other proposition (distinct from the proposition that '*s*' has sense) is true. However, this alternative claim is false. Whether or not '*s*' has sense depends on whether the distinct proposition *that p and the earth is round* is true, and also on whether the distinct proposition *that p and* $2 + 2 = 4$ is true.

Bogen claims that there is a distinct argument for the conclusion that names cannot name complexes, the essence of which is given by the sentence:

The requirement that simple signs be possible is the requirement that sense be determinate (3.23).

I regret to say that I cannot see that this has any bearing on the issue. Let us grant that there is to be no question-begging, so that it is not presupposed that a simple sign cannot name a complex. Then the most that this remark could hope to show is that *some* simple signs must name simples. This, indeed, is the most that is shown by Bogen's gloss. He suggests that for any description there is no logical guarantee that it is uniquely satisfied, from this he concludes, quite mysteriously, that descriptions are indeterminate in *sense* (73). But even if this consequence follows (which in fact it certainly does not), the most it could show is that there need to be some determinate signs like names, or that some names must name simples. It does not come anywhere near showing that complexes cannot be named.

Thus neither in Russell nor in Wittgenstein do I find any remotely plausible argument for the doctrine that only simples can be named.

A further Russellian claim, in *PLA*, concerning simples is that some of them, namely particulars, are independent:

Particulars have this peculiarity, among the sort of objects that you have to take account of in an inventory of the world, that each of them stands entirely alone and is completely self-subsistent. . . . Each might happen to be the whole universe; it is a merely empirical fact that this is not the case (*PLA* 201–2).

Elsewhere, he has claimed that:

The only way, so far as I know, in which one thing can be *logically* dependent upon another is when the other is *part* of the one (*OKEW* 81).

This is rather too strong, since surely I could not have existed if my father had not, though I am not a part of him. None the less, the part-whole relation is no doubt one species of logically necessary relation, in the sense that things that are part-whole related are not independent. If we grant Russell his strong thesis, that this is the only way in which dependence can arise, it is easy to explain the connection between particulars and independence. Since each particular is simple, none has parts, so none is logically dependent on any other particular.

Notice that the logical independence of particulars from one another means that none of them is a necessary existent. In the idiom of possible worlds, a necessary existent is one that exists in every possible world. If a and b are mutually independent, there is a world in which a exists and b does not, and a world in which b exists and a does not. This means that neither a nor b exists in every world, and this fact is stressed by Russell, in the passage quoted, when he says that each particular might have been the only thing in existence. This marks a contrast with Wittgenstein's atomism, for it seems that his objects are necessary existents (*Tractatus* 2.024, 2.027).

The doctrine of independence is not, apparently, extended to all atoms in *PLA*, for it seems not to apply to simple universals. There is no direct evidence in the lectures, but in *PP*, for example, Russell seems to take universals as necessary existents, and this is incompatible with the kind of independence possessed by particulars. (In *PP* (57) universals are said to subsist and not exist, but the point is that, so far as one can tell, a subsistent universal could not have failed to subsist.)

This last point must not be confused with another. Whereas Wittgenstein in the *Tractatus* held that the simplest kind of propositions ('elementary propositions') are logically independent (4.211 gives part of the condition), Russell's simplest kind of propositions ('atomic propositions') are not logically independent. An example of an atomic sentence, which in general is an unanalysable n-ary predicate concatenated with n unanalysable names, is 'This is white' (*PLA* 200), and from the fact that 'red' is unanalysable it follows that 'This is red' is atomic. But these sentences (as used on the same occasion, of the same object) cannot both be true, and so they are not logically independent.

Let us call the doctrine that there are ultimate constituents of reality which are mutually independent and simple, 'simplicity-atomism'. From the fact that Russell thought it could be argued that there are no simples, but did not think it could be argued that there are no sense-data, we can infer that he did not think that sense-data-atomism entails simplicity-atomism. However, perhaps the entailment does, in reality, hold, for perhaps sense-data are simple and independent.

This is, certainly, a traditional empiricist tenet. Sensible qualities, for example a shade of colour, have traditionally been taken to be simple on the grounds of their p-simplicity: there is no distinguishing sub-shades within a given shade. Likewise, if instead of qualities one takes particulars which instantiate them, points of colour, *minima visibilia*, one might argue similarly: they are p-simple, for there is no distinguishing any spatial or other parts in a point, and thus simple. Moreover, the independence of sense-data is approximately what Hume asserts: perceptions are 'distinct existences' and so 'separable in the imagination' (see, e.g., *Treatise* Bk I, Pt 4, Sc V) and so any one might exist without any other.

Russell, however, is debarred twice over from holding that sense-data are simple. In the first place, he rejects the inference from p-simplicity to simplicity, though admittedly this rejection occurs later and is not explicit in *PLA*. In *Matter* he points out that A and B may be indistinguishable, and also *B* and *C*, but not *A* and *C* (280–1). Hence we might be presented with what appears to be a single colour shade, but which is in reality composed of two distinct but indistinguishable ones. So what is p-simple may be complex. In the second place, he defines sense-data in a way that admits complexity. For example in *RSP* (admittedly a few years before *PLA*) he says that a sense-datum is 'such a part of the whole [sensory field] as might be singled out by attention: particular patches of colour, particular noises, and so on' (109); and 'little patches of colour' are used as examples in *PLA* (179). However, one can certainly single out a complex by attention, and then single out a part of it. Since the whole cannot exist without the part, one has singled out things which are not mutually independent. Likewise, unless a patch of colour is actually a phenomenal point, one can always consider a part of it, and what one then considers is not independent of the whole. So Russell does not hold that sense-data are even p-simple, let alone simple. Thus the two doctrines, sense-data-atomism and simplicity atomism, lead separate lives.

It remains briefly to chart subsequent developments. Roughly, simplicity-atomism is abandoned early on, but the main framework of sense-data-atomism survives intact. However, there are modifications of detail, of which two are especially important.

The first of these is that from around the time of *Matter*, Russell ceased to think that every non-atom was a class ultimately composed of sense-data. In *PLA*, physical objects are such classes, but in *Matter*, and more clearly and definitely in *HK*, they come to be regarded as distinct entities, ones which could exist even if there were no sense-data. In sense-data-atomism, physical objects are classes of sense-data; after *Matter* they are causes of sense-data. Russell would say: in sense-data-atomism they are constructions, in the later philosophy they are inferences. The shift from construction to inference marks a shift in epistemological theory, exactly matching the shift from phenomenalistic to noumenalistic analysis, and is discussed in Chapter VI below.

The other main change is that in *IMT* the ultimate entities are qualities, which Russell there treats as particulars. They are not the primary data of sense, for we single them out by the analysis of a complex sensory field. Colours, then, rather than patches of colour, become basic. The main motivation is to eliminate the myth of substance. This is discussed in Chapter VII.

One rather minor change, from our present point of view, is that very soon after *PLA*, in 'On Propositions', Russell abandoned the term 'sense-datum', generally preferring thereafter 'sensation'. This marks a change in his view of the self, as discussed in Chapter VI.

The notion of a perfect language in *PLA* is that of the language with the unanalysable vocabulary. This vocabulary has meaning in, so to speak, the primary way: the way specified by the realist theory. Hence the notion of the perfect language has a claim to the attention of philosophers of language. To say that language only has meaning in so far as it approaches the ideal language is to say that words only have meaning in so far, basically, as they have meaning-relata. This basis is indispensable for any words, including defined words, to have meaning. By *IMT* this conception has changed, and the new view is even more explicit in *HK*. In these later works, what is of interest is a minimum vocabulary which will yet suffice for expressing all we know, and have various epistemological and metaphysical advantages, like not tempting us into the myth of substance. However, there is no claim that only words in the minimum vocabulary have meaning in the primary way. Rather, the qualifications for being in this vocabulary are essentially epistemological, and are not claimed to have any special bearing on the philosophy of language. This comes out in various ways.

For one thing, the possibility that complexes of qualities should be named is explicitly countenanced (*IMT* 251; cf. 320), yet these words, though genuinely names, are not included among the names in the minimum vocabulary, which includes only names of the sensory qualities themselves (*IMT* 89, 91).

There is another sign that the minimum vocabulary is not determined by special semantic role. The realist theory comes apart from the principle of acquaintance in a way that leads to the exclusion from the minimum vocabulary of some of the words which have meaning-relata:

> 'Object-words' are defined, logically, as words having meaning in
> isolation, and, psychologically, as words which have been learnt
> without its being necessary to have previously learnt any other
> words. These definitions are not strictly equivalent (*IMT* 62; cf. *HK*
> 88–9).

The 'logical' definition of an object-word makes it one to which the realist theory applies, whereas the 'psychological' definition makes it one to which the principle of acquaintance applies (possibly in some diluted form). As an example of the non-equivalence, Russell cites the possibility that someone with greater perceptual powers than ourselves might be able to learn the meaning of 'chiliagon' through acquaintance, whereas we have to learn it through a definition. Presumably, this is a counter-example to the equivalence of the definitions only if 'chiliagon' has a meaning-relatum. But it will not be included in the minimum vocabulary.

The psychological definition of an object-word makes it look as if the principle of acquaintance has been diluted almost to nothing, and as if there is a different kind of non-equivalence between the two definitions. One might think that even an empty name, and certainly a predicate which holds of nothing, can be mastered in some way other than through verbal definition: through pointing to pictures, perhaps. However, Russell's practice is to identify those words whose meaning can be learnt without verbal definition with those words which hold of something we experience, so in practice we have much the same principle of acquaintance as in the *PLA* period. As he was later to put it (*MPD* 170), the words to which it applies, and in particular those in the minimum vocabulary, 'represent the hard core of experience by which our sentences are attached to the non-linguistic world'.

The possibility of naming complexes, countenanced in *IMT*, shows that by that time simplicity-atomism had been abandoned. Its separation from sense-data-atomism is clearly marked in *LA*:

> When I speak of 'simples' I ought to explain that I am speaking of something not experienced as such, but only known inferentially as the limit of analysis (337).

However, even earlier, in *IMP*, there has been what can be interpreted as a substantial retraction. There, what count are 'relative individuals': 'terms that, throughout the context in question, are never analysed and never occur otherwise than as subjects' (173–4). Admittedly, these possibly complex entities are given not names but 'relative names' (174), but it is not possible to detect any difference between the semantic functioning of relative names and that of names. Hence the requirement that names name only simples has in effect been abandoned. However, the matter is not clear-cut. The remark from *LA* just quoted, and made some five years later, shows that there is still a hankering after simples. And in his *Outline of Philosophy* Russell says: 'Of these [proper names], however, there are no examples in actual language' (267); the surrounding discussion makes it plain that the reason that what we ordinarily call names are not properly speaking names is, in effect, that they do not name simples. In my discussion of names, I shall not consider the requirement that they must name simples, since I have already shown that it is groundless. However, I shall draw attention to the part played in Russell's account by his doctrine that they must (if logically proper) be unanalysable, for in my view this is a potent source of error in an otherwise admirable account.

Rather little has been said about universals, the meaning-relata, supposedly, of general terms. Their role in *PLA* is somewhat subdued, perhaps because Russell was still sensitive to the *PofM* difficulty about explaining the difference between a verb and a verbal noun or abstract singular term. In *Mind*, there is what may seem to be a more substantial retraction: 'Words of which the logical meaning is universal can therefore be employed correctly, without anything that could be called consciousness of universals' (228). Appearances may deceive, for in *PP* Russell in effect has identified acquaintance with a universal with the ability correctly to use a general term, an ability which he thinks requires that one be acquainted with some particular of which it holds. So it may be not that, in *Mind*, Russell is retracting the principle of acquaintance relative to general terms, but that he is there tightening the requirement for consciousness of a universal.

Russell's discussion of universals in *IMT* is a good illustration of the need the realist has, in Russell's treatment, of something like the principle of acquaintance. He there defines a universal as 'the meaning (if any) of a relation-word' (324). So one might think that there could be no doubt about whether universals exist. However, Russell reaches that conclusion only hesitantly, and after considerable discussion (cf. *PP* 55). He argues that the only way of parsing away relation-words involves using at least one relation-word, '. . . is similar to . . .'. This shows that what he is considering is not merely whether there are meaningful relation-words, which there plainly are, but whether, in addition, there are relation-words having meaning-relata. To show this, he has to show that there are unanalysable, or at any rate indefinable, relation-words, for only to such words can the realist theory of meaning be applied.

Russell mostly discusses and applies his realist theory to names: words for particulars. In the next chapter, I argue that the theory, at least in this application, is substantially correct. It can be detached from the principle of acquaintance, though we shall still need some such principle to delimit its sphere of application. It is enough to confine our attention to such names as have not been introduced into the language merely as abbreviations of complex expressions.

III

Names

Russell has two theories of names. One applies to what he calls 'logically proper' names, and is based on the realist theory of meaning and the principle of acquaintance. The other applies to what he calls 'ordinary proper' names, for example 'Aristotle', 'Troy', 'Margaret Thatcher', and is the theory that these are 'truncated or telescoped' descriptions (*PLA* 243; cf. *PP* 29). The overall account has two aspects. On the one hand, there is a body of doctrines which supposedly effect a contrast between two semantic functions, one ascribed to logically proper names, and the other ascribed to descriptions. I shall call these functions, respectively, naming and describing, and I shall call any expression which names (that is, has the naming function) a 'name'. On the other hand, there is the allocation of English expressions between these two functions. This has the effect that none (or almost none) of the expressions we ordinarily call 'names' are, according to Russell, names. In *PLA* (201) the only names are 'this' and 'that'. In *IMT* the category is enlarged to include words for sensible qualities, like 'red' and 'hot'.

Russell's account of naming poses a methodological problem. He attributes many features to a function he calls 'naming', but it is not always clear what features should be taken as defining the function, and what features should be regarded as, supposedly, ones that obtain in consequence of the defining features. The problem is intensified by Russell's view that most of what we ordinarily call names do not have this function, for it means there is no trusting our untutored intuitions about naming as a guide to what features Russell took to define this function.

The deepest roots of Russell's notion of naming undoubtedly receive nourishment from the realist theory of meaning and from the principle of acquaintance. However, we have resolved to reject the principle of acquaintance, and thus to reject the doctrine that there are unanalysable names, that is, 'logically proper' names. Thus if we rely on this feature to settle how Russell defines naming our problem is solved, though in an uninteresting way: naming will be a semantic function which no expressions possess.

However, there seems to me to be no harm in demoting the principle of acquaintance to a secondary position: a supposed (but not actual) consequence of an account of naming to be found elsewhere. This is what I shall do. I shall, in the course of the chapter, show how the doctrine of acquaintance misled Russell in his view about what expressions are names. Plainly, this could not be shown if one were to regard the principle of acquaintance as involved in the very stipulation of how, in Russell's mouth, 'name' is used.

Should we, however, retain at least the realist theory, which, applied to names, is the theory that a name's meaning is its bearer? Were we to do this, we would again *seem* to be exposed to the risk of making the naming function vacuous, or at any rate unduly limited. An appreciation of the risk is what very likely underlies Wittgenstein's view in the *Tractatus* that the bearers of names must be necessary, unchanging, and indestructible, a view similar to the one Russell held in *PofM* (44). There are, in fact, three distinguishable fears.

The first is that if the bearers of names were contingent, then our names might be meaningless, so we might all be talking nonsense. But this is absurd.

Whatever specious plausibility this argument possesses derives from a shift from metaphysical to epistemic possibility. It is logically possible that there should have been no such language as ours, but it is not the case that, for all we know, we talk nonsense all the time. If 'a' names a, then if a had not existed 'a' would not have the meaning it in fact has. (Either it would be meaningless or it would mean something else.) But there is nothing absurd in this consequence. Hence identifying the meaning of a name with its bearer does not require that the bearers of names should be necessary existents.

The second fear is that if a named object changes, then so does the meaning of a name. So it seems that to keep meanings constant we must name only unchanging things.

This argument, like the first, is mostly confusion. It is true that if the meaning (i.e. meaning-relatum) of 'a' is a, than if a changes so does the meaning of 'a', but it does not follow from this that, after the change, 'a' has a distinct meaning (i.e. meaning-relatum). Of course, we do not 'ordinarily say' that the meaning of 'Fido' is losing its fur; but then many truths ordinarily go unsaid.

The third fear is more substantial. It follows from the identification of the meaning of a name with its bearer that if Socrates no longer exists, nor does the meaning (i.e. meaning-relatum) of 'Socrates'. The danger is that it *seems* to follow, absurdly, that 'Socrates' is no longer meaningful. The consequence can be avoided in more than one way, but one can at least see why it was not unreasonable for Russell once to have held that the bearers of names should be indestructible.

Rather than discuss this issue, I shall take another way out. Let us interpret the realist theory as the claim that one adequately specifies the meaning of a name '*a*' by saying that it stands for its bearer, *a*. 'Socrates' does stand for Socrates (however you treat tense). So this avoids any tendency to think that the realist theory requires the bearers of names to be indestructible.

It may seem rather cavalier to reinterpret the realist theory in this way, but in fact most of Russell's statements of the theory (though admittedly not all: cf. *IMP* 174 and p. 16 above) harmonize satisfactorily with the reinterpretation, for example:

> 'Scott' taken as a name has a meaning all by itself. It stands for a certain person, and there it is (*PLA* 253).

I therefore propose to adopt this reinterpretation of the realist theory. Accordingly, the theory need not hold that the bearers of names are necessary, unchanging or indestructible, since *a* might change, or cease to exist, while all along '*a*' stands for *a*.

The realist theory, then, is one of the things, indeed the main thing, that will be taken to fix what Russell intends by the semantic function of naming. This gives us a fixed point in terms of which his other doctrines can be regarded as doctrines about *naming*, rather than as stipulations which partially determine his possibly idiosyncratic use of 'name'. Some of these doctrines, I shall argue, are falsehoods about naming, and I shall attempt to explain what led Russell to err. Others of the doctrines are fundamental insights, of lasting importance.

Interpreting Russell in this way has the result, I shall argue, that most of what we commonly call 'names' are indeed names, and this conflicts directly with Russell's position. However, it is a consequence that increases the importance of Russell's account of naming to an understanding of language, for it widens the sphere to which the account applies. And though such a flagrant conflict between what Russell said and what, on my reading, he should have said is *prima facie* evidence against the accuracy of the reading, the evidence does not stick: we can quite independently explain how Russell came to adopt the erroneous view that most so-called 'names' are not names.

My procedure is to consider the consequences, actual or supposed, of the doctrine that the meaning of a name consists in the fact that it names its bearer. Indeed, only through an examination of these actual or supposed consequences can we form an adequate estimate of what this cryptic doctrine amounts to. I shall start by listing these, and they will be examined one by one in the subsequent sections of the chapter.

Suppose 'a' is a name of a. Then:

1 a enters into the identity of the proposition expressed by '. . . a . . .'. (Cf. *PP* 73–4.) This has some affinities with the position that naming is a species of genuine reference (in Peacocke's sense: 'Proper Names, Reference, and Rigid Designation' 119).

2 One who believes the proposition expressed by '. . . a . . .' has a singular belief concerning a (*PP* 73–4).

3 Names are not scope-sensitive in the way that descriptions are (*PLA* 247, 251).

4 There are no empty names (*PLA* 242–3).

5 Two names with the same bearer have the same meaning (*PLA* 245).

6 If 'b' is a name, then one who understands '$a = b$' knows enough to know its truth-value (*PLA* 245).

7 'a exists' is nonsense (*PLA* 250–2).

8 'To know the meaning of a name is to know who it is applied to' (*PLA* 244).

9 No name is synonymous with any description (*PP* 31).

Before beginning the discussion, it may be useful if I reveal my hand. I shall argue that all these doctrines except 5, 6 and 7 constitute valuable insights concerning naming.

I Genuine reference

Russell held that a enters into (is a constituent of) the proposition expressed by '. . . a . . .', but that the F does not in the same way enter into (is not a constituent of) the proposition expressed by '. . . the F . . .'.

One way in which one might try to make this less metaphorical is this: a sentence containing a name is about the named object, but a sentence containing a description may not be about the described object (even if there is one). For example, 'Margaret Thatcher will have a hard time with the unions' is about Margaret Thatcher, but 'The next Prime Minister (whoever it may be) will have a hard time with the unions' is not. Margaret Thatcher is not said, by someone who uses the second sentence, to be someone who will have a hard time with the unions, even if she is in fact the next Prime Minister. However, the notion of what a sentence is *about* is slippery, so it would be well to find firmer ground.

The meaning of a name in itself determines what the bearer of it is.

But the meaning of a description may, by itself, be insufficient to determine of what, if anything, it holds. What typically settles what object, if any, it is of which a description holds is the meaning of the description *together with* the way the world is. If 'The next Prime Minister' holds of Margaret Thatcher, this is not merely in virtue of what 'The next Prime Minister' means: other facts, concerning the leadership of parties and national opinion, are vitally relevant. By contrast, that 'Margaret Thatcher' names Margaret Thatcher is settled by the meaning of the name, independently of any other facts. As the identity of a proposition is settled merely by the meaning of the words in the sentence that expresses it, the proposition expressed by the sentence 'Margaret Thatcher will have a hard time with the unions', but not the proposition expressed by 'The next Prime Minister will have a hard time with the unions', may metaphorically be said to contain Margaret Thatcher. Thus a name genuinely refers to its bearer, whereas a description does not genuinely refer to whatever object, if any, of which it holds.

A similar contrast, or a precisification of this very contrast, is found in that between 'rigid designators' and 'non-rigid designators'. Kripke says 'Let's call something a *rigid designator* if in any possible world it designates the same object' ('Naming and Necessity' 269). Thus if '*a*' is a rigid designator, and in fact designates *a*, then, holding the meaning of '*a*' constant, at any possible world at which '*a*' designates anything it designates *a*. Thus 'the next Prime Minister' is not a rigid designator. Even if it in fact designates Margaret Thatcher, there are possible worlds in which, holding the meaning of the phrase constant, it designates Anthony Benn. However, 'Margaret Thatcher' *is*, it seems, a rigid designator, since so long as the meaning of the name remains the same it will, at every possible world at which it designates anything, designate Margaret Thatcher. The key point here is that whereas someone other than the person who is in fact the next Prime Minister might have been the next Prime Minister, no one other than Margaret Thatcher could have been Margaret Thatcher. (Throughout, I shall pretend that names are unambiguous, though in reality there are no doubt many Margaret Thatchers. Tyler Burge has suggested a way of dealing with this problem: 'Reference and Proper Names'.)

Peacocke has suggested a different account of what it is to be a rigid designator, and he claims that, according to the criterion, proper names are, and some descriptions or uses of descriptions are not, rigid designators. ('Rigid designation' is just a variant of 'genuine reference'.) The first rough criterion is that a term *t* is a rigid designator iff

61

there is an object x such that for any sentence $G(t)$ in which t occurs, the truth (falsity) condition for $G(t)$ is that $<x>$ satisfy (respectively, fail to satisfy) $G( )$ (110).

To see how this criterion operates, consider the two sentences 'Edmund Hillary is bald' and 'The first man to climb Everest is bald'. There is no object x such that one can give the truth-condition of 'The first man to climb Everest is bald' as that x be bald. Edmund Hillary is not such an object, for, if he had not been the first to climb Everest, whether or not he was bald would be irrelevant to the truth or falsity of the sentence. But nor is anything else such an object, for, as things are, it is whether or not Edmund Hillary, rather than anyone else, is bald that counts for the truth or falsity of the sentence. By contrast, there is an object x such that one can give the truth-condition of 'Edmund Hillary is bald' as that x be bald. That object is Edmund Hillary. (Cf. Peacocke 110–11.)

It is one thing to give a criterion, and another thing to determine how it divides the terms in our language. The recent example shows that 'The first man to climb Everest' is not a rigid designator, but it does not show that 'Edmund Hillary' is a rigid designator, for it does not show that Edmund Hillary is such that, for *every* sentence of the form 'G(Edmund Hillary)' its truth-condition is that <Edmund Hillary> satisfy G( ). The criterion itself has something in common with Russell's notion of a named object entering into the proposition, and Peacocke explicitly mentions the similarity with one of Russell's ideas in *OD* (Peacocke 111). However, it looks as if there will be a sharp divergence between Russell's category of logically proper names, and the category of rigid designators. The reason is that whereas Russell's logically proper names are, in *PLA*, just 'this' and 'that', and also, by *IMT*, words for sensible qualities, it is plausible to maintain that most ordinary names, like 'Edmund Hillary', are rigid designators.

The difficulty of *showing* this is that one has to show something concerning *every* sentence in which the term occurs. Belief-sentences seem to offer a *prima facie* reason for thinking that 'Edmund Hillary' is not a rigid designator. Suppose that 'Edmund Hillary' is a rigid designator, and also suppose he has another name, 'a', which we stipulate to be a rigid designator. Then it may seem that a truth-condition of both 'Tensing believes that Edmund Hillary is bald' and 'Tensing believes that a is bald' is that $<a>$ satisfy the condition expressed by 'Tensing believes that ( ) is bald'. However, it may be that Tensing does believe that Edmund Hillary is bald but does not believe that a is bald (because he does not realize that a is Hillary), and thus it may be that these sentences have different truth-values.

They cannot, therefore, have the same truth-condition. Hence, one might argue, 'Edmund Hillary' is not a rigid designator. The general point is that Peacocke's criterion makes sense only if the place marked by '( )' in the schema 'G( )' is transparent, but some places in belief-sentences are not transparent.

Peacocke's strategy for avoiding the conclusion that ordinary proper names like 'Edmund Hillary' are not rigid designators consists in refusing to regard a belief sentence like 'Tensing believes that Edmund Hillary is bald' as exemplifying the form 'G(Edmund Hillary)' (126–8).

This sort of problem means that one ought to adopt the hypothesis that ordinary proper names are rigid designators rather cautiously, for it is hard to be sure that one has resolved all the problem cases. Hence it is well to found the distinction between naming and describing not on the notion of rigid designation alone, but also on other, doubtless intimately connected, phenomena. Some of these will be considered in subsequent sections.

Although it looks as if there will be more rigid designators than Russellian logically proper names, Peacocke suggests that a small modification of the criterion will include demonstratives in the class of rigid designators, and this is in harmony with Russell's selection of 'this' and 'that' as the prime cases of logically proper names (Peacocke 118 ff.).

That demonstratives satisfy the intuitive ideas underlying the criterion of rigid designation can be shown by the following consideration. The proposition expressed by 'The first man to climb Everest is bald' would be the same, even if someone other than whoever in fact first climbed Everest had first climbed Everest, but the proposition expressed by 'This is bald', as used on a particular occasion, would have been different if some other object had been demonstrated than the one in fact demonstrated.

Thus the view that ordinary names are rigid designators, to which this section has lent some support, if regarded as an elucidation or precisification of Russell's view that named objects enter into propositions, supports his selection of demonstratives as expressions which function like names, but challenges his refusal to regard ordinary proper names as, really, names.

2   Singular belief

Let us say that a sentence built on the following lines attributes a *relational* belief: 'A believes, concerning . . . , that it is —— ' (where the pronoun picks up the reference of what fills the dots). The place occupied by the dots is referentially transparent: 'A believes, concerning t, that it is F', together with '$t=s$', entails 'A believes, concerning s, that it is F'.

A sentence attributes a singular belief, with respect to an object o, iff it entails a sentence expressing a relational belief, in which the expression occupying the dots, in the schema above, denotes o. Every sentence which attributes a relational belief is a sentence which attributes a singular belief. Note, however, that 'A believes, concerning t, that it is F' does not entail 'A believes that t is F'. For example, you may believe, concerning the woman who is in fact the most miserable creature alive – viz. your wife – that she is happy, but the sentence 'You believe that the most miserable creature alive is happy' may, at least on one interpretation, be false.

According to an analysis of belief that Russell offered in *PP*, a belief-sentence expresses a relation between the believer and the meaning-relata of the believed-sentence (i.e. the sentence which says what is believed). (For later modifications of this account see Chapter VII, pp. 224–8.) Thus, for example, 'A believes that Edmund Hillary is bald' is analysed as: A is belief-related to Edmund Hillary and baldness. (I follow Russell's practice, in the *PP* account, of assuming that something which in the end he wishes to regard as *not* a logically proper name can none the less be treated as one for illustrative purposes.) Thus Russell makes every belief relational, if a name is used in the believed sentence, and in this he surely goes too far, since typically the positions occupied by singular terms in belief-sentences are not referentially transparent. For example, 'John believes that Tully is an orator' is not equivalent to 'John believes that Cicero is an orator', even though Tully=Cicero. In treating all ascriptions of belief in which a name is used in the believed-sentence as relational, Russell thereby treats them all as singular, and in this much he seems to me to be right: when a proper name is employed in the believed-sentence, the belief-sentence attributes a singular belief concerning the name's bearer. By contrast, this does not always hold if a description is employed, rather than a name.

This contrast is predictable from, or at least harmonizes well with, the idea that the bearers of names enter into propositions expressed by sentences containing names. The contrast is one of semantic role, and it is another question to say which expressions play this role. The outcome here, though, is similar to that in the last section: demonstratives play it, but so too do many expressions which we ordinarily classify as proper names, but which Russell refused to classify as logically proper names.

If you believe that Edmund Hillary is bald, it surely follows that Edmund Hillary has this property: you believe that he is bald. So it follows that you believe, concerning Edmund Hillary, that he is bald.

(This is not to say that 'Edmund Hillary' occurs transparently in 'You believe that Edmund Hillary is bald', for the reason noted in the second paragraph of this section.) By contrast, suppose that you have come across the sentence 'The first man to climb Everest is bald' in a philosophy book, by an accurate and reliable author, who offered it as an example of a truth. You have not, we shall suppose, the least idea of who the first man to climb Everest is: you have no beliefs at all in the field of mountaineering, you have never heard the name 'Edmund Hillary' and never met the man. However, you now form the belief that the first man to climb Everest is bald. Does it follow, in this case, that you believe, concerning the first man to climb Everest, that is, concerning Edmund Hillary, that he is bald? I think not. If this is right, one can ascribe a belief to someone by using a description, without thereby ascribing to him a singular belief.

The point about names and singular belief holds even when there is iteration of '. . . believes that ——— '. Thus 'John believes that Mary believes that Edmund Hillary is bald' does, surely, entail 'John believes, concerning Edmund Hillary, that Mary believes that he is bald'. It does not entail 'John believes that Mary believes, concerning Edmund Hillary, that he is bald', for a man may not believe all the consequences of what he believes.

'This' likewise results in the attribution of singular belief, when used in believed-sentences. 'John believes that this is bald' entails 'John believes, concerning this, that it is bald'.

This connection with singular belief does not hold of all expressions that are rigid designators by Kripke's standard. 'The even prime' designates the same in all worlds. Yet 'John believes that the even prime is Mary's lucky number' seems not to entail 'John believes, concerning the even prime, that it is Mary's lucky number'. The entailment fails, I am inclined to think, for if John does not know which number is the even prime we are reluctant to say that he has a belief concerning it.

One might think that the same phrase is also a rigid designator by Peacocke's standard, thus showing that this notion of rigid designation, likewise, fails to yield precisely the category of names. (Peacocke does not claim it does, for he holds that some descriptions are rigid by his standard.) Will not the number 2 serve as an object in terms of which one can give the truth-condition for every sentence G(the even prime)? If 2 is not such an object, it is not for the same reason that Edmund Hillary was not a suitable object in terms of which to give a truth-condition for every sentence G(the first man to climb Everest). However, there is a different reason which can be put roughly as follows: the resulting truth-condition would not have the same meaning as the sentence for which it was a truth-condition, and so it would not feature in a theory of truth which was adequate to serve as the core of a theory of meaning. Something close to, and inspired by the thought of, this more demanding notion of a truth-condition is in effect imposed in Peacocke's finished criterion for rigid designation (125). Thus there is no reason to think that the category of Peacocke's rigid designators will include expressions which fail to satisfy the Russellian condition of invariably resulting in the ascription of singular belief, when used in believed-sentences.

3   Scope

As applied to formal languages, scope is a perfectly precise syntactic notion. For example, in the language of *PM* the scope of an occurrence of an expression other than a parenthesis is the shortest formula in which it occurs. In this language, relative differences of scope between occurrences of expressions make a semantic difference. For example,

$$\sim(\ \exists\ x)Fx$$

says that it is not the case that there is something which is *F*. In other words, it says that there are no *F*s. By contrast

$$(\ \exists\ x)\sim Fx$$

says that something is not an *F*. The syntactic reflection of the different things said by these formulae lies in the different relative scopes of the occurrences of '$\sim$' and ' $\exists$ '. In the first, the scope of ' $\exists$ ' is '($\exists$ *x*)*Fx*' and the scope of '$\sim$' is the whole formula; so we may say that the occurrence of ' $\exists$ ' lies within the scope of the occurrence of '$\sim$'. In the second, the position is reversed. The scope of '$\sim$' is '$\sim Fx$' and the scope of ' $\exists$ ' is the whole formula, so the scope of '$\sim$' lies within that of ' $\exists$ '.

By analogy, the idea of scope may be extended in a somewhat imprecise way to natural English. For example, a pair of English sentences may differ in meaning in such a way that the only difference in their formalized equivalents is in the relative scope of occurrences of expressions. 'John is either lying, or he is drunk and unhappy' may be formalized in the propositional calculus as '*p* v (*q* & *r*)' (where '*p*' abbreviates 'John is lying', '*q*' 'John is drunk' and '*r*' 'John is unhappy'). By contrast, 'John is either lying or drunk, and he is unhappy' may be formalized as '(*p* v *q*) & *r*'. Since the formulae differ only in the relative scope of the occurrences of 'v' and '&' we can, by analogy, say that the English sentences differ only in point of the relative scopes of 'either . . . or' and 'and'.

In a similar way, some ambiguity in English may be explained as

66

due to scope ambiguity. What this amounts to is that the English sentence in question can be formalized in different ways, each formalization capturing one of its meanings, where the formalizations differ syntactically from one another only in the different relative scope of occurrences of expressions whose translations occur in the English sentence. An example frequently used is the sentence 'Everyone loves someone'. Many speakers find this ambiguous: on one reading it says that each person is such that there is someone whom he loves, and on the other it makes the stronger claim that some (enviable) person is loved by everybody. The difference is reflected in the different relative scopes of '$\forall$' and '$\exists$' in the formalizations. The first reading is formalized as '$(\forall x)(\exists y)$ loves x, y' and the second as '$(\exists y)(\forall x)$ loves x, y'. Most people find the first reading the more natural, and this corresponds to the fact that it is quite common for widest scope to be marked, in English, by leftmost occurrence.

The thesis I wish, with some hesitation, to ascribe to Russell is this: descriptions (at some occurrences) are scope-sensitive but names are not. An expression is scope-sensitive if there is an ambiguous sentence in which it occurs and whose ambiguity is explained (in the fashion described) in terms of the expression's different scope relative to some other expression. More generally, perhaps, an expression is scope-sensitive if there is a sentence in which it occurs whose meaning can be altered merely by altering the essentially scope-indicating devices in the sentence (brackets, punctuation, or, if it is a spoken sentence, inflection) in such a way that the scope of the expression relative to some other is the only syntactic change effected.

In ascribing this thesis to Russell, the hesitation attaches only to its generality. He certainly held it concerning some constructions in which names occur, and I start with two of these.

The simplest case is scope relative to an occurrence of a negation sign. Russell thinks that descriptions are scope-sensitive in this respect:

'The present king of France is not bald' is false if it means
'There is an entity which is now King of France and is not bald',

but is true if it means

'It is false that there is an entity which is now King of France and is bald' (*OD* 53).

In the first case the description is said to have 'primary' occurrence, that is, it occurs with widest scope. In the second case, it is said to have 'secondary' occurrence, that is, it does not occur with widest scope (the scope of 'it is false that' or 'it is not the case that' is wider). Thus

Russell holds that 'The King of France is not bald' is scope-ambiguous, and this qualifies the description for scope-sensitivity relative to 'not'. By contrast, Russell claims, there is no analogous ambiguity in the case of an otherwise similar sentence in which a name replaces the description.

> When you say 'Scott is human' there is no possibility of double denial. The only way you can deny 'Scott is human' is by saying 'Scott is not human'. But where a descriptive phrase occurs you do have the possibility of double denial (*PLA* 251).

The 'possibility of double denial' is just there being two non-synonymous sentences, depending on the relative scope of the expression and the negation sign. The possibility is closed when the expression is a name (or as Russell sometimes cautiously said, not wanting to commit himself to the view that 'Scott' is a name, is being *used as* a name; e.g., *PLA* 246) but is open when it is a description.

Though I think that Russell is right to draw this contrast in exactly this way, it is not clear how much weight can be placed upon it as an argument to show that names, unlike some descriptions, are scope-insensitive. The reason is that pre-theoretical intuitions may vary: some may intuit that the truth of 'Scott is not human', unlike the truth of 'It is not the case that Scott is human', requires Scott to exist. One undermines this intuition not by stating the contrary one more loudly, but by invoking the fundamental idea that the bearer of a name enters into the identity of propositions expressed by sentences in which it occurs.

A second well-known Russellian claim of differences of relative scope for a description but not a name is relative to 'wished to know whether'.

> When we say, 'George IV wished to know whether Scott was the author of *Waverley*', we normally mean 'George IV wished to know whether one and only one man wrote *Waverley* and Scott was that man'; but we *may* also mean: 'One and only one man wrote *Waverley* and George IV wished to know whether Scott was that man' (*OD* 52).

In the first case the description has secondary occurrence, and in the second case it has primary occurrence. (In fact Russell has replaced the description 'the author of *Waverley*' by the analysis required by the theory of descriptions. But I shall pretend that the description itself still occurs.) In other words, in the first case it has narrow scope relative to 'George IV wished to know whether', and in the second case it has wide scope. However, there is no true reading of 'George IV wished to know whether Scott was Scott' (*OD* 50), but there would

68

be one if the sentence were, in an analogous way, scope-ambiguous. So it is not scope-ambiguous, and so the name is not scope-sensitive relative to 'George IV wished to know whether'.

Russell certainly succeeds in drawing attention to a contrast, and the explanation in terms of scope is plausible. However, the relevant phenomena are complex, and Russell's account is very likely not comprehensive. (Cf. J. Hornsby, 'Singular Terms in Contexts of Propositional Attitude'.)

We can arrive in a more wholesale way at the doctrine of the scope-insensitivity of names relative to the constructions of *PM* by remarking that Russell viewed variables as in important ways similar to names (see, e.g., *IMP* 175-6), and that variables are scope-insensitive in *PM*. (For example, there would be no semantic difference between '$\sim(\varphi x)$' and '$(\sim\varphi)x$' and so this syntactic difference is not marked.)

There is a further batch of expressions, which Russell did not consider, but which none the less suggest scope-insensitivity for names but not descriptions: modal expressions like 'necessarily' and 'must'. For example, 'The number of the planets has to be nine' is ambiguous. In the more natural reading, the description has wide scope relative to the modal expression, and the effect of the sentence is to ascribe the property of being necessarily nine to the number which numbers the planets. Since this number is nine, it has the property ascribed, and so the sentence is true. There is also a rather less natural reading, in which the description is seen as having narrow scope relative to the modal expression, and in which the effect of the sentence is to claim, falsely, that there have to be nine planets. By contrast, 'Nine has to be nine' has no false reading, and this suggests the scope-insensitivity of the name 'nine' as opposed to the description 'the number of the planets' (cf. Peacocke 113).

Does the scope-insensitivity of names follow from the hypothesis that they are rigid designators by Kripke's standard? We have already seen that a Kripkean rigid designator like 'the even prime', as it occurs in a believed-sentence, may or may not be used to attribute singular belief, and this may be explained as a matter of scope-sensitivity. However, even if in fact all Kripkean rigid designators were scope-insensitive, I cannot think of an argument which shows that they have to be. By contrast, Peacocke is surely right to claim that scope-insensitivity follows from his standard for rigidity. In effect, Peacocke's criterion ensures that the truth-conditions for all sentences in which a rigid designator occurs can have a common overall structure, applying to the designated object in the same way, and thus the criterion ensures that there is no way for a rigid designator to be scope-sensitive.

69

4   Empty names

If it is characteristic of a name that its bearer enters into every proposition expressed by a sentence containing the name, there are no names without bearers.

If a name is a rigid designator, by Peacocke's standard, it plainly must have a bearer, for otherwise there will be no object in terms of which to give the truth-conditions of each sentence in which the name is used. (Kripke's formulation seems technically to allow empty rigid designators, since they vacuously satisfy the condition of designating the same in every world in which they designate anything. It would be easy to remedy this.)

If the occurrence of a name in a believed-sentence ensures that the belief-sentence in which it occurs expresses singular belief with respect to the name's bearer, it follows that there are no names without bearers.

Plainly, therefore, there are no names without bearers. We are faced with a terminological difficulty. It is tempting and customary to refer to expressions like 'Vulcan' as 'empty names', meaning names without bearers, but if there are no such names, 'Vulcan' is not one. I shall regard 'empty' as qualifying 'name', in 'empty name', rather as 'fake' qualifies 'diamond' in 'fake diamond': there are empty names all right, but they are not names. I shall also on occasion speak of 'syntactic names', meaning thereby expressions which look like names, but which may or may not be names (they may be empty names and thus non-names).

Setting aside expressions which are genuine names, we can distinguish two further species of syntactic name, and it is tempting to classify both as empty names. On the one hand, there are fictional and mythological names, like 'Romulus', 'Pegasus', 'Hamlet' and perhaps 'Homer'. On the other hand, there are names whose original use was not within fiction or mythology but, supposedly, sober fact: for example, 'Vulcan', as supposedly used of the intra-Mercurial planet, and 'Eldorado', as supposedly used (as the 'name' suggests) of a city paved with gold. Russell's examples are of fictional and mythological names, but there is little doubt that he would have treated factual empty names in the same way as the others: his theory is that they are truncated or telescoped descriptions (*PLA* 243). There is a good exposition of the theory in a rather later work. Speaking in *IMT* of our emotions when seeing *Hamlet*, he says:

> They are really not about anything, but we think they are about the man named 'Hamlet'. The propositions in the play are false because there was no such man; they are significant because we

know from experience the noise 'Hamlet', the meaning of 'name', and the meaning of 'man'. The fundamental falsehood in the play is the proposition: the noise 'Hamlet' is a name (*IMT* 277).

(A further refinement is added in *HK*: '"Hamlet" is a word which Shakespeare pretends to be the name of a Prince of Denmark' (93).) The overall account is smooth: every such syntactic name abbreviates a description true of nothing, and so every sentence in which such a syntactic name has primary occurrence is false.

One alternative to this account would be to hold that there are no syntactic names which lack bearers. A distinction will be made between existing and being, in such a way that certain things which do not exist, like Hamlet and Vulcan, none the less have being. An empty syntactic name would be defined as one of which nothing in the world of being was bearer. 'Hamlet' and 'Vulcan' are thus *not* empty syntactic names, for they name those familiar non-existent denizens of the world of being, Hamlet and Vulcan. This is rather the kind of account Russell gave in *PofM*, and is the sort of issue that was uppermost in his mind in his many discussions of Meinong in the early years of the century. By *IMP* he has decisively rejected any such approach, and he scorns it in a passage which I cannot resist quoting at length:

Logic, I should maintain, must no more admit a unicorn than zoology can; for logic is concerned with the real world just as truly as zoology, though with its more abstract and general features. To say that unicorns have an existence in heraldry, or in literature, or in imagination, is a most pitiful and paltry evasion. What exists in heraldry is not an animal, made of flesh and blood, moving and breathing of its own initiative. What exists is a picture, or a description in words. Similarly, to maintain that Hamlet, for example, exists in his own world, just as truly as (say) Napoleon existed in the ordinary world, is to say something deliberately confusing, or else confused to a degree which is scarcely credible. There is only one world, the 'real' world: Shakespeare's imagination is part of it, and the thoughts he had in writing Hamlet are real. So are the thoughts that we have in reading the play. But it is of the very essence of fiction that only the thoughts, feelings, etc., in Shakespeare and his readers are real, and that there is not, in addition to them, an objective Hamlet. When you have taken account of all the feelings roused by Napoleon in writers and readers of history, you have not touched the actual man; but in the case of Hamlet you have come to the end of him. If no one thought about Hamlet, there would be nothing left of him; if no one had thought about Napoleon, he would soon have seen to it that

71

someone did. The sense of reality is vital in logic, and whoever juggles with it by pretending that Hamlet has another kind of reality is doing a disservice to thought. A robust sense of reality is very necessary in framing a correct analysis of propositions about unicorns, golden mountains, round squares, and other such pseudo-objects (*IMP* 169–70).

Though the rhetoric is splendid, the argument may well be found somewhat scanty. If 'Hamlet' is an abbreviated description which holds of nothing, how can the sentence 'Hamlet is the Shakespearean character most admired by Bernard Levin' be true? The view that fictional names name objective entities, viz. fictional characters, at least has the merit of pointing towards a possible solution to that problem. However, I shall not consider fictional (syntactic) names, but only the purer cases of syntactic names like 'Vulcan' and 'Eldorado', and I shall assume that such syntactic names cannot be treated as having bearers: these are, I shall assume, uncontroversial examples of empty names.

I wish to make two connected points, both of which concern Russell's view that the syntactic names we ordinarily call proper names are abbreviated descriptions. The first is that the case of empty names supplies an ingenious argument in favour of Russell's description theory. The second point is that there is a feature of the treatment of empty names, imposed by not accepting Russell's description theory, which helps to explain why he refused to allow that ordinary proper names be counted as names.

The argument I have in mind, in favour of the description theory, goes like this:

(*i*)   Empty syntactic (non-fictional) names like 'Vulcan' are meaningful.

(*ii*) Since they have no bearers, they are not names.

(*iii*) Unless they are abbreviated descriptions or names, they are meaningless.

The immediate conclusion is:

(*iv*) Empty names are abbreviated descriptions.

But there is a further one, which relies on this extra premise:

(*v*)   The arguments which are supposed to show that non-empty syntactic names like 'Aristotle' are not descriptions apply equally to empty names like 'Vulcan'.

From which, together with (*iv*), one can extract:

(*vi*) These arguments are unsound (even if we cannot show just what is wrong with them).

Russell certainly used (*i*)–(*iii*) as an argument for the description theory (*PLA* 243), but he did not consider the ingenious twist provided by the addition of (*v*)–(*vi*), for he never considered objections to the description theory. By themselves, (*i*)–(*iii*) at best tend to show merely that empty names are descriptions. The addition of (*v*)–(*vi*), however, lends support to the wider view that all syntactic names are descriptions.

The arguments alluded to in (*v*) will be discussed in section 9 below, but one important one can be spelled out here, and shown to apply to empty names as much as to what are ordinarily called names. The claim is that what are ordinarily called names satisfy the condition that for any such expression '*a*', and any description, 'the *F*', native speakers will admit that the proposition expressed by '*a* is not the *F*' might have been true, but will not admit that the proposition expressed by 'the *F* is not the *F*' might have been true. This suggests that '*a*' does not abbreviate 'the *F*'. This contrast appears to apply to empty names like 'Vulcan' and 'Eldorado'. If we project ourselves back to the time before it was discovered that there was no such planet as Vulcan, we would surely expect, in respect of this word, just the pattern of behaviour described. Scientists would agree that such sentences as 'Vulcan is not the planet that revolves nearer the sun than Mercury' might have been true (and would have been, if there had been some upheaval in the solar system), but would not agree that 'the planet that revolves nearer the sun than Mercury is not the planet that revolves nearer the sun than Mercury' might have been true. Likewise for other descriptions. The same goes for the empty name 'Eldorado'. Those who unenlightenedly used it would accept that 'Eldorado is not the city paved with gold' might have expressed a truth (perhaps it is only paved with an aggregate rich in iron pyrites, or perhaps more than one city is paved with gold), but they would not accept that 'the city paved with gold is not the city paved with gold' might express a truth, and the same goes for any other description.

Thus (*v*) is true at least with respect to some of the arguments that are supposed to show that what we ordinarily call names are not descriptions. Thus, I think, the real choice lies between accepting (*iv*) and (*vi*) on the one hand, and, on the other, rejecting (*i*). I shall show that the latter alternative is not as implausible as it might at first sight seem.

It is natural to think that it is absurd to hold that empty names like 'Vulcan' and 'Eldorado' are meaningless. Surely they have a 'communicative use': children are taught how to use the expressions correctly, and corrected if their usage fails to match the community's; messages are imparted by the use of the sentences; in point of meaningfulness, there is no way in which any feature of the community's behaviour segregates empty names from others. Indeed, how could it, since they are themselves unaware of the distinction? Finally, one must surely admit the meaningfulness of empty names as they occur in positive and negative existential sentences, for *we* hold that such sentences are, respectively, false and true.

But if empty names have a 'communicative use' we, who know they are empty, ought in theory to be able to say what is communicated by a sentence in which one is used, and what people believe if they believe a proposition expressed by a sentence in which such a name occurs. Is something communicated, or believed, concerning Vulcan? Clearly not, for there is no such thing. Is there some other object which these communications or beliefs concern? Surely not. Perhaps, then, sentences in which empty names are used express some general proposition, or the name is functioning as a description? But there are arguments against this suggestion, drawn from the (supposed) behaviour of the users of syntactic names. These arguments have to be shown to be unsound *before* one can accept that (*i*) is true. We have already mentioned one example of such arguments, and others will be found in section 9.

The above does not entail that one cannot reasonably attribute beliefs to users of 'Vulcan' on the basis of their behaviour as it relates to that word. On the contrary, an unenlightened speaker, who utters the sentence 'Vulcan's period of revolution is 24·25 days', thereby provides us, if we have suitable background information, with good evidence that he believes that the intra-Mercurial planet's period of revolution is 24·25 days. We cannot, however, view the sentence he utters as expressing the proposition, belief in which we ascribe to him on the basis of his utterance. The reason is that we cannot regard 'Vulcan' as an abbreviation, in his idiolect, for 'the intra-Mercurial planet', or for any other description, for reasons already mentioned, and therefore we cannot regard the sentence he utters as expressing any proposition at all. But clearly there is no general difficulty about ascribing beliefs to people on the basis of evidence other than that of what propositions they express by their utterances. The 'no-sense' theorist of empty names may thus end up by giving the same overall account of the beliefs of users of empty names as the description theorist would give. Their difference will reside in how they characterize the evidence for the beliefs they ascribe.

John McDowell, in his 'On the Sense and Reference of a Proper Name', offers an explanation of why it is especially tempting to regard an empty name as an abbreviated description. We are tempted to think that a thought is something purely mental, so that our thinking entails nothing about the way the world is outside our thoughts. But some thoughts are essentially thoughts *about* objects, and there can be no thoughts about objects that do not exist: the objects are woven into the thought. (Cf. McDowell 172–5.)

The difficulty about existential sentences remains. Perhaps we should adopt the metalinguistic approach that Russell, as we have seen, recommended in the case of fictional names. Then 'Vulcan does not exist' will be analysed as '"Vulcan" is not a name', and 'Vulcan does exist' as '"Vulcan" is a name'. There are at least two kinds of criticism of this suggestion, one of detail and one concerning the general strategy.

The detailed criticism is that the supposed analysis will make 'Vulcan does not exist' come out false, whereas we want it to come out true. The reason is that someone's cat is named 'Vulcan'. (I owe this observation to Colin Phillips.) Perhaps detailed revisions will overcome this, but it is not entirely easy to see how.

The more general criticism is that it appears unjustified to give a non-uniform account of how 'Vulcan' contributes to the sentences in which it occurs. If it occurs meaningfully in 'Vulcan does not exist' surely we ought to allow that it occurs meaningfully in 'Vulcan is a planet', having, perhaps, the meaning '"Vulcan" names a planet'? Unless an expression is ambiguous, it makes the same contribution to the meaning of every sentence in which it occurs, and this single contribution is what analysis lays bare.

In the present case, however, there *is* something akin to ambiguity, and it justifies some kind of divided treatment. The division separates the employment of 'Vulcan' by the enlightened from its employment by the unenlightened. We who are enlightened will not use 'Vulcan' with the intention of expressing or imparting singular beliefs concerning Vulcan. Our enlightened use of the word will primarily be directed to giving an account of what unenlightened speakers believe, and in saying just how these beliefs are false. Since, as we have seen, we certainly will want to attribute to the unenlightened such beliefs as that the intra-Mercurial planet has a period of revolution of 24·25 days, the natural suggestion is this: the enlightened, though not the unenlightened, use 'Vulcan' as an abbreviation of a description. This suggestion squares well with another phenomenon: the enlightened speaker will not give a straightforward yes/no response to the question whether a sentence like 'Vulcan is not a planet' might have been true. He will first ask for some elucidation of what the sentence means, and the sort of elucidation that is appropriate appears to consist in replacing 'Vulcan' by some description. Once the suggestion is accepted, there is no problem about how 'Vulcan does not exist' can, in the mouth of an enlightened speaker, express a truth. (In the mouth of the unenlightened, it expresses nothing at all:

75

at the moment of enlightenment, 'Vulcan' acquires a meaning for him and he will have to distance himself from the way in which, formerly, he had tried to use the word.)

The conclusion so far is this: Russell rightly held that there are no names which lack bearers. This presents a dilemma concerning empty names: either they are descriptions, or they are meaningless. I have tried to show that the latter suggestion gives a plausible account for unenlightened speakers, the former a plausible account for enlightened speakers. This limited adoption of the description theory, however, has no tendency to suggest a more generalized adoption. The argument of the present section can, therefore, be seen as part of a vanguard action in support of the claim in section 9 that there are general reasons, which extend to at least some empty names, in their unenlightened use, for not regarding most of what are ordinarily called names as descriptions.

I said that the consideration of empty names helped to explain why Russell thought that ordinary proper names are not names. The explanation is tentative, since it depends on the attribution to Russell of the following belief, and I have no direct evidence for the attribution: the speakers of a language cannot mistake which of its expressions are names, or at least they are entitled to as high a degree of confidence on this subject as on any.[1] But Russell held that only in our sense-data beliefs are we entitled to the highest degree of confidence. Hence names can name only sense-data. Of course, Russell's principle of acquaintance gets him to this conclusion in a single step, and cannot be ignored in an account of why Russell was reluctant to regard ordinary proper names as names. But it is interesting to note that the present point gets Russell to the same conclusion independently of the principle of acquaintance, though not, of course, independently of his epistemological views in general. However, if what I have suggested in this section is correct, the premise required for this route to the conclusion is false; there were plenty of beliefs which the unenlightened users of 'Vulcan' were entitled to hold with greater confidence than the belief that 'Vulcan' was a name.

The next three sections suggest other routes which led Russell to his erroneous view that ordinary proper names are not names.

[1] Ayer seems to think that one needs to attribute to Russell an even stronger principle: that it is inconceivable that any symbol we take to be a name should not be a name. He is not explicit, but without this strong attribution, his argument on pages 43–4 of *Russell and Moore* is invalid.

5   Two names with the same bearer have the same meaning

> If one thing has two names, you make exactly the same assertion whichever of the names you use (*PLA* 245).

In other words, two names which name the same mean the same. This follows from the doctrine that the meaning of a name is its bearer, but it does not follow from the doctrine that the meaning of a name, '*a*', consists in the fact that it names *a*. The reason is that the fact that '*a*' names *a* is not the same fact as the fact that '*a*' names *b*, even if *a*=*b*. I take it that the fact that . . . is the same fact as the fact that —— only if '*A* believes that . . .' and '*A* believes that ——' are mutually entailing. But *A* may believe that 'Tully' names Tully without believing that 'Tully' names Cicero, for he may not realize that Tully=Cicero. (The point about fact-identity may be taken as stipulative, if you like, and the claim that the meaning of '*a*', if it is a name, consists in the fact that '*a*' names *a* can be rephrased so as to avoid the apparent reference to facts.)

We can thus explain Russell's adherence to the view that if two names name the same they mean the same in terms of his adherence to the view that the meaning of a name is its bearer. But we can also show how he could have avoided this conclusion, by adhering instead to the view that the meaning of a name '*a*' consists in the fact that '*a*' names *a*. In the introductory remarks to this chapter, we saw that there were independent reasons for holding that Russell should have held this last view, and that much of his doctrine concerning names can be extracted from it.

The example above showed at the same time that what we ordinarily regard as names, for example 'Tully' and 'Cicero', do not satisfy the principle that names which name the same mean the same. This helps to explain why Russell did not count ordinary proper names as names. We *might* accept the principle as part of a stipulation concerning how Russell will use 'name' (or 'logically proper name'). However, in accordance with the policy sketched at the beginning of this chapter, I shall instead regard it as a false doctrine concerning naming, the nature of naming having already been established by the other doctrines that we have considered.

The doctrine may, perhaps, be satisfied by demonstratives, but *if* this is so (and there is room for doubt) it is so in virtue of special features concerning contextual determination. Demonstratives certainly fail to satisfy the converse of the principle, that expressions which name different things have different meanings. In *PLA*, Russell accepted the consequence that this made demonstratives ambiguous, but in *IMT* he realized that this was a mistake and that a demonstrative pronoun has, in some sense, a single meaning despite the fact that it can be used, on different occasions, to demonstrate different things (*IMT* 103).

If names are rigid designators, by Peacocke's standard, then it may seem that they should satisfy the false doctrine. For will not it be possible to use the same name, in giving the truth-condition of two sentences which differ only in that a name in one is replaced in the other by a distinct name which names the same? This surely would hold of the original rough criterion. But as I have already mentioned, the finished account requires, in effect, that the truth-condition be one which could serve as the core of a total theory of meaning: in particular, that it be one which one could use to ascribe to a man such propositional attitudes as beliefs and assertions on the strength of the noises he makes. Such a truth-condition will match a name in the sentence for which it is a truth-condition with a synonym.

That names which name the same mean the same also fails to follow from the point about singular belief. For although '*A* believes that Tully is bald' entails '*A* believes, concerning Tully, that he is bald', which in turn entails '*A* believes, concerning Cicero, that he is bald', there is no route from here to '*A* believes that Cicero is bald' (cf. McDowell 173 n. 1). Hence singular belief gives no support to the view that 'Tully is bald' and 'Cicero is bald' express the same belief, and thus no support to the view that 'Tully' and 'Cicero' are synonyms, and thus no support to the view that if names name the same they mean the same.

6　*Knowing that a = b*

Russell argued that a true identity sentence in which the identity sign is flanked by names is 'just a tautology' (*PLA* 245), and he used this supposed fact as an argument for the description theory of ordinary proper names. Since such sentences as 'Tully is Cicero' can come as surprising news, they are not mere tautologies, and so it cannot be that both the syntactic names are genuine names.

In his work 'On Sense and Reference' Frege used similar considerations to come to a similar conclusion, and this was the basis on which he elaborated his theory of the general distinction between sense and reference. It led him to suppose that for any name there is some identificatory knowledge concerning its bearer which must be possessed by anyone who understands the name, and this leads naturally to the view that names are concealed descriptions.

Both Russell and Frege are wrong to suppose that there is any problem about knowing that $a = b$, even if both 'a' and 'b' are names and $a = b$. They could arrive at the view that '$a = b$' is a 'tautology' (or that it has the same 'cognitive value' as '$a=a$') only by defective arguments.

One is the argument that names which name the same mean the same, so '$a=b$' means the same as '$a=a$'. But this argument, as we saw in the last section, has a false premise: that names name the same does not guarantee that they mean the same.

Another is the related argument that if A knows that 'a' names a then he knows, concerning a, that 'a' names it; so if $a=b$ he knows, concerning b, that 'a' names it; so he knows that 'a' names b. So, if $a=b$, one who understands '$a=b$' thereby knows enough to know that $a=b$. But this argument, as we also saw in the last section, is invalid: one cannot infer from the fact that A knows, concerning b, that 'a' names it, that A knows that 'a' names b.

There is thus no good reason to suppose that a true identity sentence in which the identity sign is flanked by names cannot come as news to one who understands it. Frege's distinction between sense and reference was designed to overcome a non-existent problem. (For the connection of this point with Frege, see McDowell.)

7 Existence

'a exists' . . . is a mere noise or shape, devoid of significance (*IMP* 165: the context makes clear that 'a' is a name).

The fact that you can discuss the proposition 'God exists' is a proof that 'God', as used in that proposition, is a description and not a name. If 'God' were a name, no question as to existence could arise (*PLA* 250).

In other words, a sentence of the form '. . . exists' is meaningful iff what replaces the dots is a description. This is part of Russell's famous doctrine that existence is not a property of individuals. In *PLA*, for example, it leads him to say:

So the individuals that there are in the world do not exist, or rather it is nonsense to say that they exist and nonsense to say that they do not exist (*PLA* 252).

The cause of this view is twofold. On the one hand, Russell's theory of descriptions suggests that in some cases attributions of existence can be replaced by applications of the existential quantifier. Details are given in the next chapter. This paves the way for the denial of all attributions of existence, which is independently argued for on the grounds that if 'a' is a name, there is something that it names, and so it is not possible to say significantly 'a does not exist'. (I paraphrase a remark from *PLA* 250.)

In more detail, the argument might look like this. Any meaningful sentence has a meaningful negation. So any meaningful sentence is one which, even were it false, would be meaningful. So if 'a exists' is meaningful, it would be meaningful even if it were false. But it would not be meaningful if false, for 'a' would be bearerless. Therefore 'a exists' is meaningless, whether we envisage it to be true or whether we envisage it to be false.

This argument relies on a false step. From the truth that any meaningful sentence has a meaningful negation, we cannot correctly infer that any meaningful sentence is one which, even if it were false, would be meaningful, for this conclusion is false. This is shown by a consideration of sentences not involved in the present controversy, for example: 'some sentences are meaningful'; 'there are languages'; 'the word "meaning" has meaning'. These sentences are, uncontroversially, meaningful. But they all have the supposedly impossible property of being such that, were they false, they would be meaningless.

All that follows from the fact that names name is that all sentences of the form 'a exists' are true, and all those of the form 'a does not exist' are false, if 'a' is a name. This follows of necessity. But it does not follow that any sentence of the form 'a exists' is a necessary truth, nor does it follow that any sentence of the form 'a does not exist' is a necessary falsehood.[2] That just depends on whether or not a is a necessary existent. Confusion on this point would help to foster the view that existential sentences containing names are meaningless, and it may, perhaps, be detected in Russell's claim that

> it is perfectly clear that, if there were such a thing as this existence of individuals that we talk of, it would be absolutely impossible for it not to apply, and that is the characteristic of a mistake (*PLA* 241).

Russell may also be making another mistake in this passage: that of supposing that there cannot be a coherent predicate which applies to everything. That this is a mistake can be seen by considering a predicate like '. . . is self-identical'.

We could interpret Russell as simply *stipulating* that he will not count as a 'name' any expression which can figure meaningfully in

---

[2] In these remarks I use 'necessary' in the so-called 'strong' sense, sometimes symbolized '$\boxdot$', according to which '$\boxdot p$' is true iff 'p' is true in every possible world. In the 'weak' sense, sometimes symbolized as '$\Box$', and according to which '$\Box p$' is true iff 'p' is true in every possible world in which the bearers of any names in 'p' exist, we have that $\Box$ (Socrates is a man). We do not have that $\boxdot$ (Socrates is a man), since there are worlds at which Socrates does not exist, and thus worlds at which 'Socrates is a man' is not true. For any name 'a' we have, of course, that $\Box$ (a exists), but not in general that $\boxdot$ (a exists). For the distinction, and the problems it raises, see Davies, 'Weak Necessity and Truth Theories'.

existential sentences. However, in pursuance of the policy outlined in the introduction to this chapter, I shall not adopt this course. Rather, I shall treat Russell's doctrine about existential sentences as a mistaken doctrine about *naming*. The mistake helps to explain why Russell refused to allow that what we ordinarily call proper names are names: ordinary proper names can figure meaningfully as the subjects of existential sentences.

Since it is uncontroversial that 'exists' is a grammatical predicate, and since we know the semantic effect of concatenating a name with a predicate, no positive action need be taken to *show* that existential sentences containing names are meaningful.[3] All that is necessary is to rebut objections to this view, and this I have already done to some extent. However, a further question remains: can we explain how the utterance of a positive existential sentence whose subject is a name can serve to inform a hearer of something he previously did not know? For this is how one *might* characterize the use of 'Virgil exists', or rather 'Virgil really existed', in such sentences as 'Virgil really existed whereas Homer probably did not'.

For '*a* exists' to have a genuinely news-bearing role, I think we have to regard 'exists' as Strawson does in 'Is Existence Never a Predicate?', that is, as a predicate whose extension is the set of all non-fictional entities, and the complement of whose extension is the (non-empty) set of all fictional entities. However, it is plain that this is not the kind of predicate that Russell had in mind when he denied that existence is a predicate, for the predicate he had in mind was intended to have the universal set (of individuals) as its extension.

In any case, one might be worried by Strawson's suggestion on two other counts. One is that it requires that there be fictional objects (and we saw above how vigorously Russell resisted this suggestion – pages 71–2). The other is that, if existential sentences with names as subjects are to have a news-bearing role, it must be possible to understand a name without knowing whether it names a fictional or a non-fictional object; and some might find this implausible.

However, if we insist that 'exists' be used in the way that Russell envisaged but rejected, that is as a predicate true of everything, then one has to accept the conclusion that sentences in which the predicate is concatenated with a name will have no news-bearing use. This does not mean that there will never be any point in uttering such sentences. For example, if we suspect that someone has doubts about his own understanding of '*a*' we may utter '*a* exists' to reassure him. The

---

[3] One might, however, remark that the easiest way to explain the meaning of such uncontroversially meaningful sentences as 'Socrates might not have existed is to view them as the result of applying a modal operator to a (meaningful) sentence.

mechanism here is not that we aim to get him to believe that a exists, for if he understands 'a' it is hard to see how he can fail to believe this already. Rather, by uttering the sentence we manifest our confidence in the obtaining of some of the facts which must obtain for the sentence we utter to be meaningful, and our utterance will have point if we think that our hearer's confidence concerning his grasp of 'a' is at a low ebb. If we find Strawson's suggestion unattractive, this is one explanation we might give of the point of uttering sentences of the form 'a exists', as in 'Virgil really existed but Homer probably did not'. Again, it is always open to us to hold that in at least some of these examples we have syntactic names which are not genuine names. For the point I am making against Russell is only that the result of concatenating a genuine name with 'exists' is significant and might pointfully be uttered. I am not claiming that every sentence in which a syntactic name is concatenated with 'exists', and which can be used pointfully, is one containing a genuine name.

It would, of course, be a mistake to infer from the fact that a sentence has no news-bearing use that it is meaningless. Think of sentences of the form '$a=a$'.

Part of the explanation of Russell's adherence to the false doctrine that existence is not a property of individuals must lie in his delight at the discovery that *some* occurrences of 'exist' can be regarded as occurrences not of a predicate of individuals but of the existential quantifier: a predicate of predicates. It was tempting to think that this ruled out the possibility of there being an existential predicate of individuals. But this is a mistake twice over: not only is it an unwarranted generalization, but the lie to the conclusion is given within Russell's own formal framework. For what is '$(\exists x)(x=\zeta)$', if not an existential predicate of individuals?

Another part of the explanation might consist in the following slide: first one takes the all too easy step of confusing the truth that, necessarily, every instance of 'a exists' is true, with the falsehood that every such instance is a strongly necessary truth (see note 2, p. 80). Then one confuses a necessary falsehood with something meaningless (a view for which Wittgenstein argues in the *Tractatus*). Finally, one makes the valid move from the false premise that every sentence of the form 'a does not exist' is meaningless to the conclusion that every sentence of the form 'a exists' is meaningless.

8   Understanding names

Russell's account of what it is to understand a name 'a' of an object a is dominated by his principle of acquaintance. Since I have rejected this principle, I intend to see whether Russell has any other suggestions about what it is to understand a name.

There is in particular one remark that I intend to study. Russell at one point says that 'to know the meaning of a name is to know who it is applied to' (*PLA* 244). It seems to me that we have here a condition for understanding that is at least sufficient, and perhaps also necessary.

What is it to know to whom or what a name is applied? I suggest that it is to know, concerning the object which is in fact the bearer of the name '*a*', that it is named '*a*'. So the claim that Russell's condition is sufficient is the claim that if someone knows, concerning *a*, that it is named '*a*', he understands '*a*'. I suggest that this claim is correct.

Before giving reasons for this, I draw attention to the connection between this claim and the principle of acquaintance. On Russell's stricter and more proper view, acquaintance with an object is a necessary condition for singular knowledge concerning it. Hence Russell would interpret the present claim as consistent with the necessity for acquaintance with the bearer of any name which one can understand.

One reason that might be given for supposing that the present sufficiency thesis (that knowing of *a* that it is named '*a*' is sufficient for understanding '*a*') is incorrect is this: understanding a name involves knowing how to use it and interpret it as it occurs in sentences, but this is not vouchsafed merely by knowing, of the bearer, that it is thus named.

I am inclined to think the objection mistaken, on the grounds that knowing of an object that an expression *names* it is possible only for one who knows what *naming* is, and who thus has a general understanding of the role of names in sentences. However, the point is of small importance: for one could well relativize the sufficiency thesis to those who have the general linguistic capacities in question.

The correctness of the sufficiency thesis is suggested by such familiar cases as the following: Fido goes by; we point him out and say 'That's Fido'; our audience comes to understand the name 'Fido'. What more has happened, relevant to this understanding, than that our audience has come to know, of Fido, that he is named 'Fido'? Surely the answer is: nothing.

There seems to be only one serious source of opposition to this answer. This is that, in addition, the audience has come to associate the name 'Fido' with some description, a description which encapsulates the meaning of the name (or which will serve to encapsulate the meaning the name will have in the audience's idiolect). The inherent plausibility of the sufficiency thesis counts against this description theory. But it would be unwise to rely on this alone, and in the next section I marshal independent arguments against the description theory.

Here I wish to emphasize the incompatibility of the sufficiency thesis with the description theory. For imagine the following proposed reconciliation. A description theorist of names is extremely likely to hold a description theory of singular knowledge, maintaining that one can have knowledge *of* an object only 'under a description': in other words, that one can know of a that it is G only if, for some F, $a=$ the F and one knows that the F is G. Hence, it may seem, this theorist can accept the sufficiency thesis, since the singular knowledge that it claims is sufficient will have to be mediated by a description, just as will, supposedly, the understanding of a name.

The proposed reconciliation is spurious. The reason is that any remotely plausible description theory of singular knowledge will allow that there is a wide variety of descriptions which can, in any given case, mediate singular knowledge of an object. But there is only one description (or disjunction of descriptions) that mediates the speaker's understanding of an unambiguous name. So it is always an open possibility that the description which mediates a speaker's knowledge of a should be other than the description which mediates his understanding of 'a'; and thus always an open possibility that he should know of a that it is named 'a' without understanding 'a'.

An example might be the following. Suppose the description theorist claims that 'Tully' abbreviates the description 'the F' and 'Cicero' abbreviates the description 'the G'. Suppose, further, that a speaker, A, knows of Cicero that he is named 'Cicero'. On the description theory of singular knowledge this can obtain only if there is some proposition which the speaker knows, expressed by a sentence containing a description of Cicero, and suppose that in the present case the description is 'the F'. Then what A knows is that the F is named 'Cicero', and there is no chance of his extracting from this the appropriate association of the name 'Cicero' with the description 'the G'.

The example brings out the following important point about the sufficiency thesis. Knowledge of a that it is named 'a', together with $a=b$, entails knowledge, concerning b, that it is named 'a', but it does not entail knowledge, concerning a, that it is named 'b'. So the sufficiency thesis does not have the absurd consequence that one who understands one name for an object understands every name for it.

The remark of Russell's which we are studying identifies understanding a name with knowing who or what its bearer is, so he is claiming not only the sufficiency thesis, which we have discussed, but also an analogous necessity thesis. This emerges in other remarks, for example:

84

> To understand a name you must be acquainted with the particular of which it is a name, and you must know that it is the name of that particular (*PLA* 205).

I shall not discuss the correctness of the necessity thesis, but I shall mention two grounds for doubt. One is that it might be argued that one can grasp a name without grasping the concept of naming. If so, one can understand '*a*' without knowing of *a* that '*a*' *names* it. The other ground is this: perhaps it would be enough truly to believe, of *a*, that '*a*' names it. If so one can understand '*a*' without *knowing* of *a* that '*a*' names it.

A further question is this: what form must a proposition take, if knowledge of it is to be sufficient for understanding a name? Here one can suggest that knowing that '*a*' names *a* is enough for understanding '*a*'. (Cf. McDowell.)

Two objections may be made to this claim, but they are easily set aside. One might misread the required knowledge as amounting merely to knowledge that the sentence '"*a*" names *a*' is true, and for this latter knowledge an English speaker need only know that '*a*' is a name: he need not know what it names, and he need not understand it. But the claim that *A* knows that '*a*' names *a* is logically independent of the claim that *A* knows that the sentence '"*a*" names *a*' is true. The latter is neither necessary nor sufficient for the former. It is not necessary, since *A* might know that '*a*' names *a* without understanding English, and thus without knowing that the sentence '"*a*" names *a*' expresses what he knows, and thus without knowing that it is true. It is not sufficient, since *a* might know that the sentence '"*a*" names *a*' is true because he has heard it on good authority, but he might not know what the sentence means, and thus might fail to know that '*a*' names *a*. (Cf. McDowell 169.)

The other objection is that if *a* = *b* then knowing that '*a*' names *a* will suffice for knowing that '*b*' names *b*, and thus, absurdly, for understanding '*b*'. This would be a mistake twice over. One mistake would be to suppose that every sufficient condition is a minimally sufficient condition. If one gave a condition sufficient for understanding both '*a*' and '*b*' one would have given a sufficient condition, though presumably not a minimally sufficient condition, for understanding '*a*'. The other mistake concerns the form of the argument: as we have already seen, there is no valid argument from '*A* knows that "*a*" names *a*' and '*a* = *b*' to any of: '*A* knows that "*b*" names *b*'; '*A* knows that "*a*" names *b*'; '*A* knows that "*b*" names *a*'.

Once the view is properly understood, and these incorrect objections are set aside, there is no obstacle, so far as I can see, to its acceptance, even by the description theorist. What he will object to is not the claim that knowing that 'a' names a is sufficient for understanding 'a', but rather the claim that this is the best or most illuminating account that can be given of the relevant knowledge. He will maintain that the best account will unpack 'a' into the description that gives its sense, rather than merely reuse 'a' with that sense.

One source of the description theory is the belief that we use criteria in applying names. Then the sense of a name will comprise the identificatory knowledge which guides our use of it. I shall conclude this section by showing that, at least at one moment, Russell firmly rejected this route to the description theory. The passage comes from *Mind*:

> Understanding words does not consist in knowing their dictionary definitions, or in being able to specify the objects to which they are appropriate. . . . Understanding language is more like understanding cricket: it is a matter of habits, acquired in oneself and rightly presumed in others. To say that a word has meaning is not to say that those who use the word correctly have ever thought out what the meaning is. . . . The relation of a word to its meaning is of the nature of a causal law governing our use of the word and our actions when we hear it used. There is no more reason why a person who uses a word correctly should be able to tell what it means than there is why a planet which is moving correctly should know Kepler's laws (197–8).

The passage raises a number of points of interest. (*i*) If having habits is the essence of understanding, then presumably *how* the habits were acquired is not. Thus the thought of this passage is in tension with the principle of acquaintance. One way to resolve the tension would be to suppose that the principle of acquaintance is to be understood not as I have understood it, as intended to give the essence of understanding, but rather as a contingent truth: as things are, we only acquire the relevant habits by acquaintance with the meaning-relata of words. However, this interpretation would not sit well with Russell's insistence on the principle, from *OD* to *MPD* and at many points in between, for surely only what was offered as an analysis of linguistic understanding would be thought to deserve such prominence. (*ii*) 'The relation of a word to its meaning is of the nature of a causal law.' 'Meaning' is here to be understood as 'meaning-relatum', and the sentence offers a step towards an analysis of the relation which holds between a word and its meaning-relatum. In simple cases, at least, Russell says shortly afterwards, it consists in the fact that the word has the same causal efficacy as its meaning-relatum (*Mind* 200). I wish to point out merely that the truth of the doctrines with which we have been principally concerned in this section, the sufficiency thesis and the doctrine that knowing that '*a*' names *a* is enough for understanding '*a*', must be distinguished from the question of how the naming relation they both invoke is to be analysed. (*iii*) The behaviouristic tendency of the passage suggests that Russell would not here have held the necessity thesis. As we have seen, this contrasts sharply with his views in *PLA*, written a relatively short time before. (*iv*) Most immediately relevant to our present purpose, the first sentence of the passage contains an explicit denial of the idea that using a name requires the user to exploit knowledge of uniquely identifying facts concerning its bearer: the user may not be 'able to specify the objects to which they [the words] are appropriate'. This harmonizes well with the fact that most of us, even if we can pick Margaret Thatcher out of a crowd, cannot say how we do it. The proof is that for any description of Margaret Thatcher we can offer, as an account of the basis of our recognition, we can easily distinguish between some waxwork or identikit or other woman satisfying the description, and Margaret Thatcher. No doubt there are mechanisms whereby we recognize her, but we do not know in full detail what they are, any more than a chicken-sexer can say how he distinghishes the sexes of day-old chicks. So it cannot be correct to say that we rely on *knowledge* of these mechanisms in applying the name 'Margaret Thatcher'. (Cf. McDowell 165–6.)

It is not surprising that Russell should reject the general claim that applying words, and in particular names, is mediated by identificatory knowledge of their meaning-relata, for he believed that there are logically proper names, and that these are not synonymous with any description. To the extent that Russell held, for certain expressions that we call 'names', that they are abbreviated descriptions, he had special reasons, some of which we have already encountered: he was not relying on a general claim about the need for identificatory knowledge.

9   Names and descriptions

Russell was driven to the theory that what we ordinarily call names are really descriptions by various false doctrines about names, as we have seen earlier in the chapter. The chief culprit is the principle of acquaintance, which made Russell think that only sense-data can be named. But any of the following doctrines, if true, would entail that what we ordinarily call names are not names, and Russell held them all, except, possibly, the last: if names name the same, they mean the same; existential sentences involving names are meaningless; identity sentences involving names can be known to be true, if true, and false, if false, by anyone who understands them; one has as much right to confidence about the non-emptiness of any syntactic name which is in fact a name as about anything at all. The previous discussions have, I hope, served to block these routes to the description theory of names.

None the less, the description theory has the merit of providing solutions, correct or incorrect, to a number of problems. How does a name contribute to the truth-conditions of sentences in which it occurs? What is it for a name 'a' to name an object a? What is it to understand a name? How can empty names be meaningful? The trouble is that the solutions are, on the whole, incorrect. But can this be said to have been satisfactorily established by the foregoing discussions? I think not. For, in many cases, the most that has been shown is that names function in a different way from *some* descriptions. It has not been shown that names function differently from any description. Hence some further argument is called for, and this section aims to provide it.

In section 1, it was argued that names are rigid designators and that some descriptions are not. This, if accepted, shows that names do not abbreviate non-rigid descriptions, but this does not establish that there is no description that a name abbreviates, for perhaps, as Peacocke argues, some descriptions are rigid. If this is right (and the question is discussed more fully in the next chapter), it is on the cards that names abbreviate rigid descriptions.

The same sort of argument applies to two properties intimately linked with rigid designation: that a name's bearer enters into the proposition expressed by a sentence in which it occurs, and that the presence of a name in a believed-sentence ensures that the belief ascribed is singular. Consider the sentence 'The woman over there is likely to be the next Prime Minister', uttered when the woman over there is Margaret Thatcher. Is not there some temptation to suppose that the speaker has said *of* Margaret Thatcher that she is likely to be the next Prime Minister? If so, one who forms a belief on the basis of correctly understanding what is said will form a singular belief concerning Margaret Thatcher. So there is, perhaps, some temptation to suppose that this description's denotation enters into the proposition the sentence expresses, and that the presence of this description in a believed-sentence ensures that the belief ascribed is singular. I do not say that it is proper to yield to this temptation (the question is discussed in the next chapter) but only that until it is shown to be improper we cannot reject the view that names abbreviate certain types of description.

Exactly the same point applies to scope. We saw that some descriptions are scope-sensitive, whereas names are not, and this shows that there are some descriptions which names do not abbreviate, but it fails to show that no descriptions are abbreviated by names. We could imagine a device for desensitizing a description with respect to scope. For example, in many formulations of the propositional calculus it is customary to rank the operators in order of dominance, usually with '$\sim$' lowest, so that '$\sim p$ v q' abbreviates '$(\sim p)$ v q' and not '$\sim(p$ v $q)$'. Likewise perhaps some descriptions, or some occurrences or intonations of descriptions, have their scope-ambiguity resolved, and perhaps it is these kinds of description that proper names abbreviate. Or, indeed, perhaps what proper names abbreviate are not descriptions but scope-desensitized descriptions, regardless of whether or not the latter are, as they occur in the language, physically distinguishable from scope-sensitive descriptions. Thus the mere fact that names are scope-insensitive and some descriptions are not does not show that no name is an abbreviation of some description. (However, cf. Peacocke 113.)

No name can lack a bearer, for then it would be meaningless. But a meaningful description, like 'the golden mountain', may denote nothing. However, this only shows that names do not abbreviate *empty* descriptions. How about non-empty ones?

We must be clear at the outset precisely what is involved in asserting or denying the description theory of names. One thing that cannot sensibly be held is that it is impossible for what is syntactically a name to abbreviate a description. The reason is that, given any description, you could introduce a simple abbreviation for it. This will be a syntactic name which, by stipulation, has the same meaning as a description. This fact is not open to dispute.

I can imagine two grades of description theorist. One accepts that naming, characterized as a function which, if possessed by 'a', is adequately specified by saying what is the bearer of 'a', is a coherent semantic function, which in theory might be possessed by words in a language, but which in fact is not possessed by any words, or almost any words, in actual languages. This is more or less Russell's position. It is not that there could be no genuine names, but that there just happen to be rather few (only 'this' and 'that', or these together with names for the sensible qualities). A deeper grade of description theorist denies that naming is a coherent semantic function. He will insist that there is no way of understanding an expression, whose intended role is that it stand for an object, except by regarding it as expressing some property of a kind which we could use to determine concerning an arbitrary object whether or not it is the one for which the expression stands. This position is approximately that of Dummett's *Frege*.

The case against both grades of description theorist can be developed in the same way. One takes examples of what are ordinarily called 'names' and shows that they are really names; or at

89

any rate, one shows that they cannot satisfactorily be viewed as disguised descriptions.

The essence of the case is that whatever description you take a name to abbreviate you will get the semantic properties of some sentence wrong. Consider, first of all, one of the implausibilities that Russell freely admits attaches to the description theory. Concerning the thought in the mind of one who uses an ordinary proper name he says:

> The description required to express the thought will vary for
> different people, or for the same person at different times. The only
> thing constant (so long as the name is rightly used) is the object to
> which the name applies (*PP* 29–30).

The idea is that, for example, when I use 'Bismarck' I mean 'the first Chancellor of the German Empire', and this is what I understand when you use 'Bismarck', even though you associate the word with a different description. 'The particular description involved usually makes no difference to the truth or falsehood of the proposition in which the name appears' (*PP* 30). However, in many cases it does make a difference. For example, in the envisaged circumstances, if you utter 'Bismarck was an astute diplomatist' I cannot correctly say that you said that Bismarck was an astute diplomatist, for that would be to attribute to you the thought that I associate with that sentence which, by hypothesis, is different from the one which you associate with it. Indeed, I have no direct way of reporting what you said, since I may not know what you said. I shall have to report you as having asserted some singular proposition which would be made true by Bismarck's being an astute diplomatist. This highly implausible conclusion, about what others say and about my ability to report it, is forced on the description theorist by the admission that names abbreviate different descriptions in different mouths. This admission in turn is forced on the description theorist by the fact that, for any description, 'the F', of an object, a, there will always be users of a word for a who do not know that a is the F. Bismarck's mother did not know, at the christening, that Bismarck was (or was to be) the first Chancellor of the German Empire, so this description, or the property it expresses, cannot have been what she meant by 'Bismarck'.

Even if we swallow this implausibility, it none the less appears to be a plain fact that users of names typically do not have before their mind a description which can be regarded as being abbreviated by the name. The way to reveal this fact is by an examination of the modal properties of sentences, in the way already mentioned in section 4. (It is an analogue of Kripke's examination, in 'Naming and Necessity', of the properties of modal sentences containing names.) Take a name, say 'Napoleon Bonaparte', as used by me. What description could it abbreviate? 'The first Emperor of France'? If so, then the sentence 'Napoleon was not first Emperor of France' and 'The first Emperor of France was not first Emperor of France' should mean the same, in my idiolect. But they do not, since I think the first but not the second, holding constant the meaning of both, might have been true (Napoleon might have died young). The same goes for all the definite descriptions I can think of: 'the husband of Josephine', 'the most famous person to be exiled on St Helena', 'the victorious general at Marengo', 'the commander of the vanquished at Waterloo', and so on. Moreover, other speakers, so far as I know, have similar beliefs about the modal properties of the relevant sentences. And what goes for 'Napoleon' goes for other names.

Scope raises its ugly head again: when I say that 'The first Emperor of France is not the first Emperor of France' could not have been true, I mean 'not' to have narrow scope relative to the first occurrence of the description, for if it has wide scope the sentence could have been true in virtue of France never being an Empire. But now someone might raise the following objection. 'Napoleon', too, is scope-sensitive, relative to 'not', and when you think that 'Napoleon is not the first Emperor of France' might have been true you are effecting a different disambiguation from the one you effect in the other case, and this explains the different modal properties.

The objection is worthless. The shortest way to deal with it is to add a conjunct to each of the sentences under discussion. To the one containing the name one adds 'Someone was Napoleon'; to the one not containing the name one adds 'Someone was the first Emperor of France'. The discrepancy of modal property persists, and shows that the two sentences differ in meaning, and thus that the meaning of the name is not the same as the meaning of the description.[4]

In this argument, it was assumed that the speaker knew that certain (definite) descriptions held of the bearer of the name, and so what had to be shown was that none of these descriptions was synonymous with the name. The assumption can be challenged, and this constitutes a distinct argument against the description theory.

---

[4] The argument here might not take this relatively simple form for anyone who believes that some descriptions, on some occasions, are rigid designators by Peacocke's standard, and effect genuine reference. However, someone in this position will already have rejected the deeper grade of description theory (the one I attributed to Dummett's *Frege*), and will therefore find himself in agreement with the main conclusion I seek to establish.

Someone wishing to come to understand the name 'Narvik' might usefully consult *Chambers's Encyclopaedia* (1901 edition). He will find this entry:

A port in Norway, sheltered by the Lopoden Islands, and open all the year, which ships vast quantities of iron ore brought by railway from Gellivarce in Sweden; pop. 5000.

It would not be unreasonable to say that someone who knows that this is the entry for 'Narvik', and who knows what the entry says, understands 'Narvik'. Yet the entry ascribes no property to Narvik which it claims to be unique, so he who knows what the entry says does not thereby know, concerning any property, that it has unique application, and so he cannot know any truth of the form 'Narvik is the F'. Hence, though he understands the name, there is no description which it abbreviates.

One should not place too much weight on this argument, for the notion of understanding a name (or any other expression) is vague, and it may be that the encyclopaedia reader does not come to understand 'Narvik'. However, the general point that we are often at a loss to come up with descriptions holding of bearers of names we are certain we understand is not nugatory.

Russell more than once suggested a standardized way of reaching, for any name 'a', a suitable description: one takes 'the thing called "a"' (*PP* 32, *PLA* 243). However, one could understand every word except 'a' in the sentence 'a is the thing called "a"', and know that the sentence is definitionally true, yet not understand 'a', and this shows that the description in question is insufficient to mediate understanding of the name. Moreover, this description, like any other, induces modal properties which are different from those induced in sentences in which the name replaces the description. The proposition expressed by 'a is not called "a"' might have been true.

It remains to attempt to unmask causes of belief in the erroneous description theory. I have already done this so far as Russell is concerned, but I shall now consider three more general causes.

One is the mistaken belief that since a description may well be used in the course of teaching someone the meaning of a name, the description is part of the meaning. That this is false is illustrated by the fact that the description may turn out not to hold of the bearer of the name, understanding of which was mediated by the use of the description. In Kripke's splendid example ('Naming and Necessity' 294), many of us were first introduced to the name 'Gödel' by a process involving the use of the description 'the first man to prove the incompleteness of arithmetic', but it is conceivable that this should turn out to be a description that does not hold of Gödel. This shows that even if our coming to understand 'Gödel' somehow involved a description, it does not follow that the description gives the meaning of the name, for it does not even follow that the description applies to the same thing as the name. (It is not easy to give a correct account of learning names. Exposure to the speech of someone who already understands the name seems sufficient, but it is doubtful whether we can say anything more useful about what the exposure does than that it enables the hearer to 'latch on' to the use of the name. We cannot say anything of interest about the mechanism whereby this happens. This point has some relevance to both parties to the dispute about whether one can learn the meaning of a word like 'pain' from 'one's own case': if one can or cannot, this has nothing to do with whether one can or cannot *state* a criterion.)

A second cause of belief in the description theory springs from a difficulty about explaining how we could apparently have evidence for sentences of the form '*a* does not exist'. Discoveries which would lead us to accept such a sentence could not be discoveries concerning *a*, so they must be discoveries to the effect that certain descriptions fail to hold of anything. But this can bear necessarily on whether or not *a* exists only if there is some analytic connection between the name and the description (cf. Searle 'Proper Names').

All goes well with this argument until almost the end. It is indeed true that, if we believe that *a* is *F* or is the *F*, but then discover that nothing is *F* or, for the second case, that more than one thing is, we *may* simply decide that *a* is not, after all, *F* or the *F*, but we may instead begin to wonder whether what we take to be singular beliefs expressed by sentences like '*a* is *F*' or '*a* is the *F*' are really singular beliefs, and whether these sentences actually express anything. In short, we may come to decide that '*a*' is bearerless. But this phenomenon requires no analytic connection between the name and the predicates or descriptions, since the evidence, even the sum of the evidence, does not *entail a*'s non-existence. We may be obliged wholly to revise our beliefs about *a*. This point is reinforced by the consideration of the third cause of belief in the description theory.

If two speakers both use a name, '*a*', and we believe that they have a common vocabulary with, perhaps, the exception of '*a*', and if there is a very widespread disagreement concerning the truth-values of sentences in which '*a*' is used, we may conclude, and indeed reasonably, that the speakers mean different things by '*a*'. This fosters the view that the meaning of a name is settled, if not by a description (i.e. a definite description), at least by a predicate or set of predicates. Otherwise, there could surely be total disagreement about the properties of one and the same thing, yet it is this possibility that, in the case envisaged, we refrain from countenancing.

Now it is true that this sort of discrepancy of assignment of truth-value to sentences containing a name is good ground for the conclusion that the speakers do not mean the same by the name. But it is a mistake to conclude from this that a degree of harmony in assignment of truth-values is necessarily required for shared understanding, and thus an even greater mistake to conclude that any area of overlap of truth-value assignment which happens to support the hypothesis of shared understanding identifies the predicates which must be believed, by anyone who understands the name, to result in true sentences when concatenated with the name.

The second error involves a modal fallacy. One cannot pass from the premise that necessarily there are shared judgments to the conclusion that there are judgments such that these are necessarily shared. The first error is more illuminating, and the way to show it up is to show that there is nothing impossible about all of a man's beliefs concerning an object, beliefs which he would express by using a name of that object, being false. A criminal once had an honest employee called '*a*', and when the police eventually caught up with him he tried to cover his tracks by attributing all his crimes to *a*, who, he claimed, was once his partner. The police may have no true belief about *a*, yet they understand '*a*'. In an extreme case it is admittedly sometimes arbitrary whether we say there was complete make-believe, or falsehood concerning *a*. But the latter possibility is open in many cases. In the present example, we could well imagine *a* having a case for suing for defamation of character. To take another example: everyone agrees that some of a man's beliefs about an object *a* may be false. But it is surely logically possible that he should one by one forget all the true ones and be left with only the false beliefs about *a*. Under the assumption that the man can express his beliefs about *a* by using a name of *a*, both examples are subject to one possible limitation: perhaps the man must know that this name names *a*. Evidently, this concession would go no way towards resuscitating the idea that anyone who understands a name must thereby know, concerning some significant range of predicates (properties), that they hold of the bearer of the name.

The moral is that we can allow no end of false beliefs about *a* so long as we know about the mode of acquisition of the beliefs, and can thus account for the error. In the absence of such evidence, we do generally deny that the name is understood, or is understood in the same sense. But the evidence is inductive: it does not entail the conclusion we draw, and this shows that true belief, or shared belief, is not part of the essence of understanding.

IV

Descriptions

Russell's theory of descriptions was first presented in the famous article 'On Denoting' (*OD*) which appeared in 1905. In that article he discusses various quantifier phrases, including those of the form 'all so-and-so' and those of the form 'a so-and-so' (indefinite descriptions). However, by 'Russell's theory of descriptions' I shall understand his theory of the proper analysis of definite descriptions, initially characterized as phrases of the form 'the so-and-so', and I shall continue the implicit convention of previous chapters of using 'description', *tout court*, to mean any such phrase, unless there is explicit indication to the contrary.

The theory of descriptions has two aspects, one informal and the other formal, and within each aspect there are two parts, one part to deal with existential description-sentences ('The *F* exists'), another to deal with all other description-sentences. The informal aspect offers an analysis of descriptions in ordinary English. The formal aspect consists of definitions of the non-primitive *PM*-symbol '$\imath$' (inverted iota), a symbol whose role in the formal language is intended to be close to the role of 'the' in English, and of the non-primitive symbol 'E!'. A full account of the scope of descriptions in English is to be obtained only through the formal aspect of the theory.

In the informal aspect, the theory is this: one part holds that any sentence of the form 'The *F* is *G*' is to be analysed as 'At least one thing is *F* and at most one thing is *F* and whatever is *F* is *G*'. The other part holds that any sentence of the form 'The *F* exists', or an equivalent sentence like 'There is such a thing as the *F*', is to be analysed as 'At least one thing is *F* and at most one thing is *F*'. Russell's doctrine that 'exists' is not a predicate means that it is not one of the intended

95

substitutes for 'is G' in 'The F is G', so sentences of the form 'The F exists' are not, in the theory, provided with two distinct patterns of analysis.

Turning now to the formal aspect, the symbol '$\imath$' has the intended reading, roughly, of 'the'. At first sight, one might think that it could be regarded simply as a variable-binding operator which forms singular terms out of open sentences (I shall call the results '$\imath$-descriptions'), and that the spirit of the informal account would be recaptured by defining every sentence of the form '$G(\imath x)(Fx)$' (roughly, 'the object x, such that Fx, has G') as an abbreviation of the corresponding sentence '$(\exists x)(Fx \ \& \ (\forall y)(Fy \rightarrow y=x) \ \& \ Gx)$', or of its terser equivalent '$(\exists x)((\forall y) \ (Fy \leftrightarrow y=x) \ \& \ Gx)$'. However, this plan pays insufficient attention to possible scope-ambiguities. Russell gives the example of the formula '$G(\imath x)(Fx) \rightarrow p$' (PM 173). Different ways of applying the present plan will give different results. One possibility gives '$(\exists x) ((\forall y)(Fy \leftrightarrow y=x) \ \& \ Gx) \rightarrow p$', in which the existential quantifier has merely the antecedent of the conditional as its scope, and which may be read in English as: if the F is G, then p. Another possible application of the present plan yields '$(\exists x)((\forall y)(Fy \leftrightarrow y=x) \ \& \ (Gx \rightarrow p))$', in which the existential quantifier has the whole formula as its scope, and which may be read in English as, roughly: the F is such that if it is G then p. There is a semantic difference: $\sim(\exists x)Fx$ suffices for the truth of the first formula, and for the falsity of the second. This gives ground for saying that the original formula ('$G(\imath x)(Fx) \rightarrow p$') was ambiguous, but as there are no ambiguous formulae in PM a device must be found for removing the ambiguity before we can regard expressions containing $\imath$-descriptions as well-formed.

Russell's device is somewhat clumsy. (I have replaced his scope-indicating dots by parentheses, and this makes for a notation that is even clumsier than his own.) It involves having a second, scope-indicating, occurrence of the $\imath$-description, enclosed in square brackets, at some point to the left of what I shall call the 'proper' occurrence of the $\imath$-description. The scope of the $\imath$-description (that is, the scope of the proper occurrence of the $\imath$-description) is the formula whose leftmost symbol is the first round bracket to the left of the scope-indicating occurrence, and whose rightmost symbol is the mate of this bracket. (Suitable formation rules are required to ensure that there is a suitable formula: for example, it must include the proper occurrence of the $\imath$-description.)

The result is that we can distinguish between '$[(\imath x)(Fx)] \ G(\imath x)(Fx) \rightarrow p$', which abbreviates '$(\exists x) ((\forall y)(Fy \leftrightarrow y=x) \ \& \ Gx) \rightarrow p$', and '$[(\imath x)(Fx)]G(\imath x)(Fx) \rightarrow p)$', which abbreviates '$(\exists x)((\forall y)(Fy \leftrightarrow y=x) \ \& \ (Gx \rightarrow p))$'. In effect, the scope-indicating occurrence of a description can be regarded as a kind of quantifier, and we could replace the proper occurrence by merely the variable which follows '$\imath$', and which would then be regarded as bound by the scope-indicating occurrence. For example, the formulae recently given could be written, more simply, as, respectively, '$[[(\imath x)(Fx)]Gx] \rightarrow p$' and '$([(\imath x)(Fx)](Gx \rightarrow p))$'. (The bracketing could be further simplified.) This is why it would be misleading to think of '$\imath$' as a term-forming operator. However, Russell does not adopt this simplification, so that his formation rules require that for each proper occurrence of an $\imath$-description there is a scope-indicating occurrence of that $\imath$-description, and conversely.

Having settled on suitable formation rules, Russell can now give the definition of '$\imath$', as follows:

$$([(\imath x)(Fx)]G(\imath x)(Fx)) =_{df} (\exists x)((\forall y)(Fy \leftrightarrow y = x) \,\&\, Gx) \qquad *14 \cdot 01$$

The idea is that the definition need be given only for a schema in which the (schematic) $\imath$-description has the whole schema as its scope, for where an $\imath$-description has as its scope a sub-formula in a formula, one can first apply the definition to the sub-formula, and then reinsert the result in the whole formula.

Since, on Russell's view, no predicate letter in *PM* can be regarded as standing in for 'exists', we need some fresh notation, if it is to be possible to formalize sentences of the form 'The *F* exists'. This is the second part of the formal theory, and it is provided in terms of '$E!$', defined as follows:

$$E!(\imath x)(Fx) =_{df} (\exists x)(\forall y)(Fy \leftrightarrow y = x) \qquad *14 \cdot 02$$

The scope of a description in an English sentence is to be the scope of the corresponding $\imath$-description in the sentence's formalization. Russell also gives a test for distinguishing between the primary occurrence of a description (when the description has the whole sentence as its scope) and the secondary occurrence (non-primary occurrence), a test which is independent of the syntax of *PM*: if a description 'the *F*' has primary occurrence, the whole sentence is false unless the *F* exists (*PM* 70). The converse does not in general hold, so the test may not be decisive, and in any case it enables one at best to distinguish primary from secondary occurrence. It does not in itself enable one to differentiate the various different sorts of secondary occurrence. The general point is that no merely two-way distinction can adequately reflect scope-distinctions. Thus the idea of the scope of a description leans on that of the scope of an $\imath$-description, and this is why one cannot give a fully adequate account of the informal aspect of the theory without introducing the formal aspect.

I have so far only roughly indicated the intended sphere of application of the theory of descriptions, in its informal aspect.

Russell at one point described it as the doctrine of the word 'the' in the singular (cf. *IMP* 167), but this would seem both to understate and to overstate the case. If the theory works at all, it should also apply to phrases which have more or less the same meaning as phrases of the form 'the so-and-so', but which do not contain 'the'. A large class of such phrases contain genitives: 'my cat' ('the cat I own'), 'John's father' ('the father of John'). Let us extend the use of 'description' to include phrases which can be thus paraphrased. Then the theory of descriptions applies more widely than to the word 'the' (in the singular).

According to Russell, it also applies less widely. He accepts from Moore the suggestion that it does not apply to 'The whale is a mammal', and explains: 'For this the blame lies on the English language, in which the word "the" is capable of various different meanings' (Schilpp 690). Again, he says in *PM* (30), concerning 'the': 'We shall use this word strictly, so as to imply uniqueness'. The suggestions are unnerving, since they prompt the thought that it will be hard to test the correctness of the theory of descriptions. Apparent exceptions can be blamed on the ambiguity of 'the' or on our failure to use it 'strictly'. However, I shall adopt the methodological principle of ignoring these escape clauses. We should not impute ambiguity unless we have to, and it is *prima facie* evidence against a theory that it has to treat 'the' as ambiguous.

Russell calls descriptions (and $\imath$-descriptions) 'incomplete symbols' (*PM* 66), and this metaphor appears to be equipollent with another: descriptions do not 'have meaning in isolation' (*PM* 66, cf. *OD* 42). The corresponding literal truth is that, for Russell, descriptions do not have meaning-relata; this is fortunate, since sentences like 'The golden mountain does not exist' are both true and meaningful. If 'the golden mountain' had to have a meaning-relatum, then this would have to be a non-existent entity for the sentence to be true. Russell attributes this 'intolerable' ontology to Meinong, and I discuss the issue further in the next section. An unkind critic, impressed by Russell's lavish ontology in *PofM*, might pretend to identify Meinong with Russell's earlier self, but this would be unfair. Though Russell's *PofM* theory of denoting has no plausibility at all when the predicate in the denoting phrase is empty (see above, page 18), and though he does indeed allow there to be non-existent entities, he does not explicitly counsel this move for the case of empty descriptions.

It is customary to suppose that a further characteristic of incomplete symbols, over and above their lacking a meaning-relatum, is that they are not to be analysed by being provided with a synonym, but are rather to be provided with a recipe whereby the symbol can be eliminated from any sentence in which it occurs (cf., e.g., Ayer, *Russell* 55). However, if one extracts from 'There is exactly one F and it is G' everything save what corresponds to the description, one is left with 'There is exactly one F and it', which one might say (assuming the truth of the theory) is synonymous with 'The F'. Moreover, just like 'The F', it is in some sense a 'logical unit': it takes a predicate to make a sentence. Russell's only point can be that it is not the sort of 'unit' to which anyone would wish to attribute a meaning-relatum. So this source of the idea that the theory of descriptions is not intended to provide a synonym for descriptions results either in a mistake, or else in a confusing reiteration of the point that descriptions do not have meaning-relata.

The *point* of applying the theory of descriptions to English description-sentences is clarity: the result is something whose meaning is totally perspicuous. The point of applying the theory to $\imath$-descriptions is somewhat different. The aim is that the syntax of *PM* should be minimal, while yet permitting the formalization of description-sentences. From these two aims flow both the need for '$\imath$' and 'E!' and the need for these to be defined rather than primitive symbols.

Russell at one point spoke as if the theory of descriptions marked the abandonment of the realist theory of meaning (*MPD* 63). In reality, the theory of descriptions is a substantial step towards making room for a suitably restricted realist theory. The idea is that every language is analysable into a perfect language, and the realist theory applies to all the extra-logical expressions of such a language. The logical constants are treated differently, in a way mentioned in Chapter II (pp. 24–5). Thus Russell thinks he can give an adequate account of all simple symbols of the perfect language: extra-logical vocabulary by the realist theory, logical constants by another method. But how is he to deal with descriptions? The theory of descriptions by, in effect, defining 'the' in terms of the logical constants, shows that there is nothing new to deal with: what suffices for extra-logical simple expressions, and for logical constants, suffices for descriptions.

To put the point in terms of an example: how can one, granted the realist theory and Russell's treatment of the logical constants, analyse a sentence like 'The F is G'? The answer is simple: the meanings of 'F' and 'G' (assuming the predicates indefinable) are treated by the realist theory, and once the word 'the' has been analysed away, every other symbol will be a logical constant, for which Russell had another account.

2 Russell's arguments for the theory

In the earliest exposition of the theory (*OD*), Russell's arguments for it are mostly negative:

(*i*) The attempt to treat descriptions as names ('Meinong's theory') has 'intolerable' consequences, ontological and other.

(*ii*) Distinguishing between the meaning and the denotation of descriptions, and indeed of denoting phrases generally ('Frege's theory'), leads to 'an inextricable tangle'. On the positive side:

(*iii*) Russell's theory, unlike the foregoing two, is capable of dealing with certain 'logical puzzles'.

(*iv*) In some subsequent expositions (e.g., *IMP* 176–7) he stresses that the theory correctly analyses description-sentences, and this means at least that analysandum and analysis are necessarily equivalent (i.e. that every possible circumstance in which the one would be true (false) is a circumstance in which the other would be true (respectively, false)).

I shall consider these arguments in turn, drawing as convenient on Russell's various expositions of his theory.

(*i*) Descriptions are not names. Russell uses various arguments to establish this.

(*a*)

If you understand the English language, you would understand the phrase 'The author of *Waverley*' if you had never heard it before, whereas you would not understand the meaning of 'Scott' if you had never heard it before because to know the meaning of a name is to know who it is applied to (*PLA* 244).

'Scott' is here being used as an example of a (logically proper) name, despite the fact that, on the finished theory, it must be held not to be a name but merely an ordinary proper name, that is, an abbreviated description. So presumably the intended generalization is to the conclusion that names are simple and descriptions are not, so descriptions are not names.

On the surface, we have here nothing but a trivial point of terminology: it is convenient to restrict 'name' so that only simple expressions count as names, and to restrict 'description' so that only complex expressions count as descriptions.

The quotation suggests, however, that this surface distinction is meant to reflect a deep distinction, the distinction between functioning as a name and functioning as a description, as this distinction was drawn in the first section of Chapter III. For Russell explains the simplicity of 'Scott' (the fact that you cannot work out its meaning on the basis of knowing the meanings of its parts) in terms of its having the naming function (to know the meaning of 'Scott' is to know who it is applied to). However, Russell cannot really have intended that the simple/complex distinction should exactly match the naming-function/describing-function distinction. For he thought that some simple expressions, ordinary proper names, function as descriptions, not as names. Hence he should not argue from being simple to functioning as a name.

Perhaps, in the quoted passage, the argument is in reality in the reverse direction: from having the naming function to being simple. But this argument is unsound. We have seen that Russell rightly allowed that demonstrative pronouns like 'this' function as names. But then he surely ought to have allowed that complex demonstrative phrases like 'that man' also function as names. Indeed, it has been suggested (by Peacocke) that some descriptions function, on occasion, as names (for they can be used indifferently in place of corresponding complex demonstratives). Hence we cannot, without further ado, move from the fact that an expression is complex to the claim that it lacks the naming function. This issue is taken up again in later sections.

Hence the only thing Russell can be said to have established in the argument under consideration is the stipulation that only simple expressions be called 'names', with the consequence that descriptions are not to be called 'names'.

(b) An identity sentence both of whose terms are names is trivial if true, but an identity sentence one of whose terms is a description can be non-trivially true (OD 55, PM 67, KAKD 164, PLA 245–6, IMP 174–5, MPD 85). Thus no description means the same as any name, and to treat a description as a name would be incorrect.

The argument is valid, but it has a false premise (cf. Chapter II, section 6).

The same falsehood underlies Russell's argument that if we treat descriptions as names, and thus say 'the F' means the F and 'the G' means the G, we will be obliged to hold that 'the F' means the same as 'the G' (KAKD 165).

(c) There are no empty names but there are empty descriptions (e.g., IMP 179). (In accordance with the convention of Chapter III, section 4, we should express the first part of this as follows: no empty names are names.)

This point is important, and might be rephrased: the semantic function of a name requires it to have a bearer, but the semantic function of a description leaves open whether or not it has a denotation (i.e. it leaves open whether there is a unique satisfier of the predicate in the description). The sign is that one can understand a description without knowing what its denotation is, or even whether it has one, but one cannot understand a name without knowing what its bearer is. A sentence containing an empty description can be used to say something (cf. section 4 below), as Russell stresses with his example of the sentence 'The King of France is bald', which, he says, says something false (*OD* 46). But now consider an expression with this characteristic: if it is meaningful at all, then it is a name. A sentence containing such an expression cannot say anything, if there is nothing the expression names. Correspondingly, if someone utters a description-sentence, and you know the context of the utterance, you know enough to know what the speaker said, without knowing what the denotation of the description is or even that it has one. By contrast, if someone utters a sentence containing a name, and you know the context of utterance, you do not know enough to know what he said unless you know what the bearer of the name is.

The bald point that there can be no meaningful names without bearers but that there can be meaningful descriptions without denotations seems to establish only that denotationless descriptions cannot be treated as names, but the considerations of the last paragraph show that the point extends more widely to a general contrast of semantic function between descriptions and names. However, Russell at one time relied on a method of extending the point which, for someone with his particular views, is rather dangerous. He relied on the idea that one must give a uniform account of both denotationless and other descriptions in virtue of their 'parity of form' (*KAKD* 162): expressions alike in form must be analysed alike. The danger is that the doctrine could be put to the following use: ordinary proper names, according to Russell, abbreviate descriptions so, by parity of form, all simple singular terms abbreviate descriptions, so there are no genuine names.

It is worth remarking that Russell sometimes (e.g., *IMP* 179) attempts to explain the possibility of a description's being meaningful yet empty (denotationless) by its complexity. This is an instance of a confusion, which I noted in connection with (*a*) above, between having the function of describing (or naming) and being a complex (respectively, simple) expression. Russell himself holds that simple expressions (ordinary proper names) may be empty yet meaningful, and I mentioned that there is a case for the view that some complex expressions (complex demonstratives, or even on some occasions descriptions) cannot be meaningful and empty.

We have so far assumed that there *are* empty or denotationless descriptions, but in *OD* Russell considers an alternative, which he attributes to Meinong (this is what I call 'Meinong's theory'). One makes a distinction between subsistence and existence in such a way that some things which do not exist none the less subsist. What were previously called 'empty' descriptions will be reconstrued as descriptions which describe some non-existent but subsistent entity. (Russell's terminology differs from time to time. I have used the terminology of *PofM* and *PP*, but in *OD* he uses 'subsists' for 'exists' and 'is an object' for 'subsists'.)

Russell argues that Meinong's theory involves infringement of the law of contradiction, for it involves the contention that, for example, the round square is round and also not round (*OD* 45). How, exactly, is Meinong's theory committed to this? Presumably, the Meinongian is supposed to argue that every instance of 'the *FG* is *F*' and 'the *FG* is *G*' is true. Then, granted the truth of 'whatever is square is not round', he will have to conclude that 'the round square is round' and 'the round square is not round' are both true, and so, therefore, is their conjunction. Finally, Russell can reasonably argue that, on the Meinongian assumption that there is exactly one round square (in the world of subsistence), this conjunction is equivalent to 'the round square is round and it is not the case that the round square is round', which is satisfyingly contradictory.

The only escape for the Meinongian is to deny the principles of inference involved, and the only plausible general solution seems to be to say that if a description holds of a subsistent non-existent entity a sentence containing it is neither true nor false, unless the predicate of the sentence happens to be 'subsists' or 'does not subsist'. In this way the Meinongian could deny that there is any contradiction which he holds to be true. However, the alternative is very unpalatable: the world of subsistence is shadowy indeed if nothing true or false can be said of its contents, save that they subsist. So even if it is not exactly right to say that Meinong's theory involves contradictions, Russell is none the less right to reject it.

(*d*) If the blank in '——— exists' or '——— does not exist' is filled by a name, the result is nonsense. Not so with descriptions. So descriptions are not names. (Cf., e.g., *IMP* 178–9.)

We saw in Chapter III, section 7, that the first premise of this argument is false.

(*e*) Names are scope-insensitive but descriptions are not (*OD* 52).

This argument is inconclusive, since what is shown is only that some descriptions are scope-sensitive. Perhaps there are scope-insensitive ones that can be treated as names. Moreover, one would have to show that scope-insensitivity is an essential property of being a name. For it is clear that there could be scope-sensitive simple singular expressions, and Russell himself thought that ordinary proper names were examples.

Apart from (*c*), the arguments we have considered have been inconclusive. That of (*c*), however, points in the direction of the general contrast of function between naming and describing: the bearer of a name enters into or is a constituent of propositions expressed by sentences in which the name is used, but the denotation, if any, of a description does not thus enter into propositions expressed by sentences in which the description is used. However, even if we agree, as we must, that descriptions cannot in general be regarded as functioning as names, this goes only a very small way towards establishing Russell's theory of descriptions. For there may be (and indeed are) many different ways of treating descriptions differently from names. Russell's theory is not entailed by the fact that descriptions are not names.

(*ii*) Frege's theory. In *OD* there is an obscure passage (48–50) in which Russell criticizes the view, which he attributes to Frege, that one should distinguish between the meaning and the denotation of denoting phrases. A similar view is discussed and rejected in *KAKD* (162–4), where it is attributed to Miss E. E. C. Jones.

In 'On Sense and Reference' Frege distinguishes two components in meaning, which he calls '*Sinn*' and '*Bedeutung*', usually translated as 'sense' and 'reference'. Russell, however, translates these terms as 'meaning' and 'denotation' respectively, and I shall keep to his usage in this discussion. Frege's view is that meaning and denotation are properties of expressions. Every meaningful sentence, general term, and singular term possesses meaning, and some in addition possess denotation. He would have accepted Russell's example of 'the present King of France' as a singular term with meaning but with no denotation. The meaning of a sentence is determined by the meaning of its meaningful parts, and the denotation of a sentence, which he identifies with its truth-value, by the denotation of its meaningful parts. If a meaningful part of a sentence lacks denotation, so does the sentence, that is, the sentence is truth-valueless. This conflicts with Russell's account of sentences containing descriptions which hold of nothing (lack denotation), since Russell, as we have seen, took them to be false. But it is not on these grounds that he at this point attacks Frege's position.

Quite what Russell's grounds are is hard to determine. (See, e.g., Searle's 'Russell's Objections to Frege's Theory', and Watling 65–9.) He makes the point that in order to speak of the meaning of an expression we have to speak about the expression and not about what, if anything, the expression denotes. Hence a phrase which denotes the meaning of an expression will normally contain a part which denotes that expression. For example, the meaning of the first line of Gray's Elegy is the meaning of 'The curfew tolls the knell of parting day'. It is not the meaning of 'The first line of Gray's Elegy'. But how is this relevant?

Two possibilities are suggested by his claim that one of the difficulties with Frege's theory is 'that meaning cannot be got at except by means of denoting phrases' (*OD* 49). This could be taken to be established by the remarks of the previous paragraph, and in turn to establish that *if* it is assumed that meaning and denotation are distinct the theory is incoherent: for every meaning is a denotation. This objection is simply a confusion. Frege held that, in any use of an expression, its meaning and its denotation are distinct, but he did not hold that no meaning could be a denotation. Quite the contrary: he held that in special circumstances (intensional contexts) an expression denotes that entity which, in ordinary circumstances, is its meaning. Russell thus establishes nothing that contradicts Frege's position.

The other possibility, which emerges particularly in *KAKD* (164), is that the fact that meaning can only be 'got at' through denoting phrases involves Frege's (or Jones's) theory in an infinite regress. Suppose we are trying to analyse a sentence like 'Scott is the author of *Waverley*'. Then, since the meaning of 'the author of *Waverley*' is relevant to this proposition, we must hold that it is the meaning of the phrase which does the denoting. Call the meaning of the phrase 'M'. Then the analysis is 'Scott is the denotation of M'. 'But here we are explaining our proposition by another of the same form, and thus we have made no progress towards a real explanation' (*KAKD* 164). However, whatever Miss Jones may have held, Frege held that expressions, not meanings, denote. Moreover, it is unclear what sort of explanation is needed, and why the circularity is vicious. This objection is therefore inconclusive.

The claim that the meaning must denote the denotation is also made in *OD* (49), on the grounds that 'the relation of meaning and denotation is not merely linguistic through the phrase: there must be a logical relation involved'. Frege's view was that the meaning of an expression, together with the way the world is, fixes its denotation (if any), but that the denotation of an expression, together with the way the world is, does not fix the expression's meaning. It is not clear what Russell means by saying that this is a 'merely linguistic' relation between meaning and denotation.

The true source of Russell's complaint consists, I think, in his supposition that the only way in which the meaning of an expression could be relevant to the identity of the proposition expressed by a sentence containing it is by the meaning being denoted. Granted this supposition, Frege's theory will not work. But Russell gives no reason for the supposition, though that he makes it is an interesting manifestation of the grip that the realist theory of meaning has over him: a proposition is made up of meaning-relata, of what the expressions in the sentence *hold of.*

This interpretation is substantiated by an examination of the argument whereby Russell tries to refute the suggestion that Fregean meaning alone is relevant to the identity of the proposition a sentence expresses. In abstract, there are, as Watling points out (67), three possibilities: that denotation alone is relevant, that denotation and meaning are both relevant, and that meaning alone is relevant. Frege's view is the last one. Russell argues, reasonably enough, that the first two possibilities are ruled out by the existence of denotationless descriptions. It is his argument against the third that is less than satisfactory.

Let us use '*C*' as a schematic letter whose substitutes are descriptions, and adopt the convention that the result of enclosing '*C*' in asterisks is an expression which denotes the meaning of '*C*'. (Russell uses single quotation marks for the same purpose: *OD* 48.) Now Russell argues that the denotation of the expression 'the meaning of *C*' is not $*C*$ but the meaning, if any, of the denotation of '*C*'. To form an expression denoting what '$*C*$' denotes we may write 'the meaning of "*C*"'. This shows that when '*C*' occurs unquoted in a sentence, $*C*$ does not occur in, and is thus irrelevant to determining the identity of, the proposition expressed by the sentence; and that when $*C*$ does occur in a proposition, and thus determines its identity, the sentence must contain not the denoting expression '*C*' but a distinct expression whose denotation is $*C*$. Thus the meaning of '*C*' is irrelevant to the proposition expressed by a sentence containing '*C*', which is not what is intended. (Cf. *OD* 50.)

The trouble with the argument is that it simply presupposes that only what is denoted is relevant to the identity of the proposition expressed. The presupposition is required for the move from the fact that when '*C*' occurs unquoted in a sentence it may be that nothing in the sentence denotes $*C*$, to the conclusion that $*C*$ is irrelevant to the identity of the proposition the sentence expresses. The presupposition is the opposite of Frege's view, for Frege held that meaning alone fixed the identity of the proposition ('thought'). But to presuppose something with which your opponent disagrees is not to show that he is mistaken. Thus Russell's arguments against Frege's theory fail.[1]

(*iii*) The 'logical puzzles'. In *OD* Russell gives three: (*a*) concerns the law of identity, (*b*) the law of the excluded middle and (*c*) existential sentences.

(*a*) The problem is to effect a reconciliation between the 'law of identity' and the fact that though Scott was the author of *Waverley*,

[1] For an opposing view, see Blackburn and Code.

George IV wished to know whether Scott was the author of *Waverley* but did not wish to know if Scott was Scott. Thus, the 'law of identity':

> If *a* is identical with *b*, whatever is true of the one is true of the other, and either may be substituted for the other in any proposition without altering the truth or falsehood of that proposition (*OD* 47).

The proposed solution is that, according to the theory of descriptions, 'Scott is the author of *Waverley*' is not really an identity sentence but has the form ' "Scott wrote *Waverley*; and it is always true of *y* that if *y* wrote *Waverley*, *y* is identical with Scott" ' (*OD* 55). Hence 'Scott is the author of *Waverley*' does not supply us with a suitable premise for an application of the 'law of identity'.

There are two points to be made. The first is that there is no such 'law' as the 'law of identity', and thus there is no puzzle. The second is that if there were a puzzle, Russell's solution would be·inadequate. Both points are established by the consideration that names cannot everywhere be interchanged *salva veritate* even if they name the same: 'John believes that Tully was bald' may differ in truth-value from 'John believes that Cicero was bald'.

(*b*)

> By the law of the excluded middle, either '*A* is *B*' or '*A* is not *B*' must be true. Hence either 'the present King of France is bald' or 'the present King of France is not bald' must be true. Yet if we enumerated the things that are bald, and then the things that are not bald, we should not find the present King of France in either list. Hegelians, who love a synthesis, will probably conclude that he wears a wig (*OD* 48).

We have already encountered Russell's solution in another connection (Chapter III, section 3). He treats 'the present King of France is not bald' as scope-ambiguous. On one reading, the theory of descriptions yields the analysis 'It is not the case that there is one and only one King of France and he is bald', and this sentence is true. On the other reading, the theory of descriptions yields the analysis 'There is one and only one King of France and he is not-bald', and this sentence is false.

To assess the adequacy of the solution, we must first make the nature of the problem more precise. One interpretation of the law of excluded middle is that it excludes a third truth-value: there is truth, falsehood, but no third value. On this interpretation, there is no problem, for one could hold that both 'the present King of France is bald' and 'the present King of France is not bald' are truth-valueless (as opposed to holding that they have the 'third' truth-value), and this is precisely Frege's view.

Russell's own statement of the 'law of excluded middle' is, according to his own theory, ambiguous, if descriptions are appropriate substitutes for the schematic letter 'A', and irrelevant if they are not. One must imagine that what he takes the law to be is this: every sentence or its negation is true. Now this 'law' entails, but is not entailed by, the exclusion of a third truth-value. To see this, notice that the law is equivalent to the principle of bivalence, i.e. the principle that anything to which truth or falsehood are significantly applicable is either true or false. The reason for the equivalence is that any operator which deserves the name 'negation' will yield a true sentence iff applied to a false one, so that if a sentence is not true, the law entails that its negation is, which means that the sentence itself is false. So, in other words, a premise to Russell's argument at this juncture is the principle of bivalence.

This principle has been challenged by anti-realists, but this dispute is not relevant here, since one who has these grounds against the principle will happily concede that it holds for some restricted class of sentences, and this is all that Russell requires. More to the point, the principle has in effect been challenged by Frege and by Strawson precisely for sentences of the form 'the F is G', when there is no F. This means that it is an open question whether there is a genuine puzzle to solve. If there is, Russell certainly has a satisfying solution: 'the King of France is not bald' is ambiguous between being the negation of 'the King of France is bald', in which case it is true, and being false, in which case it is not the negation of 'the King of France is bald'. One problem with the solution, however, is that some people profess to be unable to hear a true reading of 'the King of France is not bald', and Russell himself recognized that a false reading 'would usually be adopted' (*PM* 69).

(*c*) Existential sentences. The puzzle here is: 'how can a non-entity be the subject of a proposition?' (*OD* 48). Yet how else are we to analyse true sentences like 'The golden mountain does not exist' than as the attribution of non-existence to something? His solution, which has already been given, in effect treats 'exists' as something other than a predicate, or something other than a predicate of individuals.

This puzzle is genuine, and Russell's analysis solves it. Whether the analysis is acceptable on other grounds is another matter.

(*iv*) Russell's arguments so far have mostly been inconclusive. The fact that descriptions cannot (always) be treated as names, or that they cannot be treated in Frege's way, could not establish the correctness of Russell's theory. Nor could the ability of his theory to solve the puzzles. What would have to be shown is that *only* his theory can solve the puzzles, and in such a case the method of challenge (What solution have you?) may be less than convincing. However, Russell does, on occasion, argue more directly for his theory, as for example in *IMP* (176–7):

> The only thing that distinguishes 'the so-and-so' from 'a so-and-so' is the implication of uniqueness. We cannot speak of 'the inhabitant of London', because inhabiting London is an attribute that is not unique. We cannot speak about 'the present King of France', because there is none; but we can speak about 'the present King of England'. Thus propositions about 'the so-and-so' always imply the corresponding propositions about 'a so-and-so', with the addendum that there is not more than one so-and-so (*IMP* 176).

And on the next page Russell asserts that the analysis of a description-sentence implies and is implied by its analysandum and 'hence' may be taken as defining it. (Cf. *PM* 68.)

The first question to ask is: exactly what standards of correct analysis did Russell set himself? Is it merely that analysandum and analysis must be necessarily equivalent, as his remarks about implication suggest? Or must analysandum and analysis be synonymous, in a sense which guarantees that if 'p' and 'q' are synonymous then A asserts (believes, wishes, hopes) that p iff A asserts (believes, wishes, hopes) that q? The latter is suggested by the talk of 'definition' in *IMP* and of 'meaning' in *PM* (68), and of what is 'asserted' in *OD* (44). On the other hand, the point about necessary equivalence evidently fails to establish the claim of synonymy, so that some of Russell's arguments, if taken as arguments for the latter, must be regarded as rather spectacular *non sequiturs*.

Looking back, Russell says of his theory of descriptions:

> I was concerned to find a more accurate and analysed thought to replace the somewhat confused thoughts which most people at most times have in their heads (*MPD* 243; cf. Schilpp 691).

However, this squares ill with a remark in *PM*:

> In all propositions about 'the so-and-so' there is an apparent variable . . . in what *we* have in mind when we say 'Socrates is human' there is an apparent variable (50).

The reason for the last remark is that 'Socrates' abbreviates a description. Now if the theory of descriptions does, as the *PM* account suggests, aim to reveal what is in a person's mind in using a description, it is presumably intended that analysandum and analysis be synonymous.

Is this intention realized? The question is difficult. For one thing, as we shall see in subsequent sections, there are grounds for doubting even the logical equivalence of description sentences with their Russellian analyses, but let us for the moment firmly set these doubts aside. For another thing, the notion of synonymy is both unclear and vague. I have already suggested that one route to it is through the propositional attitudes, using the idea that synonymous sentences are those that can be used to ascribe attitudes with the same content. Pursuing this thought suggests the following principle: synonymous sentences must lean on the same conceptual resources, so that if a sentence 'p' can be used correctly to ascribe to someone a propositional attitude, and 'q' is synonymous with 'p', the use of either sentence will imply the same conceptual mastery on the part of the bearer of the attitude. Let us see how this principle would apply in practice.

Suppose a young child who has not learnt to count, but who has somehow come across the word 'hundred' and who has, we think, understood at least that if 'there are a hundred Xs' is true then there are many Xs, utters the words 'There are a hundred bees'. Has he asserted that there are a hundred bees? I think not. Someone cannot succeed in asserting, that is cannot actually assert, what he cannot intend to assert, and the child cannot intend to assert that there are a hundred bees. He has asserted, at best, that there are many bees.

Now consider another case. An alien tribe speaks a language like ours save that it includes the predicate 'malchik'. Investigation reveals that the extension of this predicate is the union of the class of males with the class of post-menstrual females. Moreover, the observable facts suggest that members of the tribe, when being taught the language, come to understand 'malchik' long before they know what menstruation is. If, in reporting alien sayings, I am confined to English, then the best I can do, if an alien utters 'There's a malchik in that hut', is to report him as having said that there's a male or post-menstrual female in that hut. However, my report is misleading, and I would do better to qualify it: he said something more or less to the effect that there's a male or post-menstrual female in that hut. The reason why it is misleading is that it misleadingly suggests that something has been said which can be understood only if one knows what menstruation is. In the particular example, there is a further misleading element. The report would imply that the alien had said something which conversationally implicates (in Grice's sense) that he does not know whether what is in the hut is male or whether it is a post-menstrual female. But we can imagine circumstances in which it is evident to the least tutored gaze which of these possibilities obtains, yet the utterance of 'There's a malchik in that hut' is utterly natural.

In such a case, the best anthropological procedure is to say that the alien said that there was a *malchik* in that hut; then one explains what a malchik is, and the way in which a person is treated, in that society, in virtue of being one. Thus it is best not to decompose an alien concept into parts, if it functions in a unitary way for the alien. One sign of the unitary character of the concept is that the alien may see nothing especially natural about dividing malchiks into men and women: nothing more natural about this division than about dividing them into fat malchiks and thin ones, or tall malchiks and short ones. The concept of being a male or a post-menstrual female, however, suggests a natural division among the things to which it applies.

Equally, one should not condense a complex concept into a unitary one, in reporting what another has said. Suppose I am investigating this very tribe, but I have not yet grasped the unitary character of the concept of a malchik. However, I have noted that in certain ways both males and post-menstrual females elicit similar behaviour in other aliens. One day, when I see an alien behaving in a certain way, I do some inferring and utter the words: 'Tom must have seen a male or a post-menstrual female'. Should the ideally rational and well-informed *alien* report *me* as having said that Tom must have seen a malchik? Surely not. Admittedly, this might be the best he could in practice do, if he possessed no separate concept of menstruation; but we surely feel that this best is not as good as it could be, if only the alien could use English.

If you utter the words 'Tom is a bachelor' I can *perhaps* correctly report you as having said that Tom is an unmarried man. We would justify this by our confidence that you arrived at your mastery of 'bachelor' through first having learnt 'un' and 'married' and 'man'. Thus we have good reason to believe that my report does not ascribe to you concepts which you lack. On the other hand, one should, I think, feel rather more hesitation about reporting you as having said that Tom is a bachelor, if you have uttered 'Tom is an unmarried man'. The reason is that in general it is unsatisfactory, as we saw in the second example concerning 'malchik', to condense a complex of concepts into a single one in reporting another's sayings.

Now consider a child who is learning to talk, but who has not yet mastered quantifiers. He understands such sentences as 'Tom is bald' and 'Mary is bald', but to sentences like 'No one is bald' and 'Someone is bald' he responds with such utterances as 'Who's no one?', 'Who's someone?'. None the less, we can imagine that such a child has mastered 'the', and so can see what phrases of the form 'the *F*' mean, so long as he understands '*F*'. Thus, perhaps, he has at first used 'cat' in what we are inclined to interpret as merely a feature-placing way, but, having learnt 'the' in other contexts, he one day comes out with the sentence, which he has never heard before, 'the cat over there is bald', and he responds in appropriate ways to questions like 'Which one?', 'Where?', 'Where did it go?'. Did he assert that at least one cat is over there and at most one cat is over there and whatever is a cat over there is bald? Bearing firmly in mind that we are still assuming that Russell's analysis is necessarily equivalent to the analysandum, the answer is negative for this reason: the child can assert something which includes that whatever is a cat over there is bald only if he has mastered the concept of quantification. How could he assert such a thing if he had not? It may take him months to latch on to 'whatever' and 'there is at least one' and 'there is at most one', even though he is adept with 'the'. But to report him as having said, in uttering the words 'the cat over there is bald', that there is at least one cat over there and at most one cat over there and whatever is a cat over there is bald, is falsely to imply that he has already mastered these quantifier concepts.

Even though we *have* mastered these concepts, it will still be wrong to report what we say in uttering description-sentences by Russell's theory, for these reports will fasely imply that we *exploit* the various quantifier concepts in asserting what we assert, and this is no more true of us than it is of the child.

If we speak Russellese, the language whose syntax is *PM* and whose extra-logical vocabulary is simple English names and predicates, the best report *we could give* of what was said by an English utterance 'the *F* is *G*' would be that $(\exists x)((\forall y)(Fy \leftrightarrow y=x) \ \& \ Gx)$. However, this would fall short of being the best report that could be given in any language. To suppose that a language with *PM* syntax will best reveal what English speakers say seems to me quite unwarranted. (Cf., however, Russell's account of the 'perfect language', discussed in Chapter V.)

Strawson has used a different argument to arrive at the non-synonymy of description-sentences and their Russellian analyses. He suggests that one who asserts that the *F* is *G* does not thereby assert, but rather presupposes, that there is an *F* ('On Referring' 116 contains the denial that existence is asserted; the technical term 'presupposes' is introduced in *Introduction to Logical Theory* 175ff.). This bears on Russell's position only if one who asserts that there is at least one *F* and at most one *F* and whatever is *F* is *G* thereby asserts that there is at least one *F*. But suppose someone did not realize that '*p* and *q*' entails '*q*'. Would it be correct to say that, in asserting that *p* and *q*, he thereby asserted that *p*? There is room for doubt.

The rule of 'conjunction elimination' within assertions is perhaps one of the most plausible rules concerning what one can infer from sentences of the form '*A* asserted that *p*'. It is much less plausible to hold that a rule of, so to speak, conjunction elimination under existential quantification holds within assertions. Thus one ought to feel very strong doubts about the inference from 'A asserted that $(\exists x)(Fx \; \& \; Gx)$' to '$A$ asserted that $(\exists x)Fx$'. *A fortiori* one should strongly doubt the inference from 'A asserted that $(\exists x)((\forall y)(Fy \leftrightarrow y=x) \; \& \; Gx)$' to '$A$ asserted that $(\exists x)Fx$'. Hence Russell has only to insist on the formalized version of his analysis of description-sentences to achieve a considerable degree of immunity from Strawson's objection, even supposing its premise, that one who asserts that the F is G does not thereby assert that there is an F, to be correct.

However, as I have said, I incline to share Strawson's overall position that 'The F is G' does not mean the same as its Russellian analysis. This leaves open the question of whether or not the two are necessarily equivalent. The subsequent sections of this chapter are addressed to this hotly disputed issue. (Of course, failure of necessary equivalence would entail failure of synonymy, but the converse does not hold.)

3 Underdetermination: failure of uniqueness

In the remaining sections of this chapter, I shall consider objections to the view that a description-sentence and its Russellian analysis are necessarily equivalent. The objector has to show that there is a description-sentence which, in some possible circumstance, would have a truth-value different from the truth-value the Russellian analysis would have in that circumstance.

It will, I think, be useful to state my conclusions at the outset. I think there is only one really serious objection to Russell's claim of necessary equivalence. This is the suggestion that descriptions on occasion function like complex demonstratives, and thus like names: they have what Peacocke calls an 'entity-invoking' use ('Proper Names, Reference and Rigid Designation' 117). If this suggestion is correct then Russell's analysis is incorrect, for it will give an incorrect account of entity-invoking uses of descriptions.

In this section and the next I consider putative objections to Russell's analysis which I think can be decisively rebutted. In section 5 I consider Donnellan's distinction between referential and attributive uses of descriptions. This at first sight looks like the distinction between entity-invoking uses of descriptions and others, but I argue that in reality this is not the distinction Donnellan makes, and that he has no effective objection to Russell. Finally, in section 6, I discuss the distinction between entity-invoking and other uses of descriptions, and I rather tentatively conclude that the facts of linguistic behaviour do not require us to recognize any entity-invoking uses of descriptions.

The objection to be considered in this section is that Russell's analysis fails when the predicate in the description holds of more than one thing: the description is underdetermined.

Suppose I own a cat. She jumps on my lap and mews. I utter the sentence

(*i*) The cat is hungry.

According to Russell's theory, this is necessarily equivalent to

(*ii*) There exists exactly one cat and it is hungry.

Now the objection is that it is easy to imagine circumstances which would make (*i*) and (*ii*) have different truth-values. For suppose that the cat in question is hungry. Then (*i*), as uttered on that occasion, is true. But, as things are, (*ii*), as uttered on that occasion, is false, since there is more than one cat in the world.

The objection, in the form of the present example, simply *states* that one who utters (*i*) in the envisaged circumstances speaks truly, whereas one who utters (*ii*) in those circumstances speaks falsely. However, both these assignments of truth-value are open to question.

The doubt springs from the fact that there is considerable room for manoeuvre in fixing the line that separates what a man (strictly and literally) *says* from what a man *means* (but perhaps does not say). (An analysis of the notion of speaker's meaning will be found in Grice's 'Meaning'. His ideas have been subsequently refined and extended by himself and others. See, e.g., Schiffer's *Meaning*.)

An example of a clear contrast between what is said and what is meant is irony: one who says ironically that *p* typically means that not-*p*, but he does not say that not-*p*.

The notion of speaking truly goes naturally with what is said rather than what is meant: a man speaks truly iff what he says is true. Thus a man who says ironically that *p* typically speaks falsely, and indeed it is the usually obvious falsehood of what he says that cues us to the irony, and thus makes us realize what he means.

It is natural to suggest that in many cases two factors conspire to determine what a man says on a given occasion: the sentence-type, a token of which he utters, and the context in which he utters it. Thus he who utters 'It's raining' in London on Monday says something which is true iff it is raining in London on Monday, whereas he who utters that sentence in Oxford on Tuesday says something which is true iff it is raining in Oxford on Tuesday. It might be that what the one said is true and what the other said is false, so they had better say different things, even though they utter the same words.

This is an example of what I shall call 'non-linguistic' contextual determination. In other cases, contextual determination may be linguistic. For example, if I say 'John will come next week. Then I shall be pleased', what is said in uttering the first sentence plays a part in determining what is said in uttering the second, by helping to determine the temporal reference. The linguistic context of an utterance consists in the immediately prior utterances, whether by the speaker or by other speakers in the same conversation.

The notion of contextual determination is at work in making plausible the idea that he who utters (*i*) in the envisaged circumstances speaks truly. For if (*i*) had been uttered when no cat was conspicuously present, there would be no temptation to regard what was thereby said as true. In virtue of the context, however, we perhaps treat one who utters (*i*) as having said that the cat on his lap is hungry, or that the prominent cat is hungry. In short, we treat the context as supplying a further determination of the predicate involved in the description.

By contrast, to make plausible the idea that (*ii*), as uttered in the envisaged circumstances, is false we have to ignore the possibility of contextual determination. But why should we do this? I shall show that it is reasonable to treat sentences containing quantifiers as susceptible of contextual determination, relative to the predicate of quantification.

If in the middle of a lecture during which I have been writing on the blackboard I exclaim 'There's no more chalk' it is natural to suppose that I do not claim that there is a world shortage, but only that there is no chalk to hand. Or again, if I utter the words 'Yesterday, I lectured on descriptions. Everyone was sceptical about my contention that . . .', it is natural to suppose that what I said, in my utterance of the second sentence, was not that everyone in the whole wide world was sceptical, but only that those present at the lecture were.

If we accept this possibility of contextual determination for such cases, then we ought to accept it for (*ii*). Then what is said by one who utters (*ii*) in the envisaged circumstances is perhaps that there is exactly one cat on his lap and it is hungry, or that there is exactly one prominent cat and it is hungry. But then what is said is true. The claimed discrepancy of truth-value between (*i*) and (*ii*), as uttered in the envisaged circumstances, has disappeared.

We might, perhaps, be able to arrive at what is, in the end, a no less satisfactory overall account of people's behaviour by resisting the possibility of contextual determination. We might interpret one who utters 'There's no more chalk' as having strictly and literally said that there is *no* more chalk (anywhere), despite the circumstances surrounding the utterance. Similarly we might interpret one who utters the words 'Yesterday, I lectured on descriptions. Everyone was sceptical of my contention that . . .' as having said, in uttering the second sentence, that *everyone* (in the whole wide world) was sceptical. To account for the speakers' behaviour, however, we will want to say that the first none the less *meant* that there was no chalk to hand, and the second *meant* that everyone at the lecture was sceptical. Applying this policy to (*ii*), we would say that what is strictly and literally said by an utterance of it, in the envisaged circumstances, is false, though what is meant is that there is exactly one cat *on my lap* and it is hungry, and is thus, we are supposing, true. But if we are going to apply this policy to (*ii*), why should we not also apply it to (*i*)? Uniformity surely requires that we should say that what is strictly and literally *said* by (*i*), as uttered in the envisaged circumstances, is false, though what the speaker *meant* is true.

There are, then, two overall policies that one might adopt about contextual determination. According to one policy, we freely allow it to determine what is said, and if we follow this policy we must hold that what is said by both (*i*) and (*ii*), as uttered in the envisaged circumstances, is true. The other strategy is to disallow the determination by context of what is said, though allowing it more freely at the level of what is meant. If we follow this policy, we must hold that what is said by both (*i*) and (*ii*), as uttered in the envisaged circumstances, is false. Whichever policy we follow, we have no divergence of truth-value between (*i*) and (*ii*), and thus no objection to the necessary equivalence of Russell's analysis with its analysandum. The only way to seem to have an objection is to apply one policy about context to one example, and another to the other. But for this disparate treatment, I can find no warrant whatsoever.

It is easy to confuse the present point with another. Perhaps there is some temptation to treat an utterance of (*i*) but not (*ii*) as, in the envisaged circumstances, saying *of* a certain cat that she is hungry. In other words, perhaps there is a temptation to suggest that (*i*) should be treated as an entity-invoking use of a description. For the moment it is enough to say that this suggestion has nothing in particular to do with the proper subject of the present section, namely, underdetermination (cf. Peacocke 117, and section 6 below).

4   Overdetermination: failure of existence

For this section, I stipulate that a description 'the *F*' is empty iff nothing is *F*. Strawson has argued that in the case of empty descriptions there is a divergence of truth-value between the description-sentence and its Russellian analysis ('On Referring').[2]

[2] For Strawson's more recent views, see his *Subject and Predicate in Logic and Grammar*.

Critics of 'On Referring' claim to discern two incompatible doctrines which are relevant to the present point. (See, for example, G. Nerlich, 'Presupposition and Entailment'.) Rather than offer any exegesis of Strawson, I shall simply consider the two doctrines in turn.

(*a*) A man who seriously utters a description-sentence whose description is empty makes a statement which is neither true nor false.

(*b*) A man who seriously utters a description-sentence whose description is empty makes no statement. Hence he does not make a false statement and he does not make a true statement.

Though (*b*) essentially requires the distinction between a sentence and a statement, (*a*) does not. We can for the moment simplify (*a*) to the contention that sentences containing empty descriptions are truth-valueless. (Both Strawsonian doctrines have to be modified to allow for positive and negative existential description-sentences.) Thus, in short, (*a*) amounts to the abandonment of bivalence for (non-existential) description-sentences with empty descriptions.

Why *should* we abandon familiar bivalence, enshrined alike in pre-theoretical intuition and classical logic? Setting aside anti-realist scruples, which are not relevant to the present issue, I can envisage two replies. One stems from Frege's theory of sense and reference. The other is Strawsonian, and involves denying that bivalence is enshrined in pre-theoretical intuition.

Frege held that the reference of a sentence, if it refers at all, is a truth-value, and that the reference of a referring expression is determined by the reference of any subsidiary referring expressions it contains. ('Referring expression' in this context must be understood not as an expression which has a reference, but as any expression which counts as a 'logical unit'.) Hence if one referring expression, say 'Pegasus', has no reference, a complex one in which it occurs, say 'the sire of Pegasus', has no reference. Likewise, a sentence containing an empty description will have no reference, that is, it will be truth-valueless.

Frege's assimilation of complete sentences to referring expressions has found little favour, in virtue of the considerable disparity between on the one hand the relation between a name and its bearer, and on the other the relation between a sentence and its truth-value. This point is strongly argued by Dummett in his *Frege* (ch 12). As Dummett also points out, if the notion of the reference of an expression is not understood on the basis of the paradigm of the bearer of a name, there will be no support for the view that a sentence containing a referring expression without a reference is truth-valueless. Thus there is no supporting the abandonment of bivalence from this aspect of Frege's philosophy.

The second reason that might be offered for abandoning bivalence is that this principle is not reflected in our linguistic practice. Thus one might urge that if a man were assertively to utter the sentence 'The King of France is bald' we would be disinclined to say that what he said is true, and disinclined to say that what he said is false, and so we should be inclined to say that what is said is neither true nor false, thus committing ourselves to the denial of bivalence.

However, as (*b*)-Strawson shows, the phenomenon requires careful interpretation. Strawson suggests that the two disinclinations could be explained in terms of the recognition that the original speaker, in uttering 'The present King of France is bald', has not produced a statement. Now a 'statement', Strawson stipulates, is any entity of which truth and falsehood are significantly predicable. Hence if no statement has been produced, it will normally be rational to refrain from saying 'That's true', and rational to refrain from saying 'That's false' *and* rational to refrain from saying 'That's neither true nor false'. For whatever would be designated by 'that', as used in this context, would not be a statement, and thus would not be something to which truth or falsehood is significantly ascribable. Hence the disinclinations to respond to description-sentences which we believe contain empty descriptions by either 'That's true' or 'That's false' do not establish that we do not hold to bivalence. For, properly formulated, this is the principle that anything to which truth and falsehood are significantly ascribable, and which is not true, is false. (The fact that neither of the sentences 'The sun is true' and 'The sun is false' is true does not show the failure of bivalence.)

It may seem as if our disinclination to respond to an utterance of an empty description-sentence by 'That's false' conflicts with Russell's theory, which holds that such utterances are false. However, the disinclination in itself establishes no conflict, for perhaps it issues from the realization that to utter 'That's false' in such a situation would be misleading. The reason is that the typical way in which a description-sentence 'The F is G' is false is that there is exactly one F but not one which is G. Hence someone who receives the response 'That's false' to his utterance of a description-sentence is likely to jump to the conclusion, if he has confidence in his audience, that there is exactly one F but not one which is G (cf. *PM* 69). Since his audience realizes all this, he will not be inclined to respond by 'That's false', despite thinking that had he uttered this he would have spoken truly, though misleadingly.

Let us, however, suppose that we actually found the inclination to respond to description-sentences containing what are taken to be empty descriptions by 'That's neither true nor false'. Would this show that bivalence fails? Surely not, or not immediately, for all it immediately establishes is that people do not believe in bivalence, and this is logically independent of whether or not bivalence is true.

Admittedly, widespread belief that p is *prima facie* evidence for p, but this evidence is undermined if we can explain how people would come to believe that p even when not-p. Russell would have such an explanation, were such an inclination discovered. It is that people confuse what it would be misleading to say with what it would be false to say. Thus they (rightly) think it would be false to say 'That's true' and they (wrongly) think it would be false to say 'That's false' and then they do some inferring and conclude that it would be right to say 'That's neither true nor false'.

This point is worthy of generalization. In giving an account of description-sentences as they occur in ordinary speech, we must, of course, take into account our actual ordinary uses of these sentences. These are our data. But we might also find, in ordinary conversation, the beginnings of a fumbling and inarticulate semantic theory concerning the nature of description-sentences, or truth or falsehood; for example, a theory which conflates speaking misleadingly with speaking falsely. There is no reason why *this* theory should be incorporated into our own. Strawson remarks that 'ordinary language has no exact logic' ('On Referring' 127). Perhaps the trouble is, not that our primary language, including description-sentences, lacks an exact logic, but that our everyday unselfconscious theorizings about this language are vague or imprecise or downright incorrect. I do not suggest that it is easy to distinguish between those aspects of our behaviour which manifest the semantic properties of our language, and those which primarily manifest our beliefs about these properties. My point, rather, is that we should be on our guard and not jump to the conclusion that relatively unreflective beliefs about our language's semantic properties are inerrant. (This conclusion would merit Russell's gibes against 'The cult of common usage'; see the essay of that title.)

So much for (a)-Strawson's denial of bivalence: it is inadequately motivated by the phenomena he discusses. However, I would put my money on the identification of Strawson with (b)-Strawson, for only (b)-Strawson crucially needs the distinction between sentence and statement of which Strawson makes much. The distinction is connected with the notion of contextual determination. If there are any context-independent sentences, it will be of no moment to distinguish each from the one and only statement it can be used to make. But context-dependent sentences say different and perhaps incompatible things, depending on the context in which they are used; they are used to make different statements.

Strawson takes Russell to task for supposing that there is a single kind of entity, let us call it a proposition, to which the 'bogus' trichotomy 'true, false, or meaningless' applies, and for using the trichotomy to argue for the falsehood of the proposition that the present King of France is bald. As we have seen, however, at least in *OD* Russell's argument takes it as a premise that this proposition is false, and so does not rely on the 'bogus trichotomy'. By contrast Strawson, more exactly (*b*)-Strawson, maintains that one who utters 'The present King of France is bald' makes no statement, and thus says nothing true, and also nothing false, and also nothing having the property of being neither-true-nor-false. But, so far, we have a straight difference of opinion. What hangs on the difference, and what arguments might be adduced on either side?

A point that might be at issue concerns the distinction between entity-invoking and other uses of descriptions. If one attempts to use an empty description entity-invokingly, one cannot succeed in saying anything. For to say that the use is entity-invoking entails that some entity, denoted by the description, enters into whatever proposition one asserts, and to say that the description is empty is to say that there is no such entity.[3] However, Strawson's example is not well-chosen, if it is intended to be an example of an entity-invoking use, since it seems that this sort of radical failure to say anything does not occur when someone assertively uses the sentence 'The present King of France is bald'. If such a person speaks sincerely, we surely want to report him as believing that the present King of France is bald, and this we could not do unless there is a statement to the effect that the present King of France is bald. Even if we wish, on the basis of the speaker's utterance, to attribute to him a smaller belief, say the belief that France is a monarchy, what more natural way to characterize our evidence than this: in uttering the sentence, the speaker sincerely said that the King of France is bald, and he would not have said this sincerely unless he believed that France is a monarchy.

To attempt to establish his claim that one who utters 'The present King of France is bald' makes no statement, Strawson relies on our disinclination to respond to such an utterance with 'That's untrue'. But we have already seen that this point can be undermined, for we

---

[3] This is an over-simplification, depending on the premise that the *F* is the entity invoked by an entity-invoking use of 'the *F*'. There are, however, other ways in which one might determine the relevant entity for entity-invoking uses of descriptions: see sections 5 and 6 of this chapter.

may be disinclined to utter a misleading truth. Russell, on his side, offers no argument. So how can the issue be resolved? Should we accept Russell's later view that his disagreement with Strawson on this point is 'a purely verbal question' (*MPD* 243)?

There is one substantial issue at stake: whether or not there are entity-invoking uses of descriptions. My main discussion of this question is in section 6. It is appropriate at this stage, however, to establish this much: there are at least some non-entity-invoking uses of descriptions. One can show this by showing that there are at least some cases in which a sentence containing an empty description can be used to make a false statement. (Of course, this much can be shown by reference to false existentials; e.g., 'The golden mountain exists'. But Strawson gives a special account of existential sentences (118), so these examples would not serve the present polemical purpose.)

Suppose a girl at a party utters the words 'My fiancé will be here soon'. She has no fiancé and utters these words in order to discourage your attentions, by trying to make you believe that her fiancé would be there soon. There seem to be plenty of reasons to support our intuitive judgment that the girl said something, and that what she said was false.

To show that the girl said something, that she made a statement, consider how natural are the following three comments on what has occurred:

(*a*) The girl intended to get you to form a certain belief, viz. that her fiancé would be there soon, by uttering the words she uttered. Now admittedly it is possible successfully to intend to get someone to have a belief, by uttering certain words, without thereby saying anything. (One might utter goobledygook in an angry voice in the presence of one whom you believe believes he does not understand your language, with a view to getting him to believe that you are angry.) But there is nothing to suggest that this is what has happened in the present case. Rather, she intended to get you to believe that her fiancé would be there soon by saying precisely that.

(*b*) You may well believe what the girl said. So she must have said something.

(*c*) You know what it would be for what she said to be true: that she have exactly one fiancé and that he be about to arrive.

To show that what the girl said was false, consider the fact that it is natural to describe her as having lied, as having deliberately caused you falsely to believe, by what she said, that she had a fiancé. Once it is conceded that the girl has said something there can be no deep reason for not agreeing that she spoke falsely.

I therefore conclude that the case of empty descriptions does not in itself tell against Russell's analysis, for this case does not as such establish a failure of necessary equivalence between description-sentences and their Russellian analyses.

5 'Referential' v. 'attributive'

In his article 'Reference and Definite Descriptions', Donnellan argues for a distinction which he calls that between 'referential' uses of descriptions and 'attributive' uses of descriptions. He claims that, through its failure to make room for this distinction, Russell's theory of descriptions is incorrect.

There are several reasons for thinking that Donnellan intends his contrast to be that between entity-invoking (referential) uses of descriptions and other (attributive) uses. His choice of the words 'referential' and 'attributive' already suggests this contrast, and it is underlined by his characterization of the referential use as 'the genuine referring use' (281). Moreover, he likens the referential use to the use of a Russellian logically proper name (282); he suggests that referential uses of descriptions express particular (singular) propositions, whereas 'one might well say' that attributive uses express purely general propositions (303); and he suggests, as if it marked a contrast with attributive uses, that 'when a definite description is used referentially, a speaker can be reported as having said something *of* something' (303).

On the other hand, there are also indications that Donnellan views not only the referential use but also the attributive use as a species of entity-invoking use. For example, his first characterization has it that 'A speaker who uses a definite description attributively in an assertion states something *about* whoever or whatever is the so-and-so' (285: my italics). It would be natural to infer that the object which the statement is *about* enters into the truth-conditions of what is stated. This suggestion is reinforced by Donnellan's consideration of attributive uses of empty descriptions. He says of such cases, as if marking a contrast with the attributive use of non-empty descriptions, that nothing has been said, by an utterance of 'The F is G', to be G (287). Moreover, he tends to equate this with a situation in which nothing at all has been said (288). This is just what one would expect if attributive uses are entity-invoking: for if in a putatively entity-invoking use of a description no entity is invoked, then nothing is said.

I am not sure that any clear account of attributive uses of descriptions is adequate to everything Donnellan says. However, there is, I think, a clear and straightforward account of his notion of referential uses. We can rely for the moment on his claim that every non-referential use is attributive (300) to make this account do duty for both sides of the distinction.

His early characterization runs:

> A speaker who uses a definite description referentially in an assertion . . . uses the description to enable his audience to pick out whom or what he is talking *about* and states something *about* that person or thing (285: my italics).

Both in an explicit later statement, and in his discussion of examples, Donnellan takes it that 'whether or not a description is used referentially or attributively is a function of the speaker's intentions in a particular case' (297). In fact, there are two sides to the account: one side settles what intentions a speaker must have, in order to qualify as having used a description referentially; the other settles what are the truth-conditions of what he thereby said. (This talk of truth-conditions squares ill with Donnellan's hesitation about calling his distinction semantic (297); but then this hesitation squares ill with his claim that Russell's theory is refuted by the existence of referential uses (283).)

> (*i*) A speaker *S* uses a description referentially, in uttering the sentence 'The *F* is *G*', only if there is a unique object *x* such that *S* intends that, through *S*'s utterance of the sentence, his audience will come to believe, concerning *x*, that it is *G*.

> (*ii*) If *S* uses 'The *F* is *G*' referentially, then the unique object *x* such that *S* intends that, through *S*'s utterance of the sentence his audience will come to believe, concerning *x*, that it is *G*, is such that *S* speaks truly iff *x* is *G*.

(To expand (*i*) into a sufficient condition, one would have to add at least some Gricean conditions about how *S* intends the belief to be caused in the hearer *H*.) I shall now show that this account of referential use harmonizes with Donnellan's discussion.

To illustrate the distinction, Donnellan suggests that if, on the basis of the horrible condition of Smith's mangled corpse, together with our knowledge of his lovable nature, we exclaim, 'Smith's murderer is insane', then we use the description non-referentially (i.e. attributively). This coheres with my interpretation, for the imagined background seems calculated to ensure that there is no object concerning which the envisaged speaker intends that his audience form a belief.

> The contrast with such a use of the sentence is one of those situations in which we expect and intend our audience to realize whom we have in mind when we speak of Smith's murderer and,

more importantly, to know that it is this person about whom we are going to say something (285–6).

This again fits my interpretation, as does Donnellan's subsequent remark that, in such a case, we can give some such answer as 'Jones' to the question 'To whom are you referring?' This could be seen as revealing that Jones is the object concerning which we had the communicative intention which the referential use requires.

On the side of truth-conditions, Donnellan says:

> Using a definite description referentially, a speaker may say something true even though the description correctly applies to nothing (298).

In a specific case in which our intention (as the speaker) concerns Jones, and we utter 'Smith's murderer is insane', Donnellan suggests that 'Jones might . . . accuse us of saying false things of him in calling him insane and it would be no defence, I should think, that our description, "the murderer of Smith", failed to fit him' (286). This suggests that in such a case we speak truly iff Jones is insane, which is an instance of the truth-condition I suggested. This does not require that the invoked object x satisfy the description, though it does entail the requirement that S believe that uttering 'The F is G' is likely to cause H to believe, of x, that it is G. The standard basis for part of this likelihood is, as Donnellan points out (290), that S believes, and believes that H believes, concerning the relevant object, that it is uniquely F.

My interpretation of Donnellan's account of referential use explains his discussion of the example of the man with the walking-stick (295–6). He is here attempting to analyse what it is for an object to satisfy the condition required for the referential use of a description. His conclusion is, roughly, that any object, however different in character from anything of which the predicate in the description holds, can satisfy the requirement, provided that the speaker, once fully informed, would agree that it was what he was referring to, and this seems to amount to the condition that the speaker regard it as the object concerning which he had the relevant intention.

Finally, my interpretation squares with Donnellan's one example of a description-sentence having only an attributive use: 'Point out the man who is drinking my martini' (298). The idea, presumably, is that no one would make this request unless they did not know who was the man drinking their martini. In this state of ignorance, there is no object x such that S can reasonably suppose that an utterance of 'Let the man who is drinking my martini be pointed out!' is likely to cause H to realize that x is to be pointed out; hence the conditions for referential use do not obtain. (Of course, they would obtain if S knew all along who was drinking his martini, and wanted to embarrass that person by having H point him out.)

However, my account has left the attributive use characterized merely as any non-referential use, whereas Donnellan seeks to provide a more positive characterization which, as we have already seen, suggests the idea that he views the attributive use as a species of entity-invoking use. The following would give effect to that idea:

(*i*) S uses a description attributively, in uttering the sentence 'The F is G', only if: (*a*) there is no object such that S intends H to form a belief concerning it; and (*b*) S intends that, through S's utterance of the sentence, H will come to believe, concerning whatever object is in fact uniquely F, that it is G.

(*ii*) If S uses 'The F is G' attributively, then, if some object x is uniquely F, then S speaks truly iff x is G; otherwise, S says nothing.

However, one can reconcile the intention of (*b*) with the absence of intention of (*a*) only in rather special cases. For example, if you have been watching the door all morning, I may want you to believe, concerning whoever entered the building first, that he is G. But if I neither know nor care who came in first, it is wrong to say that that person is the focus of (enters into the identity of) my intention: I would have had the same intention even if someone else had entered the building first. However, it is unclear that Donnellan wants the attributive use to be limited to such special cases. In particular, it would falsify his claim that all non-referential uses are attributive. For on this characterization, both referential and attributive uses are entity-invoking, whereas we saw in the last section that there are some non-entity-invoking uses of descriptions.

It will not serve our purposes to consider other possible interpretations of Donnellan's 'attributive' use. Let me, rather, summarize the important points of the discussion, so far as it bears on the question of whether description-sentences are necessarily equivalent to their Russellian analyses.

(*i*) If there are description-sentences which can be used to make statements having the truth-conditions Donnellan associates with referential uses of descriptions, then Russell's theory is wrong.

(*ii*) However, even if there are no referential uses of descriptions having the proposed truth-conditions, Russell's theory may still be wrong, for there are other entity-invoking truth-conditions which might be assigned to description-sentences (as, for example, in my positive characterization of attributive uses).

(*iii*) We cannot very well deny that there are referential uses of descriptions, but we can well question the associated truth-conditions. For example, it might be the case that there is a unique object x such that S intends that, through his utterance of the sentence 'There is at least one F and at most one F and whatever is F is G', his audience will come to believe, concerning x, that it is G. Yet we would not wish to argue from this to the conclusion that in such a case S speaks truly iff the intended object is G. For S surely strictly and literally said that there is at least one F and at most one F and whatever is F is G. Donnellan rather baldly states one way in which facts about speakers' intentions might interlock with facts about what they state. But there are other possibilities, as we shall see in the next section.

6 Are there entity-invoking uses of descriptions?

An utterance of a description-sentence 'The F is G' constitutes an entity-invoking use of 'the F' iff there is an object x such that what is said by the utterance in question is true iff x is G (cf. Peacocke 110, 117). That an utterance of a description-sentence is entity-invoking leaves open what sort of general rule determines, for each entity-invoking utterance, which entity is thereby invoked.

One could in abstract imagine various general rules, which can be roughly arranged in a spectrum. (The order is not to be taken very seriously.) At one pole, one could introduce an expression, say 'the$_1$', with the stipulation that:

(1) An utterance by S of 'The$_1$ F is G' on a given occasion is such that if there is, relative to that occasion, an object x which is uniquely F, S speaks truly iff x is G; otherwise, S says nothing.

To bring out the contrast with the Russellian 'the', which I shall designate 'the$_0$': if whatever is in fact uniquely F (relative to the occasion of utterance) had been non-G, though some G thing had been uniquely F (relative to the occasion of utterance), one would have spoken truly had one uttered 'The$_0$ F is G', but falsely had one uttered 'The$_1$ F is G'.

Near the other end of the spectrum I envisage, one might find the particle 'the$_n$', with the stipulation that:

(n) An utterance by S of 'The$_n$ F is G' on a given occasion is such that if there is a unique object x such that S intends, by his utterance of 'The$_n$ F is G' on that occasion, to bring it about that H believe, concerning x, that it is G, then S speaks truly iff x is G; otherwise, S says nothing.

In this case, we would have to make the condition for understanding S's utterance not that one know that S said that ——, but rather that one know, concerning the object with respect to which S had the communicative intention, that S said of it that —— it ——.

We can envisage various theories about the truth-conditions of 'the', and I shall call them 'theories of reference'. T_0 is that 'the' is univocal and has the truth-conditions of 'the$_0$'. $T_{0,i,j}$ is that 'the' is three-ways ambiguous, having, depending on circumstance, the truth-conditions of 'the$_0$' or of 'the$_i$' or of 'the$_j$'. $T_{1,n}$ is quite close to Donnellan's theory, as I characterized it in the last section.

I take it that in section 4 I showed that 'the' is at least sometimes used non-entity-invokingly. Accordingly, I shall assume, though this is a further step, that sometimes 'the' functions as 'the$_0$'. But beyond this, how is one to choose between the various theories of reference that remain open?

Consider, for example, the different ways in which T_0 and T_n would describe an utterance of 'The murderer of Smith is insane'. The facts are that Jones is insane and is widely believed to have uniquely murdered Smith, though Robinson, who is sane, is the true murderer. Jones is such that S intends, by his utterance of 'The murderer of Smith is insane', to bring it about that H believe, concerning Jones, that he is insane. One who holds T_0 must recognize an occurrence of 'the$_0$', and so hold that S speaks falsely. One who holds T_n must (and one who holds $T_{0,n}$ may) recognize here an occurrence of 'the$_n$', and so hold that S speaks truly. Both theories of reference may be supplemented in various ways to arrive at an overall explanation of other aspects of the behaviour of S and, perhaps, his audience. An aspect that may be troublesome to T_0 is that S may be outraged to discover that Jones is insane, if we have assured him that what he said by the utterance under discussion is false. S will accuse us of misleading him. The T_0-theorist will meet this charge, perhaps, by allowing that in uttering the sentence S meant, concerning Jones, that he is insane; and by insisting that it is not only what people say, but also what they mean, that is important. An aspect that may be troublesome for T_n is that it is not easy to swallow the suggestion that one who did not know of Jones that he was believed to have murdered Smith could not be expected to know what S said, on the strength of hearing the utterance and knowing the meaning of the sentence uttered. The T_n-theorist will meet this charge, perhaps, by distinguishing sharply between the meaning of the sentence S uttered, which he will concede that the ignorant bystander may know, and what S thereby said, which he will persist in denying could be known to one who failed to identify S's intended object of reference.

Let us use 'context' in such a way that it is true to say that nothing other than the *context*, together with the meaning of the sentence, a token of which is uttered, is involved in determining what one who utters the token thereby says. Then we can, very roughly, grade theories of reference according to how rich and complex they will require contexts for description-sentences to be. A theory like T_0 leaves context with relatively little (or even perhaps nothing) to do in the case of description-sentences. This will make for a relatively easily formulable specification of the nature of context, but there will be greater complexity at the level of the links between what a man says and his overall plan of action. A theory like T_n, however, by linking what a man says with a richer assortment of his intentions, may well be able to provide a simpler account of the links between what he says and his overall plan of action, but only at the expense of a more complicated account of the nature of context, that is, of the relationship between the meaning of the sentences which a man tokens and what he thereby says.

These considerations make it look as if more than one theory of reference can form a part of some adequate overall theory of how we behave; and thus as if more than one theory of reference can itself be regarded as adequate.

In *Subject and Predicate in Logic and Grammar*, Strawson considers a range of theories of reference, but concludes that 'there is no wholly realistic way of fitting *all* the facts within the framework of logic' (66). This amounts to the conclusion that all theories of reference are, to some degree, unrealistic. Strawson's standard of realism, however, is that a wholly realistic theory should match the output of our hesitant and often indeterminate intuitions about what, if anything, a man has said in uttering a sentence. I agree that by this standard no theory of reference will be realistic, but I would not agree that this standard is appropriate. Our pre-theoretical intuitions may be confused, and are certainly not sharp enough to figure in a decently precise theory of human behaviour. While a theory of reference would best avoid a conflict with our firm intuitions, there is no reason why it should agree at every point (though divergences will require explanation). A theory of reference is not to be seen merely as a theory of our use of expressions like 'what he said', 'true', 'refer', but rather as part of our overall enterprise of making sense of others' actions, including their utterances. Of this our utterances about utterances form a minor part, of no special significance for theory.

I claim that while it may be that some theories of reference other than T_0 are adequate to the facts, there is no reason to think that T_0 is inadequate. I also think that some methodological considerations may even tell slightly in favour of T_0, but I shall place little weight on this point.

The existence of intentions like those alluded to in T_n do not in themselves compel a departure from T_0. We can quite well imagine that there be a unique object x such that S intends, by his utterance of 'The$_0$ F is G', to bring it about that his audience believe, concerning x, that it is G. A fuller account of his intentions would reveal that he aims to get his audience, H, into this state of belief by first getting H to believe that the$_0$ F is G. H's knowledge, concerning the object S intends, that it is uniquely F, will, S calculates, lead H to the desired singular belief.

It is true that the T_0-theorist will have to maintain that if we interpret an utterance of 'The F is G', made with the intentions just mentioned, as an utterance of 'The$_0$ F is G' we shall have to view S's plan as having two stages, in which that H believe that the$_0$ F is G is an intermediate. However, there is no objection to this on the basis of introspection, for introspection will not reveal the myriad of intentions which we, as theorists, are in any case obliged to attribute to language-users (cf. Grice).

Peacocke has suggested a test for whether a use of a description is entity-invoking, and has given a putative example of such a use. A description is used entity-invokingly

if, in an utterance of 'the F is G', what is strictly and literally said would equally appropriately be said by an utterance of '*that F* is G' (117).

Let us grant that complex demonstratives like 'that F' are, on at least some occasions of their use, rigid designators (and thus entity-invoking). None the less it looks at first sight as if it will be hard to apply Peacocke's test, since only with respect to an occurrence of a description-sentence already identified as an entity-invoking use could we be sure that what was strictly and literally said by its utterance could equally appropriately be said by an utterance of 'that F is G'. Presumably the idea, however, is that we can identify situations in which a speaker would as willingly use 'that F' as 'the F', and infer that these situations are ones in which he would, strictly and literally, say the same thing whichever phrase he selected.

The general principle used here is questionable. For example, a speaker might in some situation as willingly use 'Tully' as 'Cicero', but, as we saw in the last chapter, one who utters 'Tully is bald' says something other than what is said by one who utters 'Cicero is bald'. Admittedly, what is said by the one sentence is necessarily equivalent to what is said by the other, and this would suffice for the present case, since we are only interested in whether description-sentences are necessarily equivalent to their Russellian analyses. However, it is easy to imagine cases in which a speaker is indifferent between 'the$_0$ F' and 'a' (where this last is a name). Or again, a speaker might as willingly utter 'Smith died of heart failure' as 'Smith died of a coronary', but he would strictly and literally say different things by these utterances (since coronary failure is only one species of heart failure). This indifference between the utterance-types might be displayed, on occasion, by one who was quite well aware of the semantic difference. Admittedly, one could imagine circumstances in which one who was aware of this difference would not be indifferent between the utterances, but then Peacocke does not claim that there is any utterance-type of the form 'the F' which is always used entity-invokingly, so he will have to admit that there may be circumstances in which one would not be indifferent between 'the F' and 'that F'.

Peacocke's test must in any case be applied with caution, since not every occurrence of 'that F' is a rigid designator. For example, 'that man' is not a rigid designator as it occurs in 'Margaret Thatcher wondered who the next Liberal Leader would be and whether that man would consider a coalition'. We must thus be sure not only that 'the F' is interchangeable with 'that F', but also that 'that F', in the context, functions as a true demonstrative.

Turning now from Peacocke's test to his alleged example of a case of entity-invoking use, he suggests that:

> If you and I visited the Casino at Monte Carlo yesterday, and saw a man break the bank, and on the same day saw a man break the bank at Nice, and it is common knowledge between us that this is so, then the description 'The man who broke the bank at Monte Carlo yesterday' as it occurs in a particular utterance *today* of 'The man who broke the bank at Monte Carlo yesterday had holes in his shoes' . . . is here entity-invoking both intuitively and by our criterion (117).

In accordance with my last remark about the need for caution in applying the test of the/that switching, we would have to be sure, even if we accepted that the switching could occur in this case, that 'That man who broke the bank at Monte Carlo had holes in his shoes' contained a truly demonstrative occurrence of 'That man', and that the sentence was not just a notational variant of something like:

> The man who broke the bank at Monte Carlo yesterday: that man had holes in his shoes.

Moreover, in accordance with my previous remark, we would in addition have to be sure that in this case the possibility of switching really showed that it makes no difference to what is said, or at any rate to the truth-conditions of what is said, whether 'the' or 'that' is used. But we could only show this conclusively if we had some other test for what is said by the description-sentence.

I do not mean to discredit the view that some description-sentences have entity-invoking uses. However, I do want to say that every 'hard fact' given in the example can as well be explained if we view the 'the' as 'the$_0$'.

One who lacks the common knowledge imagined in the example is none the less naturally said to be able to know what has been said by the utterance. This raises no problem for the T_0-theorist. The entity-invoking theorist will have to say that it is natural to make the mistake of confusing understanding the words a man utters with knowing what he has said.

We have already seen that the T_0-theorist can allow that in uttering 'The$_0$ man who broke the bank at Monte Carlo yesterday had holes in his shoes' a speaker should have a communicative intention concerning whoever broke the bank; and that the T_0-theorist can explain why uttering that sentence should be seen as a good means to the desired end. (Common knowledge is, of course, relevant here.) This will underpin the theorist's explanation of our tendency to hold that one who has uttered the sentence 'the man who broke the bank . . .' has said something concerning whoever uniquely broke the bank. For he will claim that this tendency, in sloppy everyday speech, is as likely to be discovered in a language whose only definite article is 'the$_0$'.

The fact that the T_0-theorist can adequately explain the facts of one supposed example of entity-invoking use shows rather little. On the other hand, it would evidently be impossible to consider all possible examples, one by one. I shall therefore consider two further examples, which exemplify the only further *kinds* of reason I can think of for regarding an entity-invoking account as especially appealing. One is the case in which the description-sentence is accompanied by some gesture such as pointing, just as it would have been if 'that' had replaced 'the'. The other case is one in which the predicate in the description has a special place in the speech of the speakers and hearers concerned.

Suppose I point to the girl at the window and say 'The girl at the window has red hair'. Metaphorically, we might feel that the pointing brings the relevant entity into the truth-conditions of what I say. Moreover, the gesture is just what one would have expected had I used a demonstrative. So this looks to be a case in which the entity-invoking use has special appeal. I do not wish to deny this, but only to say that a Russellian account seems to me to be no less satisfactory.

The T_0-theorist will have to see the pointing gesture as entirely otiose. He will add that in cultures in which it is rude to point, the gesture would have been omitted without loss; and that in any case it could be omitted without loss. Indeed, not wishing to let the girl know she is in one's thoughts, one might under only marginally different circumstances have looked away while making the utterance, yet have said just the same by it.

Suppose there was no girl at the window but only a dummy or a holograph image. The T_1-theorist will claim that by my utterance I have said nothing whereas the T_0-theorist will hold that I have said something false. Naturalness sides with T_1; but unless we have independent grounds for taking the utterance to be an entity-invoking use, this fact is hardly important enough to overthrow T_0. The T_0-theorist will explain the unnaturalness as arising from our tendency to equate '"The$_0$ F is G" is false' with '"The$_0$ F is not G" is true', and then to prefer the disambiguation of the latter which assigns narrow scope to 'not' relative to 'the$_0$'. There are no new considerations here. Only the gesture promised to make a difference.

If there are many girls at the window, then the gesture is not otiose to the overall communicative act. The T_0-theorist can meet this point in one of two ways. He may say that the gesture bears only on what is meant, not on what is said. What is said is false, but there are plenty of examples in which one deliberately conveys truth by speaking falsely (e.g., irony). Alternatively, the T_0-theorist may say that the gesture is part of the context which restricts the predicate 'girl at the window' to something like 'girl-at-the-window-to-whom-I-am-pointing'. Once more there is nothing new here, and in any case Peacocke, for one, insists that the case for entity-invoking uses is independent of the present question of underdetermination (underspecification: 117).

Finally, I consider the example 'The baby is crying', as uttered in the family circle, a case in which the predicate used in the description, or the descriptive phrase as a whole, plays a special role in the speech of the speakers and hearers concerned. Here one might feel that the baby is so conspicuously present and important that it worms its way into the truth-conditions of such a description-sentence. Less metaphorically, one might suggest that 'the baby' functions interchangeably with its proper name, 'Mary', and even though the interchange will not preserve meaning, it is natural to think that it will preserve truth-conditions (the set of worlds at which what is said by a familial utterance at a given time of 'The baby is crying' is true, is identical with the set of worlds at which what is said by a familial utterance at that time of 'Mary is crying' is true).

Against the suggestion about truth-conditions, one might put up the following case. If 'the baby is crying' is entity-invoking at any time, then one would expect not only that it be entity-invoking at all times at which the circumstances are similar and the speaker has an intention concerning Mary, but also that Mary should be the entity invoked in every such utterance. But now suppose that during a visit to the clinic Mary is inadvertently switched for the indistinguishable

Jane. The infant in the family circle is now, unbeknownst to them, Jane and not Mary. If Jane is crying and Mary is not, an utterance in the family circle of 'The baby is crying', made soon after the Jane/Mary switch, would be false if it invokes Mary, whereas an utterance of 'The$_0$ baby is crying' would be true, and this last seems the more natural treatment of the utterance. The entity-invoking theorist could react to this example in a number of ways. He might deny, as the T_1-theorist must, that 'the baby' serves to invoke the same entity on the different familial occasions. But in this case he gives up what was meant to be the special reason for finding the entity-invoking treatment appealing: that 'the baby' is interchangeable with 'Mary' in the imagined circumstances. If the special reason is the accompanying ostensions, the present case is not different in essence from that of 'The girl at the window has red hair'.

I do not wish to claim that there is no satisfactory entity-invoking account of 'The baby is crying', but only that there is no reason to think that there is anything unsatisfactory about the T_0 treatment of the case.

I have no way of being certain that my search for cases which T_0 cannot accommodate has been exhaustive, but I have considered and found wanting the candidates known to me in the written and oral tradition. If there are cases with which T_0 quite definitely cannot deal, this discussion may serve the useful purpose of eliciting them.

If it is conceded that T_0 is adequate, it is to be preferred to any account which makes 'the' ambiguous.[4] The reason is that the elements in a comprehensive theory of human action containing T_0 will be fewer than those involved in a comprehensive theory based on an entity-invoking theory of reference. Both accounts will require such elements as speaker's intentions, and how these can make it seem reasonable to produce certain utterances, and the contrast between what a speaker means and what he strictly and literally says. (Even the T_n-theorist must allow that ironists often speak falsely when what they mean is true.) But the account based on T_0 manages with only one sense of 'the', rather than more than one. Our preference for simple explanations should thus incline us to one based on Russell's theory of descriptions.[5]

[4] Some descriptions are certainly rigid designators by Kripke's standard, for example, 'the even prime'. However, we do not need to suppose that 'the' is ambiguous, in order to explain the truth-conditions of such sentences. The rigidity of the predicate (the fact that it has the same extension in each world) already serves as sufficient explanation.

[5] A stronger argument is that if 'the' is ambiguous it ought to be possible to master just one sense; but it is impossible to see what behaviour would manifest this partial understanding.

V

The Perfect Language

Speaking of a logically perfect or 'philosophical' language, Russell says, in answer to a criticism by Max Black:

> I have never intended to urge seriously that such a language should be created, except in certain fields and for certain problems. The language of mathematical logic is the logical part of such a language, and I am persuaded that it is a help towards correct thinking in logic. The language of theoretical physics is a *slightly* less abstract part of what I should regard as a philosophical language, and is, I am convinced, a great help towards a sound philosophy of the physical world. No doubt my suggestions as to how a philosophical language should be constructed embody my opinions to a considerable extent. But that does not prove that we ought, in our attempts at serious thinking, to be content with ordinary language, with its ambiguities and its abominable syntax. I remain convinced that obstinate addiction to ordinary language in our private thoughts is one of the main obstacles to progress in philosophy (Schilpp 693–4).

The charges against ordinary language are serious. (I shall consider only English, but the intended points extend to *any* ordinary language.) How are they to be substantiated? And what exactly is the role of the logically perfect (or 'philosophical') language in Russell's philosophy?

The idea of the perfect language (PL) has two aspects. One concerns syntax and logical vocabulary: these must be as in the language of *PM*, a condition I shall abbreviate by saying that PL will have *PM*-syntax. The other aspect concerns the extra-logical vocabulary: in *PLA*, as we have seen, Russell claims that this must be restricted to names and predicates which hold of simples (197), and he takes this to be equivalent to the condition that the names and predicates must be unanalysable (that is, learnable only through acquaintance), and also equivalent to the condition that the names and predicates must be indefinable. Later, he offers a more modest restriction: the extra-logical vocabulary must be a 'minimum' vocabulary, in a sense shortly to be made explicit.

Is Russell's conception of PL a vehicle for stating some doctrines in the philosophy of language, or are the PL-doctrines not intended to concern the nature of language in general? In the abstract, there are two extreme positions. It might be held that every language is PL (or some merely notational variant), so that every generalization about PL belongs to the philosophy of language. At the other extreme, PL is just one language among others, and its significance lies wholly in its potential for making graphic certain metaphysical and epistemological doctrines. Russell's own position is complex: in his account of PL one can, I think, find doctrines which would be classified as belonging to metaphysics and epistemology, and also doctrines which would be classified as belonging to the philosophy of language. The complex fusion of doctrines about PL matches the complex fusion of doctrines which go to make up Russell's logical atomism.

Russell often gives the impression that PL is what you would get to if you fully analysed ordinary language, and that this is no accident. This appears to be equivalent to the claim that any ordinary language, or perhaps more generally any learnable language, can be translated into PL. This suggests that the nature of PL will afford insight into the nature of language in general, and so it is a doctrine which one should look out for when examining Russell's position in detail. The first thing to ask is what exactly Russell thought was wrong with English.

I What makes English imperfect?

(a) Ambiguity. We saw in the quotation at the beginning of this chapter that one defect of English, according to Russell, is its ambiguity. It cannot be denied that English is ambiguous, but it is worth distinguishing two sorts of ambiguity relative to which PL might offer some insight into English. So-called 'lexical ambiguity', exemplified by the two senses of 'bank', is a trivial and not very interesting affair. Normally, such cases can be regarded as two words which happen to have the same spelling or pronunciation. However, of more interest, relative to PL, are (i) 'syntactic ambiguity' and (ii) ambiguity between quite different kinds of semantic role.

(i) A sentence counts as syntactically ambiguous if it is ambiguous and there is no way of accounting for the ambiguity by holding that one or more words in the sentence is ambiguous. The discussion of scope in Chapter III provides examples, since scope ambiguity is syntactic ambiguity *par excellence*. Thus 'Everyone loves someone' is ambiguous, but the ambiguity cannot be adequately explained in terms of ambiguity in any of the component words (cf. page 67 above). Now I argued earlier that an account of scope-ambiguity involves the notion of a language with a precisely formulated syntax. As things are, English is not such a language, but PL is. One may, therefore, hope to see in PL the basis of an explanation-by-elimination of scope-ambiguity in English. (An attempt to make this more precise is considered in section 2 below.)

(*ii*) Some English words are ambiguous in a way that tempts us to a faulty account of how they work. An example is 'is', which, on Russell's view, has three very different semantic roles. These are distinguished in PL by three different constructions: one role is marked by '∃', another by '=', and the third by concatenating a predicate with a term. Once again, this sort of fact suggests the idea that from PL one will somehow derive an insight into the workings of English. (Cf. also (*d*), below.)

(*b*) Vagueness.

> The process of sound philosophizing, to my mind, consists mainly in passing from those obvious, vague, ambiguous things, that we feel quite sure of, to something precise, clear, definite, which by reflection and analysis we find is involved in the vague thing that we start from, and is, so to speak, the real truth of which that vague thing is a sort of shadow (*PLA* 179–80).

PL is not capable of further analysis, so the quotation suggests that no truth stated in PL would be vague. This interpretation is confirmed by a passage in *LA* (338) where he says that vagueness is a difficulty facing the creation of PL, but is a defect of English 'which it is easy to imagine removed, however difficult it may be to remove in fact'. Much later, he took a rather different line on this issue. In *HK* (277) a vague predicate is introduced as one whose extension is divided into three regions. There are those things of which the predicate definitely fails to hold, those of which it definitely holds, and those (like a group of nine or ten people relative to the predicate 'crowd') of which the predicate neither definitely holds nor definitely fails to hold. Russell says that 'red' is vague by this standard, and he argues that vagueness is ineliminable. For example, you cannot replace 'red' by a non-vague predicate which holds of all the things of which 'red' definitely holds, and fails to hold of everything else, for there is no sharp line between the things of which 'red' definitely holds, and those of which it neither definitely holds nor definitely fails to hold. In other words, the lines separating the three regions into which the extension of a vague predicate divides are themselves vaguely drawn. Russell also argues that all empirical measurement is vague (*HK* 276), so one cannot eliminate vagueness by replacing 'red' by a predicate of wavelengths. (This seems to be a different sort of point: Russell is in danger of confusing whether a predicate definitely holds with whether we can know for certain whether or not it holds. A predicate specifying a wavelength might be non-vague, yet there might be no cases of which we can be sure it holds exactly, because of limitations of our measuring apparatus. However, I shall not pursue this point.)

If Russell's later self is right in holding that vagueness is never wholly eliminable, his earlier self was wrong in thinking that it would be wholly eliminated from PL. Both selves regard unnecessary vagueness as a defect. But what are the grounds for this? Vagueness indeed conflicts with certain purposes, but I know of no reason for thinking that a language with vague expressions is on this account defective as a language. A law granting tax rebates to bald men would be bad law because of the indeterminate cases, but the sentence promulgating this law would not be a bad *sentence*. (Vagueness may make it hard to give a suitable semantic theory for a language it infects, but that is a different matter.)

The benefits of the (perhaps only partial) elimination of vagueness will accrue at best to the enterprise of providing a minimally vague language for science. Its elimination or diminution will ensure that English cannot be translated into PL. Thus from the point of view of the philosophy of language we can regard PL not as a more pellucid realization of ordinary language, but at best as an abstraction from its inconvenient features, an abstraction permitting at best only preliminary or idealized generalizations about ordinary language.

(*c*) In English, meaningless sentences are counted as meaningful. (Cf. *LA* 335, 338.) The reason has to do with the paradoxes and the theory of types which was designed to avoid them. The paradoxes can be argued for in English, but the formation rules of PL will make the expression of the paradoxes impossible (since PL has *PM*-syntax), and so, *a fortiori*, the threat of the paradoxes being provable vanishes.

Consider the sentence 'I am now speaking falsely', a sentence which those unfamiliar with the paradoxes, like the traditional grammarians, would count as a meaningful English sentence. (After all, 'He is now speaking falsely' seems meaningful, and surely one can replace one pronoun by another without turning a meaningful sentence into a meaningless one?) If he who utters the sentence on a given occasion speaks truly, then he speaks falsely (for he truly says that he is speaking falsely), but if he who utters the sentence speaks falsely, then he speaks truly, for speaking falsely is what he says he is doing. So the sentence (as uttered on a given occasion) is true iff it is false, from which it follows, in classical logic, that it is both true and false, which is a contradiction. It deserves the name of 'paradox' because it is not obvious where the error in reasoning lies. (For a fuller discussion, see Chapter VIII.)

Now the informal analogue of Russell's theory of types, wherewith he purports to block the paradoxes, holds that the sentence 'I am now speaking falsely', unless interpreted in a way that threatens no paradox, is meaningless. This is not apparent from its physical make-up, and this is the present reason for regarding English as defective. In PL, by contrast, there is a clear and definite rule for preventing the formation of such sentences (i.e. a rule which will clearly and definitely exclude such expressions from being sentences of PL).

It would obviously be a serious defect in a language to include meaningless sentences: for this really amounts to there being no effective method, based wholly on physical make-up, for telling whether an arbitrary object is (a token of) a (meaningful) sentence of the language. But there is room for doubt whether an adequate treatment of the paradoxes will entail that English possesses this defect. For one thing, one arrives at the paradox only on certain assumptions (the informal equivalent of the axioms or rules of proof of a formal system). One such assumption, as I make plain in my more detailed discussion of the liar paradox in Chapter VIII, is that every meaningful sentence is either true or false. In the absence of this assumption, one could say that the utterance of 'I am now speaking falsely' is neither true nor false, and then no contradiction follows. This fact suggests an alternative and perhaps less radical way of treating the present paradox, and if the alternative way is adequate English does not have the defect Russell alleges. (Cf. Kripke, 'Outline of a Theory of Truth'.) The general point is that there seems to be no uniquely adequate way of avoiding paradox, and if some way other than Russell's is adopted, it is on the cards that this way will be consistent with the meaningfulness of all those English sentences normally thought of as meaningful.

The idea that English encourages false theories about how it works (d) and the idea that it encourages false or unwarranted metaphysics (e) are both prominent when Russell talks of the misleading effects of language ('grammar'), and when he denigrates English. It is important to stress that Russell thought that one could extract metaphysical conclusions from language (e.g., *LA* 338, *IMT* 322), but one would get the wrong metaphysics if one attempted to extract them from English rather than PL. Here are some exemplary remarks, which range in date from 1903 to 1948:

The study of grammar, in my opinion, is capable of throwing far more light on philosophical questions than is commonly supposed by philosophers (*PofM* 42).

I think the importance of philosophical grammar is very much greater than it is generally thought to be. I think that practically all traditional metaphysics is filled with mistakes due to bad grammar, and that almost all the traditional problems of metaphysics and traditional results – supposed results – of metaphysics are due to a failure to make the kind of distinctions in what we may call philosophical grammar with which we have been concerned (*PLA* 269).

It is exceedingly difficult to make this point clear [that existence is a property of properties, not of individuals] as long as one adheres to ordinary language, because ordinary language is rooted in a certain feeling that our primeval ancestors had, and as long as you keep to ordinary language you find it very difficult to get away from the bias imposed upon you by language. . . . The only way you can really state it correctly is by inventing a new language (*PLA* 234).

Language, from the start, or rather from the start of reflection on language, embodies the belief in more or less permanent persons and things. This is perhaps the chief reason for the difficulty of any philosophy which dispenses with the notion of substance (*HK* 81). (Cf. *PLA* 253, *Mind* 192, *LA* 338.)

The point at issue in the penultimate quotation is a clear case of the way in which, according to Russell, English misleads us about its workings: it makes us think that existence is a property of individuals. The last quotation is a clear example of Russell's belief that English encourages false or unwarranted metaphysics. I shall consider these two claims in turn.

(*d*) One way in which, according to Russell, English misleads us is made manifest by our tendency to regard quantifiers and descriptions as names. That we do indeed have the tendency (even if we are not Meinong) is shown by the fact that Lewis Carroll's jokes are funny.[1]

[1] For example:

'Who did you pass on the road?' the King went on, holding out his hand to the Messenger for some more hay.

'Nobody', said the Messenger.

'Quite right', said the King: 'this young lady saw him too. So of course Nobody walks slower than you.'

'I do my best', the Messenger said in a sullen tone. 'I'm sure nobody walks much faster than I do!'

'He can't do that', said the King, 'or else he'd have been here first.'

(*Through the Looking-Glass*, 143–4.)

Whether we would lack the tendency if our first language had had *PM*-syntax is a question that I do not know how to answer. Certainly, for many of us, getting rid of the tendency comes at the same time as mastering *PM*- (or rather first-order) syntax. This line of thinking opens up the prospect that we shall be able to use PL to gain a more accurate understanding of English.

Another example pointing in the same direction is the case of 'is', already mentioned. According to Russell, a further example is to be found in the case of the notion of meaning. The theory of types shows that there are many different types of meaning, but as words are all of the same type, they encourage us to forget this fact about their meanings (*LA* 332ff.).

An example that Russell gives in *PM* (2) to make the general point that similar-seeming sentences in ordinary language may none the less have quite different semantic structures is this: '. . . "a whale is big" and "one is a number" both look alike', though 'one' and 'a whale' play quite different semantic roles, and so do 'is big' and 'is a number'.

(*e*) The influence of its 'bad grammar' on metaphysics was one of Russell's main reasons for deploring English. In the early years he was particularly exercised by the influence of the subject-predicate grammatical form in encouraging monism. Under this influence 'traditional logic' held that every proposition has this form, which made it impossible to admit that there are several entities, since a proposition to this effect would not itself be of the required form (cf. *LA* 331). Later, the main point was that our assumption that words stand for something outside themselves leads to the wrong results when applied to English. PL will 'prevent inferences from the nature of language to the nature of the world, which are fallacious because they rest upon the logical defects of language' (*LA* 338).

These fallacious inferences are most likely in the case of descriptions and of ordinary proper names.

> We commonly imagine, when we use a proper name, that we mean one definite entity, the particular individual who was called 'Napoleon' (*Mind* 192).

However, Napoleon is a series of events and not a simple (single) entity, so what English tempts us to imagine is false. So, quite generally, 'proper names, as ordinarily understood, are ghosts of substances' (*HK* 88). It is because we do not understand that ordinary proper names are abbreviations of descriptions that we hold the unwarranted view that their bearers are simple substances, whereas in reality they are set-theoretical complexes.

The temptation Russell envisages seems to go like this. First, we are tempted to treat ordinary proper names as names. Secondly, we are tempted to believe that names name only simples. Hence we end up by thinking of the bearers of ordinary proper names as (*au fond*) simple and unchanging substances.

In Chapter III I argued that the first temptation is one to which we ought to succumb. In Chapter II I argued that there is no warrant for the view that only simples can be named. In Chapter VII I shall argue that nothing in our ordinary conception of enduring things commits us to the view that each has a substance, regarded as a sort of unchanging thread on which the thing's history hangs. I thus find nothing acceptable in this part of Russell's claim that PL is superior to English.

The supposed defects would be remedied in PL by having names only for ultimate simples, and letting descriptions replace what we ordinarily think of as names. If those of my views mentioned in the last paragraph are correct, this whole aspect of Russell's philosophy rests upon error.

(*f*) English contains redundant expressions. Russell may well have thought that adverbs and their modifiers, attributive adjectives, and the like, are redundant *categories* of expression in English, since there is no place for them in PL (since it has *PM*-syntax). He says nothing about them in *PLA*, nor in *IMT*, even though, in the latter, he explicitly considers the question of whether a language with *PM*-syntax is capable of translating English (*IMT* ch 19). By contrast, he discusses the analysis of belief-sentences on many occasions (e.g., *PP* ch 12, *PLA* 224–7, PM_2 App. C, *IMT* ch 19). At first sight, it appears that such sentences cannot be translated into any language with *PM*-syntax, but if some of the analyses of belief that Russell tentatively offers (e.g., in *PP*, PM_2 or *IMT*) are correct, appearances in this respect deceive. (See also Chapter VII, section 1.) However, the issue I shall briefly take up here is whether English contains redundant names.

At the time of *PLA* Russell was no doubt led to the idea that names cannot name complexes partly by the fact that it was a stipulation that no PL-name named a complex. One thing that grounded this stipulation, it seems, was the supposed redundancy of names of complexes:

> I thought, originally, that, if we were omniscient, we should have a
> proper name for each simple, but no proper names for complexes,
> since these could be defined by mentioning their simple
> constituents and their structure (*MPD* 166).

Now Russell himself held that a genuine name is not synonymous with any description, so if English contains names of complexes, it follows that PL cannot translate it. Moreover Russell did not think that it was the simplicity of the object named that prevented the name being synonymous with any description. (At any rate, he certainly should not have thought this, since one simple may give rise to a suitable description by being uniquely related to another. That Russell has reason for holding that names are not synonymous with descriptions, and which does not depend on the claim that named objects are simple, is plain from the passages referred to in Chapter III, e.g., the discussion of scope in *OD*.) If it is to be said that English expressions which seem to name complexes are not really names, there needs to be a reason independent of the claim that names name only simples. Russell has such an independent reason: the principle of acquaintance. However, we have rejected this principle, and also the view that names name only complexes. The upshot is that while there are no doubt names in English which are redundant in the sense that we could achieve many practical purposes without them, they are not redundant in the sense of being definable by means of descriptions. Hence PL, as envisaged in *PLA*, cannot translate English.

Immediately after the passage just quoted from *MPD*, Russell says he now rejects the view that it describes. The rejection first appears in *IMT*, in which, as we have seen, names of complexes are allowed. At much the same time, there is an important shift in the idea of a perfect language. In *HK* the perfect extra-logical vocabulary is no longer specified as one having expressions only for simples; rather, it is *some* 'minimum vocabulary', and Russell realizes that there may be more than one (*HK* 94, 259; *MPD* 170).

> A minimum vocabulary is defined as one having the two properties (1) that every proposition in the given body of knowledge can be expressed by means of words belonging to the minimum vocabulary, (2) that no word in this vocabulary can be defined in terms of other words in it (*HK* 274).

Russell thought that the idea of minimum vocabularies was important for two reasons. On the one hand, as we have seen, he still takes English to give rise to the unwarranted metaphysics of substance, in part via having names of complexes. By contrast 'a minimum vocabulary cannot contain names for complexes of which the structure is known' (*HK* 274). More generally, 'What mathematical logic does . . . is to diminish the number of words which have the straightforward meaning of pointing to an object' (*MPD* 237), and thereby one diminishes the number of entities one's language forces one to assume. The generalization is open to precisely the same sort of criticism as the one I offered earlier concerning the redundancy of names. If one believes there is a language containing a *name 'n'*, one is committed to no fewer entities by preferring a language in which there is no such name; and if one believes that *'n'* is not really a name, one needs an independent reason.

The other importance of a minimum vocabulary is that the words common to every minimum vocabulary 'represent the hard core of experience by which our sentences are connected to the non-linguistic world' (*MPD* 170). This, however, amounts to nothing more than the principle of acquaintance. The words common to all minimum vocabularies are those which can be defined in no (learnable) vocabulary, but which can be mastered only by acquaintance with the things (experiences) for which they stand. Similar remarks apply to what Russell in *HK* describes as 'the main conclusion' concerning minimum vocabularies (265): the conclusion is none other than that there are what I earlier called unanalysable expressions.

Thus Russell's claim that English contains redundant names depends for its content and supposed importance on errors, notably the principle of acquaintance and the erroneous view that names name only simples.

(*g*) PL, unlike English, 'will show at a glance the logical structure of the facts asserted or denied' (*PLA* 198). One could summarize the idea like this: in PL, logical form and grammatical form will be the same. In PL, but not in English, logical form is manifest at the surface. This gives rise to the idea, closely related to that of (*d*) above, that PL sentences are the deep structures which underlie English sentences. This Russellian view of logical form and logical structure is discussed in the next section.

2   Logical form

Many of Russell's criticisms of English, considered in the last section, concern its extra-logical vocabulary, and thus bring out the corresponding aspect of the perfection of PL. The other aspect is its perfect syntax (i.e. *PM*-syntax), compared with which the syntax of English is deplored as 'abominable'. It is this aspect that I shall discuss in the present section.

For the sake of the present discussion, I shall give a brief account of the syntax of *PM*, but I shall ignore those of its features which flow from the ramified theory of types, and I shall not explain the circumflexion operator (but see Chapter VIII, and my 'Note on Symbolism'). The initial idea is one which will not in fact be represented in the syntax: the idea of an atomic proposition. This is expressed by a sentence comprising an unanalysable predicate of degree n followed by n unanalysable names. If we pretend that the relevant English expressions are unanalysable, an example of an atomic sentence involving a predicate of degree 1 is 'Wise Socrates'; of degree 2 'Loves (Cassio, Desdemona)'; of degree 3 'Gives-to (John, *Anna Karenina*, Mary)'. We now introduce 'name-variables' ('individual variables'), which can properly occur in the positions occupied by names, and are written 'x', 'y', 'z'. . . . This gives rise to the idea of such expressions as 'Wise x', 'Loves (x, y)', 'Gives-to (x, y, z)', which Russell calls 'propositional functions'. These become sentences when their variables are replaced by names.[2] Next we introduce the idea of a predicate variable, written 'φ', 'ψ', 'χ', ... If we replace the names in an atomic sentence by name-variables and the predicate in such a sentence by a predicate variable the result is what I shall call 'atomic formulae': 'φx', 'ψxy', 'χxyz'. . . . Russell would regard these expressions also as propositional functions, but, respectively, propositional functions of two, three and four variables. They would become sentences expressing propositions if their variables were replaced by appropriate constants, name-variables by names, predicate variables by predicates. Atomic formulae belong to the language ('syntax') of *PM*, and are the syntactic basis of all other formulae. A 'quantifier' (universal) is an expression of the form '($\forall$)', with the blank filled by either a name-variable (in which case it is a name or individual quantifier) or a predicate-variable (in which case it is a predicate quantifier). Applying a quantifier to a formula yields a formula. A 'sentential connective' is either '$\sim$' (tilde) or 'v' (vel). The result of enclosing a formula in brackets and prefixing it by '$\sim$' is a formula, and so is the result of inserting 'v' between two bracketed formulae. (These formation rules are roughly stated.) Roughly speaking, '$\forall$' means 'all', '$\sim$' means 'not' and 'v' means 'or'. Thus '$(\forall x)\varphi x$' means, roughly, 'Everything has φ', '$(\forall \varphi)\varphi x$' means, roughly, '$x$ has every property' and '$(\forall x)(\forall \varphi)\varphi x$' means, roughly, 'Everything has every property'. '$\sim(\varphi x)$' means, roughly, 'It is not the case that φx' and 'φx v ψy' means, roughly, 'Either φx or ψy (or both)'. In these terms, one can introduce further sentential connectives (e.g., '&' ('and') '$\rightarrow$' ('if . . . then') ' $\leftrightarrow$ ' ('iff')), further quantifiers (e.g., '$\exists$' ('there is')), and a defined predicate (constant) '$=$' ('is the same as').

PL results from this language by the addition of predicates and names, with the result that atomic sentences can be formed. Even without such additions, formulae of the language which contain no variable not in the scope of some quantifier ('closed formulae') can be regarded as 'saying' something, true or false. Thus '$(\forall x)(\forall \varphi)\varphi x$' says something false, whereas '$(\forall x)(\exists \varphi)\varphi x$' says something true. The propositions thus expressed Russell calls 'absolutely general' (*OKEW*

---

[2] I here assume that propositional functions are expressions, but this is controversial. For a discussion, see Chapter VIII, section 4.

53), and it is this absolute generality which is one mark of 'logical propositions':

> Every logical proposition consists wholly and solely of variables, though it is not true that every proposition consisting wholly and solely of variables is logical (*PLA* 237).

The first part is not strictly true to Russell's intentions: a closed formula of *PM* contains constants, but all its constants are *logical* constants. The second part, indicating that complete generality is not sufficient for being a logical proposition, arises from the fact that Russell here wants a logical proposition to be not merely one expressed wholly in logical terms (i.e. by an expression all of whose constants are logical), nor even a *true* proposition of this kind, but one which is, in addition, *logically true*. For example, the proposition that there are at least 30,000 things in the world can be expressed in wholly logical terms, but even though it is true it is not a logical truth. (Cf. *PLA* 240.)

Russell offers at least two accounts of logical truth. Close to the passage just mentioned in *PLA* he says that it is sufficient for being a logical truth that the proposition be deducible from 'the premises of logic'. However, he omits to give any general characterization of these premises. Later, in the introduction to the second edition of *PofM*, he says that a logical truth is one which is 'formally true' or 'true in virtue of its form', but he confesses himself unable to give any further analysis of what is involved in being true in virtue of form (*PofM xii*; cf. *OKEW* 66–7).

In *PLA*, he characterizes the logical form of a proposition as 'that which you get when for every single one of its constituents you substitute a variable' (238). (Remember that there are no constituents corresponding to the logical constants.) However, there is no routine way of identifying the constituents of a proposition until it has been expressed in PL. (For example, Socrates is not a constituent of the proposition that Socrates is wise, for constituents are meaning-relata, and 'Socrates', not being a name, according to Russell, has no meaning-relatum.) Hence this account, while adequate to characterize the logical form of a proposition expressed in PL, is inadequate as a characterization of the logical form of a proposition expressed in English.

However hard to characterize, logical form plays an important part in Russell's account of our understanding of English:

> In order to understand a sentence, it is necessary to have knowledge both of the constituents and of the particular instance of the form. It is in this way that a sentence conveys information,

since it tells us that certain known objects are related according to a certain known form. Thus some kind of knowledge of logical forms, though with most people it is not explicit, is involved in all understanding of discourse (*OKEW* 53).

The theory of descriptions aims to give the logical form of description sentences, and in doing so, according to the Russell of *PM*, it shows what is going on in the mind of one who uses such a sentence:

> Thus in what *we* have in mind when we say 'Socrates is human' there is an apparent variable (*PM* 50).

An apparent variable is one that is bound, in this case by the existential quantifier present in the description that the ordinary proper name 'Socrates' abbreviates. There are other examples, e.g.:

> Often an apparent variable is really present where language does not at once indicate its presence. Thus for example '*A* is mortal' means 'there is a time at which *A* will die'. Thus a variable time occurs as apparent variable (*PM* 50).

Making plain an English sentence's logical form is part of a whole branch of philosophy:

> It is the business of philosophical logic to extract this knowledge [of logical forms] from its concrete integuments, and to render it explicit and pure (*OKEW* 53).

At the time of this lecture, indeed, philosophical logic seems to have been thought of as the whole of philosophy:

> Every philosophical problem, when it is subjected to the necessary analysis and justification, is found either to be not really philosophical at all, or else to be, in the sense in which we are using the word, logical (*OKEW* 42; cf. *LA* 323).

Logical form is important, according to Russell, not only in our understanding of language, and not only to philosophical logic, but also to inference, for 'In all inference, form alone is essential' (*OKEW* 53).

We thus have a network of interconnected notions: the formulae of *PM*; logical constants; completely general propositions; logical propositions (i.e. logical truths); logical form, as applied both to *PM*-formulae and to English sentences; inference; philosophical logic. One way to organize the material is to take logical form as the central idea. A logical truth is one true in virtue of its form. The logical form of an English sentence is some *PM*-formula, or at any rate some PL-sentence. A logical constant is a constant which occurs in a logical form. A completely general proposition is a logical form closed by universal quantification. A logically valid inference is one valid in virtue of its logical form. Philosophical logic is the study of logical form. Logical forms 'will show at a glance the logical structure of the facts asserted or denied' (*PLA* 198).

Although Russell's explicit discussions of the notion of logical form, and even of the notion of PL, are rare, it is hard to overestimate the importance these ideas had for him, at least in the period between *OD* and *HK* (which encompasses all his most significant writings with the exception of *Leibniz* and *PofM*). It will be found that his analyses and reconstructions are generally couched in the fragment of English closest to *PM*-syntax. What is the justification for this method? The fullest of Russell's accounts comes in the second lecture in *OKEW*, of which the salient remarks have already been quoted. But this leaves at least three questions inadequately answered:

(*i*) What is a logical constant?

(*ii*) What is the criterion for determining what *PM*-formula is (or gives) the logical form of an arbitrary English sentence?

(*iii*) Given the apparent divergences between *PM*-syntax and English, how can knowledge of the former, or of what the former reveals, be of importance to understanding English, or to recognizing the validity of arguments couched in English?

(*i*) Russell's thought about the logical constants is fairly steady throughout his life. Admittedly, he includes set-theoretic membership as a primitive logical constant in *PofM* (11), whereas by the time of *ML* (and, of course, *PM*) it is treated as a defined logical constant. Admittedly, also, in *PofM* (11) he includes truth as a logical constant, but it is not clear that he means to exclude it later. In *ML* it is included among the 'primitive ideas required in symbolic logic', along with negation, quantification, and a symbol ('!') drawn from the theory of types (*ML* 83–4). In *PM* there is a tendency to equate the meaning of sentences containing constants with that of sentences predicating truth or falsehood of other sentences. Thus, for example, '$\sim p$' is said to denote the proposition asserting that p is not true (*PM* 6). This tendency is quite unequivocal in *IMT*, where each constant in a sentence marks a further remove up the Tarskian hierarchy from the basic language, free of the truth predicate (*IMT* 60ff., 74ff.). The tendency is deplorable, for it is plain that, as Russell elsewhere puts it (*PM* 41), 'the notion of *truth* is not part of the content of what is judged' when, for example, we judge that Socrates is not female.

Having made this remark about truth, I shall pretend that Russell does not treat it as a logical constant, so that for him the logical constants are, simply, some adequate set of truth-functional sentential connectives (in *PM* he selects '$\sim$' and 'v') and quantifiers binding variables taking name position, and quantifiers binding variables taking predicate position (I continue to neglect circumflexion). The only justification one can find in Russell for selecting just these expressions as the logical constants is their complete generality. He does not, for example, consider whether the same criterion would rule 'necessarily' as a logical constant or as a non-logical one.[3]

I discuss the adequacy of Russell's characterization of the logical constants in Chapter VIII, section 2. The discussion is confined to a consideration of the suggestion that there is a sharp divide between first-order logic and a system, like that of *PM*, which contains predicate quantifiers, and which, for this reason, some have seen as going beyond the bounds of *logic*, properly so-called. The reader is referred to Peacocke's 'What is a Logical Constant?' for a sophisticated criterion to underpin the intuitive idea that the logical constants are those which introduce no special subject-matter.

(*ii*) The problem of finding a criterion for matching an arbitrary English sentence with the *PM*-formula which gives its logical form cannot be discussed at any length until we have some answer to our third question, concerning the importance of logical form. However, it is plain that there is a routine way of transforming a PL-sentence into a *PM*-formula, so that the latter would intuitively be regarded as the logical form of the former: systematically replace all non-logical constants by appropriate variables. This means that the question of a criterion for the logical form of an English sentence can be reduced to the question of a criterion for an appropriate PL-correlate of an English sentence. A natural thought is that the appropriate standard of correlation is synonymy, but both Russell's intentions and his practice suggest some weaker standard. Whether such a standard can be found is a question that will be taken up later.

(*iii*) Russell's discussions of logical form in connection with understanding (*OKEW* 53, *PLA* 239) suggest that he is toying with the idea that logical form might help to solve his problem about the unity of the proposition. Take an individual, say Plato (we will share Russell's 'rash assumption' (*IMP* 175) that Plato *is* an individual), and a property, say wisdom, and all you have is two entities and not a proposition. But if you could somehow weld them together by means

---

[3] This requires some qualification. At one point, Russell denied that propositions could be necessarily true (*PLA* 231), and at another point he questioned whether there are true propositions which could have been false (*Leibniz* 24). One who could make either denial would naturally be somewhat inhibited in his discussions of modal operators. In *PLA* he seems to have held that 'necessarily' is a variant of the universal quantifier (231), and thus it would follow that it is a logical constant. But one cannot treat the words he here utters as asserting concerning modal operators (i.e. what are really modal operators) that they are logical constants.

of the logical form *monadic relation* then you would have something which *says* something, true or false. However, it is not clear, and Russell himself was not clear, how this explanation could work. The trouble is, Russell suggests, that one is tempted to regard the logical form as one of the constituents of the proposition, but 'If it were you would have to have that constituent related to the other constituents' (*PLA* 239). Russell does not pursue the suggestion; nor, therefore, shall I.

There is some indication that Russell thought that if you know the logical form of a sentence, then you know how it is that the meanings of its parts combine to determine its meaning. One such sign is in the discussion in *OKEW* from which I have already quoted: the logical form 'tells us that certain known objects are related according to a certain known form' (*OKEW* 53). (Bear in mind that for Russell the meaning of an unanalysable non-logical word is an object, and that he held that knowing the meaning of the word involved knowing the relevant object.) Another sign can be detected in Russell's discussion of the logical form of belief-sentences in *PLA* (224–6). He claims that belief is 'a new beast for our zoo' (226), by which he means something which entails that a belief-sentence does not have a *PM*-logical-form. He concludes the discussion by apologizing for this *difficulty*, so it is not unreasonable to interpret him as holding that (*a*) if one can translate an idiom into PL at least the 'logical' difficulties concerning the idiom (or, perhaps, the related subject-matter) are thereby solved, and (*b*) that if one cannot translate an idiom into PL the problems are intensified or even, perhaps, rendered insoluble. Certainly, whenever Russell offers any positive account of belief-sentences, the account invariably consists in suggesting a translation, of one kind or another, into a language with *PM*-syntax (see, e.g., *PP* ch 12; *PM*$_2$ App. C; *IMT* ch 19, and Chapter VII, section 1). With some hesitation, therefore, one might attribute to Russell the view that when (and perhaps only when) one can give the logical form of a sentence by translating it into PL, one can properly appreciate the semantic mechanisms the sentence involves.

One cannot, I think, find in Russell's writing evidence that he held any more precise version of the view just mentioned, or that he held beliefs which would justify the view. I shall try to supply both precisification and justification. However, it must be understood that, though this involves considering a precisification and justification of a Russellian view, the ideas used to precisify and justify cannot be attributed to Russell.

One relatively precise view of logical form, of which Russell's attitude might be seen as a sort of imprecise shadow, is to be found in the work of Donald Davidson (see, e.g., 'Truth and Meaning', 'The

Method of Truth in Metaphysics'). According to Davidson, the best way to provide a semantic account of English is first to translate it into some formalized language and then to provide a recursive semantic theory, which in Davidson's view will consist of a theory of truth, for the formalized language:

> I view formal languages or canonical notations as devices for exploring the structure of natural language. We know how to give a theory of truth for the formal language; so if we also know how to transform the sentences of a natural language systematically into sentences of the formal language, we would have a theory of truth for the natural language ('The Method of Truth in Metaphysics' 247).

On Davidson's view, the logical form of a sentence of English is the sentence with which it is matched in some formal language for which there is a theory of truth. (Since no doubt there is more than one such formal language, we should speak of logical-form-in-L, or L-logical-form, where 'L' denotes the formal language in question.) Since PL will count as a formal language in Davidson's sense, a 'transformation' of an English sentence into PL, which I shall call its 'PL-logical-form', will serve to prepare it for the application of a theory of truth. Since a theory of truth is precisely, in Davidson's eyes, what a semantic theory is, we may say that, on this view, the PL-logical-form of an English sentence is the proxy through which a semantic theory is applied to English.

The notion of a semantic theory here invoked is foreign to Russell. This is not surprising in connection with his earlier work, since the idea had not been developed. Though Russell was later familiar with Tarski's work on truth, he seems not have connected the results with the theory of meaning. We cannot, therefore, attribute Davidson's view to Russell. But, since many of Russell's remarks about logical form follow from Davidson's view, we might consider using the latter to justify Russell's position.

For example, how could one justify Russell's claim that 'some kind of knowledge of logical forms, though with most people it is not explicit, is involved in all understanding of discourse' (*OKEW* 53)? Granted Davidson's view, there are two possible justifications. One is that if we are explicitly to state the meaning of an English sentence, in the framework of a semantic theory, we shall have first to give the sentence's logical form; thus it is that a sentence's logical form reveals its semantic mechanisms. The other is that one may, perhaps, attribute to any English speaker an 'implicit' knowledge of a semantic theory for English, and thus an implicit knowledge of the logical forms of English sentences, forms through the medium of which the semantic theory applies to English. (One might – and I think should – resist the second suggestion even if one accepts the first: cf. Stich, 'What Every Speaker Knows'.)

To take another example, how could one justify Russell's claim that '*A* is mortal' contains a bound variable ranging over times (*PM* 50)? His own justification is simply that this sentence means the same as 'There is a time at which *A* will die', but this is plainly inadequate. Since synonymy is symmetric, what Russell says equally supports the view that the second sentence, despite appearances, contains no quantifier and no variable. However, armed with Davidson's theory, the pattern of explanation is straightforward: 'There is a time at which *A* will die' (or, if you prefer, '$(\exists x)(\text{time } x \ \& \ \text{dies-at } (A, x))$') is the transformation of '*A* is mortal' which we must give in order to arrive at a semantic theory for English by proxy of a semantic theory for PL. (I do not wish to suggest that Davidson himself would think that anything remotely like this transformation is required.) Russell's metaphorical talk of the 'real presence' of a variable in a sentence which, as written in English, does not contain one is replaced by something literal and intelligible: the variable occurs in the PL sentence by proxy of which one gives the semantics of the English sentence.

A further way in which a Davidsonian view would, if sound, justify Russell's use of the idea of logical form is this: the direct applicability of a theory of truth to PL, but not to English, gives literal content to the metaphor that PL, but not English, 'shows at a glance the logical structure of the facts asserted or denied' (*PLA* 198). The syntax of PL 'reveals structure' in that there is a relatively straightforward way of articulating the relationship between the physical make-up of PL-sentences and their semantic properties.

On Davidson's view:

> The logical constants may be identified as those iterative features of the language which require a recursive clause (not in the basis) in the definition of truth or satisfaction ('In Defence of Convention T' 81).

Since the whole idea is that there will be no definition of truth applying directly to English, this would give rise to the idea that the logical constants of English are to be identified through those of PL. This in turn might, perhaps, be developed into a justification for Russell's association of the notion of logical form with inference.[4]

Thus a Davidsonian view of logical form would, if sound, give

---

[4] For reservations about Davidson's account of the idea of a logical constant, see Evans's very illuminating article 'Semantic Structure and Logical Form' (especially 203). Davidson has discussed in some detail the connection between his idea of logical form and that of inference: see, e.g., his 'Action and Reaction'.

support to Russell's main ideas concerning logical form. Unfortunately, Davidson's view is unsound.

One reason for this, when PL is the formalized language which is to serve as the proxy whereby semantics are given for English, is that many English sentences resist translation into PL. Yet it would obviously be incorrect to give the same semantic account for non-synonymous sentences. For example, I argued in the last chapter that English description-sentences are not synonymous with their transformations into PL. Thus the semantics for the PL sentences will not in general transfer to their English counterparts.

However, the notion of synonymy is, as we have seen, troublesome. It is therefore fortunate that the present point can be generalized and extended, in such a way that it does not even rely on the premise of the impossibility of translating English into PL. The attempt to give the semantics of English by proxy confronts a dilemma: either there is a translation manual which, purely on the basis of physical make-up, matches each English sentence with a sentence of the formalized language, in such a way as to preserve the semantic structure of the original, or there is not. If there is such a manual, then semantics by proxy are needless, since one could as well supply direct semantics for English. Then the idea of logical form would be devoid of the importance which Russell attached to it. If there is no such manual, then semantics by proxy are inadequate. Obviously, if there is no translation manual of any kind, then there is no way in which the semantics for the proxy language can be applied indirectly to English. If there is a manual but it is not based purely on physical make-up, the semantics will be inadequate, since a total theory of meaning should enable one to pass from sentences, characterized purely as shapes or sounds, to their meanings. (An example of a manual which fails this condition would be one non-redundantly containing the rule: 'If in any sentence in which "is" occurs it can be replaced by "is identical to" without altering the sentence's meaning, translate it by "=".') If there is a manual based on physical make-up, but which does not preserve the semantic structure of English, the semantics by proxy will be inadequate precisely because there will be no way of extracting the correct semantic structure of English on the basis of the semantic theory together with the manual. (An example would be a manual which translated 'bach' as 'unmarried' and 'elor' as 'man': such a manual may match every English sentence with a 'synonym', assuming we have a notion of synonymy which imposes no structural constraints, but in the context of semantics by proxy it would lead to the incorrect ascription of structure to the unstructured expression 'bachelor'.)[5]

[5] This argument is elaborated in my 'Semantics by Proxy'.

The last point takes for granted the notion of semantic structure, and this is worth brief elaboration. One way of elucidating the notion is in terms of the causal structure of speakers' competence: if mastery of all the sentences in a certain set is causally sufficient for mastery of some sentence outside the set, this latter sentence will have to be treated as composed of semantically significant expressions and constructions belonging to the sentences in the original set.[6] Thus for the normal English speaker mastery of the sentences 'Bread is nutritious' and 'Rice is expensive' suffices for mastery both of 'Bread is expensive' and 'Rice is nutritious'. It is facts of this sort that justify us in regarding these sentences as involving at least two simple expressions, and having a common construction. However, the former pair of sentences might be mastered by one who did not understand the latter if, for example, he had learnt them *en bloc* from a phrase book. It would be wrong to attribute any semantic structure to these sentences in the idiolect of such a person. (In a truth-theory, the T-sentences for these sentences should be axioms.)

Any adequate semantic theory must give a proper account of the semantic structure of its object language. (If the theory is a truth-theory, we can effect the requirement as follows: iff the axiomatic resources used in deriving the T-sentences for each sentence in a set a suffice for deriving the T-sentence for s, mastery of each sentence in a is causally sufficient for mastery of s.) Hence, for semantics by proxy, the translation manual must preserve semantic structure. As I have already said, if this condition is satisfied, there is no reason why a direct semantic theory should not be given. The point I wish at the moment to stress, however, is that even if English can be translated into PL, the translation will not preserve structure.

This is easy to see in the case of descriptions, if we assume that English quantifiers are translated by PL quantifiers. For then semantics for English by proxy of PL will attribute the same semantic structure both to sentences of the form 'The F is G' and to sentences of the form 'There is exactly one F and it is G'. But then understanding sentences of the one form should be causally necessary and sufficient for understanding sentences of the other; but this is plainly not the case. Thus even if Russell's theory of descriptions matches English description sentences with PL synonyms, it would still be inadequate within a programme of semantics by proxy.

It is not, therefore, within Davidson's notion of semantics by proxy that we shall find a satisfactory way of justifying Russell's conception of logical form. We must look elsewhere.

Like Frege (*Conceptual Notation* 105), Russell mentions with approval Leibniz's vision of *characteristica universalis*, a kind of

6 Cf. Evans, 'Semantic Structure and Logical Form' (201).

generalized arithmetic which would provide definite rules for settling argumentative disputes (*OKEW* 49). The vision includes a systematic and finitely statable characterization of validity. This will take the form of a finitely stated proof-theory or model-theory (I shall refer to both indifferently as the *logical apparatus*), and the minimum requirement is partial characterization: the apparatus must bring out only valid sentences as provable, or true-in-every-model. For the moment I intend the most general notion of validity, whereby a sentence is valid iff necessarily true, and an argument valid iff necessarily truth-preserving.[7] (We need no separate treatment of arguments, since for our purposes we may equate the validity of an argument with that of its corresponding conditional.) In determining whether a logical apparatus offers a partial characterization of validity, we have to proceed informally, leaning on pre-theoretical intuitions of validity.

Validity in English is intrinsically less amenable to systematic treatment than is validity in PL, whose syntax was, of course, devised with an eye to the provision of logical apparatus (the proof-theory of *PM*). Ambiguity is one cause of the trouble, but even unambiguous English presents hard problems. In order to speak in a finite space of infinitely many sentences, a logical apparatus has to detect *patterns* of validity, but it is just these that are hard to pick out in English. One might think that every instance of the following argument-pattern is valid: 'Every *F* is a *G*, every *G* is *H*, therefore every *F* is *H*'. But it is not: put 'number' for '*F*', 'number or its successor' for '*G*', and 'even' for '*H*' (the example is borrowed from Geach's 'A Program for Syntax'). What one needs, but lacks, is a general and projectible characterization, purely in terms of physical make-up, of the sorts of expression which would yield a valid argument when inserted in the argument-pattern. This is no isolated case. The phenomenon is widespread; hence it is hard to find a logical apparatus for English.

Now the justification that I propose to consider for Russell's ideas about logical form is this: not being able to find a systematic characterization of validity that applies directly to English, for logical purposes one abandons English in favour of PL. The PL-logical-form of an English sentence will have the 'logical properties' of that sentence, but will present them in such a way that they are amenable to some logical apparatus, in particular to *PM*-logic. I shall conclude this chapter by first making this justification somewhat more precise, and then attempting to assess its worth.

For Russell, the primary application of the notion of logical form is not to sentences but to non-linguistic entities: facts or propositions.

[7] 'Necessarily' here is to be understood in what Plantinga calls the 'broadly logical' sense: *The Nature of Necessity* 2ff.

(In *PLA* (198) PL is said to show the logical structure of facts, and the role of philosophical logic is to classify the forms facts can have (216).) PL-sentences will make manifest the logical form of the facts they assert. The question of whether an English sentence (or argument) is not merely valid but also, in addition, *logically* valid, is one on which, for Russell, one has no independent grip. It can be answered only by considering whether the PL-sentence with which the English is matched, and which asserts the same fact, is logically valid, where the standard of logical validity is that its validity be captured by the logical apparatus of *PM*. The reason for saying that PL-sentences make manifest the *logical* form of the facts they assert, or the propositions they express, is that in PL all the features of the facts or propositions that bear on *logical* validity are presented in such a way as to render them accessible to treatment by the logical apparatus of *PM*. The *logical* properties of facts or propositions are just those features which, once the facts or propositions are expressed in PL, are accessible to *PM*-logic.

Let us see how some of Russell's main ideas concerning logical form could be justified, if this conception of logical form is sound. In what follows, I do not assert that the details of the justification I offer are correct, even granted the present conception of logical form. I assert merely that the Russellian ideas might seem plausible in the light of this conception.

One could justify Russell's claim that 'some kind of knowledge of logical forms . . . is involved in all understanding of discourse' (*OKEW* 53) on the grounds that speakers know (perhaps 'implicitly') the logical properties of the propositions they assert or hear asserted: they know what *logically* follows from what is asserted. This knowledge will be systematized by *PM*-logic. More generally, since the logical properties of a proposition partially determine its identity, it is tempting to think that in determining the logical form of a sentence, and thus determining the logical properties of the proposition it expresses, one is partially determining the semantics of the sentence.

Russell's claim that 'A is mortal' contains a variable can be justified as the claim that the logical form of this sentence contains a variable. The logical form will express the same proposition, but in a way that renders its logical properties accessible to *PM*-logic. Thus, for example, the logical form would reveal that the inference from 'A dies-at time t' to 'A is mortal' is *logically* valid, being an instance of existential generalization.

PL, but not English, will 'show at a glance the structure of the facts asserted or denied' (*PLA* 198) in the by now familiar sense that it will render these logical structural properties accessible to systematization by *PM*-logic.

An immediate difficulty with this conception of logical form is that, as we have seen, there are grounds for believing that English sentences are not in general synonymous with the PL-sentences which are supposed to be their logical forms, and thus do not in general express the same proposition. However, in this case, by contrast with the case of the Davidsonian conception, it is possible that we could make do with a weaker relation. If, as in the Davidsonian conception, the logical form of a sentence is a transformation of it fit to be the input to a semantic theory, with the aim that the theory should then apply indirectly to English, logical form and English sentence need to mean the same. If, however, as in the present conception, the logical form of a sentence is a transformation of it fit to be the input to a proof-theory, with the aim that the proof-theory should reveal something about the logical properties of the proposition the English sentence expresses, then it is sufficient that logical form and English sentence express propositions with the same logical properties. Since validity hinges on no more than truth-conditions, the same must hold for the narrower notion of logical validity. Hence, it would seem, the present conception requires only that logical form and English sentence have the same truth-conditions.

That the relation be weaker than synonymy harmonizes well with Russell's practice. It allows that the theory of descriptions should give the logical form of description-sentences, and it allows for such manœuvrings as the formalization of 'but' as '&', and, perhaps, for formalizing tensed sentences by quantification over times. However, it would certainly be at variance with Russell's philosophy to allow that sameness of truth-conditions is sufficient.

For one thing, unless there is some restriction on the vocabulary of PL, the question of whether or not PL contains, for each English sentence, its logical form, would be trivial instead of substantial. For example, Russell's discussions of belief can be seen as discussions of whether belief-sentences can be matched by PL-sentences. If no restriction is placed on the vocabulary of PL, the discussion is trivial: for each sentence of the form 'A believes that p' could be represented in PM-syntax as '$G(A)$', where 'G' is a predicate stipulated to have the same truth-conditions, or even the same meaning, as '... believes that p'. The minimal restriction, then, if the question of whether all English sentences have PL-logical-forms is to be of interest, is that PL should have a merely finite vocabulary. We have seen that Russell's restrictions on the extra-logical vocabulary of PL include this and are stricter. But for the moment, it is well to see what the smallest restrictions are which would yield the main feature of his idea of logical form.

We have spoken as if there is at most one PL-logical-form of an

English sentence, but, by the standards so far set, there will be infinitely many if any, since each PL-sentence has infinitely many truth-conditional equivalents. One thinks here not only of the possibility of redundant conjuncts or disjuncts, but also of the fact that the PL-vocabulary might, for all that has so far been required, contain not only the predicates 'man' and 'married' but also the predicate 'bachelor'. Then one would need somehow to choose between 'Man John & ~ married John' and 'Bachelor John' as *the* logical form of 'John's a bachelor'.

In the light of the idea I attribute to Russell, that it is primarily facts or propositions which have logical properties, a natural suggestion would be to stipulate that the logical form which maximizes the degree to which validity is *logical* validity is to be preferred: this would best reveal the logical properties of the proposition expressed. This would make one prefer a most structured PL-sentence as the logical form of the English. (This does not yield uniqueness, but it is a step in that direction.) This shows that analysis will be involved in providing a PL-logical-form, which certainly accords with Russell's thinking. The point here, though, is that whereas the need for analysis would most naturally be seen to flow from his stipulations about the nature of the extra-logical vocabulary of PL, in particular that it should have only expressions with simple meaning-relata, or should be a minimum vocabulary, in the present conception the need for analysis is already guaranteed by other considerations.

One might feel some reluctance to hold that 'John's a bachelor, so he's unmarried' is *logically* valid, yet this is what one would have to say if one accepts the Russellian notion of logical form that I am sketching. On Russell's view, the reluctance is caused by the misleading influence of grammatical form which has hidden, beneath a definable expression, some of the logical structure of the premise.

We are still some way from uniqueness of logical form, and this is particularly acute in the case of valid English sentences, each of which, for anything that has so far been said, has any valid PL-sentence, say '$(\forall x)(x=x)$', as its logical form. I shall show that many people, and not just Russell, in practice operate with the notion of a sentence's most *explicit* logical form (in a formalized language, say PL).

Without the notion of a most explicit logical form we could not ground our belief that, for example, first-order logic cannot be used to establish the validity of every valid English argument. As an example of such an inaccessible argument, an elementary logic text might give 'John is happy, so possibly John is happy'. But unless we insist that there is no more explicit logical form of the premise than something like 'Happy John', we can establish the argument's validity by first-order, and thus *PM*, means. Formalize the argument as 'Happy John & G(John) ⊢ G(John)', where 'G' is a primitive predicate which means the same as 'Possibly, . . . is happy'. This 'overstructured' formalization is not merely permitted by the requirement that English sentence and logical form must have the same truth-conditions, it is actually required by the stipulation that one should select logical forms so as to maximize the extent to which validity will be counted as logical validity. Since there are infinitely many arguments of this kind, and since each requires a fresh primitive predicate, the restriction of the vocabulary of PL to finitude rules this out as a general tactic, but it does not rule out the application of the tactic to (any finite number of) particular cases.

So long as we confine ourselves to the sorts of idea we have so far considered, there seems to be no satisfactory solution to the problem of finding a criterion for matching English sentences with PL-sentences, in a way which accords with our intuitions concerning most explicit logical form. The way forward most in harmony with Russell's approach is to reintroduce requirements stricter than finitude on the extra-logical vocabulary of PL. If this is right, then the two aspects of perfection, syntax and vocabulary, will not in the end be separated: the business of philosophical logic, of assigning logical forms, is not to be divorced from using a vocabulary that, by some standard or other, is optimal.

We could borrow from Wittgenstein's *Tractatus* a way of restricting the PL-vocabulary that would fit well with many of Russell's ideas about philosophical logic. We stipulate that this vocabulary be the smallest which is both adequate to our expressive needs and which is such that, for every atomic sentence p and every set of atomic sentences X which contains neither p nor $\sim p$, the arguments 'X therefore p' and 'X therefore $\sim p$' are both invalid. This looks enough to rule out predicates like the lately considered 'G': for expressive adequacy will require us to include 'happy', and 'Happy (John) therefore G(John)' is valid. Within such a framework, certain other problems about structure could be accommodated by stipulating that the basis of the transformations from English to PL be a matching of simple English predicates with (possibly complex) PL-predicates, of English 'names' with (for Russell) PL-$\imath$-descriptions, and English constructions and other categories of English expression (like verbs of propositional attitude) with PL-constructions.

The overall programme of transforming English into PL could be recommended on the following grounds. Logic 'aims at effecting the greatest possible analysis of the ideas with which it deals and of the processes by which it conducts demonstrations' (*PM* 1), and, as applied to PL, though not as applied to English, it can do this completely, by presenting each proposition 'in a form as characteristic of itself as possible' (*PM* 3). For in PL, as at present envisaged, all validity is logical validity. The atomic propositions are truly *atoms*, and all the validity-inducing properties of propositions are reflected by the occurrence of the logical constants. In presenting a proposition in the logical dress of PL, rather than in its messier English garb, we reveal its full logical reality, for all its validity-inducing features are accessible to the smooth and simple processes of *PM*-logic.

We cannot straightforwardly attribute this view to Russell since, as we have seen, he allows incompatible colour predicates into the vocabulary of PL. However, we can offer it as a view, or even the view, that he should have held, in order best to make sense of his idea of logical form.

We know that this exhilarating vision cannot be maintained in its pure form, for the incompleteness of arithmetic shows that if the *PM*-logic is consistent and complete for PL, then some mathematical truth cannot be expressed in PL. However, this fact need engender only a minor impurity. *PM*-logic may be as complete as is sensible or practicable, and this leaves ample room for the importance of PL-logical-forms.

One criticism that could be made of this picture is that it is quite unrealistic to suppose that any vocabulary could meet the conditions imposed. Adequacy to our expressive needs, it may be said, requires predicates which, like the colour predicates, have extensions occupying incompatible positions along a continuum, and which can be defined only in terms of other predicates having this general feature. This may be so. But the criticism I wish to advance cuts deeper, since it will apply however the restrictions on the extra-logical vocabulary of PL are imposed.

The superiority of *PM*-syntax is supposed to consist in the fact that it, but not English syntax, admits of a proof-procedure. But if this is merely an accidental truth, a reflection of our powers of ingenuity rather than of some matter of principle, then the conception of PL-logical form will be parochial, and not a fit foundation for a philosophical programme.

Something we have all learnt to do is interpret any sentence on (an infinite fragment of) English, given merely its physical make-up. Since we are finite beings, there must in principle be some way of representing this practical ability theoretically: by a finitely stated theory which is informative enough to enable one who knows the theory to interpret any sentence in (the relevant infinite fragment of) English. In short, there must be a finitely statable theory of meaning for English.

It would be absurd to use this as a basis for arguing that there must be a proof-theory for English which proves every valid sentence, for we know that this conclusion is false. However, the existence, in principle, of a systematic semantic theory for English does show that the sorts of syntactic irregularity which we noted earlier, exemplified by the fact that there are invalid instances of the schema 'Every F is a G, every G is H, therefore every F is H', can be brought to heel. For if a semantic theory is to state, in a finite space, enough to yield a suitable theorem for each of the infinitely many sentences of English, it must organize English syntax into semantically significant patterns of occurrence. This in turn shows that the only reason we were able to give for the preference for PM-syntax, namely the irregularity of English syntax, is a parochial matter: not a matter of principle, but of the current state of expertise. And this in turn shows that the greater glory of PL-sentences, from the point of view of proof-theory, may be transient, and not an eternal basis for a philosophy.

The following conjecture, for which I have no argument, might be considered: where there is a consistent proof-theory for L, and some reasonably systematic way of associating L'-sentences with L-sentences (their L-logical-forms), then there is in principle a proof-theory for L' whose set of theorems is consistent and contains every sentence whose L-logical-form is a theorem of the proof-theory for L.

It is thus at least on the cards that there is a proof-theory for English whose overall results are no less adequate than what is achieved by the proxy of PL. Then all that could make PL superior to English would be the ease with which its proof-theory can be mastered and operated. But ease is a person-dependent and culture-dependent matter. What is easy for you may be hard for me, and what is discovered today, with great difficulty, in the most arcane reaches of physics, will be easily learnt by schoolchildren tomorrow. Thus PL may have some transient heuristic importance, but nothing more. For there is no reason to think that English is not in logically perfect order as it is.

VI

Knowledge

An epistemologist may adopt either of two different approaches to his subject-matter. If he is what I shall call a *descriptive* epistemologist he will aim to give a systematic description of what we take to be knowledge. For example, he will show that we do not count every true belief as knowledge, nor indeed every justified true belief. None the less, we have fairly confident and person-invariant intuitions concerning which beliefs are knowledge, and the descriptive epistemologist will try to say what cues this discrimination. The inquiry is not radically different in approach from a psychologist's attempt to determine what cues a chicken-sexer's sexual discriminations. Those who sex day-old chickens, like those who discriminate some beliefs as knowledge, cannot give a full account of what cues they are responding to.

An alternative approach to epistemology is *critical*. Not content to say what we *count* as knowledge, the critical epistemologist will try to determine whether it is *really* knowledge. He might then, for example, end up as some sort of sceptic, believing perhaps that 'the greater part of what would commonly pass as knowledge is more or less probable opinion' (*PP* 81).

Russell offers both critical and descriptive epistemology, though his emphasis is always on the former, even when some of his remarks suggest otherwise. For example, in *HK* he stresses that he is going to take scientific knowledge for granted, and merely find out what 'postulates' must be true if the inferences scientists make are to be valid. The critical dimension is not far from the surface, for Russell maintains that what passes for scientific knowledge would not really be knowledge unless something like his postulates were true, and were known to be true (*HK* 524). Since it turns out that it is very hard to see how we could have knowledge of these postulates, of the kind

161

Russell requires, and since he himself asserts that scepticism is irrefutable, the overall position has a critical edge.

There are many ways of embarking on critical epistemology. At one time, Russell favoured Descartes' method of doubt:

> I think on the whole that the sort of method adopted by Descartes is right: that you should set to work to doubt things and retain only what you cannot doubt because of its clearness and distinctness (*PLA* 181).

His approval is somewhat qualified: we should refrain from sharing Descartes' hope of a method guaranteeing freedom from error, for there is no such method. Later, his qualifications are more extreme:

> The method of Cartesian doubt, which appealed to me when I was young and may still serve as a tool in the work of logical dissection, no longer seems to me to have fundamental validity. Universal scepticism cannot be refuted, but also cannot be accepted. I have come to accept the facts of sense and the broad truth of science as things which the philosopher should take as data, since though their truth is not quite certain, it has a higher degree of probability than anything likely to be achieved in philosophical speculation (*MPD* 207; cf. *LA* 339).

He expresses the relationship between the acceptance of these two sorts of data in a pleasing image:

> Ever since I was engaged on *Principia Mathematica*, I have had a certain method of which at first I was scarcely conscious, but which has gradually become more explicit in my thinking. The method consists in an attempt to build a bridge between the world of sense and the world of science. I accept both as, in broad outline, not to be questioned. As in making a tunnel through an Alpine mountain, work must proceed from both ends in the hope that at last the labour will be crowned by a meeting in the middle (*MPD* 205).

At different times, Russell employs different techniques to effect this meeting. One technique is that of logical construction, whereby the claims of science are so shrunk that the tunnel connecting it to sense is much shorter and safer than one might have supposed. Another technique is a different kind of diminution of the claims of science: we can know, not the intrinsic nature of the physical world, but only its structural features. This is like leaving the gap between sense and science as wide as ever, but reconciling ourselves to a short safe tunnel leading to a point from which the world of science can be dimly, and as it were merely structurally, glimpsed. Finally, in *HK* the world of science and the world of sense are connected by no lowly empiricist's tunnel but by the helicopter service of synthetic *a priori* principles.

The general form of the problem is that of induction, the problem of what, if anything, justifies our reasoning from what we have experienced to what we have not. Until we have made up our minds how this problem is to be resolved, we cannot make a satisfactory assessment of Russell's treatment of the relationship between experience and the physical world. So the first section of this chapter concerns induction. In the second section I argue for the view, which Russell consistently held, that 'Descartes' malicious demon is a logical possibility' (*Matter* 205). In the third section I consider the relationship between this fact and scepticism, and, in the fourth section, Russell's ways of avoiding or minimizing scepticism. Finally, I briefly discuss Russell's accounts of *a priori* knowledge.

1   Induction

The traditional problem of induction is whether we know, or even have good reason to believe, any proposition which lies outside the content of experience. I shall stipulate that the content of experience is closed under entailment,[1] with the result that it includes all truths which are both necessary and knowable *a priori*. The content of experience is relative to a person and a time so that what is in the content of your experience may not be in mine, and what is not within the content of my experience now may come to be so later. Other than this, little need be said, for the purposes of this section, about the content of experience. It is universally agreed that contingent propositions about the future, and about the past before we were born, and such contingent unrestricted generalizations as 'All men are mortal' lie, wholly or partly, outside the content of our experience.

The problem can be reformulated in various ways. For example, it is equivalent to the problem of whether there are any strong inductive arguments, where an argument is inductive (for *S* at *t*) iff all its premises lie within the content of experience (of *S* at *t*) and its conclusion is consistent with, but not entailed by, the content of experience (of *S* at *t*), and, as a first approximation, an argument is strong (to degree *n*) iff anyone who knows the premises is thereby justified (to degree *n*) in believing the conclusion. Alternatively, we could express the problem as that of whether there are any inductive propositions which it is rational to believe, where a proposition is

---

[1] That is, if '*p*' belongs to the content of experience, and '*p*' entails '*q*' then '*q*' belongs to the content of experience. '*p*' entails '*q*' iff it is knowable *a priori* (and thus necessary) that if '*p*' is true so is '*q*' (holding constant the meanings of the sentences).

inductive (for S at t) iff it is consistent with, but at least in part outside, the content of experience (of S at t).

We intuitively believe that some, but not all, inductive propositions are rational to believe, and that some but not all inductive arguments are strong. For example, we intuitively believe that it is rational to believe that the sun will rise tomorrow and not rational to believe that the sun will not rise tomorrow. We intuitively believe, likewise, that the first but not the second of these inductive arguments has a high degree of strength:

   (*i*) The sun has risen every day in my experience, so it will rise tomorrow.
   (*ii*) The sun has risen every day in my experience, so it will not rise tomorrow.

It would be nice if we could identify some characteristic, C, possessed by all and only those inductive arguments we intuitively regard as strong, which could explain our discrimination: C would be what cues our response. Then it would be nice, indeed even nicer, if we could show that the beliefs we claim to justify by using arguments possessing C are more likely than not to be true. Thus we now have two problems: the identification of C and the justification for using arguments possessing C.

In traditional discussions of induction, the problem of identifying C was implicitly taken as easily soluble. Roughly speaking, it was taken for granted that an argument had C iff it projected observed phenomena on to the unobserved, iff, in other words, the argument proceeded in accordance with the assumption of the 'uniformity of nature'. Russell deserves credit for being, so far as I know, the first person to show that not only is this identification of C incorrect, it is also very hard to see how to arrive at a correct one. This discovery of Russell's is now generally associated with Nelson Goodman, who made the same point, with notable clarity and elegance, some forty-three years after Russell. Before returning to the problem of justification, I shall consider this problem about identifying C.

Russell's first discussion of this is in 'On the Notion of Cause' (147–9), which was first published in 1912. He writes (148):

> Given some formula which fits the facts hitherto – say the law of gravitation – there will be an infinite number of other formulae, not empirically distinguishable from it in the past, but diverging from it more and more in the future.

Yet we discriminate among these formulae, despite the fact that all describe what we have experienced. We regard some, but not others, as being worthy of our belief as descriptions of how the future will be.

In practice, Russell suggests, what we do is to prefer the simplest formula adequate to what we have experienced.

Russell returns again to this difficulty much later.

> Suppose $a_1, a_2, \ldots a_n$ are members of α which have been observed and have been found to belong to a certain class β. Suppose that a_{n+1} is the next α to be observed. If it is a β, substitute for β the class consisting of β without a_{n+1}. For this class the induction breaks down. This sort of argument is obviously capable of extension. It follows that, if induction is to have any chance of validity, α and β must be not *any* classes, but classes having certain properties or relations (*HK* 432; cf. 422).

When he speaks of the induction 'breaking down' Russell seems to mean that the inductive argument will have a false conclusion, in this case the falsehood that the next α will belong to $\beta - \{a_{n+1}\}$. This, however, is beside the point, for we all allow that some strong inductive arguments have false conclusions. The point, rather, is that the envisaged argument, with the conclusion as just given, is not one we would regard as strong. Because Russell connects inductive strength with frequency of the truth of the conclusion, in a way that will shortly be discussed, the weakness (Russell would say 'invalidity') of the inductive argument is probably thought to follow from the fact that the way of producing the false conclusion is generalizable. What Russell successfully shows in this passage, as in the earlier one, is that there are many ways of describing, or classifying, our past experience, but only when we describe it or classify it in certain special ways do we think we can justifiably extrapolate from it to the future. Thus it is false that the arguments we intuitively regard as strong are just those that project experienced phenomena on to the unobserved.

Despite Russell's historical priority, it must be confessed that the point emerges with particular clarity in Goodman's exposition. He introduces the predicate 'grue' defined as follows: 'x is grue at t' $=_{\mathrm{df}}$ 'x is green at t and t is before 2000 AD, or x is blue at t and t is not before 2000 AD'.[2] All observed emeralds have been grue, so projecting observed phenomena on to the future would consist in concluding that all emeralds are grue. But plainly we do not regard an inductive argument with that premise and that conclusion as strong. At any rate we *should* not, for we in fact hold that it is rational to believe that all emeralds are green, and this conclusion, in the presence of the assumption that there are emeralds after 2000 AD, is incompatible with the conclusion that all emeralds are grue, despite being based on the same observations. For consider the emerald called 'α' which

---

[2] Cf. Goodman, *Fact, Fiction and Forecast* 74. This is not a verbatim account of Goodman's example, but I think it captures the essence.

exists in 2001 AD (as well as before and after). Then 'All emeralds are grue', which means 'All emeralds are grue at all times', entails 'α is grue in 2001', which in turn entails 'α is green in 2001 and 2001 is before 2000, or α is blue in 2001 and 2001 is not before 2000', which in turn entails 'α is blue in 2001'. This is incompatible with 'α is green in 2001', which is entailed by 'All emeralds are green'. This incompatibility shows that not only do we not regard all arguments which project experienced phenomena on to the unexperienced as inductively strong, but we are in addition right not to do so. It is now generally known as 'Goodman's Paradox'.

How, then, can C be identified? In the early account, Russell suggests that 'The difficulty we have been considering seems to be met partly, if not wholly, by the principle that *time* must not enter explicitly into our formulae' ('On the Notion of Cause', 149). Goodman considers a similar suggestion in response to his paradox, but argues against it on the following grounds: the predicate 'grue' contains no reference to time, so if anything is objectionable it is that 'grue' is defined by an expression which mentions a time. But whether an expression is definable, and if so how, is relative to linguistic resources. Imagine a language in which 'grue' and 'bleen' are primitive, but 'green' and 'blue' are not. ('Bleen' is defined in English in rather the way that 'grue' is, but 'blue' replaces 'green' and vice versa.) Then in that language it is 'blue' and 'green' whose definition involves mention of a time, and it is thus these predicates which, on the proposed suggestion, would be banished from strong inductive arguments.

Goodman's point might possibly be circumvented by a different account of what it is for time to enter into a formula or predicate, but it is unnecessary to pursue this since there is another objection to Russell's early proposal. This is simply that one can construct arguments which project experienced phenomena on to the unexperienced but which are not counted as inductively strong and which certainly do not 'involve time' in any way. A possible example is found in the passage already quoted from *HK*. A shadow of doubt may infect the specification of $\beta - \{a_{n+1}\}$, since a_{n+1} is the *next* α to be observed, but this is easily dispelled by a slight modification of the example. Suppose that for each observed α we introduce a name: 'a_1' ... 'a_n'. (n will be finite, since we can make only finitely many observations.) As before, each α has been found to be a β. We now define a class γ as follows:

$$'x \in \gamma' =_{df} 'x = a_1 \text{ or} \ldots \text{or } x = a_n \text{ or } x \notin \beta'.$$

Both the following arguments are inductive:

(*iii*) All observed αs are βs, so All αs are βs.
(*iv*) All observed αs are γs, so All αs are γs.

Both project experienced phenomena on to the unexperienced. Yet not both are, or should be, regarded as inductively strong. Hence we have a rebuttal of the traditional identification of C which does not lean on arguments which 'involve time'. (The use of class names is obviously inessential. The example could easily be reconstructed in terms of predicates.)

In Russell's later discussion, a new suggestion for identifying C is made. We must avoid 'manufactured classes', of which $\beta - \{a_{n+1}\}$ is an example, and we do so by defining classes 'by intension, not by mention of their membership' (*HK* 432). Then C would be the property of being an argument which projects experienced phenomena on to the unexperienced and in which the phenomena are classified by classes defined 'by intension'.

On the necessity for some such restriction, if C is to be identified, Russell is surely right. He explicitly draws the consequence that substituting co-extensive predicates will not necessarily preserve inductive strength. To use an example different from his: even if we suppose 'grue' and 'green' co-extensive (e.g., because after 2000, as a result of some cataclysm, there are neither blue things nor green things), the argument from 'All observed emeralds are grue' to 'All emeralds are grue' is not (by our usual reckoning) inductively strong.

But the condition as stated is surely not sufficient, and it is likely that Russell was aware of this. Shortly after the point about manufactured classes, he says, in summary:

> If an inductive argument is ever to be valid, the inductive principle must be stated with some hitherto undiscovered limitation.
> Scientific common sense, in practice, shrinks from various kinds of induction, rightly, as I think. But what guides scientific common sense has not, so far, been explicitly formulated (*HK* 436).

'So far' presumably includes *HK* 432. He does not give reasons for doubting the sufficiency of his restriction to classes defined 'in intension', but I will offer two.

(*i*) We have no guarantee that there could be no primitive predicate co-extensive with '. . . $\in \gamma$', yet, if there were, we still would not regard the argument analogous to (*iv*) as inductively strong.

(*ii*) The use of the class name 'γ' in (*iv*) is inessential. If we replace 'γ' by its definition, the argument will mention no manufactured class. Russell might reply that there will still be the manufactured *predicate* '$\xi = a_1$ or . . . $\xi = a_n$ or $\xi \notin \beta$'. But we will not get an accurate characterization of C if we disallow this sort of predicate in strong inductive arguments. What may seem objectionable is the use of a name in the predicate. But consider a scientist working with an accelerator named 'Charlie'. He may hold that a certain result will be obtained in the future with Charlie, his grounds being Charlie's past performance. Yet he might feel unwilling to extend this judgment to other accelerators, because he is too unconfident about the underlying laws, and is thus unable adequately to distinguish ways in which Charlie is, perhaps, idiosyncratic. He therefore uses the inductive argument 'Charlie has been F in the past, so probably Charlie will continue to be F', where there is no non-trivial way to avoid the name 'Charlie'. (He could be represented as projecting the predicate 'ζ = Charlie and $F\zeta$'.) Yet he is rational and his belief inductively justified, though it seems it would not be if Russell's suggestion, extended to predicates in the way proposed, were correct.[3]

There is at least no *prima facie* reason for thinking that the problem of identifying C will aggravate the problem of dealing with the traditional problem of induction. The traditional problem is that of whether there are any strong inductive arguments, any justifiable or rational inductive beliefs. Since we can give examples of what we take to be strong inductive arguments and justifiable inductive beliefs, it seems not to matter to this problem that we have no systematic way of saying what makes us regard some inductive arguments as strong, some as weak, some inductive beliefs as justifiable, some as unjustifiable. It is to Russell's treatment of the traditional problem that I now turn.

There are three major discussions: *PP*, *HK*, and *MPD*. In *PP* he sets out what he calls the 'principle of induction', of which this is one version:

> The greater the number of cases in which a thing of the sort A has been found associated with a thing of the sort B, the more probable it is (if no cases of failure of association are known) that A is always associated with B (*PP* 37).

[3] Salmon, in his article 'Russell on Scientific Inference *or* Will the Real Inductivist Please Stand Up?', interprets Russell differently, viz. as defining a non-manufactured class as one such that 'no explicit mention is made of unobserved members of the class' (191). However, I cannot find this suggestion in Russell. Salmon in addition holds that this solves the problem of identifying C: 'Thus, although Russell's formulation may need a little tidying up, his basic idea that an intensional class is one whose definition involves no reference to particular *unobserved* objects appears to provide an adequate method for handling "manufactured" or Goodmanesque predicates' (191). The tidying up will have to be a major undertaking, for it will have to deal with the modified version of Russell's example which I give in the text (pages 166–7): the definition of 'γ' mentions no unobserved members of 'γ'.

What role, precisely, does this principle play? Russell says that 'it is the inductive principle alone that can justify any inference from what has been examined to what has not been examined' (*PP* 38). So one possibility is that the principle, among other things, is supposed to serve as a premise which, when added to the premises of a strong inductive argument, results in a *valid* argument. Another possibility is that it is to be regarded as an inference pattern, every instance of which is a strong inductive argument. (The degree of strength will be proportional to the number of cases mentioned in the premises.) If the principle plays either role, it will serve to demarcate the genuinely strong inductive arguments. This is obvious in the case of the second role. In the case of the first, it obtains in virtue of the fact that we could characterize strong inductive arguments as just those which result in a valid argument when the premises are enriched by the principle.

At first sight, it seems as if there is a substantial difference between the two roles. Someone who saw the inductive principle in its first role could argue that, at bottom, all good arguments are valid ones, and there is no such thing as a pattern of 'non-demonstrative' inference which transmits justification, however slight, from premises to conclusion. By contrast, someone who saw the inductive principle in its second role would argue for the existence of a species of inference quite different from that with which deductive logic deals, and he might even accuse adherents of the first position of attempting to 'reduce induction to deduction'. However, I think the contrast is more apparent than real.

There appears to be this difficulty: as presently stated, the principle of induction has no chance of entailing the desired conclusions. These, it would seem, have the form 'All As are Bs', whereas if we use the principle the most we could hope to end up with is something of the form 'Probably all As are Bs'. Even to obtain this, we must make a small modification, reading the principle as:

> If n cases have been found in which things of the sort A have been
> associated with things of the sort B, and no cases of failure of
> association have been found, it is probable to degree n that A is
> always associated with B (i.e. that all As are Bs).

(This gives us rather more precision in degrees of probability than we want, but perhaps that does not matter.) Given the premises of the inductive argument, we can now detach a conclusion of the form 'It is probable to degree n that all As are Bs' by *modus ponens*. But how do we pass to 'All As are Bs'?

Since the overall aim is to see how inductive beliefs are to be justified, the notion of probability involved must be that of justified belief, relative to data: the more probable a proposition, relative to certain data, the more justifiable it is to believe it, if those data are all we have that is relevant. Russell himself stresses the relativity of probability in *PP* (37), so it would seem reasonable to make it explicit, so that the consequent of the principle will read: 'Relative to . . . , it is probable to degree n that ——', where the premises are repeated in the place marked by the dots. We could now add a further principle to the effect that if anyone believes that p, then, if he knows that . . . , and if, relative to . . . , it is probable to degree n that p, he is justified in that belief to degree n. (If he does not know the premises, but is merely justified in believing them to degree m, then his justification in believing the conclusion will somehow have to be determined on the basis of n and m, and will not be greater than the smaller of these two numbers. However, this is a complication that I shall ignore.) This result is no more, and no less, than what would be obtained by regarding the principle of induction as the inference pattern exemplified by all and only strong inductive arguments. In the pattern, 'probably' is best regarded not as qualifying the conclusion, but as qualifying its connection with the premises. Then, from an instance of the pattern, together with the premises, one can extract, not p, but only the fact that anyone who knows the premises is justified, to the relevant degree, in believing that p. Alternatively, one could take the conclusion as 'probably p', in which case, once the supposedly implicit relativization is made explicit, we have exactly what we had by treating the principle of induction as a premise. Thus there is no real difference between regarding the principle as a premise and regarding it as an inference-pattern and no real difference between regarding it as an inference-pattern with 'p' as its conclusion, and regarding it as an inference-pattern with 'probably p' as its conclusion. Hence in the end, the apparent difference between the approaches is illusory.

On neither approach is the principle satisfactory. For one thing, it fails to take into account the possibility of conflicting evidence: p may be probable relative to some of a man's data, yet if he knows that not-p he is not justified in believing that p. For another thing, as Russell stressed in *HK*, the principle fails to give a correct characterization of inductive strength. His reason was that without the exclusion of manufactured classes, the use of the principle would lead to false conclusions 'more often' than true ones (*HK* 435). At any rate the principle of induction certainly does not correctly identify C, and this alone might reasonably incline us to suppose that it fails to give a correct characterization of inductive strength. Its failure to identify C, that is, the characteristic in virtue of which we take some inductive arguments to be strong, is, of course, due to its failure to rule out manufactured classes.

The above discussion has involved an oversimplification about the relationship between inductive strength and justified belief. This must now be remedied. Suppose that $p_1 \ldots p_n$ are the premises of a strong inductive argument whose conclusion is q, and that A believes each p_i and also q. From the present definitions it follows that A is justified in believing q. However, we do not want this result. For suppose what makes A believe q is not the p_i but someone whom he recognizes as a persuasive liar telling him that q. Then his belief that q is not justified. Typically, we require that in such a case it is A's belief in $p_1 \ldots p_n$ which causes him to believe that q, if his belief that q is to be justified. Assuming that the premises of an inductive argument include everything relevant to its conclusion, we could therefore amend the definition to this: an inductive argument is strong (to degree n) iff one whose belief in the conclusion is caused by his knowledge of the premises is justified (to degree n) in believing the conclusion.

Let us set the inadequacies of the principle of induction, regarded as a characterization of inductive strength, behind us, and instead consider Russell's account of its status.

He claims that it is knowable *a priori* (*PP* 86). This claim has three parts: (*i*) the principle is knowable, and (*ii*) experience is not needed to confirm it and (*iii*) could not refute it. Let us start by considering Russell's argument for the second part.

> Experience might conceivably confirm the inductive principle as regards the cases that have been already examined; but as regards unexamined cases, it is the inductive principle alone that can justify any inference from what has been examined to what has not been examined. All arguments which, on the basis of experience, argue as to the future or the unexperienced parts of the past or present, assume the inductive principle; hence we can never use experience to prove the inductive principle without begging the question (*PP* 38).

Russell here goes for a stronger conclusion than the one he needs. Since what is knowable *a priori* may also be known *a posteriori* (as when you use a calculator to determine a mathematical sum) what Russell has to show is not that experience *could not* establish the inductive principle, but merely that it *need not*. For if experience is to play an essential part in justifying the principle, then, since it is intended to hold of unexperienced times, it would have to be used in its own justification. But this is question-begging, as Russell points out, and moreover it is inconsistent with the hypothesis that experience plays an essential part in the justification of the principle.

Now for the third part of the claim. Can experience refute the principle? Russell argues that it cannot. What would need refuting is that a proposition is probable, relative to certain data, but this is not refuted by showing that the proposition is false:

> For example, a man who has seen a great many white swans might argue, by our principle, that on the data it was *probable* that all swans were white, and this might be a perfectly sound argument. The argument is not disproved by the fact that some swans are black, because a thing may well happen in spite of the fact that some data render it improbable (*PP* 37).

Everyone would agree that some of a man's justified beliefs can be false. But is it possible for all or most of them to be false? If Russell's conclusions, drawn via the inductive principle, were found experientially to be more often than not false, would this not refute the principle?

If the principle is, as Russell claims, knowable *a priori*, then we would expect it to be a necessary truth, on the general ground that necessity attaches to everything knowable *a priori*. His detailed arguments give direct support for the necessity of the inductive principle. For, if Russell is right, its truth is not contingent upon what actually happens: the probability it assigns, relative to the evidence, will hold in every world if in any. In *HK* he takes an opposed view, as we shall see shortly.

So far we have considered only the second and third parts of the claim of *a priority*. It remains to show that the inductive principle is knowable, and a step in this direction would be to show that it is true. In *PP* Russell claims that

> we must either accept the inductive principle on the ground of its intrinsic evidence, or forgo all justification of our expectations about the future (*PP* 38).

Though Russell is not explicit, we may presume that we are expected to find the second alternative impossible, and thus embrace the first. This pattern of argument is unlikely to convince one who is sceptical about induction, that is, who holds that no inductive belief is justifiable.

A final comment before turning to Russell's later position: he emphasizes that we do not consciously use the inductive principle in forming our inductive beliefs. The claim is simply that our inductive beliefs are justified iff the principle is true. Hence the question of whether we can show that some of our inductive beliefs are justified is tantamount to the question (assuming that the principle does indeed correctly identify *C*) of whether we can show that the principle is true.

As we have seen, in *HK* Russell rejects his earlier inductive principle because it is vulnerable to the difficulty about manufactured classes. He replaces it with a set of what he calls 'empirical postulates'. I shall briefly discuss these later.

Whereas in *PP* Russell had viewed probability in such a way that whether or not a proposition is probable, relative to certain data, obtains independently of experience and necessarily, in *HK* he changes his mind:

> If 'probability' is taken as an indefinable, we are obliged to admit that the improbable may happen, and that, therefore, a probability-proposition tells us nothing about the course of nature. If this view is adopted, the inductive principle may be valid, and yet every inference made in accordance with it *may* turn out to be false; this is improbable, but not impossible. Consequently a world in which induction is true is empirically indistinguishable from one in which it is false. It follows that there can never be any evidence for or against the principle, and that it cannot help us infer what will happen. If the principle is to serve its purpose, we must interpret 'probable' as meaning 'what in fact usually happens'; that is to say, we must interpret a probability as a frequency (*HK* 420).

Russell overstates the case when he says that the view he had adopted in *PP*, that the principle of induction can be neither supported nor refuted by experience, makes it impossible to use the principle to 'help us infer what will happen'. What he should have said is that, on the *PP* view, even the truth of the inductive principle will not guarantee that conclusions justified by it will be true more often than not.

Overstatement apart, we should surely feel some sympathy with this argument. Suppose someone asked: why should I adopt the beliefs that are called 'justifiable'? One wants to answer: because if you do you will believe truly more often than falsely. This is precisely Russell's position in the passage just quoted, for what is probable is to be identified with what it is justifiable to believe.

It is not easy to decide whether to adopt Russell's early account, from which it follows that statements of the form '. . . is a strong inductive argument' are knowable *a priori*, if true, or whether to prefer the view, which has something in common with his later account, that such statements are knowable only *a posteriori*, if at all.

Most of the judgments of this kind that we habitually make are, it seems to me, contingent, and so *a posteriori*. For example, it seems to me to be a contingent fact that the statistics about smoking and lung cancer *show* that one is more likely to get lung cancer if one smokes cigarettes than if one does not. It is contingent on, among other things, the fact that other tissues can be made to develop cancerous growths merely by contact with certain chemicals, and on the fact that smoking involves chemicals coming in contact with the lungs. Suppose, by contrast, that statistics connected the letters in a person's name with the incidence of lung cancer, with a degree of 'significance' (in the statistical sense) as high as that which in fact obtains between the incidence of smoking and that of lung cancer. These statistics do not support the belief that, outside the observed sample, one is more likely to get lung cancer if one's name is spelled a certain way. The point is that everything we believe about disease is inconsistent with there being a causal connection between the spelling of a person's name and his state of health.

However, this contingency may not be fundamental. It may arise simply from the fact that the inductive belief has not been relativized to all the relevant data. It might be contingent that the smoking statistics give good reason for an inductive belief about the future incidence of the disease, but necessary, and knowable *a priori*, that this belief is justified relative to all the data we in fact possess.

Russell's arguments do not, I think, settle the issue. Against what I shall call the necessity thesis (the claim that true statements of the form ' . . . is a strong inductive argument' are knowable *a priori*, and thus are necessarily true) at least two points can be adduced. One we have already in effect come across, when we noted that the frequent falsity of the conclusion of a pattern of inductive argument appeared to cast some doubt upon its strength. More generally, the point is that for any inductive argument we can perhaps imagine a world in which its premises are true, and not merely is the conclusion false, it is so wide of the mark that, even relative to the premises, it is not justifiable to believe it. The second point is that on the necessity thesis it is hard to see how we are to say what the point is of being rational, or forming justifiable inductive beliefs: for, it seems, on this thesis, that point can have nothing to do with how the world actually is, and in particular it can have nothing to do with truth. We feel that what makes it worthwhile to have justified beliefs is that they are more often than not true. Against the contingency claim, there is an epistemological objection. Claims of the form ' . . . is a strong inductive argument' will, on this view, be inductive claims, for they will be contingent, yet not part of the content of experience. So on this view there seems to be no way of refuting the sceptic who urges that no inductive belief is, or at least none can be shown to be, justifiable.

A miraculous way through this dilemma would be to combine the *a priority* of the necessity thesis with the truth-linked notion of justification permitted by the contingency thesis. Then the epistemological problem confronting the latter would be swept away, and we would also be spared the unsatisfactory features of the necessity thesis (that there is some doubt about its truth and, in any case, if it were true there would be no connection between having justified beliefs and having beliefs which are, more often than not, true). This is precisely the line which Russell takes in *HK*.

To establish *a priority*, he uses much the same argument as in *PP*, though now it is expressed more colourfully:

> Either, therefore, we know something independently of
> experience, or science is moonshine (*HK* 524).

By adding the premise that science is not moonshine, we conclude that something is known independently of experience, that is, *a priori*. This 'something' is designed to be such as to transform a strong inductive argument into a valid one if added to its premises: it is the set of propositions that Russell calls the 'empirical postulates'. He holds that these are *contingent*, yet, if science is knowledge, are knowable *a priori*.

One can sympathize with the pressures that led Russell to adopt this position, but one cannot seriously entertain it, unless one is offered a very great deal of further argument. Presumably Russell would accept that science is in principle refutable by experience, so he would be under some pressure to explain how the empirical postulates, on which science is supposed to rest, would survive the experiential refutation of science. This sort of question might indeed lead to a radical reshaping or even destruction of the traditional contrast between *a priori* and *a posteriori* knowledge. For example, it might be reworked in terms of a continuum along the dimension of relative immunity to revision (cf. Quine, 'Two Dogmas'). But one who, like Russell, uses these notions in the traditional way must accept the traditional view that only what is necessary is knowable *a priori*, for the traditional reason that experience alone can tell us about how our world *happens* to be. Thus Russell's account of the epistemological status of the empirical postulates is unacceptable, and precisely the same sort of difficulty threatens any attempt to develop a contingency thesis about statements of inductive strength.

Despite the unacceptable side of the postulates, I shall none the less digress for a moment to give an example of one, which captures the flavour of them all.

'The postulate of quasi-permanence':

> *Given any event A, it happens very frequently that, at any neighbouring time, there is at some neighbouring place an event very similar to A* (*HK* 506).

Russell says that this is chiefly used 'to replace the common-sense notions of "thing" and "person", in a manner not involving the concept "substance" ' (*HK* 506). Russell reconstructs things as series of events, as we shall see in the next chapter, and part of what is involved in a single series is similarity among the members. Thus this postulate is, in part, a reconstructed version of the postulate that there are enduring things.

This makes concrete the unacceptable epistemological status Russell assigns to the postulates. For it is intolerable to suppose that it is a *postulate* that there are enduring things, and that this 'cannot even be made probable by argument from experience' (*HK* 436). If experience gives us grounds for anything, it gives us grounds for the existence of enduring things. It was Russell who once said of the method of postulating the results one desires that it has many 'advantages': 'they are the same as the advantages of theft over honest toil' (*IMP* 71).

Because of its epistemological status, the postulate cannot contribute to the traditional problem of justifying induction, but perhaps it can contribute to the problem of identifying *C*. In particular, one might hope that the postulate would help us to identify manufactured classes, for these should not figure in any inference which deserves 'validation'. This hope is quickly dashed. The postulate relies on a notion of similarity. If this is allowed to include 'manufactured' similarities, like grueness, the postulate will 'validate' the illegitimate projection of such similarities. If manufactured similarities are excluded, then the postulate itself fails to give the criterion for this exclusion, and thus has presupposed rather than provided a solution to the problem of identifying *C*.

Similar criticisms apply to the remaining four postulates: they cannot have the epistemological status which Russell claims for them, and they do not provide a characterization of *C*. This does not finally resolve the question of whether or not *some* version of the contingency thesis for claims of inductive strength can be sustained. My negative answer to this question is introduced by a discussion of Russell's claim that 'Universal scepticism cannot be refuted, but also cannot be accepted' (*MPD* 207), in other words, that 'Scepticism, while logically impeccable, is psychologically impossible' (*HK* 9). On a certain interpretation of what it would be to *refute* scepticism, I agree with Russell that this cannot be done. However, I dispute his claim that scepticism is psychologically impossible.

Taking the last point first, Russell writes, in illustration of his position:

I once received a letter from an eminent logician, Mrs Christine Ladd Franklin, saying that she was a solipsist, and was surprised that there were no others. Coming from a logician, this surprise surprised me (*HK* 196).

As Russell himself says in *HK*, there are at least two versions of solipsism. One version, which we may call 'dogmatic solipsism', holds that nothing exists save what is given in the content of one's experience. The other, 'sceptical solipsism', holds merely that no inductive beliefs are justifiable.[4] No doubt it is psychologically impossible for anyone to be a dogmatic solipsist, and perhaps it is logically necessary that no sane man is, but the case is quite different with sceptical solipsism. It is psychologically necessary to have a large number of inductive beliefs, but the sceptical solipsist will view these as ones he cannot rationally justify: for him, they will be of a kind with obsessive beliefs, like the belief that walking on the cracks in paving stones will lead to disaster. This solipsist will, of course, allow that some but not all of his inductive beliefs are what others *call* 'rational' or 'justified', but he will not accept this as a proof that his beliefs *are* rational or justified. Most philosophers have surely been sceptical solipsists for at least a few days, and some, like Hume, are often credited with having held the position for longer. Hence Russell's claim that scepticism, or sceptical solipsism, is psychologically impossible appears to me to be false.

What does refuting the sceptic concerning induction involve? The sceptic says that no inductive beliefs are justified. (I shall not consider the position of one who, while rejecting this form of scepticism, maintains that justified inductive beliefs do not merit the title 'knowledge'.) So to refute the sceptic is to show that some inductive beliefs are justified, and for this to be done properly, it may be said, none of the premises in the refutation may be ones with which the sceptic could reasonably cavil.

Russell himself offers no argument that I can discover for the irrefutability of scepticism. His remarks suggest that the logical possibility of scepticism consists simply in the logical possibility of the premises of an inductive argument being true and its conclusion false; or, perhaps, the logical possibility of this happening for every inductive argument. This identification would be a mistake: for one might properly accept the logical possibility of false belief in a certain area while also maintaining the actuality of justified belief in that area. To justify an inductive belief is to show that there are some, good or conclusive reasons for holding it. To justify an inductive belief one does not have to perform the impossible task of deducing it from the content of experience.

[4] A solipsist must also hold that the content of experience at *t* consists exclusively of intrinsic experiential propositions true of him at *t*. Discussion of this sort of claim is deferred until section 3 of this chapter.

To assess Russell's claim of irrefutability, I shall consider some putative refutations, and ask if they succeed. My coverage will be far from exhaustive. The reader is referred to Skyrms for some further suggestions.

(*i*) The verificationist maintains that every meaningful sentence is one whose truth-value can in principle be known to us. This at first sight seems to be incompatible with scepticism: for the sceptic accepts the meaningfulness of the sentences which express our inductive beliefs, yet denies that we have any justification for believing them true.

The situation is more complex than at first appears. In the case of singular inductive beliefs about the future (e.g., that the sun will rise tomorrow), or some restricted generalizations (e.g., that there will be snow somewhere within a month), there *is* a way 'in principle' of determining their truth-value: one awaits until the appointed time. Hence scepticism about these kinds of *inductive* beliefs is compatible with verificationism.

Admittedly, scepticism concerning unrestricted generalizations and concerning the past in so far as it lies outside the content of experience *is* incompatible with verificationism, assuming the meaningfulness of the relevant sentences, and it seems incoherent to refrain from scepticism on these matters while retaining scepticism for singular inductive beliefs about the future and certain restricted generalizations. But it is an open question whether this incoherence springs from scepticism or from verificationism. My own view, which I state without argument, is that it is verificationism which is to blame. (Russell argues against verificationism in, e.g., *IMT* chs 21–2; see also below, pp. 190–1, for another version of verificationism employed against scepticism.)

(*ii*) Let us call a set *k* of propositions foundational relative to a set *u* iff any knowledge of a member of *u* has to be justified by, and only by, some sub-set of *k*. The sceptic about induction identifies the set of inductive beliefs with *u*, and the content of experience with *k*, and claims that since *k* is insufficient to justify any member of *u* there are no justified inductive beliefs.

Foundationalist views have recently come under attack (e.g., by M. Williams, *Groundless Belief*), and if these attacks are successful it may seem that scepticism is thereby refuted. This looks fairly plausible in such cases as scepticism about the external world. Here *k* is the set of sensory beliefs and *u* the set of physical object beliefs. If we are not confined, as the foundationalist would have us, to *k* when we are offering justifications of a member of *u*, the prospects of an adequate justification seem much brighter. However, this line of attack against scepticism looks very much less plausible in the case of scepticism about induction for the following reason: we who are not sceptics about induction will still reckon that there are strong non-valid arguments, whatever the upshot about foundationalism, and this is the view the sceptic challenges.[5] In justifying an inductive belief p drawn from u, the other members of u we think it proper to use, together with k, will still typically fail to entail p. Abandoning k as the foundation of u does not necessarily involve abandoning the view that there are strong non-valid arguments.

(*iii*) One might seek to refute scepticism about induction head-on by showing that the inductive beliefs we take to be strong, that is, those which are the conclusions of arguments which possess C and have premises which lie within the content of experience and are known, are indeed justified in the truth-linked sense: that is, believing C-propositions will maximize true belief. An attempt on these lines is associated with Reichenbach (cf. Skyrms).

Modified to the present terminology, Reichenbach's conclusion is that the C-pattern of argument will lead to truth, if any pattern will. This is based on two conditionals: the first is that if nature is uniform, then C-arguments will lead to truth, in the end; the second is that if nature is not uniform, then no pattern of argument will lead to truth. Hence, either way, it is best to use C-arguments: for either they will lead to truth or nothing will.

I wish to challenge not the claim that it is, in some sense, 'best' to use C-arguments, but rather the claim that doing so will lead to truth, if the use of any pattern of argument will.

An initial point is that the argument must be modified in the light of what has been learnt from Goodman's paradox. It is trivial that nature is uniform relative to some system of classification, and impossible that it be uniform relative to every system of classification. Accordingly, let the antecedents of Reichenbach's conditionals speak of uniformity which is humanly discernible: for short, of hd-uniformity.

How could we show that, if nature is hd-uniform, the use of C-arguments will lead to our holding true beliefs in the end? The idea is that we abandon beliefs which prove false, and form new beliefs which are closer to the truth, in that they are consistent with longer stretches of the history of the universe than those they replace. Moreover, the C-pattern is self-correcting. An argument or kind of

---

[5]Popper's view of induction might seem to constitute an exception. (See his rejection of 'inductivism' in *The Logic of Scientific Discovery* 27ff.) However, he thinks that the more you have tried and failed to falsify a hypothesis the better it is corroborated (251ff.), and this seems no different from saying that an argument having as premises statements of failure to falsify a hypothesis, and the hypothesis itself as conclusion, is, though non-valid, strong.

argument that proves to have a false conclusion, or to have false conclusions more often than not, may be modified in the light of this experience, and expelled from the set of C-arguments.

Though superficially attractive, this argument seems to me totally spurious. Considering, for convenience, just future beliefs, the claim is, in effect, that there will come a time when anyone who forms all of his beliefs on the basis of C-arguments has only, or mostly, true beliefs. But even if this is in fact true, we have no *a priori* reason for thinking that it should be. The reason is simply that how things have been up to now (whenever now may be) cannot put any logical constraints on how things will be. At any moment, there is no logical guarantee that there is not a surprise around the corner.

It may be objected that I have forgotten the requirement of hd-uniformity. How things have been cannot logically constrain the future. But, it may be said, how they have been, together with their hd-uniformity, does logically constrain it, and in such a way that, given enough evidence, only one course of events in future is possible.

To meet this objection, one must consider various possible characterizations of hd-uniformity. We should not be too restrictive: the British climate does not show that nature is not hd-uniform. Nor would this conclusion follow from the grueness of emeralds. We could quite well accommodate such a colour change within a deeper underlying regularity. For example, perhaps the emeralds are affected by radiation from a distant star, or perhaps they are inherently unstable in hitherto unsuspected ways.

A fairly generous suggestion is this: nature is hd-uniform iff creatures more or less like ourselves could comprehend every aspect of the uniformity. The idea is that the predicates that would have to be used to classify the observed parts of nature in such a way that the classification is correctly projectible should not be too complex for us to grasp them. On this account, my criticism of Reichenbach's first conditional stands. A radical 'change in the course of nature', relative to an existing system of classification, may be accommodated as a uniformity within a radically amended, but none the less humanly graspable, system.

Perhaps a narrower construal of hd-uniformity would help Reichenbach's argument. Let us say that nature is hd-uniform iff a time must come when C-arguers have wholly or mostly true beliefs. We now obtain Reichenbach's first conditional with ease, but the second becomes suspect. If nature is not hd-uniform in this sense, we might none the less come to form true and comprehensive inductive beliefs, perhaps by opening ourselves to divine revelation.

There are intermediate accounts of hd-uniformity, but I claim that whatever the account, one or other of Reichenbach's conditionals will fail. A wide account knocks out the first conditional, a narrow one the second.

To make this abstract argument more convincing, one can flesh it out with a Cartesian fable. The inductive analogue of Descartes's evil genius can bring it about that as many as he pleases of A's inductive beliefs are false, even though, we shall assume, A consistently puts his trust only in C-arguments. In any finite stretch of the fantasy, A's false beliefs might not manifest their falsity and so might go undetected. If the evil genius chose to make manifest to A the falsity of his beliefs, A, if he managed to remain sane, would no doubt refrain from having inductive beliefs: reckoning himself in a chaotic universe, he would think no inductive belief worthy of credence. To bring it about that A once more has false beliefs, the evil genius has only to engineer an 'orderly' stretch, luring A back into false beliefs. (Admittedly, during this time the evil genius may have to let some of A's singular inductive beliefs, like his belief that this piece of bread will not poison him, be true.)

Meanwhile, the evil genius treats B quite differently. B uses no pattern of argument to arrive at or justify his beliefs. Instead, his policy is to believe the first thing that comes into his head, provided it is consistent with beliefs he already has. Obligingly, the evil genius matches the world to B's beliefs, making each one true. So B, though no C-arguer, does much better than A. So it cannot be a necessary truth that C-arguments will lead to truth if any pattern of argument will, for in the present situation C-arguments never or almost never lead to truth, whereas the policy of believing the first thing that comes into one's head (B's policy) leads almost or almost always to truth.

One point about B's situation must be admitted: after a while, he could use a C-argument to justify any inductive belief he has. For the following is a C-argument: 'Every time in the past that I have formed an inductive belief by believing the first thing that came into my head, the belief has been borne out by experience; so probably the next belief I form in this way will be borne out by experience.' (This point is stressed by Strawson, *Logical Theory* 259.)

However, this does not, I think, detract from my argument against Reichenbach. For one thing, I think it would be widely agreed, though I admit that the point is controversial, that the quoted argument is a C-argument only in virtue of the supposition, built into the example, that there is indeed a causal connection between B's inductive beliefs and the way the world is. If B had no reason other than his past successes not to think merely that he had been spectacularly lucky, then, I suggest, the quoted argument is not a C-argument: that is, it is not an argument that we would take to be inductively strong, any more than we would take as inductively strong the argument from a long run of reds in a very carefully checked and balanced roulette wheel to the conclusion of the non-equi-probability of red and black.

Since this point is, I acknowledge, controversial, it is fortunate that I do not have to rely on it. Instead, the example could be modified slightly so that *A* is, as before, a dismal failure, but this time *B* is only marginally more successful. This removes the premise for a *C*-argument to the conclusion that all or even most of *B*'s inductive beliefs are true, while still falsifying the claim that *C*-arguments will catch more truth than anything else.

(*iv*) Hume once said, as if pronouncing a necessary truth, that 'A wise man . . . proportions his belief to the evidence' (*Enquiry* § 10). A similar position has been more recently defended by Strawson (*Logical Theory* ch 9, Pt II). The essence of the idea is that there is a necessary and *a priori* connection between wisdom (rationality, justified belief) and *C*-arguments; but there is no attempt to connect wisdom with truth.

Strawson argues that the meaning of the word 'rational' dictates that it is properly applied to one who forms his opinions by inductive procedures, that is, to one who believes the conclusions of inductive arguments when he knows the premises (*Logical Theory* 261). We apply the standards of inductive argumentation to determine whether, in a given case, a man has offered good reasons or bad reasons for his beliefs. But we cannot intelligibly ask whether or not there are good reasons for adhering to these standards (257).

In order to assess this position, we must ask what Strawson means by 'inductive argument'. If he adopts my wide usage, his position is obviously false. 'The sun has risen every day in my experience, so it will probably not rise tomorrow' is an inductive argument (in my usage), but it is obviously not rational to believe the conclusion simply because you know the premise. We must look for other interpretations of Strawson. I claim that there are at most two further possibilities, and that whichever we choose Strawson's argument fails.

One possibility is to identify an inductive argument with what I have called a *strong* inductive argument. Then what Strawson says is true, indeed trivially so, but it has no tendency to banish scepticism. A strong inductive argument is defined as one whose conclusion it is rational to believe if one knows the premises. But now the question arises: *are* there any strong inductive arguments? We have seen that the sceptic says that there are not. Strawson needs a further argument to show that there are, and this he does not provide.

The other possible interpretation of Strawson's use of 'inductive argument' equates it with '*C*-argument': then Strawson's position is that the meaning of 'rational' dictates that it is properly applied to one who forms his opinions on the basis of C-arguments. This the sceptic will deny. He will grant that we do indeed apply the word 'rational' to those who form their beliefs in this way, but he will challenge the claim that such people are really rational. In the sceptic's eyes, Strawson's position will amount to nothing more than the unargued assumption that C-arguments, those we *take* to be inductively strong, are *really* inductively strong.

If the sceptic is asked what other standard there could be for inductive strength than our widespread belief in it, he has a ready reply: an argument is inductively strong, he will say, if its conclusion is more likely than not to be true. He will interpret 'more likely' in some way to do with frequencies: for example, he may say that what is required is that the pattern of argument be one such that, by adhering to arguments instantiating the pattern, one will end up with more true inductive beliefs than false ones.

There is no short way to connect C-strength with strength for the following reason: once upon a time, it was generally agreed that it was rational to argue from the shape of a plant's leaves, flowers or roots (e.g., spear-like) to the plant's dominant planet (e.g., Mars), and from this in turn to the plant's medicinal properties (e.g., an emetic). Today, this line of argument would be thought to be arrant superstition. Since we and the early herbalists cannot both be right, the example shows that an inductive argument may be widely held to be strong, yet fail to be so.

The way forward consists not in any sweeping identification of what we take to be rational with what is really rational, but rather in a detailed and step-by-step investigation, aimed at isolating principles of inductive reasoning. As so often in philosophy, the investigation will have critical as well as descriptive aspects: the data for what arguments are strong cannot in the end transcend facts concerning what people, on due reflection, take to be strong, but we are not committed merely to reporting and systematizing these facts. By the investigation itself, we may come to change our minds about what sorts of argument are acceptable. For example, we may come to represent ourselves as having viewed an argument as acceptable in virtue of a supposed, but, as investigation reveals, non-actual similarity with an uncontroversially acceptable argument. There is interaction between the principles we isolate and intuitions of inductive strength. The intuitions are what the principles systematize. But a principle which systematizes a large mass of intuitions may be used to criticize and reject other intuitions. (Cf. Goodman 63–4.)

If I am right, there is much to be said for Russell's position in *PP*. It is correct to say that we need a *principle* (or principles) of induction, and that there is no possibility of proving to the sceptic's satisfaction that the principle isolates inductive arguments that are really strong as opposed to those that we merely take to be strong. Equally, there is no way in which the sceptic could prove that the principle fails to isolate inductive arguments that are not really inductively strong, unless he is willing to rely to some extent on what we take to be inductive strength. But though the Russell of *PP* was right about the need for an inductive principle, and also to some extent right about its epistemological status, he was wrong, as we have seen, about the details. Goodman's paradox shows that the prospects of taking the projection of regularities as the essence of (what we take to be) inductive strength are not good.

One does better, in my view, to begin the investigation with the notion of explanation. One promising principle is that it is rational (justifiable) to believe a good explanation of known facts. Some principle of this kind must be involved in a theoretical representation of the practice of providing justifications in science, and it would be interesting to see if one could not use it to reconstruct justifications in more mundane areas of supposedly justified belief, such as beliefs about other minds and the external world. I do not, of course, suggest that this principle is consciously employed, in science or in common sense. The suggestion, rather, is that one could perhaps show that the beliefs we take to be justified would indeed be justified if the principle is granted.

It is important to stress that the notion of a 'good' explanation must not be truth-linked, if the principle is to serve the envisaged purpose. In the reconstruction, we will represent people as knowing that an explanation is good simply on the strength of its intrinsic qualities, and not in virtue of knowing how the explanation relates to reality. For there is no access to reality except through the explanation.

The fact remains, however, that we have here no refutation of scepticism, if you refute a man only by showing that something incompatible with his position follows from premises he will accept; in other words, if you refute a man only by showing that he is willing to assert both limbs of a contradiction. For the sceptic will certainly not accept any such principle as that it is rational to believe a good explanation of known facts. More exactly, the sceptic will say that we have no reason to believe that there *are* any good explanations, if 'good' is used in a truth-linked sense, and that if 'good' is used in some other sense, it is simply false that an explanation which is good in this sense is one which deserves rational assent. We can offer the sceptic no *reason* why he should accept what we identify as principles of inductive argumentation. For us, they are self-evident. But this is simply another way of saying that there is nothing we can do to justify them, which in turn means that there is no refuting the sceptic (on the present interpretation of what refutation involves). Either we accept some such principle 'on the grounds of its intrinsic evidence' (*PP* 38), or else we must be sceptical. So Russell was right to say that scepticism about induction is irrefutable.

This conclusion requires two comments. The first is that its apparent scandalousness is modified by the reflection that an analogous conclusion would hold for a sceptic about deduction. We can give the sceptic who rejects an independent axiom of a deductive logic no decisive *reason* for accepting it. The most we could hope to do is to persuade him that he does in fact accept it. The second is that the conclusion applies to inductive scepticism, but cannot without further argument be extended to one who is no sceptic about induction but claims to be a sceptic about, say, the external world or other minds. For perhaps a proper account of induction will show the relevant principles to be powerful enough to enable belief in the external world on the basis of experience, and in other minds on the basis of behaviour, to be justified inductively.

The claim that a proposition, *p*, is indeed a principle of inductive reasoning, that is a principle which systematizes critically scrutinized inductive practice, is a largely *a posteriori* one, resting on *a posteriori* facts about what our inductive practices are. On the other hand, the claim that *p* is not happily classified as *a posteriori*, for this would imply the falsehood that its truth or falsehood can be established by experience. Moreover, it is obvious that the facts that lead to the identification of *p* are not facts about the course of man-independent nature, but facts about human practices. This view of the matter is thus much closer to Russell's view in *PP* than his view in *HK*. It amounts to something very close to a necessity thesis concerning claims of inductive strength, and is certainly incompatible with the contingency thesis of *HK*. This, then, is my answer to the question raised some pages back, about the status of claims of inductive strength. It is not that every such claim is necessary and knowable *a priori*, for typically the inductive arguments we in practice use are regarded as strong only in the light of our theories. (It is because of our theories about emeralds that we think we should not project 'grue'; and it is because theories are rich, complex and subject to change that the task of identifying *C* in some formal way is impossible.) Rather, the claim is that once we make explicit the bearing related theories have on the assessment of strength in a particular case, the ultimate connection between evidence and conclusion is one not vouchsafed by experience, and is independent of the way our world happens to be.

2 Experience and the physical world

From as early as *PP* to as late as *HK* and *MPD* Russell maintained that we have no 'immediate perception' of physical objects. It is this fact which, in his eyes, leads to the gap between the 'world of sense' and the 'world of science'.

You look up at the sun on a clear day. What do you see? *Not* the sun, according to Russell. Here are some statements of, and arguments for, this apparently preposterous claim:

> Thus it becomes evident that the real table, if there is one, is not the same as what we immediately experience by sight or touch or hearing (*PP* 3).

> When we look at the sun we wish to know something about the sun itself, which is ninety-three million miles away; but what we see is dependent upon our eyes, and it is difficult to suppose that our eyes can affect what happens at a distance of ninety-three million miles. . . . Starting from a common-sense acceptance of our seeing, physics has been led step by step to the construction of a causal chain in which our seeing is the last link, and the immediate object which we see cannot be regarded as that initial cause which we believe to be ninety-three million miles away, and which we are inclined to regard as the 'real' sun (*UCM* 101–2).

> What astronomers call an eclipse is a public event, whereas what I am seeing may be due to a defect in my eye or my telescope. While, therefore, the belief 'there is an eclipse' may arise in me without conscious inference, this belief goes beyond the mere expression of what I see (*IMT* 128).

> If I see the sun and it makes me blink, what I see is not 93,000,000 miles and eight minutes away, but is causally (and therefore spatio-temporally) intermediate between the light-waves striking the eye and the consequent blinking (*HK* 220).

The most convenient way to bring out what is wrong with Russell's position, and also and more importantly what is right, is to sketch rather dogmatically what I take a correct analysis of perceptual verbs to involve. I confine myself to sentences of the form '*A* sees *X*', where '*X*' may be replaced by a name, or definite or indefinite description or quantifier phrase (e.g., '*A*' see Fido/a dog/the dog in the manger/every dog'). All I want to establish is that when 'see' is being used strictly and literally to report visual perception, '*A* sees *X*' is true only if *X* causes in *A* an appropriate kind of experience by an appropriate causal route.

A cannot see what does not exist. We can be sure that no one has ever really seen a unicorn. If a child says in the morning that he saw a lion in the night he must be corrected: he did not really see a lion, he only dreamed he did. Similarly, the drunkard does not really see pink rats, but only thinks he does.

If *A* sees *X* he has certain visual experiences. Moreover, not just any sort of visual experiences will do. *A* does not see a kangaroo if at that moment his whole visual field is occupied by an elephant. You have to look in the right direction to see things.

X must cause *A*'s experience. For suppose *A* is near a kangaroo and his head is turned in the right direction for seeing it, his eyes are closed, but by some coincidence a hallucinogenic drug or a cunning neurophysiologist makes him have just the kind of visual experience that he would have had if his eyes had been open. All the conditions we have so far mentioned are satisfied yet he does not see the kangaroo, because the kangaroo does not cause the kangaroo-like visual experiences.

The causal route between *X* and *A*'s experience must be appropriate. While it is hard to be more specific, it can be shown that some such condition is required. Suppose *A* is sitting with his head turned towards a window facing on to a busy street. His eyes are closed and his brain is wired to a machine controlled by a neurophysiologist who has resolved to bring it about that *A* has just the kinds of visual experiences he would have had if his eyes had been open. A girl goes past in the street, and this makes the neurophysiologist make *A* have girl-like visual experiences, of the very kind he would have had if his eyes had been open. Did *A* see the girl? I think not. The causal route was inappropriate, perhaps because the causal route was unreliable, in view of the whimsical nature of neurophysiologists.

Russell assumes that a long causal route is an inappropriate one, but this is simply false. The length of the causal chain between the sun and our sun-like experience does not make it inappropriate: we do see the sun. To this extent, Russell's account is mistaken.

On the other hand, he emphasizes that if a perceptual belief is to count as knowledge, it must be appropriately caused in the sense that the causal links are mirrored by inferential links: what caused the belief would have been a suitable basis for consciously inferring the belief (cf., e.g., *OKEW* 77, *HK* Pt 3, ch 4). Thus the idea of appropriate causal chains has, at least on some occasions, a part to play in Russell's theory of knowledge, though it enters at a somewhat different point.

We have seen that an analysis of the notion of seeing requires the notion of experience, and requires it in such a way that a man may have an experience of a certain kind which is not caused by an object

187

of the corresponding kind, and can have experiences of kinds to which no kinds of physical objects correspond. This is part of what Russell aims to establish in his discussions of perception. Another part is that all our empirical non-inferential knowledge concerns the intrinsic nature of our experiences, and does not, for example, extend to physical objects. (We may say that an experiential proposition is intrinsic, that is, reports only the intrinsic nature of experiences, iff the truth of the proposition does not require the existence of anything other than experiences and, perhaps, experiencers.)

With these points in mind, let us look back at the quotations given earlier. The claim that we do not 'immediately experience' the table (*PP*) involves two claims. One is that table-like experiences are logically independent of tables, that is, they could exist even if tables did not. The other is that all we immediately, that is, non-inferentially, know is the intrinsic nature of the experiences: the table itself is known inferentially, if at all.

In the quotation from *UCM* the incorrect assumption that length of causal chain suffices for its inappropriateness is conspicuous. The earlier argument (what we see depends on our eyes, the sun does not, so what we see is not the sun) has an ambiguous premise. On the more natural reading it is the falsehood that if A sees X, changes in A's eyes suffice to cause changes in X. On the less natural reading, 'what we see' refers to the visual experience we have in seeing. Then the premise is true, and the argument is valid, but the conclusion now amounts to the banality that the sun is distinct from the experience we have when we see it. Similar remarks apply to the remaining quotations.

Perhaps my criticism of Russell stems from an uncritical acceptance of 'naïve realism'. Let us see what Russell says about it. He characterizes it as the doctrine that 'things are what they seem' (*IMT* 13) and argues as follows:

> Naïve realism leads to physics, and physics, if true, shows that naïve realism is false. Therefore naïve realism, if true, is false; therefore it is false (*IMT* 13).

However, no one, so far as I know, and certainly no non-philosopher, has ever held naïve realism, as Russell characterizes it. For presumably the view that things are what they seem amounts, in Russell's mouth, to the claim that the inference-pattern of which the following is an instance is sound: 'I am having the sort of visual experience that I would be having if I were looking at an ellipse oriented at right-angles to my line of sight; therefore I am seeing an elliptical physical object'. But this suggestion is preposterous, and anyone who has thought about the matter at all knows that it is false.

What sort of view of the nature of perception *could* physics show to be false? Presumably, only something like the view that there are no causal intermediaries between the experience involved in seeing and the object seen. But no one has held this view, and we have seen that it is false that there can be no long causal chain between the object seen and the experience involved in seeing it.

I regard this criticism of Russell's account of perception as a minor one. I have already mentioned what I take to be its major constituents. One is that experiences are logically independent of the physical world. The other is that only experiences are known non-inferentially. The first of these is, I think, correct, and I shall attempt to establish it in the remainder of this section. The other is more dubious: I discuss it in the next section.

> No logical absurdity results from the hypothesis that the world
> consists of myself and my thoughts and feelings and sensations,
> and that everything else is mere fancy (*PP* 10; cf. *OKEW* 101–2, *HK*
> 188).

The only way to argue for a claim of this kind is to spell out the hypothesis in some detail, and yet fail to discover a contradiction, despite vigilant searching. Thus Descartes suggests that there is no contradiction in the supposition that all my 'thoughts and feelings and sensations' are like dreams, that none of them reflects an independent reality. If it is objected that dream-experiences are qualitatively different from waking ones, it could be replied, on Descartes' behalf, that dream-experiences *might* be qualitatively indistinguishable, to him who has them, from waking experiences. Hence any series of experiences, including our actual series, might exist, even if no physical world did.

We believe that our experiences are caused by physical objects. But Descartes suggests that there is no contradiction in the supposition that they are caused not by physical objects but by some 'evil genius' whose malignant aim is to cause our beliefs to be false. We could imagine the evil genius as a neurophysiologist who creates 'artificial' experiences in his subject by direct stimulation of the afferent nerves leading from the sense-organs to the brain. These delusive experiences can be made as realistic as you like, quite independently of the subject's environment, since they can be made to involve precisely the same pattern of electrical discharge, or whatever, as occurs in veridical experiences. There is no limit to the length of a series of such experiences, and no limit in principle to the coherence and regularity of the series. The subject might have a total delusion of living a life of leisure in the Caribbean whereas he is in fact the victim of a prolonged experiment in London. This does not have quite so strong a conclusion as Descartes' fantasy. That showed that experiences were independent of the physical world. This shows only that experiences are independent of the truth of the beliefs they normally cause us to form. The weaker conclusion suffices for Russell's purpose, for, in the presence of the assumption that only experiences are non-inferentially known, it makes the question of how, if at all, we know the physical world a live issue. But it is important to notice that the present point is not epistemological but logical.

When I say that any series of experiences might exist, even if the physical world did not (or, in the weaker claim, even if the physical world was not as the experiences caused the person who had them to believe it to be), am I referring to particular experiences or types of experience? If you think that a particular event's causes are essential to it, then it is false that a particular experience which is caused in the appropriate way by the physical world could have been caused by an evil genius or neurophysiologist. Then the claim must be that for any series of particular experiences there might have been a series indistinguishable to the subject even if there had been no physical world, or, for the weaker claim, even if the physical world had been quite other than the way the experiences caused him to believe it to be.

Bouwsma has argued that Descartes' fantasy of the evil genius is incoherent, and that it thus fails to show the logical independence of experience and the physical world. The idea of a total delusion, he says, makes no sense, for there is no distinguishing such a delusion from reality.

The argument is unsound, for it confuses the question of whether we can *know* that our experiences are veridical with the distinct question of whether they *are* veridical. It may be true that someone who is being totally deceived cannot find out that he is being deceived, but this does not mean that he is not being deceived. The victim of the evil genius believes that there are physical objects, persisting when he is not perceiving them; but, by hypothesis, there are no such objects.

Does this argument presuppose the rejection of verificationism? There are several species of verificationist, and I shall consider one, which I believe to be the most plausible. This verificationist will argue that any possible state of affairs is such that, if it were to obtain, then were anyone with more or less our sensory and intellectual powers suitably placed, there would be at most merely technological obstacles to his coming to know that the state of affairs in question obtains. Then, it may be said, the allegedly possible state of affairs, in which someone is totally deceived about the physical world, is one which fails to satisfy the condition, and thus is not a genuine possibility at all. (The verificationist will typically hold not that this is an impossible state of affairs, but rather that the sentences which allegedly require its existence for their truth are meaningless. However, I leave aside this aspect of verificationism.)

There does indeed seem to be a clash between our verificationist and the claim that the physical world is independent of experience in the way that Descartes envisaged. The alleged possibility is that my experiences should be indistinguishably the same, though there be no physical world at all. But if the alleged possibility obtained, how could anyone be 'suitably placed' to know this? One could not establish it by sense-experience, for only veridical sense-experience gives knowledge beyond itself, and if there were no physical world there could be no veridical sense-experience. One could not establish it by *a priori* means, for *a priori* conclusions are necessary if true, but it is not necessary that there be no physical world. Hence our verificationist would conclude that the alleged Cartesian possibility is not a genuine possibility. My rejection of Bouwsma's position thus does presuppose the rejection of verificationism.

Russell himself at various points rejects verificationism (e.g., *HK* 465). However, in the present connection there is no need for me to attempt to justify this rejection. For the possibility envisaged in the fable of the evil neurophysiologist is consistent with the present version of verificationism (and also with any verificationist position having even a semblance of plausibility), yet is enough to establish a thesis of independence strong enough for Russell's purposes. The reason is that were this possibility to obtain, it could perfectly well be known to obtain. The neurophysiologist will know at the time of the deceit he is practising, and his victim can be brought to know about it subsequently.

This possibility yields a thesis of independence strong enough to raise the epistemological questions which ·Russell thought so important. It shows that all the specific features of the physical world are logically independent of experience in this sense: for any series of particular experiences there might have been a series indistinguishable to the subject even if the physical world had been quite other than the way the experiences caused him to believe it to be.

This thesis of independence is consistent with the principle of acquaintance, for though this principle requires either a phenomenalistic or a noumenalistic analysis of physical object words, such analyses may leave open the possibility that any one person's experiential history should be reduplicated in a world without physical objects. However, at one point (*RSP* 116) Russell held a phenomenalistic analysis to be defective if it identifies physical objects with sets of sense-data whose members are drawn from the experiential history of more than one person. Were that 'defect' remedied, the resulting analysis would be inconsistent with the thesis of independence, since the existence of a given person's sense-data would suffice for the existence of all the physical objects he could know. However, Russell does not attempt to remedy the supposed defect, either in *RSP* or elsewhere, so that the analyses he in fact offers are consistent with the thesis of independence.

If this thesis is true, it should be possible to ascribe experiences to a person in such a way that the ascription does not entail the existence of any specific features of the physical world. One way is to say things like 'John has a visual experience as of a kangaroo', where 'as of' is seen as generating an intensional context, with the result that this sentence does not entail 'There is a kangaroo such that John is having an experience of it'. Russell, however, takes a different course, guided by epistemological considerations, as well as by the one just mentioned.

In *PP* he introduces the terminology of sense-data, which are 'things that are immediately known in sensation: such things as colours, sounds, smells, hardnesses, roughnesses, and so on' (*PP* 4). Russell normally treats these qualities as universals. But we are later told that a universal, 'not being particular, . . . cannot exist in the world of sense' (*PP* 52), so perhaps sense-data are not so much colours as patches of colour, that is, particulars, as they are implied to be in *PLA* (179), where their transience is stressed (203). The important point in the present context, however, is that a truth of the form '. . . senses such-and-such sense-data' does not entail anything about the specific features of the physical world.

By the time of *Mind* the term 'sense-data' has been dropped. The aim is to mark a doctrinal change. From being tentatively an object of acquaintance in *PP* (28), the self becomes in *Mind* a 'logical fiction' (141). In *PP* sense-data are essentially terms in a binary relation whose other term is a subject: with sense-data, to be is to be sensed by something. While the doctrine that the self is a logical construction is not at first glance incompatible with this, since it might seem that an adequate reconstruction would reconstruct these relational facts, there is an incompatibility at a deeper level. For the elements of the construction are going to be things like sense-data, and if these introduce, in virtue of their essential relationality, the very entities to be constructed, the construction will be circular. Thus by *Mind* 'sense-data' have given way to 'sensations', where a sensation is not essentially relational, and thus, Russell thinks, is a fit basis for the construction of the self. In the present context, the main point is still that truths of the form '. . . has such-and-such sensations' do not entail anything about what we would normally call specific features of the physical world, though as Russell in that book aims to construct the physical world out of sensations, they may entail the existence of some set-theoretic parts of Russell's substitutes for physical objects.

Perception involves more than sensation, since it involves noticing and believing. 'Percept' is a term introduced in *Matter* to mark the content of perception: roughly, a percept is the interpreted noticed part of a sensation (see *Matter* 189, *MPD* 143). It remains that the percepts might exist even if the physical world were quite other than our percepts make us take it to be (*Matter* 199).

In *IMT* the objects of perception are held to be complexes of compresent qualities (318), where qualities are firmly distinguished from their instances. Still, the 'perceptive experiences', as he calls them, are logically independent of the physical world (*IMT* 115).

The changes in doctrine and terminology just chronicled represent important shifts in Russell's epistemology and metaphysics. The epistemological issues are taken up in this section and the next, the ontological ones in the next chapter.

3   Foundations and scepticism

In some form or other, Russell consistently held the view that experience is the foundation of all our knowledge of the physical world. However, it is not easy to characterize this view with any precision, and the present formulation masks an important shift in his later philosophy.

Both these difficulties flow from the problem of interpreting the phrase 'knowledge of the physical world', or, as Russell sometimes puts it, 'empirical knowledge' (*MPD* 227). The idea is that one excludes *a priori* knowledge to do with physical things, such as the knowledge that all bachelors are unmarried. But if *a priori* knowledge is what can be known independently of experience, it seems trivial to say that all non-*a priori* knowledge is founded on experience. And in any case, to say this masks an important change in Russell's philosophy. Whereas, until *HK*, he held that the foundation of knowledge is experience, together with necessary truths knowable *a priori*, in *HK* he held that one needed, in addition to experience, contingent truths knowable *a priori*: the empirical postulates.

The simplest solution for our purposes is to understand by 'knowledge of the physical world' just contingent non-experiential knowledge. (Admittedly, this leaves open how non-*a priori* necessities are to be known, but as Russell does not recognize such a category, an exposition of him will not thereby be impeded.) Then we shall have to say that it was only until *HK* that Russell held the doctrine that all

193

knowledge of the physical world rests on experience as its foundation.

An important role which this doctrine played for him is this: it made scepticism a live and pressing problem. The reason is that the thesis of independence makes it unclear how the foundation can adequately justify what it is supposed to justify. This worry informs much of Russell's epistemology. In this section, I aim to make somewhat clearer exactly what Russell's foundationalism amounts to, and to suggest that there is a good case for his view that the sceptical question, 'Granted your experiential beliefs, how are your physical object beliefs justified?', is a coherent question which demands an answer.

On one issue, there can be little disagreement: experience is the *causal* foundation of our knowledge. This is one point that Russell could be interpreted as making in this passage:

> I think it may be said without any exception or qualification that every piece of empirical knowledge that a given person possesses, he would not possess but for some sensation in his own life. This, I should say, is the essential truth on which empiricists rely (*MPD* 227).

Russell's formulation is ambiguous: it is one thing to say that our knowledge is caused by experience, and another thing to say that it is justified by experience. The first is an uncontentious truth. The second does not follow (at least in any obvious way) and is contentious. To bring out the point, it is uncontentious that to some extent our moral beliefs are formed by the causal action of upbringing and milieu. But citing these causes will not normally make any contribution to justifying the beliefs. Russell's position requires that experience be not merely the causal, but also the *epistemic*, foundation of knowledge.

Russell explicitly denies that this position involves the absurdity that we form our beliefs about the physical world in these two stages: first we note what experiences we are having, and then on this basis we make an inference to how the physical world is (e.g., *PP* 78). The position concerns justification rather than genesis: a person's belief about the physical world is justified iff it *could* in principle have been correctly inferred from propositions which report merely that person's experiences (*PP* 78, 81; *OKEW* 76–7).

A problem for any foundationalist view is to specify correctly the asymmetry, in view of which experiences, or experiential beliefs, are the foundation of physical object beliefs, but physical object beliefs are not the foundation of experiential beliefs. For it is a plain fact that, for ordinary purposes, physical object beliefs are often regarded as justified, without any experiential beliefs being cited in justification; and we do on occasion cite physical object beliefs in order to justify experiential beliefs, as when we say that the clock shows seven, in order to justify our claim to have just heard seven chimes. What needs to be shown is something like this: every fully stated justification of a physical object belief would terminate with exclusively experiential propositions, whereas no justification of an experiential proposition, if fully stated, will terminate with a physical object proposition. In short, we need a ground for the epistemological preference for experiential propositions.

A traditional ground is this: a person's beliefs about the nature of his current experiences are inerrant, that is, if sincerely held, they cannot be false. This would mark a contrast with physical object beliefs, and would show why experiential beliefs should be taken as basic. They provide an infallible basis for justification, so that to show of something that it is justified by them is to bring doubt to an end, since they cannot themselves be doubted.

Russell emphatically denies this position, and with good reason. We can see this in his *PP* account, where we can also see how his notion of the foundations of knowledge interlocks with his notion of acquaintance:

> All our knowledge, both knowledge of things and knowledge of truths, rests upon acquaintance as its foundation (*PP* 26).

It does so in two ways. First, the principle of acquaintance makes acquaintance a precondition for understanding which is in turn a precondition for knowledge. Secondly, acquaintance is involved in grounding all knowledge of truths. It is this second claim that is relevant to the present discussion.

Since acquaintance is officially a species of knowledge of things, rather than knowledge of truths (see pages 29–30 above), it has the advantage that there is no possibility of error: the sense-data which are the objects of acquaintance are neither true nor false, but simply exist (*PP* 55). By the same token, it has the disadvantage that there is no possibility of truth. The point is that only propositions can serve as the premises of an argument, and thus only propositions can be used to justify other propositions, but acquaintance does not consist in knowledge of propositions. How, then, can acquaintance serve as the foundation of knowledge?

Russell is tempted by two superficially distinct ways of overcoming this difficulty. One way is to admit acquaintance with facts: '"my seeing the sun" is an object with which I have acquaintance' (*PP* 27). The other way is to allow that from acquaintance with sense-data one 'immediately derives' judgments of perception, to the effect that such-and-such sense-data exist or have such-and-such properties (*PP* 65). But whichever route is adopted, Russell admits that there are no beliefs which are immune from error (*PP* 78). One may falsely believe that one is acquainted with one's seeing the sun, and there is no absolute guarantee that a judgment of perception is true (*PP* 80). His main reason is that judgment involves analysis, and in this there is always room for error. One could put much the same point like this: judgment involves bringing things under concepts, but this can in theory be done incorrectly, otherwise there could be no false judgment. Fallible as we are, there surely can be no logical guarantee that we will not do what it is logically possible to do. But now the problem arises: if experiential beliefs are not inerrant, why should we prefer to justify physical object beliefs on their basis, rather than, say, on the basis of other physical object beliefs?

We can raise the same question in another way by using some terminology from *PP*. Russell contrasts 'intuitive' beliefs with 'derivative' beliefs, and claims that experiential beliefs are intuitive whereas all physical object beliefs are derivative. A derivative belief is justifiably held only if it can be derived from intuitive beliefs by intuitive principles of reasoning (cf. *PP* 81). By contrast, an intuitive belief is 'self-evident' and requires no justification outside itself. But if experiential beliefs are liable to error, why should they be self-evident? Can we not in fact offer physical object beliefs to justify them, as in such cases as the hearing of seven chimes already mentioned? And in the case of the experiences of others, surely we must always cite physical object beliefs? So there seems to be a case for not counting all experiential beliefs as intuitive. Moreover, surely my current belief that there is a typewriter before me is self-evident, if any belief is, and thus requires no justification outside itself. So there is a case for regarding at least some physical object beliefs as intuitive.

Russell offers the following argument for the claim that there must be some intuitive beliefs:

> Since inferences start from premises, there must be knowledge which is uninferred if there is to be any knowledge (*HK* 181).

However, the argument presupposes rather than substantiates Russell's foundationalism. Every act of providing a justification is finite and so must end with some belief that is, at least for the moment, taken for granted. But it does not follow from this that a belief which terminates a justificatory act is one concerning which there is no question of justification in terms of other beliefs. A belief which terminates a chain of justification on one occasion may be its starting point on another, unless, of course, foundationalism is true.

On more than one occasion, Russell suggests that the asymmetry required by the foundationalist picture consists in the fact that experiential beliefs are 'more certain' than physical object beliefs (*PP*

67; *HK* 186). Then the idea would be that even if, on occasion, an experiential belief were justified in terms of a physical object belief, in a fully explicit justification the chain would not end there. The physical object belief would in turn have to be justified by experiential beliefs, or else one would have ended up 'justifying' the more certain by the less certain, which would be unhelpful. Similarly, if one physical object belief is justified by another, this only shows that the justification has not been completely stated. The second physical object belief would, in a fully explicit justification, be justified by some experiential belief, or else one would have done the pointless thing of 'justifying' one proposition by another equally uncertain.

It should be obvious that this is quite unsatisfactory as an argument for foundationalism. Either the notion of certainty is intended in a purely psychological way, in which case it is a flat falsehood that experiential beliefs are more certain than physical object ones: I am not more certain of anything than that there is a typewriter now before me. Alternatively, the notion of certainty is intended in a genuinely epistemic way, so that only the more certain can provide a warrant for the less certain. But then the claim that experiential beliefs are more certain than physical object beliefs is not an argument for, but simply a restatement of, the foundationalism that Russell is concerned to establish.

In *HK* he considers the idea that we can distinguish experiential beliefs as those for which no further reason can be given. It is beliefs having this characteristic

> that are of most importance for theory of knowledge, since they are the indispensable minimum of premises for our knowledge of matters of fact. Such beliefs I shall call 'data'. In ordinary thinking they are *causes* of other beliefs rather than premises from which other beliefs are inferred; but in a critical scrutiny of our beliefs as to matters of fact, we must, wherever possible, translate the causal transitions of primitive thinking into logical transitions, and only accept the derived beliefs to the extent that the character of the transitions seems to justify. For this there is a common-sense reason, namely, that every such transition is found to involve some risk of error, and therefore data are more nearly certain than beliefs derived from them. I am not contending that data are ever completely certain, nor is this contention necessary for their importance in theory of knowledge (*HK* 181).

It turns out that 'Only sensations and memories are truly data for our knowledge of the external world' (*HK* 185: it is not clear exactly how this claim is meant to interlock with the role of the empirical postulates). Thus the 'intuitive' beliefs of *PP* reappear as 'data' in *HK*, and in the quoted passage one might hope to find an argument for taking experiential beliefs as data, as being more certain, in an epistemic sense, than physical object beliefs.

However, the argument appears to depend on the false assumption that the longer a causal chain the less the epistemic warrant. In discussing perception in the last section we saw that the long causal chain running between the sun and ourselves is perfectly sound epistemically, and yields knowledge of the sun. So there is no reason to think that a causal chain with a large number of 'transitions' is inherently less reliable than one with a smaller number. Quality counts as well as quantity. Nor is it that, in our ordinary concept of knowledge, we *arbitrarily* hold that long causal chains can be as sound as short ones. There is a justification for this position. For example, it is common for a telephone call from England to Australia, beamed by satellite, to result in clearer and more reliable transmission than a local call, involving antiquated equipment.

When arguing for the primacy of experience, Russell is apt to insist upon the thesis of independence (e.g., *PP* ch 1, *HK* 186ff.). However, the fact that the course of experience might have been indistinguishably the same, even if our physical object beliefs had been false, does not of itself establish that experiential beliefs must be the terminus of every fully stated justification of a physical object belief. The course of events in Alpha Centauri might have been indistinguishably the same even if our beliefs about how things are on Venus had been false, but this does not show that all fully explicit justifications of these latter beliefs must terminate with propositions about how things are on Alpha Centauri.

A rather dilute foundationalism is, I think, fairly uncontroversial. I shall briefly state what this is, and then show that it is a weaker doctrine than the one Russell espouses.

This dilute foundationalism is based on the simple point that a man's beliefs about the physical world count as justified only if they are causally related in some way to appropriate perceptions. This is obvious in the case of those justified beliefs one has acquired simply by looking, and it holds also for those beliefs one has acquired by testimony, since perception is involved in the receipt of testimony. Likewise, theoretical beliefs are justifiably held only if one knows evidence for them, and any way of knowing evidence runs back to perception. Perception involves having experiences. So a man's beliefs about the physical world are justified only if he has formed them as the result of having certain appropriate experiences. This rules out, for example, beliefs which are pure guesswork, or are based on misperceptions or illusions or hallucinations.

It follows from this that in order to establish that *A* is justified in believing that p one would have to establish that A has had p-appropriate experiences. This gives some substance to the claim that experience plays a fundamental role in the justification of our physical object beliefs, but it does not amount to Russell's foundationalist theory. One reason for the discrepancy is this: dilute foundationalism is consistent with the denial of Russell's view that every fully explicit statement of the justification for a physical object belief will terminate in experiential propositions. For the dilute foundationalist might combine his view with the doctrine that, where a physical object belief is formed on the basis of perception, the belief is justified only if the experiences are caused by whatever physical objects make the belief true. This is perhaps too strong merely for justified belief, though it is not too strong for knowledge. My present point is not that the claim is correct but only that it is, apparently, consistent with dilute foundationalism yet inconsistent with Russell's foundationalism. This establishes a divergence between the two sorts of foundationalism.

Russell would try to argue from dilute foundationalism to his stronger version on the following lines: suppose one is trying to show that A is justified in believing that p. Then indeed one may well take it for granted that p, and focus on whether A is *justified* in his true belief. But one can always raise the question of one's own justification for believing that p, where the real doubt is whether or not it is the case that p. Then the most immediate and natural course would be, if possible, to show that one has had p-appropriate experiences. If, in addition, one uses other physical object beliefs in one's justification, these too must be justified, and this involves showing further facts about one's experiences. So long as one continues to introduce further physical object beliefs, the statement of the justification cannot terminate. Hence, ultimately, a fully explicit justification must terminate only in experiential propositions.

There are at least two highly questionable moves in this argument. One is the assumption that every physical object proposition introduced into a justificatory chain calls itself for justification, and thus causes a lengthening of the chain. The other is the assumption that the introduction of an experiential proposition into a justificatory chain does not in a similar way cause a lengthening of the chain. The assumptions are, in fact, justified only if we have already assumed the epistemic priority of experience, in the full Russellian way. On other conceptions of justification, these assumptions will appear unwarranted.

For example, suppose we say that any process of justification must take something for granted. 'A is justified in believing that p' will then be seen as elliptical for 'A is justified in believing that p, relative to X', where X is a set of propositions that are taken for granted. We might argue that what is taken for granted is itself not something to be decided in advance of genuine doubts and genuine attempts to allay them, but is relative to particular situations. Then it is plain that X may contain physical object propositions, and may fail to contain experiential propositions. There is no room, on this view, for the idea that some set of propositions is uniquely privileged, so that it and nothing else is always to be taken for granted. (Cf. Williams, *Groundless Belief*.)

As I said at the beginning of the section, one of the main roles that the foundationalist position plays in Russell's philosophy is to make scepticism a living issue. I shall not discuss whether his full foundationalist doctrine is correct (for a negative view I refer the reader to Williams), but I do wish to suggest that we can at least extract something sufficient for scepticism to have the importance which Russell attached to it. What is required is not that every 'adequate' or 'fully stated' justification of a physical object belief should terminate with nothing but experiential beliefs, but simply that one justificatory question that can be raised is this: granted all your experiential beliefs, how are your physical object beliefs to be justified?

The possibility of this question seems to me to flow immediately from the thesis of independence, and this fits well with Russell's insistence on the thesis when attempting to justify his foundationalism. The thesis holds that it is logically possible that our experiences should be indistinguishably the same, even though all our physical object beliefs are false. Now there is nothing in this possibility that makes any experiential beliefs we may have unjustified. Hence, in raising the sceptical question, we are not in the silly position of asking for a justification, while being prepared to take nothing for granted. On the contrary, since experiential beliefs may be justified when physical object beliefs are false, we surely have all we need to ask whether the latter can be justified, given just the former.

This question is a special case of the question of whether inductive beliefs can be justified, and the reader will be able to see, from my discussion of induction, how I would answer the sceptical question about the external world. Russell's answers, however, are on different lines, as we shall see in the next section.

4 Construction and inference

Russell uses two techniques to try to make our knowledge of the physical world more secure from sceptical attacks. One is the method of construction, the other I shall call the method of inference. The terminology springs from Russell's claim that:

The supreme maxim in scientific philosophizing is this: *Wherever possible, logical constructions are to be substituted for inferred entities* (*RSP* 115).

The method of construction consists in reconstructing physical objects as sets of sense-data or sensations, and in thus bringing physical objects closer in their nature to the experiential foundations of our knowledge, it supposedly makes these objects easier to know. This method is the epistemological aspect of Russell's adoption of the phenomenalistic mode of analysing physical object expressions (cf. above, pp. 31–2, and it holds sway from 1914 until the middle 1920s.

The method of inference is the epistemological aspect of Russell's adoption of the noumenalistic mode of analysing physical object expressions (cf. above, pp. 31–2). Physical objects are seen as the causes of experiences, and the difficulty of having knowledge of entities apparently so remote from the experiential foundation is supposedly mitigated by a reduction in its content: we do not know the intrinsic nature of physical objects, but only their structural properties.

In this section, I consider in turn these methods of answering the sceptic. Details of Russell's logical constructions are given in the next chapter (sections 3 to 7). Here I shall be concerned only with the epistemological motivation, and I shall consider only the construction of physical objects out of sense-data or 'sensibilia'.

Russell acknowledges a debt to Whitehead for having first suggested the application of the method of construction to empirical material. In mathematics, it had been employed to sweep away 'the useless menagerie of metaphysical monsters with which it used to be infested' (*RSP* 115). In *RSP*, the same method is employed to sweep away physical objects, to the extent that they are more than sets of sense-data, and, as in mathematics, the result is supposed to be a reduction in the area of doubt.

Though, as we have seen, Russell's ideal construction 'would exhibit matter wholly in terms . . . of the sense-data of a single person' (*RSP* 116), the construction he in fact proposed contained other entities, both the sense-data of other people, and also 'unsensed sensibilia'. The latter are 'those objects which have the same metaphysical and physical status as sense-data' but which are not sensed by any mind (*RSP* 110). For any given person, both the sense-data of others and also unsensed sensibilia will be inferred entities: that is, that person's knowledge of them will be derivative and not intuitive. So how has the construction of physical objects out of these entities obeyed the 'supreme maxim in scientific philosophizing'? Admittedly, physical objects have been dispensed with, but each physical object has been replaced by a whole gamut of inferred entities, so that the replacement looks, if anything, harder to know than what it replaces. The overall effect of construction is to increase, rather than diminish, the number of inferred entities.

The same sort of objection can be made in terms of the principle which Russell often quotes with approval, under the title 'Occam's razor': entities are not to be multiplied beyond necessity. Since we are not the lords of creation, the principle must be regarded as wholly epistemic: we should not believe that something exists unless there is good evidence. The reason is that the more you stick your neck out, the more chance there is of its being chopped off: 'you run less risk of error, the fewer entities you assume' (*PLA* 222). Construction, however, requires us to 'assume' more entities than does the straightforward belief in physical objects. The reason is that each physical object is made up of sensibilia, some of which are unsensed. The latter have to be 'assumed'.

To meet this objection, one must insist that economizing is intended to apply not to the number of entities, but to the number of *kinds* of entity. We have in any case to accept the existence of sensibilia, since we are acquainted with some of them. But it is best to avoid assuming any other kind of entity, for example, physical objects (as these are ordinarily thought of). The justification for this might run as follows: being inferred would be part of the essence of a physical object, regarded as something over and above sensibilia, but it is not part of the essence of sets of sensibilia. In Ayer's useful phrase, logical construction replaces 'vertical inferences' (to essentially inferred entities) by 'horizontal inferences' (to only accidentally inferred entities) (*Russell* 39). The essence of Russell's position is that vertical inferences are less secure than horizontal inferences, and from this results the epistemological value of the method of construction. It seems to me that this position is wholly unwarranted.

One might urge in its favour that horizontal inferences are safer because they are of a kind with inferences whose conclusions have been discovered, non-inferentially, to be true. By contrast, the conclusions of vertical inferences have never been known non-inferentially.

The premise is questionable. Even if accepted, however, it has no tendency to establish the desired conclusion.

Suppose that the sentence 'this desk will be here in five minutes' time' is reconstructed in terms of a collection of sensibilia. If the unsensed sensibilia are to play any part, then the corresponding prediction will entail their existence. If the prediction is based on non-inferential premises, it will be a horizontal inference, since the conclusion involves only sensibilia. But it will not be, in any helpful way, 'of a kind with' inferences whose conclusions have been non-inferentially known, since no truth involving unsensed sensibilia has been non-inferentially known. (An unsensed sensibile may *become* sensed: but, on Russell's view, the claim that it existed before it was sensed is inferential.)

Perhaps unsensed sensibilia, and the sensibilia sensed by others, play no part in the logical constructions, or at least play no part in any conclusion in which we are entitled to believe. But in this case it is not that horizontal inferences have been taken as preferable to vertical inferences. Rather, *all* inferences have been rejected. In this case, the method of construction would provide no answer to the sceptic.

Thus the premise of the argument is, I think, false. However, even if it were true, it would not give a good reason for the greater security of horizontal as opposed to vertical inferences.

How should we understand 'more secure'? Presumably, insecurity must involve some risk of clash with what is non-inferentially known. But whether in the case of horizontal or in the case of vertical inferences, the non-inferentially known facts are the same: a vertical inference has resulted in a clash with what is non-inferentially known when, and only when, the corresponding horizontal inference has resulted in a clash with what is non-inferentially known. If it is legitimate to argue from the fact about horizontal inferences to future absence of clash, it is equally legitimate to argue from the analogous fact about vertical inferences to the analogous conclusion.

Furthermore, a preference for vertical over horizontal inferences is deeply built into our conception of rational belief. For example, we hold electronic theory to be the best explanation of certain phenomena, and on these grounds to merit our belief, even though electrons are, so to speak, a step up from the data which their existence serves to explain. Good explanations seem very often to involve the supposition of unobserved facts or entities, so that an inference to the best explanation is typically vertical.

Our preference for vertical inferences may be misguided. But, given that our ultimate basis for what is rational consists in a critical scrutiny of what we take to be rational, the onus is on him who disputes the correctness of the preference to establish his view. I can find in Russell no satisfactory discharge of this obligation. Thus Russell wholly fails to establish the superiority of horizontal to vertical inference, so that his method of construction lacks any adequate epistemological motivation.

The first signs of his turning away from this method, and towards the method of inference, are found in *Matter*:

It is impossible to lay down a hard-and-fast rule that we can never validly infer something radically different from what we observe – unless, indeed, we take up the position that nothing unobserved can ever be validly inferred (*Matter* 16).

In this book, he develops at length the theory, briefly advocated in *PP* (ch 3), that physical objects are inferred entities and are the causes of our experiences, but their intrinsic character is unknown to us. Rather, our knowledge of them is purely structural. The epistemological motivation here is so to shrink our knowledge claims that everything vital remains, yet, thanks to the shrinking, the risk of error is significantly reduced. We must first see what Russell means by the claim that our knowledge of physical objects is purely structural.

The general notion of structure is introduced in chapter 1 of *Matter* by means of the notion of an interpretation of a logical system. A logical system consists of a *syntax*, a collection of types of mark, some series of members of this collection being specified as *formulae*, together with a *proof-theory*, that is, a means of checking an arbitrary finite series of formulae to see if it counts as a 'proof'. Any last member of a proof is called a *theorem* and the member of any single-formula proof is called an *axiom*. An *interpretation* of a logical system is some method of assigning meanings to all its formulae. Roughly speaking, Russell's idea is that, concerning the sentences expressing what we take to be our knowledge of the physical world, we know that *some* interpretation of them is true, but there is no interpretation of which we know that *it* is true.

Let us say that a *theory* is a logical system together with an interpretation, and that two theories are *isomorphic* iff they have the same logical system. Now an extreme version of Russell's doctrine that we have only structural knowledge of the physical world is this: assuming that physics is a theory in the above sense, what we know is not that it is true but merely that some isomorph of it is true.

Russell does not take this extreme line. He allows in general that some interpretations of a theory are more important, or closer to what is intended. Thus, for example, he thinks that in the case of Peano's system, though there are infinitely many interpretations which make all its theorems true, one (specified in *PofM* 128) is most important. In the case of physics, Russell holds that what is important is that any interpretation or range of interpretations must make physics knowable through experience. He argues that the minimal type of inference which would lead us outside the purely experiential is based on the principle that experiences have causes which are not experiences; in other words: for each experiential event, there is a physical event which causes it. Hence every important interpretation of physics will be over a domain of events. This makes for a restriction on the extreme form of the doctrine: all we know is that some interpretation of the logical system of physics which has events as its domain is true.

This already involves a shift in what might be thought of as the natural interpretation of physics, in which enduring things like electrons occur. Russell has to show, however, that such entities can and should be regarded as series of events (*Matter* 283).

Russell uses another way of amplifying his claim that our knowledge of the physical world is structural. He asks what are the consequences of the minimal assumption that experiences have causes which are not themselves experiences. He implicitly assumes that if one particular causes another, there is a general law under which the case is subsumed. On this basis, he reaches the conclusion that if two experiences are of different types, so are their causes. Hence, in general, to each experiential type there corresponds a physical type. This holds at all levels of type: thus, if tactual experiences are *more intense than* visual ones, the physical events which cause tactual experiences must have *a corresponding relation* to those which cause visual ones. If we use the word 'relation' so as to include properties as monadic relations, Russell's position can be put quite generally: the least we know of the physical world, on the minimal assumption that our experiences are caused by events which are not themselves experiences, is that for every experiential relation there is a *similar* physical one, or, as he sometimes put it, a physical relation having the same structure.

Similarity of relations is defined as follows:

> Two relations *P*, *Q* are said to be 'similar' if there is a one-one relation between the terms of their fields, which is such that, whenever two terms have the relation *P*, their correlates have the relation *Q*, and vice versa (*Matter* 249).

What I shall call the 'positive' side of Russell's doctrine about knowledge of structure is that, granted the minimal causal assumption, we know that there is a one-one correspondence between experiences and physical events which induces, for each experiential relation, a similar physical one. (Subsequently, the doctrine is slightly modified, to take into account the fact that we sometimes learn that what was not sensibly discriminable is different, as when *A* is indistinguishable from *B* and *B* from *C* but not *A* from *C*. In the modification, similarity is replaced by partial similarity, which is like similarity except that the relevant correspondence is one-many from the field of the experiential relation to the field of the physical relation.) What I shall call the 'negative' side of the doctrine is that all we know of the physical world consists in such structural knowledge.

Positive and negative doctrines are juxtaposed in the following passage:

> This principle [that different experiences or 'percepts' are caused by different physical stimuli], together with spatio-temporal continuity, suffices to give a great deal of knowledge as to the *structure* of stimuli. Their intrinsic characters, it is true, must remain unknown; but we may assume that the stimuli causing us to hear notes of different pitches form a series in respect of some character which corresponds causally with pitch, and we may make similar assumptions in regard to colour or any other character of sensations which is capable of serial arrangement (*Matter* 227).

The doctrine may be illustrated by using Russell's own example of a map, which is a system of relations similar to the system of relations in the district mapped. There is a one-one function f correlating each point on the map (M) with some point on the district (D), in such a way that, for any M-relation R there is a D-relation S such that R holds of $<x_1 \ldots x_n>$ iff S holds of $<fx_1 \ldots fx_n>$. Thus perhaps an M-point is green iff the corresponding D-point is wooded; a pair of M-points are three inches apart iff the corresponding pair of D-points are three miles apart; a triple of M-points is between-related iff the corresponding triple of D-points is between-related; and so on. The map's key serves as a kind of 'dictionary' for matching statements about M with corresponding statements about D. Knowing of a map that it is a map involves knowing that there is a correspondence matching points on the map with points on some district other than itself. Knowing that a given map maps a given district is knowing that there is a correlation between the map and that district. To extract all the information from a map, we need to know what district it maps, and also, for each relation in the map, with what relation in the district it is supposed to be correlated.

The positive part of Russell's doctrine concerning structural knowledge is that we know that our experiences make up a map of the physical world, and that the elements of the physical world are events. Hence we know that there is a 'key': a way of transforming experiential truths into truths about the physical world. It is in this sense that experience gives us knowledge of the physical world. The negative part of his doctrine is that we do not know what the key is. For any experiential relation, we know that there is a matching one holding of correlated events, but we do not know what this matching relation is. Thus we know the structure of the physical world, but not its intrinsic nature. We know that some interpretation of physical statements is true, but not which.

This fact is masked by the ambiguity of our language. 'The word "blue" will have a different meaning as applied to a light-ray from that which it has when applied to a percept' (*HK* 493). Applied to a light-ray it really means 'some relation similar, under the given correspondence, to blue'. If we try to mean more than this, we make what we say unknowable.

The idea is that if we claim to know only the structural properties of the physical world, our claim is smaller and safer than if we claim to know the intrinsic properties of the physical world. Yet this shrinking of what we claim makes no practical difference: our ability to predict, explain and control the world remains unimpaired.

It is not easy to find an argument for the negative part of the doctrine. Can it be supposed to follow simply from the fact that if structural knowledge is enough for practical purposes, it would be rash to claim any intrinsic knowledge? Perhaps the idea is that the less you say, the less likely you are to be wrong. But although there is some truth in this, it is hardly adequate for Russell's purposes.

The way of scepticism is generally to expose a series of epistemological hurdles. My experience now is taken for granted. Surmounting the first hurdle involves extending my knowledge of my experience back into the past, by memory, then forward into the future, on the strength of well-grounded expectations. Then, in Russell's order, we have a hurdle to surmount in order to arrive at other minds, and the final hurdle takes us to physical objects. In the usual dialectical situation, once it is conceded that a hurdle can be crossed at all, the details of how often it can be crossed are irrelevant. Once you have somehow overcome scepticism about other minds, it is irrelevant whether you claim that there is one other mind or two or more. Now, you clearly make a logically stronger claim if you claim that there are two other minds than if you claim only that there is one. But as both lie within the same epistemological hurdles, this difference of logical strength has no bearing on the usual problems of epistemic strength. There is no general epistemological reason for supposing that the claim that there are two other minds is shakier than the claim that there is at least one.

Thus, if Russell is to establish the greater security of structural knowledge, it is not enough for him to point out that the claims involved are logically weaker than if intrinsic knowledge were claimed. He must also show that structural knowledge is on the nearer side of an epistemological hurdle than intrinsic knowledge. He would attempt to do this by means of the claim that only structural knowledge is licensed by his 'minimal assumption' that experiences have causes which lie outside themselves. The boundary of what can be known without this assumption marks one hurdle, and the boundary of what can be known with it marks another. Between these two hurdles lies all and only our purely structural knowledge of the physical world. If we can confine ourselves to this knowledge we are safer than if we cross the hurdle which marks its outermost bound.

To assess the negative side of this doctrine, that is, the denial of knowledge of intrinsic properties, it will be useful to have some examples of what we supposedly do not know. Colour, as we have seen, is one, but this case has special complexities. For one thing, there is a danger of confusing the sense of 'intrinsic' in which it contrasts with 'structural', and the sense in which an intrinsic property of a thing is one such that the fact that a thing possesses it does not entail that anything else exists. Now some philosophers, like Locke perhaps, have held that colours are not intrinsic properties in this latter sense, in that their existence requires the existence of a suitable sensory organ. Hence it might appear, if we interpret Russell through this Lockean view, that in denying that we have knowledge of the intrinsic colour properties of things, Russell is simply denying that we could know any necessary falsehoods, e.g., the necessary falsehood that this pen is *intrinsically* blue. I think this is not Russell's view. He seems to think that it is logically possible that physical things should be blue, though we cannot know it.

A further complication is that Russell thinks that 'blue' can be 'applied to a percept' (*HK* 493). The application is not straight-forward, since there are no blue percepts if, as Russell suggests in *HK* (218), percepts are mental events. Applying 'blue' to a percept must be claiming either that the percept is of the colour blue, or else of something which is blue. Here, and in *IMT*, Russell prefers to say the former, so let us confine ourselves to that. What is claimed is that we cannot know that that colour is part of the physical world. All we can know is that some similar property is, and a likely candidate is some specific wave-length.

What other intrinsic properties of physical objects might we be tempted to claim to know? Private space is distinguished from public space, so the spatial properties of physical things are not immediately known. But geometrical properties are 'logical', in the sense that they are definable in purely logical terms, and these are held to be invariant between similar systems of relations. That is, for any logical property, there is no difference between it and any similar property: similarity (in the technical sense) suffices for identity. Hence geometrical properties are in any case structural, and hence are known. (Cf. *Matter* 251.)

A similar argument appears to apply to spatial relations. The mistake we tend to make is to suppose that physical space can be identified with the private space each of us is given in experience. In reality, it is, according to Russell, something constructed on the basis of private space, and knowledge of it is, he thinks, validated by the minimal causal assumption. Hence in this case what we really mean, when we attribute spatial relations to physical things, is something we can know without going beyond the assumptions Russell is prepared to allow. In short, space is not a case in which Russell is inviting us to make do with less than we had thought we wanted.

How convincing is this theory overall? One point to notice is that there is some divergence between the notion of a structural property, understood as a property about which all we know is that it is similar to some property given in experience, and that of a property whose existence and distribution can be inferred on the basis of the minimal causal assumption. Why, for example, should we be entitled to infer that physical objects are really square, just because squareness is given in experience? It is plain that we are not entitled to this conclusion merely on the grounds that the given squareness is caused, for perhaps it is caused by rhomboidal physical objects, and distortions in our perceptual apparatus account for the rest. The general point is that the causal postulate does not tell us how to distribute likely causes between our perceptual apparatus and the rest of the world. The physical world, outside our perceptual apparatus, might have less structure than we currently suppose, for perhaps it suffers enrichment through our eyes and nerves.

No doubt satisfying-sounding principles of simplicity and so on could be seen to inform our practice. But it is dangerous for Russell to adopt the following modification of his doctrine: we are entitled only to those beliefs about the physical world which must be invoked to give a satisfactory explanation of our experience. The danger is that in this case the doctrine will come as no surprise, and will, after all, involve no diminution of the content of our ordinary beliefs. Instead of the glamorous picture in which our everyday epistemological extravagances are pruned by the judicious application of an austere philosophy, we are liable to find that all our everyday beliefs that we unreflectingly took to be justified are, after all, genuinely justified in the light of experience.

We have seen that one example of a property which we rashly attribute to physical objects when, in Russell's view, we should instead claim only that physical objects have some similar property, is colour. The only other definite example of such a property that I have been able to find is sound (*Matter* 253). Conceivably, in these cases, it is right to say that the attribution of the properties to physical objects is not justified by the aspiration of finding the best theory to explain our experience. Perhaps we can make do with wavelengths or surface textures and with vibrations in the air, and perhaps these things are not to be identified with colours or sounds. If so, then I would agree with Russell's conclusion: our attribution of colours and sounds to physical objects is not justified by experience. I do not in fact accept the antecedents of the conditionals which led to this conclusion, and I cannot find any explicit independent argument for them in Russell. The principal difficulty is this: the physicist may indeed never use colour or sound words in his descriptions of physical things, but that leaves open the question of whether or not he refers to colours or sounds: perhaps colours and sounds *are* respectively kinds of texture or vibration.

To sum up: one must, I think, agree with Russell that if we cannot justify our physical object beliefs in terms of experience, we must abandon them, or reduce or change their content. Moreover, I agree that the overall way in which experience justifies physical beliefs is that the latter should be involved in an explanation which, in the end, explains experiences. However, it does not follow from any of this that the only properties we can justifiably ascribe to physical objects have the form '. . . has a property similar to *P*', where *P* is some property given in experience. Nor does it *follow* that we are not justified in ascribing colours and sounds to physical things, though there is, perhaps, an independent argument to this conclusion.

I said earlier that there was no necessary inconsistency between the method of logical construction and the method of inference. It remains to trace the interaction of the two.

The method of construction rules unchallenged between approximately 1914 and at least 1921. However, in *Matter*, published in 1927, the method of inference, which made its first brief appearance in *PP*, is resurrected. In some ways there is no tension. Although physical things are now inferred entities, they are still regarded as sets of events. This piece of reconstruction is motivated by the desire to eliminate substance, and the construction and its motivation are discussed in the next chapter. There is no obvious clash between regarding a physical object both as a construction out of events and as something whose only known properties are structural.[6] At another point, however, there is a clash. In *Matter* Russell espouses neutral monism, with the result that physical objects must ultimately be constituted out of the same materials as are selves. But if mind and matter are constituted from the same materials, it is hard to see how any property of matter could be unknowable by mind. For example, the very colour involved in a sensation will be a set-theoretical part of a physical object. How then can our attribution of colours to physical objects be unjustified? Either we cannot *know*

[6] If a physical object a is a class, 'a causes experience e' will have to be read as elliptical for 'a member of a causes e', for classes are not causes.

that the neutral monistic construction is correct, or else blue cannot be an example of a property that we cannot, with epistemological propriety, ascribe to physical objects.

Perhaps *Matter* is a transitional work. By *HK*, neutral monism has been abandoned, and the method of inference holds undisputed sway. There are still constructions, however: physical things out of events, and persons out of their histories. But these are not constructions which tend to conflict with the method of inference.

5   A priori *knowledge*

An *a priori* truth is one which can be known to be true without appeal to experiential evidence. Likewise an *a priori* falsehood is one which can be known to be false without appeal to experiential evidence. What *can* be known without appeal to experience *may* none the less on occasion be known in virtue of experience. Thus you may come to know a logical truth, even though it is knowable *a priori*, by the *a posteriori* means of being told it by a competent logician of high moral character.

Given Russell's central interest in mathematics, it is surprising that he wrote so little on *a priori* knowledge. He never failed to regard mathematical truths as *a priori*, and necessary and certain, but he says very little about how they can be known. That experience in some way gives knowledge seems to require neither demonstration nor explanation; but that there is a source of knowledge other than experience requires both.

His only substantial discussions of the problems are chapter ten of *PP*, and the late essay 'Is Mathematics Purely Linguistic?' dated 1950–2, and first published posthumously in *EA*.

In the earlier discussion, Russell summarizes his solution to the problem of how *a priori* knowledge is possible:

All a priori *knowledge deals exclusively with the relations of universals.*
This proposition is of great importance, and goes a long way towards solving our previous difficulties concerning *a priori* knowledge (*PP* 59).

It is not easy to see how this could be even the beginnings of a solution to the problem, for the property attributed to *a priori* knowledge seems not to be exclusive to it. Dealing exclusively with universals presumably amounts to mentioning no particulars. But even if this holds of all *a priori* truths, the difficulty is that it also holds for plenty of *a posteriori* truths like 'All men are mortal'. Perhaps in the case of *a priori* truths, the relations between the relevant universals are what makes the proposition true. But this, too, holds of *a posteriori* truths: nothing except the relation between humanity and mortality makes 'All men are mortal' true. But let us look at Russell's argument for his doctrine, in the hope of finding a more promising version of it.

From the fact that a statement 'deals exclusively with the relations of universals' Russell takes it to follow that it 'may be known by anybody who is acquainted with the universals concerned and can perceive the relation between them which the statement asserts' (*PP* 60). Since a universal is the meaning (i.e. meaning-relatum) of a general term, this consequence can reasonably be interpreted as that an *a priori* truth may be known by anyone who understands the sentence expressing it *and* can perceive the relations between the meanings involved.

This, I think, is the full extent of the account of *a priority* to be found in *PP*. Any idea that there is something mysterious about the implied capacity of non-sensory perception is met by the insistence that:

> It must be taken as a fact, discovered by reflecting on our knowledge, that we have the power of sometimes perceiving such relations between univerals (*PP* 60).

But the mystery remains. In the case of some meaning-relata, we can perceive the relevant relations in a non-sensory fashion, but not in the case of others. For example, we can perceive the relation between humanity and animality, but not that between humanity and mortality, without relying on our senses. But *how* this is possible is simply the original problem in different words.

One might advance an explanation on the following lines: *a priori* truths are true wholly in virtue of meanings, are made true exclusively by linguistic facts. These are the very facts one learns in mastering a language. This explains how understanding an *a priori* truth suffices for knowing its truth, and how an *a priori* truth requires no experiential justification. To show that you really know an *a priori* truth you need only show that you know the language. (We do not attribute *a priori* knowledge to non-language-users.)

Can an explanation of this kind be attributed to the author of *PP*? The situation is unclear.

In favour of the attribution, we can stress that universals are meanings, and knowledge of universals is held to be the key to *a priori* knowledge. The problem is that we have to know not just meanings, but also relations between them, and it is not clear that Russell wants to build this knowledge into that required for linguistic mastery.

Against the attribution, one might mention the insistence that the law of non-contradiction, an instance of *a priori* truth, 'is about things' (*PP* 50): Russell rightly holds that if we say of something that it is not both a beech and not a beech, our belief concerns that thing, and not merely our thoughts about it. However, the general doctrine, which comes later, seems somewhat to qualify this point: no tree is a universal, yet 'all *a priori* knowledge deals exclusively with the relations of universals' (59).

Perhaps a stronger reason against the attribution is Russell's acceptance of synthetic *a priori* truths. He defines a synthetic truth as one which is not analytic (*PP* 47), and many philosophers regard an analytic truth as one true in virtue of meanings. On this account, one holding the proposed explanation of *a priori* knowledge cannot hold that any such knowledge is synthetic. But this reason is not decisive in the case of *PP*, for Russell does not there define an analytic truth as one true in virtue of meanings. Rather, he gives Kant's two criteria: that the idea of the subject-term contains the idea of the predicate-term; and that the proposition can be established by the law of contradiction (*PP* 46–7). Hence it is conceivable that Russell's main example of synthetic *a priori* knowledge, mathematical knowledge, is true in virtue of meanings, even if it comes out as synthetic by one or more of Kant's criteria. (In fact, Russell applies only the first of these to the issue, and it is likely that he still at this time held that logical truths, like the mathematical ones which he thought he had reduced them to, were synthetic. Cf. *PofM* 457, *Leibniz* § 11.) Thus Russell's belief in the syntheticity of some *a priori* truths is not a decisive reason for thinking he repudiates the explanation we are considering. In many ways, his philosophy in *PP* is in transition, and it is probably so on the present question. In *Leibniz* there is no hint of *a priori* truths being in any way 'linguistic' or based on meanings, though this position is explicitly adopted in writings after *PP*, at least partly as a result of Wittgenstein's influence. In *PP* there is no single definite view, but an indefinite position in which one can detect both 'linguistic' and 'non-linguistic' tendencies.

The development of Russell's thought on the question is not smooth. In *OKEW* he claims that 'some kind of knowledge of logical forms, though with most people it is not explicit, is involved in all understanding of discourse' (53), and in the same lecture he claims that logical truths are true in virtue of their form alone (66–7). Putting these claims together we have the doctrine that those *a priori* truths which are logical truths can be known simply in virtue of being understood. This seems to point decisively towards the 'linguistic' position. This is reinforced by a discussion in *Matter*. Again considering logical truths, he claims that they are really concerned with symbols. We can know their truth or falsehood without studying the outside world, because they are only concerned with symbolic manipulations (*Matter* 171).

Yet ten years later, in the introduction to the second edition of *PofM*, while he admits that 'logic becomes more linguistic than I believed it to be at the time when I wrote the "Principles"' (*xi*), he seems to have some doubts about so 'linguistic' an account as Carnap's (cf. *xii*). By the time of the *EA* essay, a linguistic view has been definitely adopted, at least for those *a priori* truths that belong to logic and mathematics. Before considering this in detail, it will be useful to show that the linguistic explanation we considered in connection with *PP* is quite definitely false.

The explanation was that *a priori* truths are true wholly in virtue of meanings, and hence one learns the facts in virtue of which they are true in learning the language. If true, the explanation would be satisfying. But it is false.

What the linguistic facts determine is what a sentence says, what proposition it expresses, and in learning a language one comes to be able to understand each of its sentences, and thus to be able to know, for each one, what proposition it expresses. However, the linguistic facts cannot determine whether the proposition, which a given sentence expresses, is true or false. It is a purely conventional and contingent matter that the series of marks 'everything is self-identical' states the law of self-identity, but what is stated is neither conventional nor contingent. No changes in linguistic facts or conventions could make the law of self-identity false, though of course we could easily imagine other conventions, in the light of which the series of marks just quoted would not state the law of self-identity. We sometimes say that sentences like 'All bachelors are unmarried men' are true by definition, and perhaps this implies that they are true in virtue of conventional linguistic facts. But this is false. What is true is that it is a linguistic and conventional fact that the mark or noise 'bachelor' has the same meaning as the mark or noise 'unmarried man' (to make the usual oversimplification). Hence it is a conventional and linguistic fact that 'All bachelors are unmarried men' is synonymous with 'All unmarried men are unmarried men'. But it is not the linguistics facts that make the latter true, so these facts do not make the former true either. The linguistic facts may ensure that a sentence states something, where that something is true, but they cannot in general be held responsible for the truth of what is stated.

It is hard to resist the belief that there is some connection between mastering a language and putting oneself in a position to know *a priori* truths. But the explanation under consideration fails to identify this connection. Let us look now at the details of Russell's later account, in the hope of finding a better explanation of the same general kind.

In 'Is Mathematics Purely Linguistic?' Russell appears to mean by a 'linguistic proposition' one which is made true by the nature of language. There are claimed to be two kinds: 'those that depend upon vocabulary and those that depend upon syntax' (*EA* 299), the dependence being dependence for truth. As an example of a linguistic proposition of the first kind he gives 'Napoleon is Bonaparte', on the grounds that this means either 'Napoleon had another name, to wit, "Bonaparte"', or 'There was a man who had two names, to wit, "Napoleon" and "Bonaparte"'. It cannot mean both, since the two do not mean the same as each other for a reason that Russell himself gives: the first supposed synonym mentions Napoleon, but the second does not. In my view, 'Napoleon is Bonaparte' means neither of the things Russell suggests. The reason is that this sentence is a necessary truth, whereas Russell's proposed analyses are both contingent truths.

Even if this criticism is set aside, the idea that the original identity statement is linguistic is suspect. The translations are supposed to show that it is linguistic on the grounds, one presumes, that being a name of Napoleon is a linguistic property of the symbol 'Napoleon'. But, by the same token, being true of Napoleon could as sensibly be taken to be a linguistic property of the symbol 'was a great general', and the distinction between sentences true in virtue of vocabulary and those not thus true lapses.

This point can be put in another way. The mark of being a linguistic proposition, one might suggest, is having a translation into a sentence in which a piece of language is mentioned – into a 'metalinguistic' sentence, as I shall call it. Presumably, it is only in virtue of the supposed existence of such translations that 'Napoleon is Bonaparte' is said to be linguistic. However, by this test, any sentence comes out as linguistic. This is thanks to the use of 'disquotational' devices like '. . . names ———', '. . . denotes ———', '. . . is true'. We could as well 'translate' 'Napoleon was the First Emperor of France' by the metalinguistic 'Napoleon is denoted by "the First Emperor of France"'; or, in general, 'translate' any sentence *s* by the metalinguistic ' "*s*" is true'. As I have said, I do not think these are correct translations. But my present point is that even if they were, the criterion of translatability by a metalinguistic sentence will not demarcate two non-empty classes, one containing 'linguistic', the other 'non-linguistic' sentences.

As an example of a linguistic proposition that depends upon syntax, Russell gives 'unmarried women are unmarried'. 'Syntax-word' means 'logical constant', and syntax comprises the meaning of logical constants, and the semantic roles of concatenation and pattern of occurrence of extra-logical expressions. Syntax alone, says Russell, makes the quoted sentence true, and in this respect it is akin to mathematical and logical propositions (*EA* 299).

I have earlier given a general argument for thinking that though facts about meaning determine what a sentence says, they cannot make what a sentence says true (unless, of course, the sentence happens explicitly to state some linguistic fact). Can a counter-argument be found in Russell? I fear there is no argument, merely assertion, for example:

> Everyone would agree that the statement . . . 'no old maids are married', is a linguistic statement (*EA* 298).

And later:

> If I say 'Socrates was wise or not wise' I say something which requires no knowledge of history; its truth follows from the meaning of words (*EA* 203).

However, there *is* an argument for the claim that logical propositions are linguistic and non-logical propositions are not. The negative part of the claim is argued first, and the conclusion, with which I agree, is that it is not in general true that 'p' means the same as ' "p" is true':

> A man who knows no English can see that a dog is brown, but does not know that the sentence 'that is a brown dog' is true; on the other hand, he may hear an Englishman of high moral character pronouncing the words 'that dog is brown', and will conclude that the sentence is true without knowing what it means (*EA* 300).

This argument is impeccable. It is the, admittedly hesitant, claim that logical propositions *are* metalinguistic that is dubious, and indeed I cannot understand how Russell came to make it:

> When words such as 'or' and 'not' come in, it is always necessary to bring in 'truth'. . . . Take such a statement as 'it is not raining'. This has not the direct application to fact that belongs to 'it is raining'. When we say 'it is not raining', the proposition 'it is raining' is first considered, and then rejected. 'Not-p' may be defined as ' "p" is false'; it is, in fact, a statement about p in quotes. When we assert 'p or not-p', the 'or' must connect two propositions having (so to speak) the same syntactical status, therefore the 'p' also must be replaced by ' "p" is true'. Thus the correct way to state the law of excluded middle becomes: ' "p" is true or "p" is

false'. . . . If the above is accepted, it is obvious that the law of excluded middle is purely verbal; it is a definition of 'false' or 'not' according to taste (*EA* 304).

I have quoted at length because it is hard to understand how Russell failed to see that this point is open to the very objection he has earlier made to identifying the meaning of '*p*' with that of ' "*p*" is true'. A man may know that that dog is *not* brown but, as he speaks no English, may fail to know that the sentence 'that dog is brown' is false. Likewise, he may know that the sentence is false, thanks to hearing an Englishman of high moral character pronounce it, without knowing what it means, and so, perhaps, without knowing that the dog is not brown. This point seems to me entirely decisive against Russell's claim that logical propositions are metalinguistic.

But even setting aside this objection, there is clearly something wrong with the whole structure of the argument. If it established anything, it would establish that every sentence containing a logical constant is metalinguistic, but since plenty of these are obviously not knowable *a priori*, we would be unable to use the supposed fact that a certain proposition is metalinguistic to explain the possibility of our knowing it *a priori*. Russell arrives at the view that logical truths, like the law of excluded middle, are linguistic only by counting as linguistic an endless number of truths which are not knowable *a priori*.

Yet even if all this is set aside, it still would not follow from the fact that the law of excluded middle makes the metalinguistic assertion Russell claims, that it is made true by linguistic facts: ' "*p*" is true or "*p*" is false' is, given Russell's logic, made true by whatever makes '*p* or not-*p*' true, and that, as we have seen, cannot be the meanings of words.

Thus I can find nothing of value in Russell's later attempt to explain *a priori* knowledge, or rather, to explain that sub-class of it constituted by our knowledge of logic and mathematics. On the other hand, two points must be borne in mind. The first is that Russell did not publish this later essay, and so presumably he thought it unfit for publication. It is not fair to make an adverse judgment of a philosopher's worth on the basis of papers he has deliberately refrained from publishing. The second point is that there is, so far as I know, no glimmer of the kind of explanation we seek to be found elsewhere. When Russell said in *PP* that the phenomenon of *a priori* knowledge requires us to admit a non-sensory cognitive faculty he was surely right. What we need, but lack, is an account of the location of this ability within the framework of our other abilities, of perception, language-use and reasoning.

VII

Ontology

This chapter contains discussion of various issues that Russell counted as ontological.

There is a section on facts, for in *PLA* Russell suggested that the most important task for philosophical logic was to determine what forms of fact there are. The issue is perhaps miscalled 'ontological', for it amounts to the question of what language is minimally adequate to describe the world. Russell maintains, in contrast to Wittgenstein of the *Tractatus*, that in addition to atomic facts there are probably negative facts, certainly general facts, and, he sometimes thinks, possibly in addition facts 'with more than one verb', that is, facts involving propositional attitudes.

There is a section on pluralism, for Russell holds that his break with idealism came with his realization that there is more than one entity in the world (*MPD* 54). The issue is connected with the 'doctrine of external relations' and the question of the propriety of philosophical analysis.

The remaining sections concern Russell's logical constructions in non-mathematical areas. The motivation is epistemological: the constructions correspond not to the whole of what they replace, but merely to the parts that can be known, and thus purport to offer an epistemologically safer world view. Horizontal inferences replace vertical ones. If the argument of the last chapter is correct, this motivation is misguided, but Russell's constructions have an interest that is independent of their motivation.

1   Facts

'The world contains facts' (*PLA* 182), and they are just as much part of the world as are tables and chairs (*PLA* 183). That facts exist is one of those 'truisms . . . so obvious that it is almost laughable to mention them' (*PLA* 182).

> I think one might describe philosophical logic, the philosophical portion of logic which is the portion I am concerned with in these lectures . . . , as an inventory, or if you like a more humble word, a 'zoo', containing all the different forms that facts may have (*PLA* 216).

Facts are what make propositions true, if they are true, or false, if they are false. They contain things as constituents, but they differ from things in that they cannot be named, but can only be asserted, whereas things cannot be asserted, but can only be named (*PLA* 187–8, 200). A name corresponds to an object in just one way, whereas a proposition may correspond to a fact in two ways: the way in which the fact makes the proposition true, and the way in which the fact makes the proposition false.

Though the existence of facts seemed truistic, Russell thought that what forms of fact there are required argument. In the purest atomistic vision, represented by Wittgenstein's *Tractatus*, there are only atomic facts. By contrast, though Russell in *PLA* denies conditional, conjunctive and disjunctive facts, he admits general facts with certainty, and also, though with some hesitation, negative facts and 'facts with more than one verb'. We must try to extract a principle of existence for facts, which will generate Russell's position.

Russell gives as his reason for asserting the existence of general facts that 'You cannot ever arrive at a general fact by inference from particular facts, however numerous' (*PLA* 235). The first point to raise is how one is supposed to distinguish between particular and general facts. For example, should we say, and if so on what ground, that the fact that $(\forall x)(\text{place } x \rightarrow \text{is-at } (\text{God}, x))$ is a general fact, but the fact that (ubiquitous (God)) is particular? The natural answer to attribute to Russell, though he is not explicit, is that to each truth expressed by a sentence in the perfect language containing a quantifier there corresponds a general fact, and to each truth expressed by a sentence in the perfect language which does not contain a quantifier there corresponds a particular fact. The idea can be generalized: conditional, conjunctive, negative and disjunctive facts are what correspond to conditional, conjunctive, negative and disjunctive truths in the perfect language.

However, this must be regarded as only a preliminary characterization, since Russell held that there are not really any conditional, conjunctive, or disjunctive facts. We could put it this way: the existence of a truth of a certain form in the ideal language establishes that there is, in an ontologically weak sense, a fact of that form, but leaves open the question of whether this fact is a *genuine* entity. Hence we can identify facts of certain forms by reference to the ideal language, and then go on to ask, of these facts, whether they are genuine entities. What makes a fact genuine?

The following accords well with some of the things Russell wants to say: a fact stated by a true PL-sentence '*p*' is genuine iff there is no non-empty set *X* of true PL-sentences, each shorter than '*p*', such that *X* entails '*p*'. (For this purpose one needs to stipulate that one PL-sentence is shorter than another iff the first contains fewer symbols than the second, where parentheses are not counted as symbols, and each name and simple predicate counts as a single symbol.) This principle has the desired consequence of making all atomic facts genuine, on the assumption that no atomic sentence whose predicate is of degree *n* is entailed by a set of atomic sentences, each of whose predicates is of a degree less than *n*. (Russell's doctrine of external relations, discussed in the next section, maintains that at least some atomic sentences of degree 2 are not entailed by sets of monadic atomic sentences.) The principle also makes each disjunctive fact that $p \vee q$ non-genuine, since either $\{p\}$ or $\{q\}$ will be a non-empty set of true sentences, each shorter than '$p \vee q$', and such that it entails '$p \vee q$'; it makes each conjunctive fact that $p \And q$ non-genuine, since $\{p, q\}$ will be a non-empty set of true sentences, each shorter than '$p \And q$', and such that it entails '$p \And q$'; and it makes each conditional fact that $p \rightarrow q$ non-genuine, since either $\{\sim p\}$ or $\{q\}$ will be a non-empty set of true sentences, each shorter than '$p \rightarrow q$', and such that it entails '$p \rightarrow q$'.

Russell claims that general facts are genuine, on the ground that they are not entailed by any collection of particular facts. Thus in *PLA* (235) he argues that even if *A* and *B* and *C* are all the men there are, the fact that *A* is mortal, together with the fact that *B* is mortal and the fact that *C* is mortal, does not add up to the fact that all men are mortal. To extract the general conclusion, one would have to add to the premises the fact that *A* and *B* and *C* are all the men there are; but this is a general fact.

It is surely correct to claim at least that there are some genuine general facts. Notice that even if it is a necessary truth that everything is identical with a_1 or a_2 . . . or a_n, this does not show that $\{Fa_1, Fa_2, \ldots Fa_n\}$ entails '$(\forall x)Fx$'. For '*p*' entails '*q*' iff it is knowable *a priori* that, necessarily, if '*p*' is true so is '*q*'. Thus for a complete set of particular truths to entail the corresponding generalization it would have to be knowable *a priori* that the set is complete, and this is not generally possible.

However, it is sometimes possible, as Pears has pointed out (*Bertrand Russell* 263). The generalization 'All the Seven Sages of antiquity were born within a thousand miles of Athens' is entailed by the set of singular propositions affirming, of each sage by name, that he was born within a thousand miles of Athens, for it is knowable *a priori* (we may reasonably assume) that these are all the sages. However, as Pears says, this is a rare kind of exception, and it does not impugn Russell's claim that there are *genuine* general facts.

One way in which Russell tries to illustrate this last claim is by considering what counts as a complete description of the world. If you fail to state at least some general fact, he suggests, you fail to give a complete description:

> When you have enumerated all the atomic facts in the world, it is a further fact about the world that those are all the atomic facts there are about the world, and that is just as much an objective fact about the world as any of them are. It is clear, I think, that you must admit general facts as distinct from and over and above particular facts (*PLA* 236).

Ayer takes Russell to task on this issue. He makes the indisputable point that a list does not fail to be complete through not having been said to be complete, and then goes on to say that 'if you were able to list every atomic fact, you would have given a complete description of the world' (*Russell and Moore* 91). However, this last claim is not established by the first. If the world contains general facts, the list is incomplete if it does not list them. Russell's complaint is not that the list fails to say of itself that it is complete, but that it is not complete.

Russell's standard of completeness seems to be that a complete description of the world must entail every truth, and by this standard a list of all the atomic facts is not a complete description. We could envisage other standards of completeness, but Russell's seems entirely reasonable, and Ayer has neither offered an alternative, nor shown that Russell's is improper.

In addition to general facts, Russell argues, somewhat more tentatively, for the existence of genuine negative facts. The argument partly consists in the claim that negative facts are needed to make non-negative propositions false, and negative propositions true (*PLA* 211ff.). What could make the false proposition that Socrates is alive false, unless the negative fact that Socrates is not alive? And what could make the true proposition that Socrates is not alive true, unless just this negative fact? However, this sort of consideration is unconvincing: the fact that Socrates is dead will do both jobs, yet it does not *appear* to be negative.

If 'p' is non-atomic, any sentence of the form '$\sim p$' is equivalent to some sentence not of this form. So if a negative fact is to correspond to a negative sentence in the perfect language, it is plain that we would not be compelled to recognize negative facts expressed by negations of non-atomic sentences. Here we rely not on the original principle, but on the idea that we recognize as few forms of fact as possible. The supposed fact corresponding to the true negation of a non-atomic sentence will reduce either to a positive general fact (and such facts have already been admitted as genuine) or else to atomic facts. Hence the question of whether there are any negative facts reduces to the question of whether there are genuine facts corresponding to true negations of atomic sentences (for short, 'true atomic negations').

Negative facts would be shown to be non-genuine, according to our original principle, if the perfect language contains, for each simple predicate, its simple contradictory. Then negative sentences would not be required in a complete description of the world. This is the possibility which Russell takes Demos to have urged (*PLA* 212), but Russell himself rejects it. His argument is not easy to follow, but he appears to offer two explicit reasons for the rejection: that allowance has not been made for the application of negation to predicates of degree higher than one, and that negation is required to apply not just to predicates but also to whole sentences (*PLA* 212). However, both these points are unsound. For every predicate of degree n, '$F\zeta_1, \ldots \zeta_n$', we could introduce a simple predicate stipulated to mean the same as, or at least be necessarily equivalent to, '$\sim F\zeta_1, \ldots \zeta_n$'. Since for atomic negations there is no distinguishing the case in which the predicate is negated from the case in which the whole atomic sentence is negated, any atomic negation is equivalent to the result of deleting the negation sign and replacing the predicate by its simple contradictory. In the case of non-atomic negations, there are well-known ways of finding, for any such sentence, an equivalent in which the negation sign is applied only to atomic sentences (this assumes that the language contains universal and existential quantifiers and both 'v' and '&'). Hence the negation sign could be eliminated from every sentence, provided every predicate has a simple contradictory.

Russell's true reason for rejecting negative facts seems to be that he is unwilling to allow that, in a perfect language, there will be a simple contradictory of every simple predicate. This emerges in the exchange after the third lecture (*PLA* 215):

Question: Do you consider that the proposition 'Socrates is dead' is a positive or a negative fact?
Mr Russell: It is partly a negative fact. To say that a person is dead is complicated. It is two statements rolled into one: 'Socrates was alive' and 'Socrates is not alive'.

Question: Does putting the 'not' into it give it a formal character of negative and vice versa?

Mr Russell: No, I think you must go into the meaning of words.

The reason that one must go into the meaning of words is, I am inclined to think, that Russell is simply presupposing that a simple predicate may be analysed in a way that involves the negation sign. Since analysis in terms of negation is permissible, and since the perfect language contains no analysable predicates, it will not contain the simple contradictory of any predicate it contains. Thus the quoted passage may be interpreted as turning on the point that 'is dead' is analysable into 'is not alive', and so is not a predicate that would appear in a perfect language. Hence the fact that Socrates is dead is in reality a (partly) negative fact. Thus the reduction of negative facts that could be effected by having, for each predicate, its simple contradictory, is rejected on the grounds that this would involve a redundancy of vocabulary which would not obtain in a perfect language.

However, one should not conclude from this that every true atomic negation in the perfect language corresponds to a genuine negative fact. For example the truth of '~red (this)' will not, according to our principle, generate a genuine negative fact, since it is entailed by the shorter '(white (this))', and, as we have seen, Russell appears to allow that both predicates will occur in the perfect language. Perhaps his tentativeness about negative facts in *PLA* may be in part explained by the fact that until one has the vocabulary of the perfect language clearly fixed in one's mind, one cannot give any definite examples of negative facts.

Much later, in *HK*, Russell firmly rejects negative facts:

If the sun is shining, the statement 'the sun is shining' describes a fact which takes place independently of the statement. But if the sun is not shining, there is not a fact *sun-not-shining* which is affirmed by the true statement 'the sun is not shining' (*HK* 520).

He gives no reason for this view, and generalizes it to the conclusion that 'not' is not required for a complete description of the world. Plainly he is no longer following the principle that I attributed to him in *PLA*, but as his discussion is brief, there would be a large element of speculation in working out an alternative principle.

The principle concerning genuine facts that I attribute to the Russell of *PLA* does not square with everything he there says. For example, he says 'it is not so difficult to admit what I might call existence-facts – such facts as "There are men", "There are sheep", and so on' (*PLA* 236). Yet these are entailed by shorter truths. None the less, I cannot think of any principle other than the one I offered which is a closer fit with what he says. For example, if instead of entailment one puts necessary equivalence, disjunctive facts will become genuine, since some disjunctive sentences are not equivalent to any shorter sentence. I am therefore inclined to regard Russell's apparent inclusion of existence-facts among the genuine facts as a mistake.

The last item in Russell's *PLA* inventory of facts is the category of facts with more than one verb, that is, facts whose expression in English requires verbs of propositional attitude like 'believes', 'hopes', 'wonders whether', and so on. I shall consider just the case of belief.

There are two questions about belief. One is: is the fact that *A* believes that *p* a *sui generis* form of fact, or is it of a form we have already discussed? The other is: is it a genuine fact? If it is *sui generis* it is genuine, but if it is expressible in the perfect language it may or may not be genuine, depending on whether it is atomic or general, in which case it is genuine; or disjunctive, conjunctive or conditional, in which case it is not genuine.

Russell's earliest theory is in *PP*, where he holds a view that entails that belief facts are not *sui generis*, but they are genuine. The reason is simply that they are atomic. Thus 'Othello believes that Cassio loves Desdemona' is analysed as the concatenation of the four-place predicate 'believes' with the terms 'Othello', 'Desdemona', 'loves' and 'Cassio', in that order (*PP* 73). (We have to assume, for the purposes of the example, that the names are logically proper.)

In *PLA*, Russell rejects this early theory. He says that it was 'a little unduly simple' of him to have treated the verb 'loves' on a par with the names 'Desdemona' and 'Cassio' (*PLA* 226):

> When A believes that B loves C, you have to put a verb in the place where 'loves' occurs. You cannot put a substantive in its place.
> Therefore it is clear that the subordinate verb (the verb other than believing) is functioning as a verb (*PLA* 225).

The point is surely correct. By way of contrast, consider a sentence like 'Love is better than hate'. Here 'love' occurs as a substantive and not predicatively, so that other substantives like 'justice' can replace it *salva congruitate*, whereas expressions like 'loved', which are fit only for predicative occurrences, cannot. However, it is unclear why the point should have made Russell think that the *PP* analysis was incorrect. In some ways it would have been in keeping with the spirit of his philosophy to dismiss the point as one concerning superficial grammar. In the logical form, he might have replied, 'loves' has substantive role, despite the misleading suggestions of grammatical form. He is prevented from taking this course in *PLA* by his doctrine that 'a verb . . . cannot occur otherwise than as a verb' (*PLA* 225; see Chapter II above).

Russell's criticism in *PLA* of the *PP* theory of belief is confused also with the old problem about the unity of the proposition, for he holds that the fundamental puzzle is how there can be *false* belief (*PLA* 225). All that is required to disperse this problem, in this form, is the distinction between whether a verb occurs predicatively, and whether it 'really relates' its terms.

We have already seen that the *PP* theory of belief is defective in that it makes all belief relational, and all occurrences of names in the believed-sentence transparent (see page 64 above). A further difficulty is that it is hard to see how the theory is to be extended to cases in which the believed-sentence is non-atomic. In *PLA* he offers no positive theory of belief, taking beliefs as a new species of genuine facts *sui generis*. However, in his next major discussion of the topic, he offers a suggestion which might repair the present defect in the *PP* account. The difference between 'Othello believes that Desdemona loves Cassio' and 'Othello believes that Desdemona does not love Cassio' can be expressed, Russell suggests, as a different relation among the same terms, rather than as the same relation among different terms. Then we would have as it were a relation of positive belief, exemplified in the first case, and a relation of negative belief, exemplified in the second (*OP* 311). However, it is easy to see that this cannot be the general form of a solution to the problem, since there will need to be as many different belief-relations as there are forms of sentence capable of expressing the content of a belief. But the number of such forms is infinite. Hence we cannot overcome the problem by introducing into the ideal language a fresh primitive belief-predicate corresponding to each of these forms, for, as we have seen, claims about the ideal language become trivial unless only finitely many primitives are permitted.

In *OP* Russell gives a further reason which, he claims, shows the inadequacy of the *PP* account: it wrongly accepts the subject (307). That is, the *PP* account assumes that believers are genuine entities as opposed to logical constructions. But why should this render the *PP* account incorrect? Admittedly, a sentence like 'Othello believes that Desdemona loves Cassio' cannot be taken seriously as an example of a fully analysed sentence, since the various personal 'names' will be abbreviations of descriptions, and analysis unpacks abbreviations. None the less, it might be argued, the essence of the *PP* account is that the belief-relation is just a relation like any other, and this essence survives the complexity of the subject. The belief-predicate will still be just that, i.e. a predicate (though presumably a multigrade one), and the only difference is that whereas in the *PP* account its gaps were supposedly filled by names, now they will be filled by the variables involved in the descriptions those 'names' abbreviate.

Why, then, did Russell suppose that the rejection of the subject entails the rejection of the *PP* account? The explanation seems to be that in his neutral monistic period, which *OP* inaugurates, he aims to construct the self out of such entities as beliefs. If these essentially involve a relation to a self, simple or complex, they cannot without circularity be used in the construction of the self. The alternative provided in *OP* has something in common with the *PP* account, in that it refuses to take at face value the idea that belief-sentences 'have more than one verb'. The changes concern the terms of the belief-relation. Instead of the subject we have a feeling of assent, and instead of the constituents of the proposition expressed by the believed-sentence we have their corresponding images. From our present point of view, the success of the *OP* analysis would have the same effect as the success of the *PP* one: beliefs would cease to form a *sui generis* kind of fact, but they would be genuine, because atomic, facts. The general point is that if belief-facts are analysable, their analyses will belong to one of the species of fact already considered: for, in Russell's view, the language of analysis has *PM*-syntax.

To complete the historical record of Russell's attempt to analyse belief-sentences we must mention the account in PM_2 and that in *IMT*.

In Appendix C of PM_2 Russell develops what he believes to be a generally Wittgensteinian account of belief. The inspiration comes from the *Tractatus*, 5.54:

> But it is clear that 'A believes that *p*', 'A thinks *p*', 'A says *p*', are of the form ' "*p*" says *p*'.

In *PM* Russell starts by introducing the notion of a thought, satisfying the condition that a thought of *x* means *x*, and thoughts are partitioned into classes alike in meaning (*PM* 662). A relation *P* of belief-predication is introduced, to hold between a pair of thoughts iff what the first thought means is believed to possess what the second thought means. Then 'A believes that Socrates is Greek' is analysed as: 'There is an *x* and a *y* such that *x* belongs to the thought-class Socrates and *y* belongs to the thought-class Greek and *x* is *P*-related to *y* and both *x* and *y* belong to *A*'.

The similarity between this account and that of the *Tractatus* is unclear. On one reading, the relevant thought-class is specified by reference to Socrates, in which case the only resemblance between Russell's theory and Wittgenstein's is that both share the Fregean feature that expressions occurring in a believed-sentence have an extraordinary sense. For Russell, 'Socrates' normally means Socrates (assuming it is a genuine name), but, on the present reading, when 'Socrates' occurs in a believed-sentence it means the class of thoughts which mean Socrates. For Wittgenstein, a believed-sentence, instead of having its ordinary sense, means itself or the proposition it expresses. However, there is another reading of Russell which brings him closer to Wittgenstein. Perhaps the relevant thought-class is specified not by reference to Socrates but by reference to 'Socrates'. In this case, his view shares with Wittgenstein the position that in a believed-sentence some expressions are mentioned rather than used. However, there is still a divergence. For one thing, in Wittgenstein, but not in Russell, this goes for all the expressions. (On Russell's analysis 'is' is used, though in an extraordinary sense.) For another thing, in Wittgenstein the believed-sentence is simply mentioned, whereas in Russell parts of it are mentioned in the service of picking out thought-classes.

This account leaves room for the opacity of names as they occur in believed-sentences. (Later in this discussion, Russell introduces the word 'transparent', in much the sense later taken up by Quine.) For we could say that if Socrates had another name, say 'a', this would be associated with a thought-class different from that associated with 'Socrates', so that there would be no inference to 'A believes that a is Greek'. However, it is not clear that Russell wishes to exploit this possibility. He says that one relevant thought 'means' Socrates, and as a thought-class is a class of thoughts alike in meaning, he perhaps would be tempted to the view that the thought associated with 'a' likewise means Socrates, and then he would be landed with the unwanted inference.

The account is defective for a reason which will by now be familiar. Every distinct form of believed-sentence will require a fresh primitive predicate, analogous to 'P'. But there are infinitely many forms of sentence which may be believed-sentences. Hence there would have to be infinitely many fresh primitive predicates. But this cannot be permitted by any satisfactory analysis.

Finally, I consider the IMT theory, in which Russell rejects the view, which he takes himself to have held in PM_2, that we should say 'A believes "p"' rather than 'A believes p', and advances a theory with a more behaviouristic cast.

> Let us put for 'p' the sentence 'B is hot'. When we say that A believes that B is hot, we are saying (roughly) that A is in a state which will lead him, if he speaks, to say 'B is hot' or something having the same significance. We are not saying that these words are in A's mind; he may be a Frenchman who, if he spoke, would

say '*B a chaud*'. We are, in fact, saying nothing about the *words* 'B is hot', but only about what they signify. Therefore there should be no inverted commas, and we should say: 'A believes *p*' (*IMT* 255).

This passage is unconvincing, since it is apparently inconsistent. On the positive part of the theory, we are saying something about the words '*B* is hot' when we say that *A* believes that *B* is hot. What we are saying is that *A* is disposed to utter some synonym of these words. Yet Russell explicitly denies that we are saying anything about words. The trouble is that we have to mention words, if we are to specify what those words signify (at least if the specification is to have the slightest chance of occurring in the analysis of belief).

The apparent contradiction could no doubt be dissolved in various ways as issuing from careless formulation. What then of the positive theory that the analysis of '*A* believes *p*' is, roughly, '*A* is disposed to utter some synonym of "*p*"'? I take it that the roughness lies in the specification of the relevant behaviour, and that it is part of the essence of the analysis that belief consists in a relation of some kind between a person and a sentence. If so, the analysis is fundamentally faulty. The reason is that if I understand '*A* believes that *p*' I know what *A* is said to believe. But I may not know this if I understand '*A* is related in such-and-such a way to "*p*"'. Hence the analysis does not mean the same as the analysandum. Furthermore, a man may surely have a belief, yet not be disposed to give voice to it, even under torture.

Shortly afterwards (*IMT* 256–7) Russell gestures towards an account of belief in terms of actual physical occurrences. It seems impossible that any such account could match belief-sentences with sentences capable of serving even roughly the same communicative purposes. But Russell's gesture is so slight that it would be inappropriate to argue weightily against it.

To sum up: except in *PLA*, Russell believes that belief-facts are not a form *sui generis*, needing to be added to the inventory of atomic, negative and general facts. The *PP* account, in making belief facts atomic, also makes them 'genuine'. In the other accounts, they are perhaps molecular, and so not genuine, or perhaps, as explicitly in PM_2, general, and thus genuine.

I have followed Russell's *PLA* line of treating these issues as ontological, as the question of what forms of fact there are. However, it must by now be apparent that there is something spurious about this procedure.

There is indeed a non-spurious ontological question, though one I cannot believe to be of great moment: are there facts? Russell's *PLA* answer to this question is surely correct: that there are facts is truistic.

For it is truistic that some sentences like 'There is an important fact which you have overlooked' are true. What is controversial is whether facts are 'nothing but' truths, and whether the notion of a fact can help to explain the notion of truth.

The main burden of Russell's discussion, as followed in this section, can only spuriously be regarded as ontological. For it concerns questions about the logical relations between general sentences and belief-sentences on the one hand, and, on the other hand, sentences of other logical forms. If Russell's premise, that what sorts of fact exist is to be measured by what forms of sentence in the ideal language would be required for a complete description of the world, is accepted, these questions do indeed take on an ontological turn. However, by the same token, just about any philosophical question could be seen as ontological, and this is why it seems to be spurious to use this classification in the present connection. I shall have similar remarks to make at the end of the next section. In the third and subsequent sections I turn to what I conceive to be ontological questions proper.

2 Internal relations and pluralism

The doctrine of pluralism, that there are many things, must seem to us extremely banal, yet according to Russell its adoption was a turning point in his philosophical career, marking the rejection of the idealism with which he had been infected during his undergraduate years at Cambridge (*MPD* 54–5). In the hands of Bradley, this idealism incorporated the monistic doctrine that 'in the end' there is only one thing, the Absolute. In the present climate, it is not easy to make this debate seem a living issue. However, Russell took the doctrine of pluralism to be connected with other doctrines which require discussion in virtue of the interest and importance which Russell and others have claimed attach to them. Of these I shall mention three: the doctrine of internal relations, the distinction between essence and accident, and the propriety of the method of analysis.

Russell states the doctrine or axiom of internal relations as follows: 'Every relation is grounded in the natures of the related terms' (*PE* 139). It would perhaps be better known as the view that relations are reducible, for Russell makes it plain that the axiom is vindicated iff every relational fact can be shown to amount either to two facts, one concerning simply the one of the apparently related terms, the other concerning simply the other, or else to a non-relational fact concerning the two apparently related terms taken as a whole. The first type of reduction he calls 'monadistic' (*PofM* 221), the second 'monistic' (*PofM* 221). The denial of the axiom of internal relations he calls the axiom or doctrine of external relations, and this last is the position for which he argues on a large number of occasions (*PofM* 221–6, 447–9; *PE* 139ff.; *OKEW* ch 2; *LA* 333–9; he had earlier held a monadistic theory, according to *PofM* 223*n*).

Russell claims that the doctrine of internal relations is equivalent to monism (*PE* 142). Certainly, if there is only one thing, relations will be reducible to monadic properties, for relational expressions like 'ζ loves ζ' will be equivalent to non-relational ones like 'ζ self-loves'. (In terms of model-theory, any expression of the form 'φxy' will receive the same interpretation as the corresponding expression of the form 'φxx', so long as we consider only interpretations over single element domains.) The converse implication is trickier. In *PE* Russell seems to argue that since difference is an irreducible relation, if the doctrine of internal relations is true there can be no such thing as difference and hence at most one thing in the world. But this looks a somewhat back-handed proof: for if difference is irreducible and if the doctrine of internal relations is the claim that no relations are irreducible, then the doctrine is false, and Russell perhaps relies on the point, here as elsewhere (*PE* 144), that a falsehood materially implies everything. However, this clearly does nothing to establish the necessary equivalence of monism and the doctrine of internal relations.

In his work on *LA* (333) Russell admits obscurities in his earlier views on relations, and there he makes it plain that what is required for his position is the existence not merely of some irreducibly relational propositions, but of some irreducibly relational *truths*. This improves the argument for the equivalence of monism and the doctrine of internal relations. For if difference is irreducible, then, if the doctrine of internal relations is true, there are no *truths* asserting difference: hence there is at most one thing. Since the *LA* modification improves the *PE* account, let us imagine it incorporated into that account.

Before we can assess the position, we must understand what it would be to reduce a relational fact, or what appears to be a relational fact, to a non-relational one. Russell gives various examples at various times. The latest one in date (*MPD* 54) must, I think, be regarded as simply a mistake. He suggests that 'If A loves B, this relation exemplifies itself and may be said to consist in certain states of mind of A. Even an atheist must admit that a man can love God.' However, the inference from '*A* loves *B*' to 'There is something *A* loves' is surely valid. Hence *A*'s love for *B* cannot consist simply in his states of mind. The atheist should not admit that some men love God, but only that some men (falsely) believe they love God. Now an expression that possesses the features Russell seems to want is 'worship': the fact that the Greeks worshipped Zeus does not involve Zeus himself for there is no such thing, and we cannot validly infer that there is something which the Greeks worshipped. However, anyone who thought that all relational truths were like this truth about the Greeks would be mad. There would be no case for the doctrine of external relations to answer.

In *PofM* (223) he gives a more helpful example of a reducible relational truth. '*A* differs in colour from *B*', he seems to suggest, could be analysed as 'there is some colour which *A* has and *B* lacks', where this fact or facts is non-relational. The overall point he is making is that this tactic cannot be used in the case of asymmetric relations. For example, in trying to reduce '*A* is greater than *B*' we are faced by a dilemma: either we assign *A* and *B* suitable magnitudes, but then we are still left with the unreduced fact that the magnitude assigned to *A* is greater than that assigned to *B*; or else we start by saying that *A* differs from *B* in magnitude, but then there is no way of injecting the correct direction of asymmetry.

At one time (*OKEW* 58), Russell thought that identity and difference might be examples of reducible relations, and he suggests that this reducibility is bound up with their symmetry. Elsewhere he rejects this view. For example, in *PE* (141) he relies, as we have seen, on the irreducibility of difference in order to connect irreducibility with pluralism, and he argues for the needed premise as follows:

> If there really are two things, A and B, which are diverse, it is impossible to reduce this diversity wholly to adjectives of A and B. It will be necessary that A and B should have *different* adjectives, and the diversity of these adjectives cannot, on pain of endless regress, be interpreted as *meaning* that they in turn have different adjectives (*PE* 141).

This argument must seem surprising in the light of the definition of identity in *PM* (*13.01):

$$x=y =_{df} (\forall \varphi)(\varphi!x \rightarrow \varphi!y),$$

whereby identity seems to be reduced quite nicely. I think the *PE* argument is in fact fallacious. If *a* differs from *b* then by the *PM* account of identity *a* has some property which *b* lacks. Now having a property differs from lacking that property, but this fact is not part of what is *asserted* when it is asserted that *a* has some property which *b* lacks. Hence the analysis of '*a* differs from *b*' can properly terminate with '*a* has a property which *b* lacks', for the latter does not have the form of the former.

However, questions about reducibility, though these examples give some guide to their nature, cannot readily be decided until we have some reasonably precise account of what is involved in reducing a relation to something non-relational. The closest Russell comes to such an account is in *LA* (335):

> Given a relational propositional function '*xRy*', it is not in general the case that we can find predicates α, β, γ, such that, for all values of *x* and *y*, *xRy* is equivalent to $x\alpha$, $y\beta$, $(x, y)\gamma$ (where (x, y) stands for the whole consisting of *x* and *y*), or to any one or two of these. This, and this only, is what I mean to affirm when I assert the doctrine of external relations; and this, clearly, is at least part of what Mr. Bradley denies when he asserts the doctrine of internal relations.

On the face of it, we have here quite a different doctrine from the one about the irreducbility of relational truths; for only closed sentences can state truths, and propositional functions are not closed. So it is best, I think, to understand the variables in the quoted passage as schemata, the claim being that there are true sentences of the form *Rab* which are not equivalent to any conjunction of sentences of the form *Fa*, *Gb*, *H(ab)*.

Where are we allowed to look for such monadic predicates? If our attention is confined to English as it actually is, Russell's claim is surely correct, but thus understood it seems unimportant. If our attention is confined to Russell's perfect language, his claim again seems correct, but this time it is question-begging. The following example suggests why it is correct. Suppose there were a predicate '$F\zeta$' which means 'ζ loves Mary'. This enables the reduction of sentences of the form '*a* loves Mary' to monadic sentences. (If there are only finitely many names and predicates, this kind of reduction would be possible for every atomic relational sentence.) But '*F*', it could reasonably be said, is analysable, and thus not a predicate that will occur in the perfect language. So it seems that, understood in this way, Russell's claim is correct. But it begs the case against Bradley, who will certainly deny that Russell's perfect language correctly reveals the nature of reality.

Suppose, now, that there is no restriction save finitude on monadic predicates. Then, as mentioned parenthetically in the last paragraph, Russell's claim, as we are interpreting it, is false. So perhaps we should strengthen it to this: it is not the case that, for every sentence containing two or more terms, there is a necessary equivalent, in some language whose primitive predicates are finite in number, which contains at most one term. (Names and variables, and nothing else, are terms.) Surprisingly, this claim is false, at least if the envisaged sentences containing more than one term are first-order. This is a corollary of the technique described in Quine's paper

'Variables Explained Away': he shows how to eliminate variables from any sentence in favour of just six predicate-forming operators on predicates (a language with names would call for more predicate-forming operators in the reducing language). By halting Quine's process before the last step, we would have reduced every sentence in the first-order language to a sentence in the new language, having just the predicates of the old together with finitely many new operators, and in which there is at most one term. (The predicates, as they occur in the new language, can be regarded as monadic, regardless of their degree in the old language, since in the new language they never have more than one argument.)

So far, then, we have found no Russellian claim which is both true and appropriate to an attack on Bradley. Perhaps the cause is our taking an excessively syntactical view. What matters, it may be said, is not whether the sentences are relational, but whether or not the facts to which, if true, they correspond are relational. Relational facts will still be asserted in the non-relational language envisaged by Quine.

How shall we define a relational fact? The idea is plain: it is a fact which involves more than one thing (though statable by a sentence free of sentential connectives). We can see clearly the relationship to pluralism: iff there are relational facts in this sense monism is false. But it now becomes hard to see how there could be any serious philosophical dispute. However the notion of a fact involving more than one thing is made precise, it will be as plain as a pikestaff that there are such facts. If this is what the doctrine of external relations asserts, its opponent is surely a man of straw. So let us look at the principal official opponent, Mr Bradley. In *Appearance and Reality* (574–5) there occurs the following attempt to clarify a question, the negative answer to which constitutes the doctrine of internal relations:

Are terms altered necessarily by the relations into which they enter? In other words, are there any relations which are merely extrinsical? . . . I am asking whether, within the whole and subject to that, terms can enter into further relations and not be affected by them. And this question is not, Can A, B, and C become the terms of fresh relations, and still remain A, B and C? For clearly a thing may be altered partly and yet retain a certain character, and one and the same character may persist unaltered though the terms that possess it are in some other ways changed. . . . Further, our question does not ask if terms are in any sense whatever qualified by their relations. For everyone, I presume, admits this in some sense, however hard that sense may be to fix. The question I am putting is whether relations can qualify terms *A*, *B* and *C*, from the outside merely and without in any way affecting and altering them internally.

I think it would be forgivable to regard this as something other than the most successful example of philosophical clarification. However, one feature which Russell discovered in such expositions, and which we can perhaps detect in the first two sentences of the passage quoted, is the claim that all of a thing's relational properties are essential to it: if *Rab*, then necessarily *Rab*.

Russell imagines the following argument for this view:

> 'If A and B are related in a certain way', it may be said, 'you must admit that if they were not so related they would be other than they are, and that consequently there must be something in them which is essential to their being related as they are' (*PE* 143).

He rejects this argument as invalid, essentially on the correct grounds that whereas it is indeed impossible that (*Rab* & not-*Rab*), this does nothing to show that if *Rab* then (necessarily *Rab*).[1]

Here, then, we see another of the promised connections between the doctrine of pluralism and other doctrines. The connection is that Russell thought that pluralism was equivalent to the doctrine of external relations, and that one thing that is involved in this doctrine is the claim that some relational properties are non-essential. For, as we can see in the passage just quoted, he felt that if all relational properties are essential, there would have to be something in the nature of the terms themselves which makes this so, with the consequence that relational properties, or what appear to be such, are reducible to non-relational ones. As he puts it on the same page, characterizing the position he opposes:

> If two terms have a certain relation, they cannot but have it, and if they did not have it they would be different; which seems to show

---

[1] Colin Phillips has suggested that this account is overgenerous to Russell. The actual words are somewhat unclear:

> Now if two terms are related in a certain way, it follows that, if they were not so related, every imaginable consequence would ensue. For, if they are so related, the hypothesis that they are not so related is false, and from a false hypothesis anything can be deduced. Thus the above form of statement must be altered. We may say: 'If A and B are related in a certain way, then anything not so related must be other than A and B, hence, etc.' But this only proves that what is not related as A and B are must be *numerically* diverse from A or B; it will not prove difference of adjectives, unless we assume the axiom of internal relations. Hence the argument has only rhetorical force, and cannot prove its conclusion without a vicious circle (*PE* 143-4).

Russell's analysis can be usefully compared with Moore's in his 'External and Internal Relations'.

that there is something in the terms themselves which leads to their being related as they are.

Despite the cautious 'seems', Russell does not, as far as I know, explicitly reject the envisaged connection. However, it deserves rejection. If all relational properties were essential, this would show that part of what a 'term itself' is, is how it is related to other things.

The view that all relational properties are essential has a spurious connection with monism, and bringing this out may throw some light on the debate between Russell and Bradley. Since everything is related in some way or other to everything else, it would follow that if saying anything about anything involved stating that thing's essence, you could not say anything true without stating every truth. Russell attributes the consequent of this conditional to the monists, and seems to presuppose (*i*) the conditional's truth and (*ii*) that the truth of the antecedent would follow from the doctrine that everything is essentially related to everything else. Hence his feeling that he needed to deny the latter doctrine. But he should have denied the second presupposition. Since you do not have to state a thing's essence in order to refer to it, there is no valid route from the claim that all things are essentially interrelated to the claim that you cannot say anything true without stating every truth.

This leads to the last of the promised connections between pluralism and other doctrines, in this case Russell's belief in the propriety of the method of analysis. Analysis involves reducing complex truths to simpler truths, and complex things to simpler things. Unless the simple truths were really true, the method would be unsound, and according to the monists, nothing short of the whole truth is really true. Hence monism conflicts with the method of analysis. One can see why it was important for Russell to show that the monistic view was based on a mistake.

By way of summary I shall list various doctrines, most of which have already been considered, and simply note whether they are, in my view, obviously false, obviously true, or controversial.

On the question of whether relational properties are essential there seem to me to be two obviously false doctrines: one is that all relational properties are essential, the other is that none are. As a counter-example to the first, it is surely not a necessary truth that I was in London some time in July 1977, so this relational property is not part of my essence. As a counter-example to the second, I could not have been Margaret Thatcher. Difference is an example of a relation which, if it obtains, obtains essentially. Together with the fact that self-identity is essential, it follows quite uncontroversially that everything has some essential relation to everything. (When I say that these doctrines are obviously or uncontroversially false, I do not mean that they have never been seriously held, but only that this is how things seem to untutored intuition. In the grip of a theory, things may take on a different aspect. The first doctrine has been attributed to, for example, Leibniz, and the second to the positivists.)

On the question of whether relational sentences are irreducible, we have found no true version of this claim which could properly be used in dispute with Bradley.

On the question of whether there are genuinely relational facts, that is, facts involving the existence of more than one thing (though statable by sentences free of sentential connectives), it seems to me that the answer is obviously that there are. No less obviously, a fact involving the existence of more than one thing cannot be identified with any fact involving the existence of at most one thing. This is in a way on Russell's side, but in another way it tells against him: for it means that his arguments for this claim have been needless.

The issue has been largely a cloud of confusions. To the extent that there have been serious issues, they have not been ontological. Hence there is something spurious about regarding the issue of internal relations in Russell's way: as, *au fond*, ontological.

3 *Logical construction and ontological reduction*

Russell held that numbers, classes, the self, the physical world, space, time and events are not 'genuine entities' but rather 'logical constructions' or 'logical fictions'. In this section I offer a general account of Russell's conception of logical construction, and I try to make sense of the idea that constructions are not genuine entities. In subsequent sections I examine some of the constructions in detail.

I interpret Russell's constructions as designed not so much to recapture our everyday beliefs as to provide epistemologically superior alternatives to them. The alternatives are held to be close in overall import to what they replace, but to be free of the ontological extravagance which makes our unreformed beliefs incapable of achieving the status of knowledge. For example, Russell takes substances to be unknowable, so he replaces beliefs that involve the concept of substance by beliefs that involve, instead, the concept of series of events. The latter are offered as the closest knowable approach to the former.

Thus I interpret Russell as what I shall call a reformist, rather than as what I shall call a conservationist. The conservationist takes himself to be providing an account of the very things we have been talking about all along. He may require that we repudiate some of our beliefs, but the repudiated beliefs are beliefs about beliefs rather than beliefs about the entities with which the construction is concerned. By contrast, the reformist asks us to abandon the use of certain concepts in favour of others. Russell's ground for reform is that, supposedly, we have no evidence for the existence of objects answering to the old concepts, but ample evidence for the existence of objects answering to the new concepts. To take an example of the contrast as applied to phenomenalistic accounts of physical object sentences: the reformist sees our everyday use of these as requiring an ontology of sense-data-transcending physical objects. He advocates the abandonment of this talk in favour of talk of sets of sense-data, in terms of which we can recapture only the knowable component of our unreformed talk. By contrast, the conservationist claims that our ordinary talk, quite unreformed, requires an ontology merely of sense-data and classes of sense-data: nothing else need exist for what we ordinarily say to be true. However, we have, no doubt, wrongly supposed that the ontology of our ordinary talk is richer, requiring sense-data-transcending physical objects.

The reformist offers his constructions as substitutes for dubious entities. I shall call such constructions 'substitutional'.

In one paper written when the programme of logical construction was in its heyday, Russell shows clearly that his constructions are meant to be substitutional. One sign is found in the wording of the epistemological principle which motivates the enterprise: 'logical constructions are to be substituted for inferred entities' (*RSP* 115; cf. *LA* 326). The discussion reinforces the suggestion. The old sentences, aimed at speaking of the supposed inferred entities, are to be given 'a new and less doubtful interpretation' (*RSP* 116). This is plainly incompatible with conservationism.

Using the old sentences in a new sense can be confusing. I argue in the next chapter that Russell's construction of cardinal numbers as classes of classes is meant to be substitutional (pp. 299ff.). However, his informal gloss of the defined symbols of *PM*, and in particular his gloss of 'Nc' as 'is the cardinal number of' (*PM* II 4ff.), gives the impression that a certain provable *PM*-formula ('$(\exists x)(\exists y)\text{Nc}(x, y)$') says that there are cardinal numbers (in the *ordinary* sense of 'cardinal numbers'). But if the construction is substitutional, this cannot be so. Rather, classes of classes are offered as substitutes for cardinal numbers, and it is the existence of such classes that the formula mentioned must be taken to assert.

The account so far leaves at least two difficulties. One is: why should logical constructions be regarded as 'fictions' rather than as 'genuine entities' (as, e.g., in *PLA* 270ff.)? The other is: why should the theory of descriptions be seen as an application of the method of construction (as, e.g., in *LA* 327–8)? The only answers I can think of involve regarding Russell's distinction between genuine entities and fictions as a conflation of several different distinctions, not all of which sit happily with the implication that a fiction is ontologically inferior (whatever exactly that means) to a genuine entity.

(*i*) One suggestion is that the first problem is easily dispelled by dispelling the confusion that arises from using old sentences in a new sense. Thus, it may be suggested, when Russell says that physical objects are fictions he means, in his phenomenalistic phase, not that classes of sense-data are fictions, but that sense-data-transcending physical objects are fictions in that they cannot be known to exist.

The dominant line of Russell's thought runs counter to this suggestion. Consider, for example, the following passage:

> You find that a certain thing which has been set up as a metaphysical entity can either be assumed dogmatically to be real, and then you will have no possible argument either for its reality or against its reality; or, instead of doing that, you can construct a logical fiction having the same formal properties . . . that logical fiction can be substituted for your supposed metaphysical entity and will fulfil all the scientific purposes that anybody can desire (*PLA* 272).

This makes it plain that it is the new entity, the construction, which is held to be a fiction. But on what grounds?

(*ii*) One contrast, which explains the connection with the theory of descriptions, is that between those entities which, according to the realist theory of meaning, must exist for the language to be meaningful, and all other entities. In a logical construction a syntactic name (e.g., 'Snowdon') will be interpreted or reinterpreted as a description (e.g., 'the series of entities belonging to *this*', where 'this' denotes a suitable mountainous sense-datum; cf. *HK* 93). The result is that the existence of the denotation of the description is shown not to be required for the meaningfulness of the syntactic name. We might have thought that 'Snowdon' was a genuine name, so that the existence of English would entail the existence of Snowdon. But when we are persuaded that the expression is, or can be reinterpreted as, an abbreviated description, we see that our assumption was mistaken, or at any rate that there is no need to speak (unreformed) English.

This view packs more punch in its conservationist form. But even at its best it appears to offer no justification for regarding as fictional those entities not required for the meaningfulness of language. The denotation of a description must exist, if sentences in which it has primary occurrence are true. What is non-genuine about this existence?

(*iii*) Constructed entities are ontologically dependent on the elements of their construction, and the dependence is asymmetric: the constructions could not exist unless the elements did, but the elements could exist without the constructions existing. For the constructions are non-empty classes, and these very classes could not exist without their members. This makes constructions not particulars (in the sense Russell invokes in *PLA*): they are not simple, they are not independent, and thus they are not part of the ultimate furniture of the world.

Put like this, it is still hard to see why constructions are fictions. My father might have existed without me existing, but I could not exist without him having existed. This asymmetric relation of ontological dependence does not make me a fiction.

(*iv*) One might try to understand Russell's thought in terms of translation or of supervenience. Translation is discussed towards the end of the section. Supervenience does not require translation. For example, it is often held that nations are supervenient upon their nationals, even though there is no translating talk of nations into talk of individual nationals. The supervenience consists in this: once all the facts about the nationals are fixed, the facts about the nation are fixed.

I have not found the word 'supervenience' in Russell's writings, and I am not sure how the notion is to be analysed. On the face of it, a fictional entity is not an entity at all, whereas presumably supervenient entities *are* entities. So the notion does not promise to provide an explanation of Russell's treatment of constructions as fictions.

(*v*) We get closer to his thought if we recall that all Russell's constructions are classes. Admittedly, Russell regards classes as fictions, so that this seems to have brought us no nearer to an understanding of his position. However, for the special case of classes there is an account which makes sense of calling them fictions. For reasons which I shall set out in the next chapter (pp. 285–6 and 329–30), Russell takes a fundamentally anti-realist view of classes. That is, he regards their nature as in part determined by our abilities. (This needs some qualification, for the basic source of this anti-realism relates to properties, in terms of which Russell defines classes.) It is only in terms of this view of classes that one could hope to justify Russell's treatment of constructions as fictions.

I conclude this section by exploring the connection between construction and translation, a connection which some have seen as essential (e.g., Ayer, *Russell* 40). I shall consider two types of translational construction, and consider how they relate to Russell's substitutional constructions.

Let us say that *A*-type entities are *impure translational constructions* out of B-type entities iff every sentence containing a syntactic name denoting an A-type entity or a predicate capable of being true of an A-type entity is translated by some sentence containing no name of an A-type entity (though perhaps there are names of B-type entities) and no simple predicate capable of being true only of A-type entities (though containing predicates capable of being true of B-type entities). (I assume that we have to deal only with first-order sentences. I stipulate that a predicate 'F' is capable of being true of an A iff, holding meanings constant, it is possible that there be an A of which 'F' is true.) This is a very weak requirement, as can be seen from the fact that Russell's noumenalistic analysis requires physical objects to be impure translational constructions out of sense-data. Any predicate capable of holding only of physical objects, for example '. . . is a table', must, on this view, be analysed by some predicates which are capable of holding of sense-data. The 'impurity' of the translation consists in the fact that it allows some predicates in the B-translations of A-sentences to be capable of holding of A-type entities as well as of B-type entities. In Russell's noumenalistic analysis, one impure predicate is 'causes', capable of holding of pairs of sense-data, of pairs of physical events, and also of mixed pairs.

An impure translational construction does not even give the *impression* of 'doing away with' entities. There may be no A-entities, but whether or not this is so is independent of the translation. The predicates used at the foot of the translational ladder cannot be empty, by the principle of acquaintance, whereas translated predicates may be. But this does not mark the difference between a *Russellian* construction and a genuine entity. The reason is that Russell counts the noumenalistic translations of physical object sentences as an abandonment of the method of construction. In other words, an impure translational construction is not a *construction* at all, in Russell's view.

We can impose purity of translation by restricting the predicates allowed in the translating sentences to ones which are capable of being true only of B-type entities. Where A-type entities are physical objects and B-type entities are sense-data, traditional phenomenalist theories entail that the former are pure translational constructions out of the latter.

Translation cannot reduce the number of entities to which we are committed, since two synonymous sentences have the same ontology: that is, just the things that must exist for the one to be true must exist for the other to be true. However, pure translation might, in certain cases, reveal the ontology of the original sentence more clearly. Thus the supposed translation of a sentence like 'John sees a red after-image' by a sentence like 'It is with John visually as if he were seeing a red object', might persuade us that the original sentence does not, despite appearances, have an ontology of mental objects. Such an argument can cut both ways; and it has no special bearing on Russell's constructions.

More positively, pure translation can reduce the number of ontological categories, or, rather, show that there are in reality fewer than we had thought. If the translation runs in only one direction, it shows that whereas the existence of A-entities requires the existence of B-entities, some of the latter could exist even if none of the former did.

In Russell's phenomenalistic phase, from 1914 to the middle 1920s, he can easily be read as claiming that physical objects are pure translational constructions out of sense-data. However, this interpretation requires two modifications. The first is that he thought of physical objects as classes, and this was essential to his treatment of them as fictions. This feature, though consistent with pure translation, is not required by it. The second modification is that, as we have seen, his attitude is reformist. Unreformed language, infected with 'the savage superstitions of cannibals' ('Mind and Matter' 143), is not translated. Reform is effected by stipulating that the sentences are to be *re*-interpreted as sense-data sentences. Only with these important modifications can we use the notion of translation to characterize Russell's theory of construction. Otherwise we shall miss the importance of the anti-realist view of classes, and of the substitutional nature of the constructions.

4   The physical world

The first applications of the technique of logical construction to non-mathematical material are in *RSP* (published 1914) and, in a somewhat abbreviated form, in *OKEW*. Russell'a aim is to construct the physical world (that is, an adequate substitute for the physical world) on the basis of actual and possible sense-data. The overall problem is epistemological: to explain how physics is knowable. The solution involves reducing its content, so that it no longer speaks of sense-data-transcending physical objects.

The problem arises because the objects of physics, molecules, atoms, and, Russell might have added, more mundane things like pennies, are not among the things given as immediate data of sense, for these latter are things like 'patches of colour, sounds, tastes, smells, etc.' (*RSP* 108). What is known is either immediately given or else inferred from what is immediately given. So, if physics is knowable, there must be some kind of correlation between its objects and immediately given objects, and physics is known through knowledge of this correlation.

But how can this correlation be known? Either there is some principle known *a priori* which assures us, for example, that our sense-data have causes other than themselves, or else the objects of physics must be re-interpreted as 'functions of sense-data' (*RSP* 109): i.e. logical constructions out of sense-data.

Later, as we saw in the last chapter, Russell was to opt for this first alternative, but here he rejects it on the grounds that if adopted 'physics ceases to be empirical or based upon experiment and observation alone' (*RSP* 108). Here, then, the aim is to show the viability of the second alternative.

A sense-datum is not the whole content of a sensory field at a moment, but rather 'such a part of the whole as might be singled out by attention' (*RSP* 109). A sense-datum is distinct from a sensation: sensation is the relation which relates a subject to a sense-datum, and a sense-datum is a term in this relation. Russell thinks that ideally, since a single person can know physics, the basis of the construction would be confined to a single person's sense-data. However, he finds he needs to broaden this basis in two directions (*RSP* 116): he includes the sense-data of more than one person, and he includes possible as well as actual sense-data.

A possible but non-actual sense-datum is not a possible but non-actual object, but an actual object having 'the same metaphysical and physical status' as a sense-datum though not in fact present to any mind (*RSP* 110). To avoid confusion, the word 'sensibilia' is introduced to apply to those objects having the same status as sense-data except, perhaps, their relationship to a mind. Russell illustrates the idea as follows. If two men are sitting side-by-side in a room, they are acquainted with similar sense-data. If a third man comes and sits between them, he will also be acquainted with similar sense-data. 'Still it is not unnatural to suppose that, from the position which he now occupies, *some* appearance of the room existed before his arrival' (*RSP* 114). Although all sense-data are sensibilia, such an appearance, before the third man arrived, would have been a sensibile but not a sense-datum. We could think of an unsensed sensibile as the radiations at a place which are capable of interacting, but do not in fact interact, with sense-organs; though we could not use this as a *definition* of a sensibile, since it presupposes physics, and physics has to be constructed on the basis of sensibilia.

Sensibilia are said to be physical, on the ground that each sensibile, including those that are in fact sense-data, might exist even if there were no minds (*RSP* 112).

The general idea is that 'things', for example pennies, are to be identified with classes of sensibilia, or, as Russell also calls them, 'appearances'. He thinks that there are two obstacles to this identification: one is the problem that a thing may appear differently and incompatibly to two different people, but it seems that these different appearances could not co-exist in the same place. The other is that we want to say that a thing's appearances may change even though the thing remains the same. There is also a third obstacle, to which Russell gives rather scant attention: how are we to gather sensibilia or appearances into the appropriate classes without specifying the class as the class of appearances of a given thing?

He thinks that the first of these obstacles is to be overcome by distinguishing between public and private space. Private space is formed by the spatial relations in which sensibilia stand. Thus, for example, the red patch in my visual field is to the left of, and further from me than, the blue patch. A system of sensibilia thus spatially related Russell calls a 'perspective'. The appearances that the world presents to a man at a given moment will constitute part of a perspective.

The next constructional step yields momentary things on the basis of sensibilia, and is a prolegomenon to the construction of public space on the basis of perspectives.

> By moving, and by testimony, we discover that two different perspectives, though they cannot both contain the same 'sensibilia', may nevertheless contain very similar ones; and the spatial order of a certain group of 'sensibilia' in a private space of one perspective is found to be identical with, or very similar to, the spatial order of the correlated 'sensibilia' in the private space of another perspective. In this way one 'sensibile' in one perspective is correlated with one 'sensibile' in another. Such correlated 'sensibilia' will be called 'appearances of one thing' (*RSP* 118).

Perspectives will form the points of public space. They will have to be interrelated in a way that corresponds to spatial relations. For example, we must be able to talk of one perspective being between two others; and the construction must ensure that things and their appearances are appropriately related in space. The problems are solved simultaneously. The first step is to form collinear collections of perspectives. For example,

> We may collect together all those perspectives in which the appearance of the penny is circular. These we will place on one straight line, ordering them in a series by the apparent size of the penny (*RSP* 119).

The place at which a thing is is defined as the intersection of all the collinear collections of perspectives to which an element of the thing belongs.

243

Russell envisages a difficulty with this definition: if we confine ourselves to *known* collinear perspectives, the intersection of these to which an element of the thing belongs may be null, since 'so far as experience goes, the penny ceases to present any appearance after we have come so near it that it touches the eye' (*OKEW* 98). The solution is to project known collinear perspectives:

> We can, for example, remove our penny and prolong each of our two straight lines up to their intersection by placing other pennies further off in such a way that the aspects of the one are circular where those of our original penny were circular, and the aspects of the other are straight where those of our original penny were straight. There will then be just one perspective in which one of the new pennies looks circular and the other straight. This will be, by definition, the place where the original penny was in perspective space (*OKEW* 98). ['Aspect' is a notational variant of 'sensibile'.]

Though this indeed guarantees the existence of *a* place for each thing, there are two reasons for doubting whether it guarantees a unique place. For one thing, the penny-appearance might occupy any of many positions in the visual field, and collinear perspectives based on different positions will assign different places to the penny. The remedy seems to be to stipulate that the penny-appearances must be central in the perspectives which determine the position of the penny. For another thing, a place is a perspective and, as we would say in unreconstructed idiom, more than one perspective can be obtained from a single place, depending on the direction of gaze. Perspectives, then, had best be gathered into co-punctual bundles, and a place identified with such a bundle. Perhaps the notion of overlap could be used: as I turn my head through about forty-five degrees, the content of the old periphery of my visual field overlaps the content of the new centre. Then one might define a co-punctual collection of perspectives as one all of whose members stand in the ancestral of the overlap relation to some perspective. However, Russell does not give this account, nor does he indicate the need for something of the kind.

A further lacuna in the account, this one harder to fill, is a construction of angularity. Once a thing's place is given, we could use it as the origin of a co-ordinate system, and thus arrive at the three-dimensional spatial continuum, if only we had the notion of the relation of, say, being at right angles, holding between collinear classes of perspectives. Russell may have missed the need for this, in virtue of his example of the penny, in which the relation of being at right angles appears to be given as the relation between the collection of perspectives in which the penny appears circular, and the collection in which it appears straight. However, it is plain that this holds in virtue of facts about pennies rather than facts about appearances, since it would be easy to construct an object involved in perspectives as the penny is, but such that two such classes of collinear perspectives were not in reality at right angles. (For example, in any one plane the thickest appearance of a cube is at forty-five degrees to its thinnest appearance.) In constructing the notion of being at right angles, then, Russell cannot rely just on the facts about appearances which were present in the example of the penny. Perhaps this difficulty is not insuperable, for, Russell says, private space is three-dimensional, so that angularity is a given, and the only problem is projecting it onto public space.

Russell argues that the success of the method, described in the last quotation, of extending known perspectives in collinear classes, is due to the empirical fact that 'any other "thing" than our penny might have been chosen to define the relations of our perspectives in perspective space, and . . . experience shows that the same spatial order of perspectives would have resulted' (*OKEW* 98; cf. *RSP* 119). The fact in question might be called the unity of space, and it consists in the fact that (i) everything spatially related to anything is spatially related to everything spatial, and (ii) everything has at most one full spatial relation to anything, where a full spatial relation is constituted by distance together with three-dimensional direction. In the construction, these go over as follows. The first is that each 'thing' x is such that everything, y, has a member belonging to a perspective which belongs to a collinear class of perspectives which can be extended to include a perspective to which a member of x belongs. The second is that for each thing there is at most one such collinear class. Some have argued that facts (i) and (ii) are necessary. If they are right, and if, as Russell implies, through his identification of the empirical with the contingent, their reconstructions are contingent, we are plainly not dealing with a translational construction. Perspective space is not space but a substitute for it.

Each sensibile (or aspect) is associated with two different classes: the thing to which it belongs, and the perspective to which it belongs. The place 'at which' a sensibile appears is stipulated to be the place occupied by the thing to which it belongs. The place 'from which' an aspect appears is stipulated to be the place of the perspective to which it belongs, and this is simply that perspective itself.

The account of a 'thing' is now subjected to two refinements. First, a thing is distinguished from its 'matter'. Since we want to say that a thing may appear other than as it really is, we need a narrower class than the class of all similar sensibilia, and this is supposed to be provided by that which constitutes a thing's matter. Secondly, we need to allow for changes in a thing over time.

The idea is to make a thing's matter the proper sub-set which contains just what one would call, in unreconstructed idiom, its veridical appearances; but this notion cannot be used in the construction since it covertly and illicitly introduces the idea of a real thing. Russell tentatively suggests the following definition: 'The *matter* of a thing is the limit of its appearances as their distance from the thing diminishes' (*RSP* 121). It may be doubted if this yields precisely what is required. Of course, it does not matter that some veridical appearances are excluded, but the trouble is that perhaps some non-veridical ones are included. The series of visual appearances does not change continuously as one approaches a thing, since after a certain degree of proximity it becomes increasingly out of focus. However, some further ingenuity might well overcome this difficulty.

The question of a thing's persistence through time arises only once time itself has been constructed. The first stage in this phase of the construction is to collect perspectives into biographies, where any two members of one biography have a 'direct' time-relation of earlier than, later than, or simultaneous with (*RSP* 123). It is not clear to me what Russell means by a 'direct' time-relation. Perhaps it is one which is immediately knowable:[2] but then a biography will not in general be a personal biography. Alternatively, perhaps Russell simply means that this is to be taken as a primitive notion, though this would not accord well with the overall epistemological aim of the construction. However this may be, the next step is to correlate the times in the different biographies, thus arriving at public time. 'The natural thing would be to say that the appearances of a given (momentary) thing in two different perspectives belonging to two different biographies are to be taken as simultaneous' (*RSP* 123). The difficulty is that we want to say that people perceive the same thing at different times, because of the time light and sound take to travel. Hence the natural idea has to be modified, in ways not specified, so as to accommodate this fact, while also respecting logical truths like the transitivity of simultaneity, and maximizing the simplicity of causal laws.

The things and their matter that have so far been constructed are momentary things, and the final stage of the construction extends them into persisting things, allowing them to change through time. Evidently a persisting thing will be some series of momentary ones. But what series? Russell considers, but rejects, the criterion of sensible continuity, where a series is sensibly continuous iff adjacent members of the series are almost indistinguishable. He suggests that sensible continuity would only be a necessary condition for persistence

[2] This interpretation is supported by Russell's reference to Robb's *A Theory of Time and Space*: see p. 16 of this monograph.

if we stipulate it to be so: explosions, for example, are not continuous in our experience, though we may hypothesize a real continuity by postulating unsensed sensibilia. And he also suggests that sensible continuity is not sufficient since 'we can travel by sensibly continuous gradations from any one drop of the sea at any one time to any other drop at any other time' (*RSP* 126). Presumably the idea is that we might thus identify one drop (at an earlier time) with a distinct one (at a later time). But the case is not entirely convincing, since it is doubtful if one does want to regard the sea as made up of discrete persisting drops. The suggestion about necessity is also somewhat unconvincing, since explosions tend to destroy things. However, Russell's final position seems to be not that continuity must be rejected, but that it must be added to: 'The characteristic required in addition to continuity is conformity with the laws of dynamics' (*RSP*126). This leads to the following definition: '*Physical things are those series of appearances whose matter obeys the laws of physics*' (*RSP* 127). (Presumably 'appearances' is a slip for 'momentary things', since only relative to the latter has 'matter of' been defined.)

It is worth mentioning the way Russell suggests that certain facts can be reconstructed on the basis of this construction. To say that a physical thing looks larger from near to than from afar is to say that its larger aspects are nearer the thing than its smaller ones (*OKEW* 99). However, since relative nearness, in the construction, is simply a matter of relative size, larger aspects being by definition nearer a thing than smaller ones, the original fact, which seems contingent, is reconstructed as a necessity. This shows once more that the construction is not translational. A thing is 'here' if the place it is at is near (i.e. similar to) the speaker's perspective (*OKEW* 99). To say that our private world is in our head is to say that our perspective (at a time) is at where that momentary member of our head is (at that time) (*OKEW* 99–100). To say that what aspect a thing presents at a given place is affected by the intervening medium is to say that the laws according to which the perspectives radiate outwards from the place at which the thing is

> cannot be stated if we only take account of the aspects that are near the thing, but require that we should also take account of the things that are at the places from which these aspects appear (*OKEW* 100).

Russell wants the construction not only to yield the physical world but also to make room for experience. Some sense-data are accounted for, as members of perspectives and members of things. These will include what philosophers commonly count as illusory sense-data like those caused by the sight of a stick in water; they will belong to a thing but not to its matter. Even some dreams may belong to things, if things cause them (*RSP* 130). The remainder, though not part of any things, are none the less physical, in the sense that they might exist without minds.

Russell emphasizes that he has only sketched the broad outline of the construction, omitting niceties (*RSP* 131; *OKEW* 99), and I have indicated *en route* one or two relatively minor problems which require attention. However, even if we make no criticism of the atoms of the construction (cf. Ayer, *Russell and Moore* 57ff.), it has what seems to me to be a glaring and irremediable error at its very first stage, the construction of momentary things from sensibilia.

The error is this: in reality, but not in his construction, distinct momentary things may be associated with very similar sensibilia (cf. Ayer, *Russell* 82). Russell's example of a penny highlights the error, for the sensibilia of *two* pennies may be indistinguishable. Yet, on Russell's account, all their sensibilia will be collected into a single momentary thing.

Notice that even if we were to accept Leibniz's Law, say in the form that things with no distinguishably different properties are identical, we would still have the counter-example to Russell's construction. If two pennies are set against different backgrounds they will have sensibly distinguishable properties, so this form of Leibniz's Law does not require us to count them as one. But a sensibile is not the whole sensory field but 'such a part of the whole as might be singled out by attention' (*RSP* 109). Hence distinguishability by relational properties will be irrelevant, and sensibilia which are intrinsically indistinguishable but associated with distinct pennies will be gathered, by Russell's construction, into a single 'penny'.

Notice also that the present point is decisive, however relaxed our standards of substitutional construction. By no standards is one penny a satisfactory substitute for two.

The difficulty cannot be avoided by shrinking the classes of similar sensibilia to those which, in addition, appear in similar perspectives. For we can easily imagine two pennies having sensibilia in two indistinguishable perspectives, perhaps because they occupy similar positions in similar, and similarly furnished, rooms. Once again, the supposition does not conflict with Leibniz's Law, since the two rooms, and thus indirectly the two pennies, may be sensibly distinguishable, though not through any perspective in which either penny occurs.

In a later version of this stage of the construction (*Mind* 98–9) Russell offers an argument designed to show that the difficulty with which we are concerned must be superable:

Even if we assume a 'real' table, the particulars which are its aspects have to be collected together by their relations to each other, not to it, since it is merely inferred from them. We have only, therefore, to notice how they are collected together, and we can then keep the collection without assuming any 'real' table as distinct from the collection.

The suggestion is that since we can in practice tell, on the basis of the nature of the aspects with which we are acquainted, whether or not they are aspects of a given table, there must be some principle, grounded in the aspects themselves, which thus collects them together. This principle is what is needed for the construction. Notice that the argument requires only that experience causes us to make the appropriate discrimination, not that we use some criterion in so doing.

At least part of this point must be accepted: no doubt there is a causal explanation of how we make all the discriminations we make, including those of recognizing that two aspects are aspects of one thing. But it would be rash to assume that this explanation will draw only on the intrinsic nature of the aspects, and thus rash to assume that it will do the job that the construction requires. For example, I may classify two dissimilar penny-aspects as aspects of the same penny in virtue of my prior knowledge that I possess only one penny. The basis of the grouping, in other words may go beyond the nature of the aspects, and once beyond these may, for all Russell's point shows, draw on material not permitted in the construction. So we should not be convinced by Russell's short-cut attempt to establish the possibility of the construction of momentary things out of aspects.

Other stages of the construction are open to deeper criticisms than those I offered *en route*. One stage in particular is a perennial preoccupation: the construction of persisting things out of momentary things, which Russell takes to be necessary if substance is to be eliminated. I consider this in the next section.

5 *Persisting things and substance*

Are persisting material things (or as I shall in this section say, for short, 'objects') anything over and above the events which make up their histories? Russell thought that if one says they are one is committed to unknowable and unnecessary *substance*, a survival of 'the savage superstitions of cannibals' ('Mind and Matter' 143). Thus, he thought, one should identify objects with their histories, a step which has the additional merit of providing the kind of ontology required by physics (*Matter* ch 23).

In the last section we mentioned one specific way in which Russell attempted to construct objects out of events: there, the events were 'momentary things', themselves identified with classes of similar sensibilia. In this section, I shall consider the question in more general terms, without attending to the question of how the events themselves are to be constructed, or whether they are to be taken as basic. However, I shall make two assumptions about events. One is that one may justifiably call anything which has spatial location (however approximate) but which does not persist an 'event'. The other is that some events are of kinds which match the different kinds of object: just as some objects are trees and some stones, so some events are tree-like and some stone-like, some fit to form part of the history of a tree, some fit to form part of the history of a stone. In short I shall assume that some events can be divided into object-kinds.

Now there are two quite distinct problems facing the construction of objects out of events, and I shall say something about each: (i) Can we gather individual events of each given object-kind into appropriate classes, i.e. ones which correspond to individual objects of the kind in question? (ii) If we can, does such a class of events add up to the corresponding object?

One way to establish an affirmative answer to the first question is actually to supply the principles which effect the grouping. These principles have to be sufficient to give the right answer, based entirely on the character and relations of events, to all questions of the form: do these two events belong to the same *objectual series*, that is, to the history of a single object? A necessary condition, obviously, is that they should be of the same object-kind. What must be added for sufficiency? If we take seriously Russell's rejection, in *RSP*, of sensible continuity, then he must be read as offering as a sufficient condition that grouping the two events into a single objectual series would simplify, or reduce the number of exceptions to, the laws of dynamics (*RSP* 126). Russell admits that this will be the refined account, whose rough version involves 'starting from what common sense regards as persisting things'. However, it is hard to see how it is intended to operate.

Consider, for example, the laws that state what happens on a billiard-table once a ball has been hit. Suppose one ball, *A*, is travelling towards the exact centre of another indistinguishable ball, *B*. A bystander lifts *B* out of the way at the last second, and then replaces it the moment *A* has gone by. Are we to say that the laws in question would be spared an exception were we to attach the subsequent *B*-history to the previous *A*-history, and the subsequent *A*-history to the previous *B*-history; were we to pretend, that is, that the threatened impact really occurred and *A* transferred its momentum to *B*? One hopes that the answer will be 'No!'; but I have not succeeded in constructing an example in which one could reasonably rely on the laws of dynamics to assign events to appropriate objectual series.

The most obvious candidate for the appropriate principle for grouping events is spatio-temporal continuity. There is no reason why Russell should not appeal to this, since his constructions of space and time precede his constructions of persisting things, yet, apart from a brief mention in *IMT* (95), he does not. We could say that a series of events is spatio-temporally continuous iff (*i*) all the events in the series are of a single object-kind and (*ii*) for any pair of members of the series, any time between the pair, any place between the pair, there is a member of the series at that time and place. Then we can consider the suggestion that this provides a principle of grouping adequate to answer the first of our problems: events belong to a spatio-temporarily continuous series iff they are events in the history of a single object.

However, both directions of this last biconditional may be challenged. Against the 'if' direction, it may be suggested that a watch's parts may be scattered, but upon reassembly constitute the original watch. Since the scattered parts of a watch are not a watch, this is a case in which there will be two spatio-temporally continuous event-series but only one object. Against the 'only if' direction, it may be suggested that it is possible that something should suddenly cease to exist, and another thing of the same kind come into existence at an adjacent time and at the same or an adjacent place. If this really is possible, the 'only if', interpreted as a strict conditional, is incorrect.

Somehow we do in fact group events into groups, each group being united by being the history of one object, and we do so without being presented with objects in their historical completeness. Accordingly, one should in theory be able to articulate the principles whereby this grouping is effected, and, using an argument similar to that discussed towards the end of the last section, one might infer that this articulation will yield the answer to our first problem. This inference would be as rash in this case, however, as in the earlier one: perhaps the only account we can give of how we effect the grouping presupposes objects as basic. So once again we must conclude that we have found no proof that the first problem is soluble.

However, I shall assume that it can be solved, and shall accordingly turn to the other problem: will objectual series amount to objects? I shall compare objects in various respects with objectual series, in order to try to determine whether the former *are*, or *are adequately substituted for* by, the latter.

251

(*i*) There are persisting objects. Correspondingly there are objectual series having non-simultaneous members.

(*ii*) There are spatio-temporally continuous objects. Correspondingly, there are spatio-temporally continuous objectual series.

(*iii*) We distinguish between changes and enduring things which change. Correspondingly, we can distinguish between events and objectual series to which they belong.

(*iv*) We distinguish between an object's identity and its history. The future history of a middle-aged elm is not yet given, but its identity is complete: the unfolding of the history is not the elaboration of the identity. Correspondingly, we can distinguish two ways in which an event-series can be 'given'. On the one hand, it can be identified as the series which includes *this*, even if one does not know the nature of the other members of the series (beyond the fact that they belong to a single object-kind). On the other hand, it can be identified by being presented in its entirety, as when an object is continuously observed over its whole history. The future history of the objectual series corresponding to the middle-aged elm is not given in the second way, but its identity is complete and is given in the first way. The unfolding of the subsequent members of the series is not the elaboration of the identity of the series, for this identity is determined by any one member.

(*v*) There are some changes which objects cannot undergo: for example, an elm cannot change into an oak. Correspondingly, some event-series cannot be objectual: for example, any series containing both an elm-like and an oak-like event.

(*vi*) Most, perhaps all, events in an object's history are only contingently part of that history. Correspondingly, for most parts of an objectual series, it is contingent that its extension to a complete series is just as it is.

How exact are these correspondences? The first two or three will, I think, generally be thought to be close: so close that in these respects, someone in the position of Quine's radical translator (*Word and Object* ch 2) would be as justified in attributing to us beliefs about objectual series as he would be in attributing to us beliefs about objects. However, after this the exactitude of the correspondences becomes more doubtful, and especially in the sixth case. I shall argue that there is a discrepancy here, and this is quite sufficient to show that Russell's construction is not translational.

There is, perhaps, not much difficulty in interpreting '*That* elm was not chopped down yesterday' as 'None of the yesterday members of the series to which *that* belongs is an elm-being-chopped-down-like-member'. Demonstrative reference could be systematically shifted from objects to events. But how should one deal with proper names?

'Excalibur never rusted' states (I shall suppose) a contingent truth, but if 'α' denotes the corresponding objectual series, 'α has no rusty members' states a necessary truth, since the identity of a series is constituted by its members and their order: α could not have had a rusty member and still been α. Thus 'Excalibur never rusted' cannot be translated by 'α has no rusty member'. So unless some other pattern of translation can be found, we have enough to show that the construction is not translational.

One remedy, in keeping with Russell's philosophy, is to adopt the description theory of names (cf. *HK* 318–19). Thus a syntactic name for an object might be construed as a description of the form 'the series which in fact contains β as a member', where 'β' names some prominent event in the appropriate objectual series. Since β might have belonged to a series other than the one to which it in fact belongs, it follows that even if the series which in fact contains β as a member is α, it is, even relative to this, contingent that the series which in fact contains β as a member has no rusty member.

This remedy cannot be accepted, for we have rejected the description theory of names on which it depends (Chapter III). Since I can think of no other remedy, I am obliged to conclude that Russell's construction of objects out of events is not translational. However, Russell never intended it to be. Quite the contrary: he advanced it as a corrective to common sense and the 'prehistoric metaphysicians' (*RSP* 115). But the revisionary nature of the construction was not held by Russell to reside in the place we have identified. Rather, Russell saw the revision as the beneficial extrusion of substance.

Are objectual series none the less tolerable substitutes for objects? I claim that we *could* abandon objects, but that there is no compelling reason for doing so. We could do so, that is, without a drastic upheaval in our view of the world. Yet we are not obliged to by any defect, metaphysical or epistemological, in our present view of the world.

I shall support this assessment from two directions. On the one hand I shall attempt to disperse some possible objections to an ontology in which events are basic, and this helps to establish the tenability of Russell's position. On the other hand, I shall adversely criticize some Russellian arguments which might make his position appear mandatory.

In *Individuals*, Strawson has argued that objects and not events are the 'basic particulars' of our conceptual scheme, and at first sight this position might seem to clash with Russell's. Perhaps on deeper reflection there is no incompatibility, for Strawson only claims to describe our conceptual scheme whereas Russell is admittedly attempting to change it; then, the fact that the new scheme differs from the old supports rather than undermines Russell's position. However, on yet further reflection, Strawson's position requires an answer from a Russellian, for Strawson attempts to link the basicness of objects with our concept of space and time in such a way that to deny this basicness would be to repudiate the familiar spatio-temporal framework. If Strawson is right on this point, Russell's revision of our conceptual scheme would be far more radical than he intends, for he intends space and time to be left essentially unchanged: though they are to be reconstructed, the constructed notions are meant to capture all the main features of our pre-constructional notions.

We have so far left vague what restraints should be placed on a substitutional construction: just what purposes must be served as well by the substitute as by its original? The discussion of Strawson will be instructive from this point of view, for we can ask whether objectual series are capable of playing the role in our conceptual scheme which Strawson attributes to objects. My position is this: they are.

'We have, then, the idea of a system of elements every one of which can be both spatially and temporally related to every other' (31 – this and other numerals in this discussion refer, unless otherwise indicated, to pages in Strawson's *Individuals*). Objects form such a system; but so do events. So far, then, there is no discrepancy.

Strawson claims that a necessary condition of our having the conceptual scheme we have 'is the unquestioning acceptance of particular-identity in at least some cases of non-continuous observation' (35). This claim, true or false, goes over nicely as a precisely analogous claim about objectual series.

Strawson argues that 'the identification and distinction of places turn on the identification and distinction of things; and the identification and distinction of things turn, in part, on the identification and distinction of places' (37). If this is right, and if 'things' are objects, and objects are distinct from objectual series, then it seems that were we to identify only objectual series and not objects we could not identify and distinguish places. However, two points could be made on Russell's behalf. One is that we *could* (a) use the identity and difference of certain kinds of objectual series to help to establish identity and difference of place, and (b) use the identity and difference of places to help establish the identity and difference of objectual series. Series corresponding to unmoving landmarks will be as unmoving and prominent as the objects, and where spatio-temporal discontinuity counts against the identity of objects it will count against the identity of the corresponding objectual series. Second, though we indeed take our practice to be one which distinguishes and identifies objects rather than objectual series, it could be argued that an outside observer in the position of Quine's radical translator, the position, that is, of one who seeks to interpret an alien language starting from scratch, could interpret all our practice, in so far as it concerns identity and difference in objects and places, as concerned with identity and difference in objectual series and places. In short, the evidence of this part of our conceptual practice may well fail to settle the question of whether our conceptual scheme contains objects or rather objectual series.

> The only objects which can constitute it [our spatio-temporal framework] are those which confer upon it its own fundamental characteristics. That is to say, they must be three-dimensional objects with some endurance through time (39).

Both claims may be doubted. The first claim is naturally read as the claim that a system of elements must be, or include, elements having every dimension in this system. But this seems to be false, since we can surely conceive space as a system of points. The second claim, if it is to threaten Russell, must be read in such a way that objectual series are not considered as 'three-dimensional objects with some endurance through time'. But event series are certainly spread over time, and their members can and should be regarded as three-dimensional.

The last point is, at least by implication, denied by Strawson, for he implies that while events have spatial position they lack spatial dimensions (57). However, this is simply a matter for stipulation. Russell can stipulate that, for example, every tree-like event, providing it forms part of an objectual series, occupies the same volume as some tree: the volume at time t of the tree which corresponds to the objectual series to which the tree-like event at t belongs. There need be no circularity here: the relevant circumscriptions can be regarded as involved in the relevant predicates of events, or if events are constructed out of sensibilia, as in *RSP*, an extension of the method for assigning a place to a momentary thing will assign it a volume also. (A momentary thing could be said to occupy every point which is the intersection of some pair of collinear perspectives containing any of the thing's members.) Admittedly, this probably does not correspond to the ordinary sense of 'event', in which case the point is no criticism of Strawson.

The above quotation from Strawson is perhaps best interpreted as a rough preview of his later points about the asymmetrical relation of identification-dependence. He wishes to show that whereas it is in general possible to identify objects without employing any identification of events, it is not in general possible to identify (public and observable) events without invoking the identification of objects. He offers two reasons for this claim, of which the first is taken to be the weightier. It is, roughly, that events do not have the right properties of stability to serve as the basis of the identification of other types of particular. However, if events permit the identification of places and times, they will form a basis for the identification of other types of particulars. Objectual event series will be as monotonous as objects are stable, and thus, as we have seen, could interact just as objects do with the identification of places and times.

His second argument for an asymmetrical relation of identification-dependence hinges on a claimed dependence of a slightly different sort. Some events, he claims, can exist only if appropriate objects exist, but there is no converse dependence. Hence having the concept of some events carries with it having the concepts of, and thus being able to identify, certain objects. But the ability to identify certain objects does not in this way carry with it the possession of certain event concepts, and thus does not in this way guarantee the general possibility of identifying certain kinds of event (51).

Let us for the moment accept the first part of the dependence, which goes over nicely into Russell's construction as the fact that some events must belong to some objectual series.

Strawson himself puts, and tries to rebut, an objection to the other part of the dependence. For example, does not 'This is an animal' entail 'Something is the birth of this'? And in general, are there not objects which can exist only if certain events exist? Strawson's rejoinder is unconvincing. It is that we can paraphrase away the apparent quantifications over events, replacing 'Something is the birth of this' by 'This was born'. But this will not do. He concedes that the truth of 'Something is the birth of this' requires the existence of events. Therefore, if it means the same as, or even is entailed by, 'This was born', the truth of the latter also requires the existence of events. Hence it remains that the existence of animals requires the existence of births. That this remains is equally plain if it is denied that 'This was born' and 'Something is the birth of this' are synonymous or mutually entailing, so long as 'This is an animal' entails 'Something is the birth of this'.

It is possible that I have not correctly identified the dependence Strawson has in mind. The ontological dependence is meant at most to underlie an identification-dependence, so perhaps it is on the latter that we should concentrate. Then, it may be said, the paraphrase of 'Something is the birth of this' as 'This was born' shows not that we can eliminate events but that we can eliminate the *concept* of events. Even if this is accepted (and it could hardly be said to be established by appeal to a single example), the overall position is now in danger on its other front. For how shall we establish that having the concept of an event requires us to have the concept of an object, as opposed to the concept of an objectual event series? It is precisely for this that an argument was sought, so it should not appear among the premises.

Towards the end of his discussion of this issue, Strawson explicitly considers the concept of an objectual series or, as he calls it, a 'process-thing' (57), and concludes that this category 'is one we neither have nor need'. If to say that we do not have the category means that we do not ordinarily take ourselves to employ the concept, Strawson is right. If, on the other hand, he means that we could not employ the concept, and end up with an overall view of the world close to our present one, he seems to me wrong. A very great deal of our ordinary talk of things might be construed by a radical translator as talk of objectual series, without our being able to fault the rationality of his hypothesis on the basis of the evidence of linguistic usage available to him. If this theory is ultimately a less good account of our practice than the theory that we talk of objects, it is because it will be unable to account satisfactorily for those relatively recondite elements of linguistic behaviour which manifest our beliefs about the necessity-value of certain sentences which we normally construe as being about objects.

On the other hand, when Strawson says we do not need the category of process-things, I agree. That is, I think that Russell's construction is not one that we are forced to accept.

Russell offers three reasons for its acceptance: one to do with perception, one based on the requirements of science, and one on the need to eliminate substance.

In, for example, *Matter* (284) Russell summarizes the joint operation of the first two arguments:

> By defining a 'thing' as the group of what would formerly have been its 'states', we alter nothing in the detail of physics, and avoid an inference as precarious as it is useless.

The second clause springs from his claim that since percepts are transitory and are the foundation of our knowledge, it is safer to construe objects as groups of percepts and thus as groups of events. The point rests on the premise, which I rebutted in the last chapter, that horizontal inference is safer than vertical inference.

The first clause of the quotation springs from two arguments, both of them dependent on the claim that since physics is the most systematic and refined knowledge we have, the view of the world taken by the physicist in his professional capacity is the view that every rational man should adopt. The first argument is based on the claim that physics has abandoned the doctrine of the indestructibility of matter (*Matter* 283). However, this is relevant only if the existence of

objects entails the indestructibility of matter, which, as Russell admits
(*Matter* 238), it does not, though there is a historical and psychological
association between the doctrines. The second argument is more
convincing. According to Russell, physics actually treats the world as
fundamentally composed of events, which are the terms of its
fundamental laws. Thus 'Heisenberg's theory . . . , in effect, resolves
the electron into a series of radiations' (*Matter* 283). Assuming this to
be generally true, we need only the premise that it is rational to see the
world as physics does to arrive at the conclusion that it is rational to
reject objects in favour of events.

Russell summarizes his position concerning the relationship
between philosophy and physics in Schilpp (700–1). He claims that it
is rational to accept the truth of physics (while recognizing that
today's supposed truths are tomorrow's inaccuracies or even
falsehoods), though 'it is for the philosopher rather than the physicist
to ascertain just what physics asserts' (701). The acceptance of objects
is not incompatible with the truth of physics, so if physics is to *make* us
reject objects we must regard it not only as true but as the whole truth.
But this view of physics goes beyond what Russell claims, and beyond
what it is reasonable to claim.

Perhaps it will be said that physics will none the less *incline* us to
reject objects as gratuitous assumptions: it is not that physics rules
them out but rather that, since it does not require them, we should be
as well off without them. However, this case is really no different from
the last, for it again assumes not just that physics is knowledge but
that it is, or can reasonably be believed to be, the whole of knowledge.

I have said that this position is unreasonable, and now I shall show
this. The reason is simply that, assuming Russell is right about
physics, it does not contain the concept of an object. This means that
the physicist would be unable to give an adequate account of our
speech-behaviour, for such an account requires the attribution to us
of the concept of an object. Hence the physicist cannot express
everything that can be known, and so it is wrong to think that physics
constitutes the whole of knowledge.

The point deserves elaboration. First of all, I shall assume without
argument that we do not understand another's behaviour unless we
know what concepts he possesses. Moreover, I am simply assuming
that Russell is right in his account of physics, according to which
physics does not employ the concept of an object (not even to deny
that nothing falls under it). Given these assumptions, that physics falls
short of being the whole of knowledge follows from the substitutional
nature of the construction. If there is no translating object talk into
series talk, we cannot catch the concept of objects merely through the
concept of series. The theorist who tries to explain our behaviour

without attributing to us the concept of an object, but only the concept of event series, will find himself quite unable to explain how a man who clearly and explicitly realizes that a series has its members essentially should believe that Excalibur might have rusted; in general, this theorist will have to attribute to us a mass of inexplicably false belief. One who ascribes to us the concept of an object does better. Under suitable conditions the best theory constitutes knowledge. Hence the concept of an object must play a part in the expression of our knowledge.

This is not to say that we are forced to concede that there are objects. One might hold that there are none, and that the community is mistaken in thinking that there are any. (The resulting false beliefs will be explained by the community's predilection for the concept of an object rather than of a series.) However, one will need some reason other than the fact that the concept is not used in physics to show that nothing falls under it.

An important general point is that Russell grants the intelligibility of the concepts he wishes to supersede, like the concept of an object. What he is denying is our claim to know that anything answers to them. A philosopher who thought these concepts were unintelligible would need no argument from physics.

This argument, then, wholly fails to establish Russell's position. I now turn to his claim that the acceptance of objects amounts to the improper acceptance of substance, and is thus untenable.

In *Matter* (238) he defines substance as 'that which can only enter into a proposition as subject, never as predicate or relation'. The notion of substance has played many roles in philosophy, but I shall mention two which seem especially germane to Russell's discussion. On the one hand, substance is what mediates the identity of a thing through its changes, and thus Russell at one point glosses a 'substance' as 'A single simple entity persisting through time' (*Matter* 401). On the other hand, substance is conceived as that which bears, but is distinct from, all of a thing's properties. As Russell puts it tendentiously in his chapter on Aristotle's logic in *A History of Western Philosophy*, substance in this role is 'a mere imaginary hook, from which the occurrences [which form an object's history] are supposed to hang' (212). The two roles are at least superficially connected by the fact that in both cases substance could be seen as the ultimate bearer of a thing's identity.

In the first of its roles, substance is intended as an *explanation* of such facts as that an object can persist through time and survive change. Now it is true that in the closest possible reconstruction of these facts in Russell's framework, this explanation is quite out of place, and indeed perhaps no explanation is required: it is obvious that we can collect non-simultaneous events into series, and that some members of the series may be dissimilar. However, accepting objects does not require us to accept the explanation in terms of substance, so although one way of avoiding this explanation is Russell's another way would be to show that the facts about objects require no explanation, or have a different one from the one in terms of substance. Doing this would take us too far from Russell, but here are two points which should raise optimism. We take ourselves sometimes to know that a given object has changed. But however we know this it is not by knowing that object's substance, not by knowing some unchanging component of the object. The second point is this: I have shown that objects are 'something over and above' event series. But in showing this I have not shown that in addition to the series of events there is some further unchanging entity. I have merely shown that facts about objects cannot be construed as facts about event series. Thus, the claim that objects transcend series of events is not, and does not entail, the claim that they are a collection consisting of a series of events plus something else, substance.

Can Russell's construction extrude substance from its second role, the holding together of a thing's properties? It seems doubtful, since events, too, have properties. And if properties need substance to inhere in, this will go for properties of events as much as for properties of anything else. At best, it seems, one sort of substance has been traded for another.

This may be too swift, as the events themselves may be constructed out of different sorts of entity. In *RSP* and for many years subsequently, events were the atoms of the construction, and although the events, series of which substituted for objects, were themselves constructed entities, they were constructed out of events. But in *IMT* and beyond, the atoms of the construction are qualities, rather than events. Russell is quite explicit that one motivation concerns substance: 'All the well-known difficulties of substance remain so long as we retain a "this" which is not a bundle of qualities' (Schilpp 686). Now perhaps qualities avoid substance, in its role of a hook for properties, in a way in which events do not.

But qualities have properties just like anything else. If properties in general need a hook, so will the properties which qualities have.

Perhaps it will be said that the quality itself is the hook. Then it is not so much that substance is rejected, but that it is accepted and identified with something else which is acceptable. But why should not the same procedure be adopted with objects? Let us identify the substance of the tree with that object, the tree.

I discuss the role of qualities at greater length in section 7 below. To summarize the present conclusion: Russell thought that his construction was revisionary in that it excluded substance, regarded as an additional component in a thing. In this he was mistaken, for the acceptance of objects is quite independent of the acceptance of substance, thus conceived. Rather, the revisionary nature of his construction consists in the fact that there is no room in it for translations of our talk about objects.

6   The self and neutral monism

The doctrine which Russell calls 'neutral monism' holds that both mental things like selves and also physical things are constructed out of entities belonging to a single category, and themselves neither mental nor physical. In other words, the atoms of the construction are 'neutral' between the mental and the physical. Russell gives this vivid account of the doctrine, at a time when he was still unwilling to accept it:

> 'Neutral Monism' – as opposed to idealistic monism and
> materialistic monism – is the theory that the things commonly
> regarded as mental and the things commonly regarded as physical
> do not differ in respect of any intrinsic property possessed by the
> one set and not by the other, but differ only in respect of
> arrangement and context. The theory may be illustrated by
> comparison with a postal directory, in which the same names
> appear twice over, once in alphabetical and once in geographical
> order; we may compare the alphabetical order to the mental, and
> the geographical order to the physical. The affinities of a given
> thing are quite different in the two orders, and its causes and effects
> obey different laws. Two objects may be connected in the mental
> world by the association of ideas, and in the physical world by the
> law of gravitation (NA 139).

Russell envisages the atoms to be not merely neutral, but also transitory. Hence there are two problems in the construction, which are in general independent. One is to construct enduring things, selves or physical objects, out of transitory things. The other is to construct the mental and the physical out of some entities which are neither mental nor physical.

The construction in *RSP* introduced in section 4 has some of the features required by neutral monism. Admittedly, he there counts sensibilia as physical, and thus they are not neutral atoms. But this may be merely a terminological matter. There he defines the physical as what is 'dealt with' by physics (*RSP* 111), but if instead he had said 'referred to or quantified over' it seems likely that sensibilia would have come out as non-physical. The main impediment to using the

RSP construction as a version of neutral monism is that Russell never moves from biographies to selves. As he makes plain in *NA*, it is precisely the difficulty of capturing what is involved in an experiencing and knowing subject that held him back from neutral monism until about 1919.

This section is devoted to Russell's construction of the self, and in particular his neutral monistic construction of it. One general point can be made at the outset: it will be a substitutional and not a translational construction. The reason is that it involves constructing an enduring thing out of transitory elements. The arguments of the last section, though directed at the specific case of the construction of material objects, apply more generally to any attempt to construct the enduring out of the transitory. For example, such a contingent fact as that Galileo believed that the earth moved cannot be reconstructed as a contingent fact about a whole or partial series of events (experiencings and believings), if 'Galileo' is treated as a genuine proper name and not a description.

However, Russell gives very little attention to this part of the construction. For example, he does not try to deal with the rather obvious, though perhaps not insuperable, difficulty that a self exists even at moments at which it has no experiential history, as in dreamless sleep. However lax our standards, it seems that only a continuous thing could be a decent substitute for a self, and this seems *prima facie* threatened, in a Russell-style construction, by the discontinuities in a self's history. As I say, this is not a problem which worried Russell. What worried him, and for some time prevented him accepting neutral monism, is whether one is entitled to the immediate elements of the construction, say experiencings or believings, or whether even these surreptitiously require the notion which is supposedly being constructed. It is as if, in the construction of enduring things, what worried Russell was not the move from momentary things to enduring ones, but the construction of momentary things out of sensibilia.

In the case of the self, these worries are most fully set out in *NA*, and are there taken, as I have said, to constitute a sufficient refutation of neutral monism. In that essay, I believe one can detect six distinguishable arguments.

(1) It is logically possible that a mind or self should have exactly one experience. But this is logically impossible according to neutral monism, since something belongs to a mind in virtue of having relations to distinct things which are not minds (*NA* 148).

Neutral monism does have the consequence Russell claims, but whether this counts as a decisive objection is doubtful. Intuitions about the possibility or impossibility of a mind having exactly one experience are variable, and generally tentative. It would seem reasonable to allow a theory of the mind to resolve this question as it will. In *Mind*, Russell's fullest defence of neutral monism, this question is not explicitly mentioned.

(2) The neutral monist cannot account for false belief. Suppose I falsely believe that today is Wednesday. That today is Wednesday seems to be involved in the belief, but this cannot be part of the physical world (*NA* 149).

Since that today is Wednesday cannot be part of the mental world either, it seems that the difficulty is a general one, not one that specially counts against neutral monism.

If the analysis of belief is to introduce propositions, the neutral monist will require that propositions should not be intrinsically mental. In *Mind*, Russell tries to construct them out of sensations and images, both of which are held to be neutral (though there are reservations about images). In the context of the analysis of belief, this construction is notably unsuccessful, since the 'meaning' of an image, on which its propositional role hangs, has to be defined in terms of beliefs (*Mind* 251, 291). However, one should not take this as proving that it is impossible to devise an analysis of propositions acceptable to the neutral monist.

(3) The construction of beliefs, that is acts or states of believing, constitutes a special problem for the neutral monist, especially when what is believed is a fact that is independent of time (*NA* 150), for example, that $2+2=4$. The difficulty is that acts of believing or states of belief cannot honourably be counted as neutral, since one wants to hold that anything which believes has or is a mind. Hence these acts or states must be constructions out of neutral material. Whatever neutral material is used must, Russell suggests, be temporal, since actively believing that $2+2=4$ is an intermittent state. But since this material must also construct the fact believed, that fact, too, must be intermittent, and in such cases as the fact that $2+2=4$ this is hard to swallow.

One might have some doubts about the special role of 'facts independent of time', but the general problem of belief is a severe one for the neutral monist, and one which Russell failed to solve even when he adopted the doctrine. The construction of belief in *Mind* involves both images and belief-feelings as primitive. Russell himself admits doubts about the neutrality of the former (*Mind* 156; cf. 302), and allows that further analysis may eliminate the latter (*Mind* 250). This shows that he was aware of the difficulty, but he does not provide a solution.

(4) How can the neutral monist analyse the event of my remembering some past event? He cannot identify the remembering with its content, for its content is the past event and not any present event. On the other hand, if we analyse the present remembering in terms of some 'idea' of the past event, we get into familiar epistemological difficulties about how the trustworthiness of memory is to be established (NA 151).

Russell's argument veers off course. He starts by saying that the fourth problem is analogous to the third, and in fact he need only make the point that an act of remembering is an act of believing. Instead, he offers the neutral monist a possible solution, in terms of ideas. But Russell gives quite the wrong reason for the unsatisfactoriness of the solution. The neutral monist could handle the epistemological problem in various ways, from embracing scepticism to accepting the reality of the past as the best explanatory hypothesis. Rather, the real reason why the neutral monist should find the introduction of ideas unsatisfactory is that they cannot be counted as neutral: ideas are essentially mental, and so cannot be taken as primitive.

(5) Russell gives two reasons for doubting the adequacy of the neutral monist's account of knowledge. One is that William James, the leading exponent of neutral monism at the time of NA, gives an account of knowledge which Russell convincingly shows to be unsatisfactory (NA 151–3). However, I shall not discuss it, since there is no reason to believe that James' account of knowledge is essential to neutral monism. The other is that the neutral monist cannot give an adequate account of relational knowledge, e.g., of knowing, concerning the Memorial Hall, that it is at a certain place (NA 154).

The second point is not well developed, but presumably the idea is that the neutral monist cannot allow something which is both extra-mental and not one of the neutral atoms as a component in a particular state of belief, since a mind is composed of whatever composes beliefs, etc. Hence all such components apart from the neutral atoms themselves must count as mental and not extra-mental.

The neutral monist should simply deny this last assertion, and keep instead to the plain truth that beliefs may involve extra-mental things, in that some beliefs can exist only if some extra-mental things exist. Since the notion of a physical thing has, supposedly, an independent definition (in terms of the sorts of causal laws connecting the neutral atoms), the neutral monist, if pressed for a definition of a mental state, could hold that it is any component of a mind that is neither one of the neutral atoms nor a physical thing. This may be a little too simple, but it seems likely that the neutral monist could meet the present objection in some such way.

(6) We can now retort on neutral monism with the demand that it should produce an account of 'this' and 'I' and 'now'. I do not mean merely that it should produce an account of particularity and selfhood and moments of time; all this it might accomplish without in any way touching the problem. What I demand is an account of that principle of selection which, to a given person at a given moment, makes one object, one subject and one time intimate and near and immediate . . . it seems to me obvious that such 'emphatic particulars' as 'this' and 'I' and 'now' would be impossible without the selectiveness of mind. I conclude, therefore, that the consideration of emphatic particulars affords a new refutation, and the most conclusive one, of neutral monism (*NA* 169).

It is not easy to see what this 'most conclusive' objection amounts to. The neutral monist seems easily able to meet the challenge: what makes some things intimate to a person, in a way that other things are not, is that some, but not others, are part of that person. What could be more intimate? Degrees of intimacy above zero could be reconstructed in terms of the size of sensibilia in the relevant perspectives, an idea already exploited, in another connection, in the *RSP* construction. Perspectives seem to have, built into them, some kind of selectivity.

It is just conceivable that this passage is the manifestation of a worry that is explicitly stated elsewhere in *NA*:

It may be urged that different people can know the same object, but cannot have the same presentation, and that this points to something other than the object as a constituent of a presentation. As against neutral monism, the argument is valid if its premise is granted; but in our theory, the difference between the subjects suffices to distinguish the two presentations, and therefore no problem arises (173).

Is the premise conceded? As I read Russell, it is. Admittedly, the technical uses of expressions like 'presentation' make it hard to be quite sure. Russell is anxious to urge that it is logically possible for two people to be acquainted with the same particular (*NA* 156), where the particular in question is intended to be a sensation. (By this time, a sensation is no longer essentially relational.) None the less, he is no less anxious to urge that 'when an object O is experienced by two different persons A and B, the experiencing of O by A is one fact, and the experiencing of O by B is another' (*NA* 162). Presentations seem to me to be playing the role of experiencings: hence I think Russell grants the premise of the argument.

The difficulty to which it points is that of giving an account of the difference between distinct particular experiences of the same kind. If the subject is granted, distinctness of experiences can be explained in terms of difference of subject: however similar experience e is to experience e', they are distinct if e belongs to one subject, e' to another. This explanation is not available to the neutral monist, and this is supposed to be a defect. I suggest that this is the very defect to which Russell was drawing attention in the earlier passage where he says that the neutral monist is refuted by a consideration of emphatic particulars.

However, it is not clear that the supposed defect is genuine. Some identity and difference has to be taken for granted and not grounded in the identity and difference of other things. It is unclear why it should be better to take for granted the identity and difference of subjects rather than the identity and difference of experiences. Indeed the latter choice might be preferred on this ground: if we suppose that subjects endure, having now one experience now another, they are more complex than the experiences which help to form their histories, and hence are less suitable to be regarded as ultimate.

The issue is unresolved in *Mind*. We have already seen that it is at best, according to Russell, a contingent fact that two people cannot have the same sensation. Presumably, then, it is contingent that no two people have all the same sensations. Yet Russell's construction of a person in *Mind* is based on the notion of a biography, as defined in *RSP*: a perspective is a set of 'simultaneous' sensations, where 'simultaneous' means in effect able to be co-experienced, and a biography is a set of sensations that are earlier or later than or simultaneous with a given sensation. It is, then, merely contingent that two people do not have the same biography, and in virtue of the way in which the notion of a biography is elaborated to yield, supposedly, the notion of a person, it follows that it is merely contingent that two people are not one. Plainly, something has gone wrong. A precisely analogous criticism applies to Russell's construction of the self in *IMT* (216–17).

The dilemma for the neutral monist is this: either he starts with logically non-private atoms, as Russell's sensations are supposed to be, in which case he will be hard pressed to reconstruct distinct persons, or he starts with logically private atoms, like experiencings, in which case the claim of neutrality looks thin.

We have, then, discovered two severe difficulties for the neutral monist: the one just mentioned, which can hardly be attributed in quite this explicit form to Russell, though some of his remarks perhaps manifest an underlying awareness of the difficulty; and the related problem which Russell clearly identified and tried in *Mind* to resolve, of the construction of particular states of belief (argument (3), above).

One of the principal contributions to the construction of the self offered in *Mind* is the development of selves out of biographies. Any series of sensations in the same place in perspective space would constitute a biography, even if all the sensations were unsensed. What is required to make a biography a self, Russell suggests, is that the sensations be connected by mnemic relations (*Mind* 129). These relations are described in lecture IV: it seems that two events are mnemically related iff one is the mnemic cause of the other, where a mnemic cause is a proximate cause which is temporally remote from its effect. Thus when we explain a burned child's behaviour manifesting fear of fire, we must include as a *proximate* cause not merely the present stimulus (the fire) but also the past event of his having once been burned. Breathtakingly, at the end of the lecture Russell tells us that he thinks it is a sensible working hypothesis that there are *no* mnemic phenomena in this sense, in that further discoveries may show that what we regard as proximate causes are not really proximate. (For example, it is not the past burning, but the present state of the child's brain, that must be added to the current stimulus to yield a full causal explanation. The past burning would be a remote and not a proximate cause.) Hence, quite absurdly, Russell is committed to the view that one could reasonably adopt the hypothesis that there are no selves, since selves require mnemic relations!

Even setting aside these doubts about mnemic relations, the account of the self in terms of them is inadequate. Interpersonal relations are plainly mnemic, if any relations are: for example, I tell you that mushrooms of the species Agaricus Xanthodermus are dangerous, and so you avoid them in future. Hence events in different people would be collected into a single Russellian 'self'.

The case against neutral monism is strong. What are the arguments in its favour? Russell offers two: that it coheres well with the fact that we are not acquainted with the subject, and that it is parsimonious.

Russell soon abandoned the view, tentatively suggested in *PP* (28), that we are acquainted with ourselves. But this is not enough to force the adoption of neutral monism, as he himself stresses in *NA* (168–9).

If neutral monism is adopted, knowledge of selves, to the extent that it extends beyond the specious present of our own self, will be inferential. The argument from parsimony, since it cannot suggest that we cease to believe in the existence of what we know exists, must hold that the inferences involved on the monistic view are safer than those involved if the subject is admitted as primitive. This is simply a version of the claim which we found no reason to accept (Chapter VI), that horizontal inferences are safer than vertical ones. The case for neutral monism is thus weak.

By the time of *HK*, Russell has abandoned neutral monism. Anything known without inference is said to be mental. The existence of physical objects as causes of percepts is inferred, but it is held that we know nothing of these objects except their structural properties: these features, 'because of their abstractness, do not suffice to show whether the physical world is, or is not, different in intrinsic character from the world of mind' (*HK* 240). It is not that earlier he had supposed one could *prove* neutral monism. The most that could be hoped is to show that it is consistent with all the known facts, and that there are some grounds for believing it true. It is this hope that seems to have been abandoned in the later work.

7   *Qualities*

We saw in section 5 that the reconstruction of objects in terms of events does not eliminate substance, if substance is required for the inherence of properties: for events have properties, and so will be substances if anything is. We saw also that in the 1940s Russell held that substance could be eliminated only by having qualities as atoms. If one could grant the success of the construction of objects out of events, all that would now be required is the construction of events out of qualities. This is the task which Russell sets himself in *IMT*. He freely admits the substitutional nature of the construction, relative to objects, or, as he calls them, 'things': he refers to the result of the construction as 'the nearest approach to "things" that our theory allows' (*IMT* 92). The justification for the substitution is the elimination of unknowable substance.

Qualities are not just any old properties, but are such things as 'redness, hardness, etc.' (*IMT* 92), properties with which we are acquainted in perception. This selection could be justified in one of two ways. Either qualities, but not properties in general, are free of substance; or the aim is not merely to eliminate substance, but to eliminate it in favour of what is given in experience. The latter motivation is enough to explain Russell's choice, but we shall also, at the end of the section, examine the former point.

Qualities are held to be 'scattered particulars': particulars because they are the bearers of proper names like 'redness', scattered because, for example, 'redness may be in America, and in Europe' (*IMT* 95), though it is not in fact everywhere in either continent, e.g., not where this page is. (This is an explanation and not a definition, for space is to be constructed out of qualities.)

Qualities are vague. Shades, for example, have vague boundaries. Russell suggests a way in which precision can be obtained, if we are prepared to pay the price of being unable to know truths of the form 'this is the same colour as that'. We cannot say that two colours are the same if indistinguishable, for identity is transitive but indistinguishability is not. Instead we should say that 'two' colours are the same iff every colour indistinguishable from the one is indistinguishable from the other. Knowing a colour identity 'requires a complete survey of the visible universe, past present and future' (*IMT* 99), and hence is impossible. Some might say it requires more than this, on the grounds that there might be a colour distinguishable from each of two indistinguishable colours but which did not manifest itself at any part of the universe.

So much for the basis. The details of the construction are not easy to follow. There are two main discussions in *IMT*, at 95ff. and 318ff. Each ignores the other, and they seem not to offer precisely the same account. Both terminate at the construction of space and time, without giving any details of the promised construction of things. The earlier discussion seems more metaphysical in orientation, the later more epistemological, concerned more with the question of how a person can, on the basis of what is given, construct his view of space and time, than with the question of how space and time can be defined in terms of qualities, known or unknown. My exegesis is clearer than the original, though as a result it may be an over-simplification.

The fundamental notion is of compresence: we can know that certain qualities are compresent when we perceive them within a single experience, but they can *be* compresent when similarly related, whether or not they are known to be. A space-time point is a maximal group of compresent qualities (i.e. all the members of the group are compresent and nothing outside the group is compresent with all its members; cf. *IMT* 321). The construction of spatio-temporal order 'is by no means a simple matter, as Einstein has shown' (*IMT* 321), and it is not attempted. However, one can explain how one in practice identifies places in space and time: one selects a rich group of compresent qualities and, thanks to the fact that spatial direction and temporal relations are immediately given, one proceeds outwards along these co-ordinates.

'I should claim it as the principal merit of the theory I am advocating that it makes the identity of indiscernibles analytic' (*IMT* 97). It does so since a thing will be a series of groups of compresent qualities, so two things cannot agree in all their qualities. Nor can two times or two places, since each time and place is defined by its qualities. At one point Russell says that 'we may find reason to think a large-scale exact recurrence very improbable' (*IMT* 98). This remark is of interest for the implicit constraint imposed on the substitutional construction. The remark comes from within our existing scheme, for in the proposed scheme such recurrence would be impossible, not improbable. The remark is made in order to suggest that in virtue of how, very probably, things are, the adoption of the new scheme will not involve a huge upheaval in practice. However, there plainly is a huge upheaval in theory: whether or not history repeats itself, there is a great gap between those who think that qualitative repetition is logically possible and those who think it is not. Why should we be obliged to adopt the new scheme, which entails what we take to be a blatant falsehood?

Presumably Russell sees this entailment as an advantage because it is the manifestation of the elimination of substance. If any two things must differ qualitatively, difference no longer need be mediated by substance. However, the elimination of substance does not require this version of Leibniz's Law, since difference may be a matter of difference of properties which are not qualities. This, certainly, is nearer our actual view: qualitatively indistinguishable things like peas and pins may differ in such non-qualitative properties as position. Thus even granted Russell's desire to eliminate substance, it is hard to see any merit in the acceptance of this version of Leibniz's Law.

Is the only way to eliminate substance to have qualities as the only atoms? On one understanding of the question, the answer is no. There is no such thing as substance, regarded as some further component in a thing that ought to be listed along with its properties in a complete description. Hence there is nothing that needs eliminating. He who denies that a thing is just a bundle of qualities should not be taken to assert that it is a bundle plus a substance. Rather, he asserts such banalities as that we take things to have some of their properties contingently.

On the other hand, one can get into a mood in which there seems to be some mystery about how groups of properties cohere, and an analogous mystery about how a thing can survive changes. In such a mood, both the coherence of the attributes of a quality, and its persistence through changes in its attributes (e.g., changes in its distribution), seem quite unmysterious. In this mood, something would seem to be explained by a Russellian construction which takes qualities as atoms. Only those who have experienced this mood can have any sympathy with Russell's attempt.

However, I think the proper corrective is not Russell's construction, but closer attention to the alleged mystery. All that grounds it, in my view, is that qualities are so easily and obviously identifiable and re-identifiable. But this fact has no bearing on whether the notion of how properties cohere or how a thing survives change is or is not mysterious. The identity and persistence of things must be distinguished from our knowledge of their identity and persistence, which is what identifying and re-identifying them involves. It may be, none the less, that the ease of obtaining the knowledge makes us feel that what is known is unmysterious, and the more problematic nature of the identification and re-identification of objects makes us feel that what is known contains a mystery. If this is its only cause, the feeling is groundless, and hence the apparent transparency of the identity and persistence of qualities is illusory: from the metaphysical point of view, qualities and objects have the same status as regards substance.

My conclusion in this case is just as it was for the other constructions I have discussed in this chapter. They are substitutional, and intended to be so; yet Russell has, in my view, given no adequate reason, epistemological or metaphysical, for preferring the substitutes to their originals.

VIII

Mathematics

1   The logicist programme

Russell aimed to show 'that mathematics and logic are identical' (*PofM v*). The main ideas which he used to try to establish this are set out in *PofM*, and a much more detailed treatment, incorporating the theory of ramified types, is given in *PM*, written in collaboration with Whitehead, and originally conceived as a second volume to *PofM*.

The logicist thesis of the identity of mathematics and logic can be analysed into three contentions:

(*i*) Every mathematical truth can be expressed in a language all of whose expressions are logical; for short, every mathematical truth can be expressed as a true logical proposition.

(*ii*) Every true logical proposition which translates a mathematical truth is a *logical truth*.

(*iii*) Every mathematical truth, once expresssed as a logical proposition, is deducible from a small number of logical axioms and rules.

To bring out the difference between (*i*) and (*ii*): 'There are at least three things' is a true logical proposition, for it is true and can be expressed in a language all of whose expressions are logical, but it is not a logical truth. (However, see below, pages 305–7.) A logical truth is 'true in virtue of its form' (*PofM xii*), and part, though not all, of what this requires is that it be necessarily true.

Russell never explicitly gives this tripartite formulation of logicism, and part of the explanation is that he never envisaged any divergence between the class of truths that he wished to count as logical truths, and the class of truths that he thought would be deducible from a small number of logical axioms and rules. Hence, as in the following passage from *PofM*, one sometimes finds logicism represented as the conjunction of (*i*) and (*iii*):

All mathematics deals exclusively with concepts definable in terms of a very small number of logical concepts, and . . . all its propositions are deducible from a very small number of fundamental logical principles (*PofM* xv).

For two reasons, however, it is best to separate (*ii*) and (*iii*). One is that, at least in a later discussion (*PofM*, second edition, 1937), Russell insists that in specifying the 'fundamental characteristics of logic . . . the question of demonstrability cannot enter in' (*xii*), the reason being that we have to define the admissibility of a logical system in terms of whether its theorems are logical truths. Being demonstrable is not part of the essence of belonging to logic, and so the point about mathematical truths being translatable as logical truths should be one thing, and the point about mathematical truths being translatable as demonstrable truths should be another.

The second reason is that the separation of (*ii*) and (*iii*) enables the logicist better to modify his programme in the face of Gödel's incompleteness result. It follows from this theorem of Gödel's that no consistent logical system with a small number of axioms and rules will permit the derivation of every mathematical truth. (For an account of Gödel's result for non-mathematicians, see De Long 160ff.) Thus (*iii*) is false (assuming the intended logical system to be consistent). So the logicist programme, as I have described it, and as Russell describes it in the passage recently quoted from *PofM*, cannot succeed. What is the minimum weakening that can save it from this result?

The answer is that the logicist should claim not that every mathematical truth is derivable, but rather that a substantial part of mathematics is derivable. Though this sounds very vague, it creates no difficulty in practice, for critics of logicism cite specific mathematical results which, they claim, cannot be proved in the logicist's system, and there is general agreement both that the success of logicism would require these results to be derivable, and that this cannot properly be achieved simply by taking them as axioms.

We can now see the value of separating (*ii*) and (*iii*). A logicist who started by asserting just (*i*) and (*iii*) would have to modify the latter in the face of Gödel's theorem along the lines just envisaged. But then he has no way of distinguishing mathematical truths from those true logical propositions which are not mathematical truths. It is therefore important that the logicist should claim that a distinguishing mark of mathematical truth is logical truth: thus he should assert (*ii*) as well as (*i*), and both must be distinguished from (*iii*).

Many of the key ideas in Russell's logicism did not originate with him, as he firmly acknowledges. To Peano he owes techniques for reducing certain mathematical notions to those of elementary arithmetic, and in *PM* he acknowledges also a debt to him in respect of notation. He also acknowledges debts to Frege, whose discovery of the definition of numbers as classes of similar classes anticipated his own work in *PofM*;[1] and to Cantor, Schröder, and others (see *PM viii*). I am not competent to judge the degree to which Russell was innovative in mathematics, in trying to execute the logicist programme (see his complaint at the way the mathematical aspects of *PM* were ignored: *MPD* 86). From the philosophical point of view, however, his own most original contributions concern the paradoxes and the ramified theory of types which he created to avoid them, and which led him into doctrines concerning the fundamental nature of language. It is, therefore, on these contributions that I shall concentrate in this chapter.

2   The domain of logic

A well-known criticism of logicism is that it succeeds in reducing mathematics not to logic but to logic plus set-theory (see, e.g., Quine, *Philosophy of Logic*, especially 66ff.). One who would adopt Russell's logicism must thus show that set-theory, or rather, in Russell's case, the theory of higher-order quantification, is genuinely part of logic. In this section I aim to specify some of the main features of this controversy, to state Russell's rather sparse contribution to it, and to gesture towards ways of defending his position.

One kind of objection which Quine levels against higher-order quantification rests on the claim that a variable capable of being bound by quantification can properly occur only in a position fit to be occupied by a name (cf. Quine *op. cit.*, 66–7). Since predicates are not names, a claim of this kind suggests that there cannot be such things as higher-order quantifiers, that is, quantifiers which bind variables which occupy predicate position. I defer discussion of this kind of objection until the next section, in which I describe Russell's theory of quantification. For the moment, I shall assume that there are genuinely higher-order quantifiers.

In order to determine the domain of logic, one must answer the

---

[1] Russell cannot be credited with the independent discovery of the definition of number. For one thing, as I mentioned in the Introduction, there is the likelihood that he had read Frege with sufficient care to have extracted it, before the composition of *PofM*. For another thing, he reports in that book on Peano's discussion (and rejection) of the definition. We know that Russell read 'every word' Peano had written before the composition of *PofM* (*A* I 144).

following four questions. What makes an expression a *logical* expression? A truth a *logical* truth? An axiom a *logical* axiom? A rule a *logical* rule? A criterion adequate to answer any of these questions must harmonize with our firm intuition that the truth-functional sentential connectives and the first-order quantifiers are logical expressions, that instances of valid first order quantificational schemata are logical truths, and that any set of axioms and rules affording a sound and complete systemization of first-order logic are logical axioms and rules. Much of the debate concerning the domain of logic turns on what are the continuities and discontinuities between first-order logic and higher-order 'logic', and on how these continuities and discontinuities are to be weighed.

Once we have a criterion for being a logical constant, we have a criterion for being a logical proposition, for a logical proposition is one expressible by an expression all of whose constants are logical. Russell's usual procedure is simply to *list* what he takes to be the logical constants. On the question of a criterion, one can extract only two suggestions. One, implicit in his account of logical form in *PLA* (238: 'I mean by the form of a proposition that which you get when for every single one of its constituents you substitute a variable'), depends on the notion of a constituent (meaning-relatum), which in turn depends on the realist theory of meaning, which in turn depends on how expressions can be analysed in the perfect language. Since the perfect language is supposed to have *PM*-constants as its only logical constants, this suggestion presupposes, rather than provides, a criterion for being a logical constant. The other suggestion can be extracted from Russell's idea that a logical proposition should have complete generality (e.g., *PofM xii*), from which one can infer that a logical constant should introduce no special subject matter. It is indeed tempting to suppose that the *PM*-constants are in this way subject-neutral. If Russell is right, part of the interest and boldness of the logicist claim is that it forces us to conclude, in the face of pre-theoretical intuitions to the contrary, that numerical expressions, numerals for example, introduce no special subject-matter: if number is regarded as forming a special subject-matter, then mathematics is not the study of number.

One difficulty with the notion of subject-neutrality as a criterion of being a logical constant is that it is vague. Perhaps even propositional logic has a 'special subject-matter': the truth-functions. Perhaps even first-order quantifiers introduce a 'special subject-matter': individuals. Until the criterion is made firmer, there can be no firm debate about whether a second-order quantifier is to be counted as introducing a 'special subject-matter' on the ground that it 'introduces' properties.

275

In his 'What is a Logical Constant?', Peacocke offers a criterion which harmonizes with our intuition that sentential connectives and first-order quantifiers are logical constants, and which, he says, permits a natural generalization as a result of which higher-order quantifiers would also count as logical constants. (The criterion is too complex to be given here.) Peacocke's discussion thus provides support for the conception of logic's domain that logicists require.

One would not be happy to count higher-order quantifiers as logical constants unless there were some way of extending the notion of logical truth from first-order to higher-order languages. Russell's rather scant remarks about logical truth fail to suggest any such natural extension. For example, in *PofM* (second edition, *xii*) he suggests that a logical truth is one 'true in virtue of its form', though he professes himself unable to give an account of what truth in virtue of form amounts to. The phrase, however, suggests that a logical truth is one which remains true for every uniform substitution over its extra-logical expressions. (Bound variables count as logical expressions.) For example, one possible justification for our belief that 'All bald men are bald' is a logical truth is that a true sentence results from every uniform substitution of expressions of appropriate categories for 'bald' and 'men'. The account appears to accommodate our inclination to count '$(\forall x)x = x$' as a logical truth. For this sentence contains no extra-logical expressions, so that the proposed condition holds vacuously. However, the account cannot be satisfactorily extended to second-order logic, for the following sentence satisfies the condition but is not a logical truth:

$$(\exists \varphi)(\exists_3 x)\varphi x.$$

('$\exists_3 x$' abbreviates 'there are at least three things, x, such that'.) Thus the logicist must find another account of logical truth.[2]

Boolos, in his 'On Second-Order Logic', suggests that there is no difficulty about extending the notions of validity and consequence from first-order to second- and higher-order languages. Indeed, on his view the required account is entirely general: a valid sentence is one true under all its interpretations; and one sentence follows from others if it is true under all those of its interpretations under which the others are true (513). All that is needed is an account of what is to count as an 'interpretation', and as 'truth under an interpretation', for second- and higher-order languages. Boolos suggests that the usual notion of an interpretation will remain unchanged, and that the recursive clause that attends to quantifiers, in the definition of 'truth under an interpretation', can be generalized to the following:

[2] The account of logical truth in terms of substitution is in any case not satisfactory in general: cf. Peacocke, 'What is a Logical Constant?' 223.

An existentially quantified sentence $\exists\, \alpha F(\alpha)$ is then true under an interpretation I just in case $F(\beta)$ is true under some interpretation J that differs from I (if at all) only in what it assigns to the constant β, which is presumed not to occur in $\exists\, \alpha F(\alpha)$ and presumed to be of the same logical type as the variable α (513).

Boolos says that two symbols are of the same logical type if they are of the same degree and are either both predicate symbols or both function symbols; names are included as o-place function symbols. Hence the single clause attends both to name quantifiers and to predicate quantifiers. (One should beware lest the usual notational conventions lull one into assuming that, in Boolos's account, 'α' occupies exclusively name position.)

Once we have the notion of validity for higher-order languages, we thereby have the notion of logical truth. Any valid sentence containing no free variables and no schemata will be a logical truth, and so will any instance of a sentence containing schemata or free variables, an instance being a sentence which results by uniformly replacing the free variables or schemata by constants of the appropriate category. Thus '$(\exists\varphi)(\forall x)\varphi x$' is an example of a logical truth, and so is every instance of '$(\forall\varphi)(\varphi x \to \varphi y) \to x = y$' (cf. Boolos 512).

The continuity of the notion of validity as applied to first-order and higher-order languages supports the Russellian view that there are higher-order languages which belong to logic. It leaves the question of what are appropriate axioms and rules as the relatively trivial one that Russell describes in *PM* (v): as axiom one may select any logical truth, as rule any valid pattern of consequence. In determining which truths are logical truths we do not have to rely merely on intuitions concerning isolated propositions; we can also draw on systematic considerations. For a genuinely logical rule, applied only to genuinely logical truths, can yield only logical truths. (Cf. *EA* 194.)

Two main points needed to establish the domain of logic in a way consistent with logicism are that higher-order quantifiers are logical constants (logical expressions), and that there is a way of extending the notion of logical truth so that it includes some higher-order sentences. These points are rendered plausible by the arguments of Peacocke and Boolos respectively. For the logicist programme what is also required, of course, is that the higher-order sentences which supposedly translate mathematical truths should themselves be logical truths. Whether this is so is, as we shall see, a much more questionable matter.

What, then, is the case *against* regarding higher-order 'logic' as logic? Doubts about the intelligibility of higher-order quantification are important, and will be discussed in the next section. I shall conclude this section by a brief mention of one characteristic which Quine takes to mark an important discontinuity between first-order logic and higher-order 'logic'. This is that the former, but not the latter, is complete.

One criticism is that the claimed divergence is less impressive once suitably qualified: for some second-order systems *are* complete, relative to a suitable, and non-standard, notion of validity (see Henkin's 'Completeness in the Theory of Types'). This suggests that one might even use the notion of completeness to illustrate a continuity between first-order logic and some second-order logics, and then use other continuities to move from the latter to Russell's system which, in its intended interpretation, is indeed incomplete.

A perhaps more important criticism is this: why should we regard completeness as a suitable mark of the domain of logic? Why not instead, for example, regard this domain as fixed as that area for which there is a decision procedure? By this criterion, not even all of first-order 'logic' would come out as logic, though some of second-order 'logic' would count as logic (cf. Boolos 523). Plainly, this outcome would cut through more important continuities. If it is said that the notion of completeness captures the pre-theoretical idea that what is logical is amenable to proof, so that completeness is part of the essence of logic, it can be replied that there is a pre-theoretical notion of long standing that whether a truth is logical is a question amenable to mechanical treatment. Yet if we take the existence of a decision procedure as the technical correlate of the notion of amenability to mechanical treatment, one could as well argue that decidability is of the essence of logic, which, as we have seen, leads to results we do not in fact want. Thus the incompleteness of Russell's *PM* system does not provide a compelling argument for not regarding it as part of logic.

3   Quantification

A variable bound by a first-order quantifier occupies name-position in a sentence, whereas a variable bound by a second-order quantifier occupies predicate-position in a sentence. For example, the quantifier in 'For some x, x is a man' is first-order, since the position occupied by 'x' in 'x is a man' is name-position: 'x is a man' can be turned into a sentence by replacing 'x' by, for example, 'Socrates'. By contrast, the quantifier in 'For some φ, Socrates φ' is second-order, since the position occupied by 'φ' in 'Socrates φ' is predicate-position. 'Socrates φ' can be turned into a sentence by replacing 'φ' by, for example, 'ζ is a man', and inserting 'Socrates' into the gap; but it cannot be turned into a sentence by replacing 'φ' by something other than a predicate, for example the name 'humanity'. To mark this contrast, I shall sometimes speak of first-order quantifiers as name quantifiers, and second-order quantifiers as predicate quantifiers.

Russell's ramified theory of types has an important bearing on his predicate quantifiers, for it is intended to restrict them in such a way as to avoid paradoxes. But though he supplies these restrictions, Russell gives no general account specifically directed at the nature of predicate, as opposed to name, quantifiers. His account of quantification early in *PM* (15; cf. *ML* 66, 83) is not explicitly restricted to name quantifiers, and it is conceivable that one should regard it as an entirely general account, applying alike to name and predicate quantifiers. In practice, however, it is easier to start by regarding it as an account of name quantification. We shall turn later to the question of how Russell understood predicate quantification.

Russell says that quantification is a primitive idea (*PM* 15; cf. *ML* 83). None the less, he offers, as glosses of '$(\forall x)\varphi x$', 'φx is always true' (*ML* 66; cf. *PM* 15, 41) and 'All propositions in the range of $\varphi\hat{x}$ are true' (cf. *PM* 15). Here '$\varphi\hat{x}$' (or perhaps $\varphi\hat{x}$) is said to be a 'propositional function' (or 'function' for short). This notion plays a crucial part in Russell's theory of quantification, and one task is to attempt to clarify it. A question to be borne in mind is: are functions expressions, or are they non-linguistic entities?

It will be useful to introduce some terminology, in the light of which one can distinguish what kinds of expression functions are, if they are expressions at all. Since we are at the moment considering only name quantifiers, if a function is an expression, it is one which can be turned into a sentence by somehow introducing a name. This means that it must be either a predicate or an open sentence. A *predicate* is an expression having at least one gap (I shall mark gaps by inserting Greek letters 'ζ', 'ζ'') such that if the gaps are filled systematically by names the result is a sentence. For example, 'ζ loves ζ' is one predicate, and 'ζ loves ζ' another. If the gaps in a predicate are filled by variables, the result is an open sentence; e.g., 'x is brave', 'x loves y'. If a function is a non-linguistic entity, it must be one which stands in some sort of relation to one or both of the foregoing sorts of expression: it must be what I shall call a *property*. If one is granted the idea of *proposition* as a non-linguistic entity, that which a sentence expresses, one can introduce the idea of a property in a way analogous to the way in which predicates were introduced: a property is something which, in a singular proposition, is applied or ascribed to one or more things. Thus being brave and loving oneself are monadic properties, and loving is a dyadic property.

Russell introduces a special notation to form from an open

sentence an expression which is or denotes a function: one applies a circumflex accent to each variable in the open sentence. The result can be called a *function abstract*. If functions are properties, function abstracts denote properties: '$\hat{x}$ is brave' denotes the property of being brave, '$\hat{x}$ loves $\hat{x}$' denotes the property of loving oneself, and '$\hat{x}$ loves $\hat{y}$' denotes the property of loving. When I use a function abstract to denote a property, I shall call it a *predicate abstract*.

A property must be thought of as having 'gaps' analogous to the gaps in a predicate. Just as we must distinguish between the predicates 'ζ loves ζ' and 'ζ loves ζ', so we must distinguish the relational property of loving and the monadic property of loving oneself. This is effected by the notation of predicate abstracts. Likewise, just as a predicate is associated with a *range of significance*, the class of those things names for which, when inserted in the gaps in the predicate, yield a significant sentence, so, in an exactly parallel way, a property is associated with a *range of significance*, the class of things to which it can be significantly applied.

If functions are expressions, then, in their uncircumflexed form, they are open sentences.[3] If functions are not expressions, then presumably they are properties.

Consider this initial account of functions in *PM* (14–15):

> Let φx be a statement containing a variable x and such that it becomes a proposition when x is given any fixed determined meaning. Then φx is called a 'propositional function' ... 'x is hurt' is an ambiguous 'value' of a propositional function. When we wish to speak of the propositional function corresponding to 'x is hurt', we shall write '$\hat{x}$ is hurt'. Thus '$\hat{x}$ is hurt' is the propositional function and 'x is hurt' is an ambiguous value of that function. .... Thus corresponding to any propositional function φx, there is a range, or collection, of values, consisting of all the propositions (true or false) which can be obtained by giving every possible determination to x in φx.

(Here 'φ' must be regarded as a schematic letter, and not as a variable, though Russell does not make the distinction.) I shall suggest that this account, even taken in conjunction with Russell's account of first-order quantification, leaves open the question of whether functions are, or are not, expressions.

If functions are expressions, then a value of a function, which results by giving a determination to 'x', will be a sentence. It will result from the function by replacing all occurrences of variables systematically by names. The range of values of a function will be the

---

[3] They are not function abstracts, as is shown by the quotation from *PM* 38 given on page 293 below.

class comprising 'every possible' sentence which can be obtained in this way. This will give the result Russell intended only if these sentences include non-*PM*-sentences (for there are no individual names in *PM*), and, indeed, only if they comprise exactly the sentences which can be formed by replacing '*x*' by some name drawn from a class of names such that every object in the intended domain of quantification has a name in the class, and such that every name in the class names some object in the intended domain of quantification. This domain is to include everything within 'the range of significance of the function' (*ML* 72). On the present interpretation, therefore, the relevant class of names will not include any which, were they to replace the variable in the function, would not yield a significant sentence. The class will, however, include every other genuine name, in every possible language. Finally, on this view, circumflexion will be just like quotation: a way of forming a name of an expression. This is why circumflexion is used when we wish to speak of the function (=expression) itself.

If functions are properties, then a value of a function is a proposition, regarded as a non-linguistic thing, as what a sentence expresses. The range of values of a function will be the class of all possible propositions involving the ascription of the property to something. The range of significance of a property will play a role exactly like that of the range of significance of an open sentence, on the alternative interpretation. On the present view, circumflexion will form predicate abstracts, which is why it is used when we wish to speak of the function (=property) itself.

Whether we regard functions as expressions or as properties, Russell's account of quantification can be interpreted in such a way that it assigns correct truth-conditions to every quantification '$(\forall x)\varphi x$', where '*x*' occupies name position. On the first interpretation, his gloss of universal quantification ('All propositions in the range of $\varphi\hat{x}$ are true') requires him to hold that '$(\forall x)\varphi x$' is true iff every significant sentence obtainable from 'φx' by replacing '*x*' by a name is true. With the relevant names given as before (everything in the range of significance of 'φx' has a name, and only names of objects within the range are relevant), this amounts to the condition that 'φx' be true of everything (nameable by any name occurring in a sentence in its significance range), which is what was wanted. On the second interpretation, his gloss requires him to hold that '$(\forall x)\varphi x$' is true iff for every object o (in the range of significance of the property $\varphi\hat{x}$), the proposition to the effect that o has $\varphi\hat{x}$ is true. This, also, is a true biconditional (though it would not be a suitable axiom for quantification in the usual kind of recursive truth-theory).

Russell's gloss of quantified sentences can thus be interpreted as providing a truth-conditional equivalent, whether we treat functions as expressions or as properties. However, if functions are expressions, the gloss is certainly not a synonym, and synonymity would also be at least open to question if functions are properties. If functions are expressions, one could know that every sentence resulting from the function 'φx' by the kind of substitution we have envisaged is true, and yet not know that $(\forall x)\varphi x$. The reason is that one might not understand 'φx'. The converse also obtains, and for the same reason. One might know that $(\forall x)\varphi x$ without knowing that every sentence resulting from 'φx' by the kind of substitution we have envisaged is true.

Even if we interpret functions as properties, Russell's gloss, regarded as supposedly a synonym, is open to question. Russell himself gives a reason for this: when we judge that $(\forall x)\varphi x$ 'the notion of *truth* is not part of the content of what is judged' (*PM* 41). This reason may be doubted, on the grounds that anyone who can be credited with any linguistic abilities can be credited with mastery of the concept of truth, so that on this score we do not misrepresent a person's conceptual repertoire if we use the concept of truth in reporting his judgment. However, it moves Russell to withdraw the original 'less accurate' gloss in favour of the more accurate 'φx always'. Since we have no independent grasp of this locution, it is not easy to assess whether or not it is synonymous with that which it is intended to explain. I think we do well to regard this later passage as a tacit withdrawal of his implicit earlier claim that '$(\forall x)\varphi x$' and 'φx is always true' are synonyms (cf. *PM* 15; *ML* 66).

Thus, so far as I can see, Russell's account of quantification, in so far as it applies to name quantifiers, does not compel us to choose between regarding functions as expressions and regarding them as properties. The reason is that the glosses which figure centrally in the account ('φx is always true' and 'All propositions in the range of $\varphi\hat{x}$ are true') can be interpreted as truth-conditional equivalents of '$(\forall x)\varphi x$' whether functions are expressions or properties; and we are not compelled to think that Russell regarded either gloss as a synonym. When one turns to predicate quantification, however, it seems that the problem will become more acute. For at first sight it looks as if the function variables will require functions as values, and thus as if it would be essential to decide whether these values are expressions or properties.

In the remainder of this section I shall consider various interpretations of Russell's function quantifiers, and it will be useful to chart these briefly at this stage.

(*i*) I start with some general comments about predicate quantification.

(*ii*) I then consider the substitutional interpretation of predicate quantifiers.

(*iii*) There are various ways in which one might regard function quantifiers as name quantifiers, and *PM* as a system of many-sorted first-order quantification. One way is to regard function quantifiers as name quantifiers ranging over classes, but this is plainly at variance with Russell's intentions.

(*iv*) Another way is to regard function quantifiers as name quantifiers ranging over functions. I suggest that this is a good representation of Russell's intentions. There are two sub-cases, according as functions are expressions or properties.

(*i*) We saw earlier (Chapter II) how Russell stressed the similarity in meaning between a predicate like 'ξ is human' and a corresponding abstract singular term like 'humanity'. This similarity led to some of Russell's problems about the unity of the proposition, but there is no need for this, so long as we keep in mind the dissimilarity: 'ξ is human' occupies predicate position, but 'humanity' occupies name position. The similarity should incline us to the view that one who assertively utters 'Socrates is human' thereby ascribes humanity to Socrates (cf. Strawson, 'Positions for Quantifiers' 77). What phenomena would make a radical translator prefer 'Socrates is human' to 'Socrates possesses humanity' as a translation of an alien sentence? One kind of phenomenon that would be relevant concerns quantification; but, in the present case, this establishes no difference. Just as we can generalize from 'Socrates is human' to 'Socrates is something' (or 'For some φ, φ(Socrates)') using a predicate quantifier, so we can generalize from 'Socrates possesses humanity' to 'Socrates possesses something' (or 'For some x, Possesses (Socrates, x)') using a name quantifier.

This already suggests the view that we can regard a predicate quantifier as ranging over properties, and there is a more direct argument for this conclusion. Just as one who has mastered name quantification must understand that the truth of a sentence like '$(\exists x)(Fx \ \& \ Gx)$', unlike that of a sentence like '$(\exists x)Fx \ \& \ (\exists x)Gx$', requires that there be a *single* thing which is both F and G, so one who has mastered predicate quantification must understand that the truth of a sentence like '$(\exists\varphi)(\varphi(\text{Socrates}) \ \& \ \varphi(\text{Aristotle}))$', unlike that of a sentence like '$(\exists\varphi)\varphi(\text{Socrates}) \ \& \ (\exists\varphi)\varphi(\text{Aristotle})$', requires that there be a *single* property possessed by both Socrates and Aristotle. To say that predicate quantifiers range over properties is not to say, falsely, that predicates name properties, but rather that sensitivity to sameness and difference of properties is involved in mastery of the idiom of predicate quantification.[4]

[4] Cf. Gareth Evans, 'Identity and Predication'.

(*ii*) I now consider, in very rough outline, how one might give a substitutional account of predicate quantifiers, and how such an account connects with Russell's ramified theory of types (see also sections 7 and 9 below).

Borrowing Kripke's suggestions concerning substitutional name quantifiers ('Is There a Problem about Substitutional Quantification?'), a substitutional predicate quantifier could be introduced in the following way. Starting with a first-order language, L_0, and some class P of L_0-predicates, one extends L_0 to L by adding a predicate quantifier and appropriate variables and characterizing the truth of L-quantifications on the lines: '$(\exists\varphi)$ ... φ ...' is true in L iff for some member, 'ψ', of P, '... ψ ...' is true in L. The righthand side must speak of truth in L, rather than L_0, since if L-quantifiers are iterated '... ψ ...' will not be an L_0-sentence. None the less, in a Kripke-style interpretation, the characterization of truth in L crucially depends on an antecedent characterization of truth in L_0: the idea is that the characterization of truth in L_0, together with the characterization of truth for L-quantifications, should uniquely determine the class of truths in L. As Kripke stresses ('Substitutional Quantification' 331–2 (for name quantifiers) and 368 (for sentence quantifiers)), the consequence is that no member of P may contain the L-quantifier. If it did, L_0 truth could not be characterized antecedently to the characterization of L truth, and there would be a kind of vicious circularity.

To reinforce this point, suppose that P contains the predicate '$(\exists\varphi)(\varphi\xi)$'. Then we might be driven to hold that the truth or falsehood of the sentence '$(\exists\varphi)\varphi a$' turns on the truth or falsehood of the following instance of 'φa' (replacing 'φ' by the predicate '$(\exists\varphi)(\varphi\xi)$'): '$(\exists\varphi)\varphi a$'. This means that there is a sentence whose truth or falsehood has not been determined by what has been said about L_0 and L; and this is to say that an adequate characterization has not been given. (Kripke's argument for a more precise version of this conclusion (for name quantifiers) should be studied: 'Substitutional Quantification' 331–2.)

If one both desires to avoid vicious circularity of the kind just mentioned, and also desires to extend as far as possible the instances relevant to substitutional predicate quantification, one is likely to arrive at a hierarchy of predicate quantifiers, bearing a striking resemblance to Russell's ramified theory of types (cf. 'Substitutional Quantification' 368). Let us call the substitutional predicate quantifier developed on the basis of the class P, where P consists of just the predicates of some first-order language, the first-order predicate quantifier. (It will count as first-order because its substitutes are.) Then we could form a new class of predicates P^* which extends P

by including predicates containing the first-order predicate quantifier. On the basis of P^*, one could introduce a second-order predicate quantifier, giving the truth-conditions of second-order quantifications in terms of the truth or falsehood of instances in which the variable of quantification is replaced by a predicate drawn from P^*. In general, one could introduce a quantifier of order $n+1$ on the basis of a class of predicates containing quantifiers of order n. Each quantifier would be confined to some position in the hierarchy, and there could be no completely unrestricted quantifier developed on the basis of the class of all predicates.

Russell is customarily credited with a hierarchy of non-linguistic entities (properties), and this would not at once flow from the hierarchy of predicate quantifiers. The connection is provided by an anti-realist conception of properties, which can plausibly be attributed to Russell. On this view, identity and difference of properties is determined by synonymy and non-synonymy of predicates which express them, where the notion of synonymy is sufficiently tight for substantial structural differences to ensure non-synonymy. In the light of this view, one can make sense of Russell's speaking of non-linguistic entities as essentially involving quantification (e.g., *PM* 37). A predicate containing a quantifier will not, on the present view, be synonymous with any predicate which does not, so the property it expresses can only be expressed by a predicate containing a quantifier. In general, because a property is properly specified only by a predicate with a certain structure, we can regard this structure as woven into the nature of the property. By contrast with objects which can in principle be named, and thus specified by a structureless expression, in the case of properties we lack a full distinction between *our* mode of specifying them and *their* nature. We saw in Chapter II that Russell tends to identify being a genuine entity with being nameable, and the same attitude is vividly manifested in his discussion of the Axiom of Reducibility. He argues that to assume that classes are genuine entities is to assume that each is nameable (cf. *PM* 58 and section 10 below). We can interpret Russell as using 'genuine entity' of those things he thinks we should view realistically (their nature is independent of us, and in particular independent of the possible specifications open to us). By this standard, properties are not genuine entities, but are to be viewed anti-realistically.

The principle that structurally diverse predicates are non-synonymous requires modification, since for any predicate, however complex, one could always introduce an atomic abbreviation. The modification is that there is no way of grasping the abbreviation except by grasping what it abbreviates. We can call the unabbreviated specification 'canonical', and one test would be: knowledge *of* a property requires, and is afforded by, mastery of its canonical specification. A consequence is that non-canonical specifications are eliminable, and in any case cannot occur in a learnable language lacking their canonical correlates.

On the customary interpretation, Russell's function quantifiers are restricted by the order of property over which they range, where the order of a property is fixed by the order of the function quantifiers, if any, in the corresponding (canonical) predicate. The hierarchy of orders of substitutional quantifier to which one is led by Kripke's account of substitutional quantification is based on a hierarchy of predicates of ascending order which, on the anti-realist view of properties, induces a hierarchy of order of properties (the 'ramified hierarchy'). This connection between substitutional quantification and a hierarchy of orders of properties is some evidence that Russell intended his function quantifiers as substitutional predicate quantifiers. If so, he would have an argument for ramification (i.e. the hierarchy of orders) independent of the paradoxes. Instead of arguing that ramification is required for the avoidance of paradox, he could argue that ramification is required for the semantic coherence of the quantifiers. If you have an incoherent quantifier it is not surprising that you can generate what are, or seem to be, paradoxes. But you do not need to point to the paradoxes to show the incoherence of the quantifier. Although Russell is not explicit, this line of thought harmonizes well with what he says. He identifies the common essence of the paradoxes as a kind of vicious circularity and claims that this circularity is to be avoided by a proper account of quantification (one could view *PM* 38–65 as a protracted argument for this claim). Since, on the substitutional interpretation, ramification is designed to avoid circularity, this interpretation would go some way towards vindicating Russell's position.

It could not be seriously maintained that the *PM* function quantifiers are substitutional predicate quantifiers developed in just the manner so far considered, for the simple reason that *PM* contains no primitive predicate constants, and hence contains no plausible class of substitutes for substitutional predicate quantifiers. However, there is no reason why a language L should not contain a substitutional predicate quantifier whose substitutes are to be found in a distinct language, not contained in L. If the project is, as before, to characterize L truth in terms of truth in the distinct language containing the relevant substitutes, it remains the case that one cannot allow these substitutes to contain the L-quantifier, on pain of vicious circularity. We could view the *PM* function quantifiers as substitutional predicate quantifiers based on some first-order language which is never specified in *PM*. On this view, the need to avoid circularity will still provide a paradox-independent argument for ramification.

It might at first sight seem to count against this view that Russell's failure to specify the relevant base language would be quite inexplicable, since until it is given the language of *PM* is not fully interpreted. However, it is plain that Russell took his first-order function quantifiers to quantify over all first-order functions. By implication, any maximally expressive first-order language (or perhaps the union of all learnable first-order languages) would provide an adequate base for the function quantifiers. In other words, one who sees the *PM* function quantifiers as substitutional predicate quantifiers will explain Russell's failure to give any detailed specification of the distinct language containing the relevant substitutes by the fact that *PM* contains, by implication, a general specification of a class of adequate languages (those that are first-order and maximally expressive). If the class contains a plurality of members, there is no interesting choice between them.

This view of Russell's function quantifiers seems to me to be *one* possible one (though, as we shall see, there are others), and it has the merit of providing, as Russell intended, a direct link between the avoidance of vicious circularity and the coherence of quantification. However, Russell's position requires something more than we have yet provided. He did not see himself as confronted with a choice between a substitutional predicate quantifier and an unramified 'referential' one. Rather, it is plain that he thought that *any* coherent function quantifier had to meet the threat of vicious circularity and so had to be set in a ramified hierarchy. For he explicitly denies that there could be a coherent unramified function quantifier (*PM* 48–9); and he is required to hold this by his use of ramification to block the paradoxes, for if there were coherent unramified function quantifiers perhaps these could be used to reintroduce the paradoxes. Thus a full vindication of Russell's position would require it to be the case that every coherent predicate quantifier must be ramified, and for this to be shown on the basis of the ideas we are at present discussing, it would have to be shown that every coherent predicate quantifier can be substitutionally interpreted.

I do not believe that this last can be shown, but it is illuminating to see how Russell might have worked himself into such a position that it would seem to him an inescapable truth.

We have already seen that Russell glosses quantification over a propositional function in terms of the truth or falsehood of values or instances of the function, rather than in terms of a relation, like Tarskian satisfaction, between objects and functions (or open sentences). This is particularly obvious in *ML* (83), where Russell is listing the primitive ideas required in logic:

The truth of *all* values of a propositional function. This is denoted by $(x).\varphi x$. . . .

If this is the only way to understand quantification (whether name quantification or predicate quantification), then it looks as if vicious circularity would always be a threat. For it seems natural to propose that these values of a propositional function, in terms of whose truth or falsehood the truth-conditions of quantifications over the function are given, must not, on pain of vicious circularity, contain the quantifier in question.

Whatever involves an apparent variable must not be among the possible values of that variable (*EA* 198; *ML* 75).

This prohibits the variable 'φ' in a quantification '$(\exists\varphi)$ . . . φ . . .' having among its values a function containing the quantifier '$(\exists\varphi)$'; and thus seems quite justly to disallow that sentences containing this quantifier be among the instances in terms of whose truth or falsehood the quantifier's truth-conditions are stated.

In short, Russell thought, not implausibly, that quantification can always be understood in terms of the truth or falsehood of suitable instances; and it is tempting to believe that this alone is enough to pose the threat of vicious circularity, so that, given anti-realism about properties, we are tempted to believe that every coherent predicate quantifier must be ramified.

This line of thought seems to me to give a useful explanation of Russell's position concerning quantification, circularity and ramification. None the less, it is unsound. The truth is that there is at least one way of explaining quantification in terms of the truth of suitable instances in which it would not matter if the quantifier occurred in the instances; on the other hand, if the permitted ways of interpreting quantifiers are narrowed so as to exclude ways like this, then there is no reason of the kind we have been considering to suppose that every coherent quantifier can be interpreted in the permitted ways. The remainder of this part of the section attempts to clarify and establish this point.

Suppose that, for interpreting a quantifier, we are permitted any way provided that it speaks only of the truth and falsehood of instances of the open sentence under quantification, and not of satisfaction. I shall show that there is one such mode of interpretation, which I call 'pseudo-substitutional', in which it is a matter of indifference if the instances contain the quantifier under interpretation. First, I shall make the point for a language L with an objectual name quantifier whose domain is everything. Instead of the usual specification of truth for quantifications in terms of satisfaction, we have something like: '$\forall v(\varphi v)$' is true in L iff every instance of 'φv' is true in L$^+$. Here L$^+$ is an extension of L containing a name for every object and no empty names, and an instance of 'φv' results from it by replacing every occurrence of 'v' by some one L$^+$-name.[5] If we further assume that a sentence consisting of an atomic predicate con-catenated with an L$^+$-name is true iff the L$^+$ denotation of the name has the property expressed (in L and L$^+$) by the predicate, we have an adequate characterization of truth in L on the basis of instances of the open sentences under quantification. Moreover, it would not matter if some of the L$^+$-'names' were to contain '$(\forall v)$'. The reason is that we never need to determine the truth or falsehood of any specific L$^+$ instance (not in L) in order to determine the truth or falsehood of an L-quantification on the basis of the stipulations made.

The point applies analogously to predicate quantification. The anti-ramificationist will agree that a pseudo-substitutional account can be given of the predicate quantifier, and he will be quite happy to include in his metalanguage the unrestricted quantifier needed to ensure that his L$^+$ contains, for *every property*, a predicate. As in the name quantifier case, it will be a matter of indifference if some of the L$^+$ instances contain the quantifier under interpretation. Such a language may be criticized on other grounds, for example, on the grounds that it leads to paradox. But there is, as far as I can see, no just criticism of it on the grounds of some general and more or less formal failure to permit an adequate characterization of truth.

If the permitted ways of giving an interpretation of a quantifier are restricted so as to ensure that the vicious circularity point obtains, there will be no reason to think that every coherent quantifier can be correctly interpreted in the permitted ways. One will simply have begged the case against the anti-ramificationist.

To sum up the conclusions of this section: it is possible to interpret Russell's function quantifiers as substitutional predicate quantifiers, based on a class of instances drawn from some unspecified, but presumably maximally expressive, language outside *PM*. This gives a partial explanation of the connection which Russell saw between the coherence of quantification, the avoidance of vicious circularity, and ramification. However, it does not explain Russell's belief that ramification was mandatory for every species of higher-order quantification. A possible explanation for this belief is that it is reasonable to suppose that every coherent quantifier can be interpreted in terms of the truth or falsehood of the instances of the

[5] Cf. Gareth Evans, 'Pronouns, Quantifiers, and Relative Clauses' 474–7.

open sentence under quantification, and natural, though erroneous, to suppose that this alone establishes the connection with vicious circularity, and thus with ramification.

(*iii*) Russell certainly did not see the function quantifiers as name quantifiers ranging over classes. One thing about *PM* (in its first edition) that is entirely certain is the sharp distinction that Russell saw between functions and classes. The identity of *classes* is fixed by the extensions of functions, but not so the identity of functions (cf. *PM* 23, 74ff., and section 4 below).

(*iv*) To view function quantifiers as name quantifiers ranging over functions is to view the system of *PM* as one of many-sorted first-order quantification. One will discern a new logical constant: concatenation of what would previously have been thought of as a predicate with its terms will express a multigrade[6] relation of holding-of, between the function and the denotata of the terms. Then a quantification like '$(\exists \varphi)\varphi(\text{Socrates})$' will be read: 'there is a function which holds-of Socrates'.

There is some evidence that Russell views his function quantifiers as name quantifiers, or, more exactly, that he sees no significant difference between viewing them as name quantifiers and viewing them as predicate quantifiers. One relevant piece of evidence is found in his account, very early in *PM*, of the distinctive use of lower case roman variables: these are to 'be used for variables whose values are not known to be functions, classes or relations' (*PM* 5). This implies that on occasion the values of 'x' might for all we know be functions. Since 'x' is often (perhaps always) used as a name variable (as in 'x is hurt' (*PM* 25)), this implies that the values of a name variable might, for all we know, be functions. Thus Russell at least countenances name quantification over functions.

A second piece of evidence in favour of the hypothesis is Russell's official indifference between the use of a function variable, e.g., 'φ', and the use of a function abstract variable, e.g., '$\varphi\hat{z}$' (*PM* 49n). A function abstract variable is a species of name variable, for a function abstract occupies name position. So if 'φ' may be used indifferently with a function abstract variable, it may, on those occasions, be regarded as occupying name position. Thus a quantifier binding it may be regarded as a name quantifier rather than a predicate quantifier.

Russell's practice is to use a function variable when the position is what we would naturally think of as predicate position, and to use a function abstract variable when the position is what we would naturally think of as name position. In this last case, we have no choice: the function abstract variable must be used 'to emphasize that

6 In Goodman and Leonard's sense: 'The Calculus of Individuals and Its Uses'.

an argument must be supplied to secure significance' (*PM* 49*n*), that is, to emphasize that the position is argument position (name position). An example Russell gives (*PM* 48) is the formula:

$$(\forall\psi)f(\varphi\hat{z}, x).$$

We are told that *f* is a dyadic relation, and though no reading is explicitly given, presumably it would be something like: *x* is *f*-related to every function.

As an example of the use of function variables, consider the axiom of reducibility:

$$(\exists\psi)(\forall x)(\varphi x \leftrightarrow \psi!x).$$

Russell's English gloss suggests that this is a case in which we could as well have used function abstract variables in place of function variables: 'given any function $\varphi\hat{x}$, there is a formally equivalent *predicative* function' (*PM* 56). ('Predicative' belongs to the terminology of the theory of types; the notion is represented by '!' in the formula.) Rewriting with function abstract variables we would have:

$$(\exists\psi!\hat{z})(\forall x)\,((\varphi\hat{z})x \leftrightarrow (\psi!\hat{z})x).$$

A consequence of indifference between using a function variable and using a function abstract variable in such circumstances is indifference between writing 'φx' and writing '$(\varphi\hat{z})x$', where the latter is to be read '*x* possesses $\varphi\hat{z}$' (cf. Quine, *Set Theory* 379). This in turn encourages indifference between regarding the 'higher-order' quantifiers of *PM* as predicate quantifiers and regarding them as a species of name quantifier. Notice that this sits well with Russell's earlier views. His difficulties about the unity of the proposition sprang in part from a tendency to conflate the doctrine that expressions in predicate position are associated with entities (universals) in a way relevant to their meaning with the falsehood that these expressions name universals. This error would encourage the arguably correct view that we can systematically reinterpret predicates as names of universals, so long as we make appropriate changes elsewhere (cf. p. 283 above); and this in turn encourages indifference between a name quantification like '$(\exists x)$ (Possesses (Socrates, *x*))' and the corresponding quantification, superficially involving a predicate quantifier, '$(\exists\varphi)$ (φ(Socrates))'.

In favour of this view I have already suggested that predicate quantification is quantification over entities, just as name quantification is. So in what respect would what is involved in mastery of predicate quantification differ from what is involved in mastery of name quantification over properties? Unless one can find an answer, which I cannot, then one must view the one species of quantification as differing merely notationally from the other. This justifies Russell's attitude in *PM*.

It remains to decide whether functions are properties, as I have tended to suppose in the above discussion, or whether they are expressions. If they are properties, then the new logical constant that must be discerned if one views function-quantifiers as name-quantifiers, must be interpreted as possession or instantiation. '$(\exists\varphi)\varphi$(Socrates)' will be read: 'Socrates possesses (instantiates) some property'. If functions are expressions, then the new logical constant will have to be interpreted as being true-of. Then the above sentence will be read: 'Some open sentence is true-of Socrates', that is, 'the result of putting a name for Socrates in place of the variable in some open sentence is true'. (In these readings, I leave aside complications arising from the theory of ramified types.)

There is a *prima facie* case against the weird and tortuous inter-pretation of functions as expressions. Viewing function quantifiers as name quantifiers, one would have to view an instance of such a quantification along the lines of, for example, '"x is a man" is true-of Socrates'. ('True-of' will have to be relativized to a suitable language.) However, this seems an inexplicable detour, since the true-of relation is explained by the use, as opposed to the mention, of predicates like '. . . is a man'. There would be no reason at all for contemplating the suggestion that functions are expressions, were it not for certain aspects of Russell's position. [7]

There are various 'surface' pointers to the conclusion that Russell thought of functions as expressions.

> By a 'propositional function' we mean something which contains a variable x, and expresses a *proposition* as soon as a value is assigned to x (*PM* 38).

Since a variable is defined as 'any symbol whose meaning is not determinate' (*PM* 4), it follows that, so long as 'contains' is being used literally, a function is an expression. Again, according to Russell,

> examples of propositional functions are easy to give: 'x is human' is a propositional function (*IMP* 156).

If quotation is being used in the standard way, this shows that functions are thought of as open sentences.

It would be natural to assign to propositional functions the same

---

[7] Since writing this, a further aspect has been pointed out to me by Saul Kripke, in the course of a helpful conversation about quantification and ramification: quantifying over expressions will induce ramification.

status as propositions, for a function 'differs from a proposition solely by the fact that it is ambiguous' (*PM* 38). However,

> We mean by a 'proposition' primarily a form of words which expresses what is either true or false (*IMP* 155).

(The qualification 'primarily' is to allow for non-verbal symbols.)

In *EA* (145), where Russell offers the earliest version of the no-class theory, he adopts a notation with the explicit aim of avoiding the 'inevitable' suggestion that a function denotes something. This seems to show a determination to regard functions as expressions, though it does not show that this survives into *PM*, where he reverts to the notation he had earlier avoided.

Finally, Russell is quite explicit in retrospect:

> In the language of the second-order, variables denote symbols, not what is symbolized (*IMT* 192).

> Whitehead and I thought of a propositional function as an
> expression (*MPD* 124).

One can find surface indications, in the writing of the *PM* period, that point in the contrary direction: towards the view that Russell thought of functions as properties. At this superficial level, nothing of great importance can be decided. We must therefore look to the rather deeper indications that Russell saw functions as expressions. One is that if functions are properties then they are 'universals', in the sense in which he used that word in, for example, *PP*. Yet his discussions of whether there are universals never exploit the premise that unless there were universals mathematics would be impossible, though this is the sort of argument he uses in other connections (e.g., external relations; cf. *PofM* 226). This suggests that he did not see functions as properties, and thus that he did see them as expressions.

His no-class theory parses apparent talk of classes into talk of functions. It is recommended on two grounds: the general ground of parsimony and the more specific ground of avoidance of paradox. If functions are properties then, it may be said, we have a less satisfactory ontology for mathematics than if we had been content with classes as 'genuine objects'. For at least the identity condition of classes is plain ($\alpha = \beta$ iff α and β have exactly the same members), whereas the identity condition for properties rests ultimately on such supposedly unsatisfactory notions as synonymy (cf. Quine, *Word and Object* 209ff., 118ff.). Moreover, if functions are properties, trading classes for functions has no tendency to help with paradox, since, as Russell well knew, the alleged property of being non-self-applicable, supposedly having all properties in its range of significance, is as paradoxical as the supposed class of all non-self-membered classes.

I aim to turn these objections. I think one cannot deny that Russell on occasion used 'function' for 'open sentence'; nor can one deny that he on occasion supposed that the correct official line had to be that functions are expressions. However, I think one can show that in this second supposition he was mistaken. Once this is shown, one can more readily take the occasions on which he departs from the official line as indicating that, at least for part of the time, he construed functions as properties. Then one would be left only with the relatively superficial point that Russell's usage of 'function' is ambiguous.

Russell may well have felt that, for the no-class theory to have the merits he desired, functions must indeed be viewed as expressions. This is what I think is a mistake. To the extent that we are in any case landed with predication, we are in any case landed with properties, for in predication some property is ascribed. Hence there is genuine advantage to be had if an ontology of classes is an ontology of no more than properties. Quinean qualms about the 'intelligibility' of properties must be met in this general fashion: though no doubt their identity is to be explained in terms of the notion of synonymy, the last notion is something which has to be accepted, whether or not there can be any reductive explanation of it. The reason is that we need as theorists both to exploit the contrast between synonymy and non-synonymy in describing and explaining linguistic behaviour (we must typically explain why a man utters some words rather than others in terms of their non-synonymy, in terms of his wanting to say different things) and to attribute an explicit grasp of the concept to those whose linguistic behaviour we explain (for they will themselves manifest some fairly conscious sensitivity to the contrast in their ascriptions of propositional attitudes). This merely gestures at the relevant reason, but it would be inappropriate to pursue it in more detail here. (Cf. Dummett, *Frege* ch 17.)

Finally, and most importantly, given the view of properties mentioned earlier, they have an immunity from paradox that classes lack. This view is that the existence of a property depends on the possibility of introducing a coherent predicate, and paradoxical predicates cannot coherently be introduced. If we regard classes as objects whose existence is wholly independent of human thought and language, there is no reason why anything should hinge on how *we* can specify them. Properties, on the present view, are different: it is quite natural that much should hinge on how we can specify them. Since part of Russell's theory of ramified types makes much of how entities relevant to mathematics can be specified, his position is better justified when these entities are, thanks to the no-class theory, properties, than were they classes. In short, despite superficial appearances to the contrary, Russell's motivation for the no-class theory is well served by regarding functions as properties.

One might very tentatively attribute to Russell the following confusion: between taking the function quantifiers as quantifying over expressions, and taking them as quantifying over distinct sorts of entity, but entities which are as finely discriminated as non-synonymous expressions, and whose existence hangs on there being certain meaningful expressions (in a coherent extension of our language). This would well explain the tendency which Russell exhibits to treat functions as expressions when he is being most self-conscious about their nature, even though, when he is using the notion of a function less self-consciously, there is no temptation to interpret him as talking of anything other than properties. It thus explains why, for example, he does not rely on the nature of mathematics when arguing philosophically for the existence of universals.

I earlier undertook to say something about Quine's objection to the coherence of predicate quantification. I conclude by summarizing the relevant points, which have already been made. One can, I think, regard second-order quantifiers as genuinely predicate quantifiers, though the overall semantic properties of a language containing such quantifiers will come out unchanged if we regard the quantifiers as name quantifiers within a system of many-sorted first-order quantification, and make appropriate adjustments elsewhere (in particular, in the interpretation of the semantic role of concatenation). In either case second-order quantification is quantification over properties. But one cannot simply deny the existence of properties, for a man who utters a subject-predicate sentence can be viewed as ascribing a property to something. In particular, one cannot deny the existence of properties on the basis of the difficulty of explaining synonymy, for synonymy relations are required to explain our linguistic practice.

4 Number defined

Numerical expressions in English divide into at least these three kinds:

(*i*) Numeral adjectives, such as 'five' in the sentence 'there are five men in the room'.

(*ii*) Numeral singular terms, such as 'five' in 'Five is prime', and such as '5 + 7' in '5 + 7 is even', and such as 'the number of the apostles' in 'The number of the apostles is divisible by three'.

(*iii*) Quantifier phrases, apparently introducing quantification over numbers, as in 'All numbers are odd or even'.

Numeral adjectives can be formalized in first-order predicate calculus with identity, but the other cases require additional expressive power. One could simply add non-logical predicate and individual constants, but this would not satisfy the logicist programme (cf. (i), p. 272 above). Russell's procedure draws only on the logical constants of *PM*, and involves two main steps: the introduction of class abstracts and the class membership sign; and definition in non-numerical terms of what it is for two classes to be similar (equinumerous). Both steps involve function quantifiers. The end result is that numbers are defined as classes of similar classes, and this single definition is applied in somewhat different ways to the formalization of all the different kinds of numerical expressions I have indicated.

There are two key definitions in the introduction of class abstracts (which have the form $\hat{z}(\varphi z)$). One is *20·01:

$$f\{\hat{z}(\psi z)\} =_{df} (\exists \varphi)((\forall x)(\varphi!x \leftrightarrow \psi x) \& f!\{\varphi!\hat{z}\})$$

This enables us to eliminate a class abstract from any sentence in which it occurs as grammatical subject: a sentence saying that the class of $\psi\hat{z}$ has the property f is replaceable by a sentence saying that some predicative property with the same extension as $\psi\hat{x}$ has the property f. (The notion of a *predicative* property is explained in section 7 below.)

The second definition is *20·02, and it is designed to allow the elimination of the membership sign '$\in$':

$$x \in (\varphi!\hat{z}) =_{df} \varphi!x.$$

Russell remarks that 'In this form, the definition is never used' (*PM* 188). It is introduced in order to permit the derivation of

$$x \in \hat{z}(\psi z) \leftrightarrow (\exists \varphi)((\forall y)(\psi y \leftrightarrow \varphi!y) \& \varphi!x).$$

(In the derivation, start by taking '$x\in$' for 'f' in *20·01.) Together with the axiom of reducibility, this leads to the more general

$$x \in \hat{z}(\psi z) \leftrightarrow \psi x.$$

This says, roughly, that x belongs to the class of ψs iff x is a ψ. The definitions bring it about that one can eliminate both class abstracts and the class membership sign, and they ensure that $\hat{z}(\varphi z) = \hat{z}(\psi z)$ iff $(\forall x)(\varphi x \leftrightarrow \psi x)$.

In the next stage of the definition of number, essential use is made of the fact that sentences containing numeral adjectives can be formalized in such a way that these adjectives introduce no concepts other than logical ones. This involves introducing what I shall call 'numerical quantifiers', and I shall begin by explaining how this may be done.

We can start by providing an inductive definition of 'there are at least n φs' as follows:

$$(\exists_1 x)\varphi x =_{df} (\exists x)\varphi x$$
$$(\exists_{n+1} x)\varphi x =_{df} (\exists x)(\varphi x \,\&\, (\exists_n y)(\varphi y \,\&\, y \neq x)).$$

On this basis, we can define 'there are exactly n φs' as follows:

$$(nx)\varphi x =_{df} (\exists_n x)\,\varphi x \,\&\, {\sim}(\exists_{n+1} x)\varphi x.$$

(Note that these 'numerical quantifiers' are not quantifiers over numbers.)

The first use that is made of the numerical quantifiers is in the definition of a one-one relation, which draws on the 'exactly' quantifier '$(1x)$'. (Russell writes this '$(\exists! x)$'.) The domain of the relation R is defined as the class of things each one of which is R-related to something, and the converse domain of R as the class of things each one of which has something R-related to it. A relation is said to be one-one between two classes α and β iff α is the domain of R, β its converse domain, and

$$(\forall x)(x{\in}\alpha \to (1y)(y{\in}\beta \,\&\, Rxy)) \,\&\, (\forall x)(x{\in}\beta \to (1y)(y{\in}\alpha \,\&\, Ryx))$$

(cf. *70). Thanks to the possibility of defining '$(1x)$' in purely logical terms, this definition of a one-one relation is consistent with the logicist programme of defining all mathematical concepts in purely logical terms.

Two classes are said to be similar iff there is a one-one relation between them (*73·02). It is clear that two similar classes have the same number of members. Now Russell suggests that we cannot ascribe numbers to individuals: if, for example, we say that there are five men in the room we are not ascribing five to any of the men in the room but rather to the class of men in the room. Hence what has to be defined is *the number of a class*, and Russell proposes that it be defined as the class of classes similar to that class. In other words, a number is a kind of class, viz. a class all of whose members are classes and all of whose members are similar to one another.

Russell defines the number o as the class consisting of all classes similar to $\hat{x}(x{\neq}x)$, i.e. as the class of all classes similar to some o-membered class, i.e. as the class whose only member is the null class. In general, though Russell is not so explicit, an expression of the form 'the number n' is supposed to be eliminable in favour of a corresponding expression of the form 'the class of classes similar to some class α such that $(nx)x{\in}\alpha$'. This is the second, and this time full, use of the definition of numerical quantifiers.

Though this full use is essential to the definition of particular numbers, Russell does not explicitly advocate it in the formalization of numeral adjectives, and tends to suggest that 'there are five men in the room' should be formalized as 'the class of men in the room belongs to five', where 'five' is to be defined, in the way we saw in the last paragraph, as the class of 5-membered classes. (*IMP* 14 points in this direction, though it is not explicit.)

Numeral singular terms like 'five' in 'five is prime' are treated in the obvious way (predicates like 'prime' will, of course, require definition). The arithmetic functors like '+' and '×' receive set-theoretic definition, in terms of union and intersection respectively, and this leads to a treatment of singular terms like '5+7' and '5×7'. Phrases like 'the number of the apostles' have to be rendered 'the class of classes which are similar to the class of the apostles'.

Quantification apparently over numbers becomes, in the first instance, quantification over classes. By the no-class theory, quantification apparently over classes becomes quantification over properties. 'Numbers are, as it were, fictions at two removes, fictions of fictions' (*PLA* 270).

Before discussing the adequacy of Russell's definition of number, it will be useful to consider the various positions which the definition might be taken to exemplify. (See Chapter VII, section 4, where I divide the possibilities in a slightly different way.)

(1) One might try to translate arithmetical sentences into class theoretic sentences, in the literal sense of 'translate' in which, if one sentence translates another, the two have the same meaning. In this way, one might hope to reduce numerical concepts to class theoretic ones. This goal would be an example of what I called in Chapter VII the goal of providing a translational construction of numbers out of classes.

(2) Another goal is this: one accepts that arithmetical sentences, in their ordinary meaning, require for their truth the existence of entities other than classes: let us call them 'Numbers' (as opposed to numbers). However, for one reason or another one finds one cannot stomach Numbers. So one sets out to offer classes as substitutes for Numbers, reinterpreting arithmetical sentences as class theoretic sentences, and abandoning any claim to *translate* Number theoretic sentences into class theoretic ones. In the mouth of one having this goal, the sentence 'numbers are classes', used to express the position in question and to make a substantial claim, must be understood as affirming that Numbers can with advantage be replaced by classes in one's thought and talk.

On one interpretation, the claim that selves are bundles of perceptions is an example of this sort of position. One might feel that personal sentences, as ordinarily understood, require for their truth the existence of simple enduring mental substances – Selves – but that precisely in virtue of this fact one has no adequate warrant for the truth of personal sentences. Hence one offers bundles of perceptions as substitutes, reinterpreting personal sentences so that, in their reformed sense, they require for their truth not that Selves exist but rather that there be bundles of perceptions. Once again, if the position is expressed by the sentence 'selves are bundles of perceptions', 'selves' must be understood in the unreformed sense of 'Selves', and the whole claim is that Selves can with advantage be replaced by bundles in our thought and talk.

(3) One might hold that numerical sentences, in their ordinary meaning, do not require for their truth that Numbers exist, but only that classes exist: numbers, those things whose existence is required by the truth of such sentences, *are* classes. However, the claim continues, people have mistakenly supposed that numbers are Numbers. This position in one sense leaves 'our ontology' unchanged, though in another sense it modifies it. It leaves unchanged what things true arithmetical sentences require to exist; but it corrects false or perhaps incoherent *beliefs* about what things true arithmetical sentences require to exist. In one sense it does, and in another sense it does not, call for a 'new interpretation' of arithmetical sentences. It corrects the customary *account* of what they mean, but leaves unchanged what they actually mean.

One might, but need not, establish a position of this kind by means of a translational construction.

The claim that selves are bundles of perceptions could be viewed as an example of this third sort of position, and it should be so viewed if it is coupled with the claim that the concept of the Self is incoherent. That personal sentences have a meaning such that they require for their truth the existence of Selves is, under the present assumption, something that cannot coherently be said. Hence this theorist cannot adopt position (2). He can more happily accept that, strictly speaking, those philosophers who have used the word 'Self' (or another word supposed to have the same meaning) have not thereby asserted anything or expressed a belief, true or false. For it is one thing to hold that philosophers have talked (literally) nonsense, and quite another and graver thing to hold that a huge body of sentences in daily usage are, in reality, without significance.

Which, if any, of these positions did Russell hold? Direct evidence is rather scant. He speaks of logicism as having 'swept away from the philosophy of mathematics the useless menagerie of metaphysical monsters with which it used to be infested' (*RSP* 115), but it is not entirely clear whether it was the old mathematics, or the old philosophy of mathematics, that bred the monsters. In the same place he says that the existence of numbers, regarded as inferred entities rather than as constructions out of classes, 'must remain in doubt, unless in virtue of a metaphysical postulate *ad hoc*' (cf. *IMP* 18). But this again leaves open the question of whether treating numbers as classes is consistent with the ordinary meaning of arithmetical sentences, or whether this treatment requires us to assign them a new meaning.

Some indirect evidence points to the conclusion that Russell did not intend the definition of number to be a translational construction on the lines of (1) above. One minor and merely permissive point is that he often uses 'definition' in a way which shows that in his mouth a definiendum need not be synonymous with its definiens (e.g., *PLA* 194–6). More positively, Russell is explicit that all constructions are 'precisely analogous' (*RSP* 115). Since there is evidence to suggest that his empirical constructions are not intended to be translational (they reform our ordinary language which embodies the savage superstitions of cannibals: cf. 'Mind and Matter' 143), we have indirect evidence that the same applies to mathematical constructions.

In any case, it seems clear that Russell *should* not have claimed translatability. I offer two arguments in support of this assertion. One is that there is a kind of possible situation which seems best described as giving us evidence that someone has mastered elementary numerical concepts, but not class concepts. He can count, add and subtract, and so, on the translation view, must thereby be ascribed grasp of class theoretic concepts. Yet when we try to introduce him to the usual class vocabulary he is an extremely poor learner, and seems unable to grasp the simplest points. This would be inexplicable if he already possessed the class theoretic concepts (some of which would have to be quite sophisticated, on the translation view, even in the mastery of relatively simple arithmetic procedures): for it should simply be a matter of learning new words for concepts one already possesses, like learning a foreign language. As I say, the natural way to describe the situation is as one in which the person has grasped numerical concepts but not all the class theoretic concepts involved in their logicist rephrasals. On the translation theory, this description is contradictory.

The other argument relies on the premise that there is an equally good case for other class theoretic constructions of number, for example, that which matches zero with Λ, 1 with $\{\Lambda\}$, and, in general, n with the class denoted by an expression consisting of n left curly brackets, followed by an occurrence of 'Λ', followed by n right curly brackets. Russell's candidate for zero is $\{\Lambda\}$, which is distinct from Λ.[8] Evidently, '$\{\Lambda\}$' does not mean the same as 'Λ'. So, on the assumption

[8] Cf. Benacerraf, 'What Numbers Could Not Be'.

of the equal adequacy of both constructions, neither expression means the same as 'o'.

If we rule out the suggestion that Russell intended his construction to be translational, the possibilities that remain are that he intended it as an example of position (2) above, or of a non-translational version of (3). I find nothing in Russell's writings to motivate a firm decision between these interpretations. However, a point made earlier can be used to supply some indirect support for the ascription of (2). In connection with empirical constructions, ordinary language is held to embody definite errors and to require reform; so these constructions are closer in spirit to (2) than to (3). But empirical and mathematical constructions are held to be 'precisely analogous'. Russell's standard of adequacy for the mathematical constructions also points in the same direction. He says simply that the definition of number is 'adequate to all mathematical uses' (*PofM* 116). He does not make the bolder claim, typical of one who held (3), that the definition reveals the true nature of numbers.

Another point previously made shows that Russell does best to offer his construction as an example of (2) rather than (3). On the earlier assumption that there are equally compelling arguments for different class theoretic constructions, the adoption of position (3) would lead to there being compelling arguments for the con- tradiction that, for example, $o = \Lambda$ and $o = \{\Lambda\}$. No such contradiction follows if position (2) is adopted. The point may be put like this: one cannot coherently hold that numbers are identical with classes, without holding that for each number there is some particular class with which (alone) it is identical. But one can quite coherently hold that there are distinct ways, adequate for our thought and talk, of dispensing with numbers in favour of classes. Thus, with some hesitation, I interpret Russell as offering his construction of number on the lines of position (2).

I have so far assumed that the non-Russellian ways of replacing numbers by ·classes are as adequate as Russell's way; but this assumption requires defending. What I shall do instead is to argue against the only argument with which I am acquainted in favour of Russell's definition as opposed to its rivals. (These remarks are due almost entirely to Bostock, 3–5.) Russell assumes that numbers can be applied to something (cf. *PofM* 112ff.; *PM* II 4). This implies that in some employments numerals function as predicates, and a putative example might be 'The number of men in the room is five'. Granted this, the question now arises: what are these supposed predicates predicates of? Given that they are plainly not predicates of individuals (for no one of the men is five), it is inferred that they are predicates of classes. The next step is to draw an analogy between, on the one hand, the supposed predicative role of numerals and their nominative role, and, on the other, the predicative and nominative roles of expressions like 'man'. The analogy is meant to be with occurrences of 'man' in such sentences as 'John is a man', where the word is, or is part of, a predicate, and its occurrences in such sentences as 'man has evolved more rapidly than any other animal' (Bostock 3), in which, it may be said, the word functions as the name of a class. Thus in its nominative employment the word names the class of entities to which, in its predicative employment, it is applied. Analogously, it is argued that numerals in their nominative employment in such sentences as 'five is prime' name the class of entities to which, in their predicative employment, they are applied. By the previous argument, numerals used predicatively apply to classes. So, the present argument concludes, a numeral used nominatively must apply to the class whose members are those classes to which the numeral applies in its predicative employment. Just as 'five', used predicatively, applies to five-membered classes, so, used nominatively, it names the class of all five-membered classes.

As Bostock convincingly shows, both the claims on which this reasoning depends are false. If 'man' in its nominative employment named a class, various sentences which are in fact ill-formed would be well-formed: for example, 'man is included in animal', 'John belongs to man', 'man has woman as a sub-class'. More importantly, the assumption that numerals have a predicative use in ordinary language is without foundation. Typically, they function as quantifiers rather than predicates, as Frege explicitly saw (cf. Bostock 5), and as Russell perhaps on occasion dimly suspected (cf. *PofM* 113; *PM* II 4). For there is clearly a close semantic analogy between the pairs 'there are no men in the room' and 'there are five men in the room'; 'most of the team came' and 'five of the team came'. The earlier putative example of a predicative employment of 'five' can best be seen as a nominative one, the whole sentence being an identity like 'half five is ten'. (Indeed, to support the analogy, the example would have to be read, quite implausibly, as a variant of 'the class of men in the room is five'.)

The upshot is that the present argument fails to show any greater naturalness of Russell's definition of number, as opposed to alternatives, and as I know of no other arguments in favour of Russell's, I must conclude that the assumption of the equal adequacy of alternatives is justified.

It remains to state what Russell takes the conditions of the adequacy of his 'definition' to be. We have already seen that he holds that it is adequate for 'all mathematical uses'; but he is also more specific. From the viewpoint of pure mathematics, he holds that it is enough that there should be an interpretation of Peano's axioms over classes of classes which brings all the axioms out true. From the viewpoint of applied mathematics, the 'definition' of number must so interpret sentences like 'Men have two eyes and ten fingers' that they come out true (cf. *IMP* 9).

We shall see in the next section that the condition of satisfying Peano's axioms holds. However, Russell's logicism is not well served by the definition of number unless there is also an interpretation, satisfying the conditions already mentioned, and such that the axioms assert not merely truths but logical truths. We shall see that this condition is not satisfied in Russell's logicism.

Russell points out that one can give a true interpretation of Peano's axioms over any *progression*, that is, any infinite series each of whose members has only finitely many precursors. Thus, in particular, one can give such an interpretation over the series of natural numbers starting from 100. Russell rightly says that this shows that we have not yet reached a satisfactory adequacy condition for the construction of numbers. For an interpretation of Peano's axioms which has 'o' denoting 100, though it can make all the axioms true, will involve ascribing meanings to the numerals ('1' being taken to abbreviate 'the successor of o', and so on) which, together with the way things are, make such sentences as 'Men have two eyes and ten fingers' false. Hence it is not an interpretation which can be regarded as giving a satisfactory account of the numbers.

Russell's construction, in the presence of the informal rules for matching sentences containing numerals with sentences that do not, satisfies this further condition of leaving undisturbed the truth values of (extensional) empirical sentences involving numerals. However, in the presence of suitably different informal rules, the same can be said for class theoretic constructions of number other than Russell's.

To a large extent, the value of Russell's construction is to be determined in the light of the success or failure of his logicist programme as a whole. If the construction mediates all the benefits one might hope for from logicism, in particular the reduction of the ontology and epistemology of mathematics, as refashioned, to that of logic, then the construction will thereby be justified. But, as we shall see, Russell's logicism is not successful, and thus his construction of number is deprived of what should have been its main source of justification.

A problematic feature of Numbers is their abstractness. On a commonly held view, this makes them unable to enter into causal relations, and, on a theory of knowledge which is generally accepted for concrete entities, this would in turn make them unknowable. One way to avoid these and similar difficulties would be to reconstrue

Numbers as concrete entities. Russell's construction is not of this kind, for classes are no less abstract than Numbers.

5 Peano's axioms

All traditional pure mathematics, including analytical geometry, may be regarded as consisting wholly of propositions about the natural numbers. That is to say, the terms which occur can be defined by means of the natural numbers, and the properties can be deduced from the properties of the natural numbers – with the addition, in each case, of the ideas and propositions of pure logic (*IMP* 4).

This arithmetization of mathematics led Russell to see the problem confronting logicism as reduced to that of logicizing arithmetic, and Peano's work afforded a further reduction of the problem. Given that his five axioms, involving just the three apparently extra-logical expressions 'o', 'successor' and 'number', permit the derivation of all the 'ordinary results' in elementary number theory (*PofM* 124), the problem for logicism was reduced to that of logicizing these axioms. In this section I shall show how Russell transformed them into logical propositions, and I shall consider some of his informal arguments purporting to establish that the logicized axioms are indeed logical truths.

In *IMP* (5–6) Peano's axioms are stated as follows:

(*i*) o is a number.
(*ii*) The successor of any number is a number.
(*iii*) No two numbers have the same successor.
(*iv*) o is not the successor of any number.
(*v*) Any property which belongs to o, and also to the successor of every number which has the property, belongs to all numbers.

Russell assumes that expressions like 'not', 'if . . . then', 'identical', 'class' and 'two' (in its adjectival occurrence) are already within the sphere of logic, so that the only apparently arithmetical expressions, requiring to be defined in logical terms, are 'o', 'successor' and 'number'.

'o', as we have seen, is defined as '$\{ \varLambda \}$'.

'x is successor of y' is defined as '$x = (y + 1)$'. This in turn is defined in purely logical terms, '1' as the class of all unit classes, and a general definition of '+' in terms of set-theoretic union is given in *110·01 and *110·02. The details are quite complicated. We can make do with the consequence that $x + 1$ is the class of classes similar to some class which results from adding to a member of the number x an entity not already belonging to it.

The definition of 'number' as 'class of similar classes' is too wide for the present purpose. It includes Λ and infinite cardinals like $\aleph_0$. Neither of these has the property, demanded by Peano's axioms, that you can reach it from o by passing through successors of . . . successors of o (cf. *PM* II 200). The narrower notion Russell calls that of an *inductive cardinal*. Let us say that a property P is hereditary for a relation R if, given that x has P and is R-related to y, y has P. Then Russell's definition is:

x is an inductive cardinal $=_{df}$ x has every hereditary property of o for the relation $+1$.

It is easy to see that every inductive cardinal is a class of similar classes. For o is a class of similar classes, and the definition of '$+1$' ensures that being a class of similar classes is hereditary for $+1$.

So much for the definitions. I turn now to the informal arguments for the claim that the results of applying the definitions to Peano's axioms are logical truths. I follow Russell's account in *IMP*, Chapter 3.

(*i*) We have to prove that $\{\Lambda\}$ is a number. (Here and hereafter I use 'number' as an abbreviation for 'inductive cardinal'.) Clearly it has every hereditary property of o for the relation $+1$, since it is o.

(*ii*) Here we have to prove that if x is a number so is $x+1$. Assume that x is a number. Then it possesses every hereditary property of o with respect to $+1$. x is related to $x+1$ by the $+1$ relation. Thus $x+1$ has all x's and thus all o's hereditary properties with respect to $+1$.

(*iii*) We have to prove that if x and y are numbers and $x+1=y+1$ then $x=y$. The definition of '$+1$' has the consequence that $n+1$ has members only if there is a class consisting of the union of some class, α, belonging to n, with some class, β, whose sole member is an individual lying outside α. If there are exactly n individuals, there is no such β, and so no such $\alpha \cup \beta$, and so $n+1=\Lambda$. Similar considerations show that, under the assumption that there are just n individuals, $(n+1)+1$ has no members and so $=\Lambda$. Hence we have that n and $n+1$ are numbers, $n+1=(n+1)+1$, yet $n\neq n+1$, contradicting what we had to prove. This axiom thus requires for its proof the thesis that there are infinitely many individuals, and Russell obtained it simply by taking it as an axiom, the Axiom of Infinity.

However, this poses a grave, indeed insuperable, problem for Russell's logicism, for the simple reason that, as Russell himself accepts (*IMP* 77), the axiom is not a logical truth. Indeed, there is room for doubt about whether it is even a contingent truth, since it is an open question whether the universe is finite or infinite. But even if there are in fact infinitely many individuals, this is not necessarily the case. Every logical truth is a necessary truth, and so the Axiom of

Infinity is not a logical truth. If logicism requires this axiom, it cannot succeed.

Russell considered two ways of avoiding this conclusion. He reports in *IMP* (134–5) that, early on, he had tried to make do with a weaker axiom, one which asserts not that there are infinitely many individuals, but merely that there are infinitely many things. The difference is that whereas individuals belong to a single type, the lowest, there are things of other types: classes of individuals, classes of classes of individuals, and so on. Now even if there are as few as zero individuals, there will none the less be at least one class in the type next above that of individuals, viz. Λ; and at least one class in the type next above that, viz. $\{\Lambda\}$; and at least two things in the type next above that, viz. $\{\{\Lambda\}\}$ and $\{\Lambda, \{\Lambda\}\}$; and so on *ad infinitum*. Given that the null class exists, and that the unit class of any existent class exists, we can be sure that there are infinitely many entities. Or so it seems.

Russell rejects this suggested proof of a weaker form of the Axiom of Infinity on the grounds that it involves a 'confusion of types' (*IMP* 135). In particular, what he takes to be involved in the argument is the admission of 'impure' classes (*IMP* 137), that is, classes whose members are drawn from more than one type (e.g., $\{\Lambda, \{\Lambda\}\}$, which has as members both a class of individuals (that is, an entity of type-1) and a class of classes of individuals (that is, an entity of type-2)). Impure classes are banned by Russell's theory of types.

There are two criticisms to be made of this analysis of the argument. One is that this ban on impure classes is not generally accepted. Systems of set-theory admitting impure ('cumulative') classes have been devised and have not been found to be inconsistent. The ban on impure classes arises from Russell's no-class theory, for a class is defined in terms of a predicate's extension, and a type in terms of a predicate's range of significance. The apparent acceptability of cumulative classes, however, simply counts against these aspects of Russell's position.

The second criticism is that Russell speaks as if the need for impure classes arose from the need to construct an infinite class by taking the union of the classes at every level in the hierarchy of types (*IMP* 135). However, for the development of finite arithmetic there is no need to have, among the entities of which the arithmetical sentences speak, an infinite class. All that is required is an infinite number of finite classes. The hierarchy we have considered, however, includes an infinite number of *pure* finite classes, each of the form $\{\ldots\{\Lambda\}\ldots\}$.

The need for an infinite class comes, rather, when one goes beyond finite arithmetic to the theory of real numbers or of infinite cardinals (cf. Hatcher 178). The existence of such a class is, however, as Russell saw, not established by the mere indication of the hierarchy just given, and, indeed, Russell's theory rules out the possibility of taking the union of the elements in the hierarchy, for this would be manifestly impure.

Thus within Russell's theory the Axiom of Infinity, as needed for the full execution of the logicist programme, must take the strong form that there are infinitely many individuals, and this is certainly not a logical truth. Whether some weaker form of the axiom, sufficient for logicism, can be proved in some system other than Russell's is an open question. For an affirmative answer, see Bostock's *Logic and Arithmetic: Natural Numbers* (114).

As I mentioned earlier, Russell considered another way of avoiding the need for the Axiom of Infinity. This consists in refraining from treating it genuinely as an axiom, but rather as a hypothesis. Rather than prove a proposition p by using the axiom ('Ax. Inf.'), he proves the conditional: Ax. Inf. $\rightarrow p$ (*PM* II 203; see, e.g., *123·33). But this device is worthless to the logicist. We could as well say that physics is reducible to logic, on the grounds that, to the extent that physics is axiomatizable (in whole or part) we can obtain it as a fragment of logic by replacing each of its theorems by a conditional whose consequent is the theorem and whose antecedent is the conjunction of the proper axioms of the original axiomatization. The point is that the result would be in no decent sense an axiomatization of *physics*, for physics makes categorical statements about how things behave, and these will not be theorems of the envisaged axiomatization. Likewise, it would be absurd to suppose that the mathematical claim that there are infinitely many numbers could be accurately translated by, say, 'If there are infinitely many individuals then there are infinitely many numbers'. The mathematician claims the consequent categorically.

Peano's remaining two axioms, however, can be seen to follow easily from the definitions.

(*iv*) What has to be proved is that for no number n does $0 = (n + 1)$. Obviously for no number n can the null class be constructed by adding an individual to a member of n, since a class thus constructed will have at least one member. So for no n can the class of all classes similar to the null class be $n + 1$, that is the class of all classes similar to some $n + 1$-membered class.

(*v*) What has to be proved is that every hereditary property of 0 with respect to $+1$ is possessed by all numbers. This follows at once from the definition of 'inductive cardinal'.

One implausible consequence of Russell's theory of types is that every numeral is infinitely ambiguous, for there are infinitely many types, and the whole series of classes of classes is constructed within each type. I have ignored this complication in this section.

307

6 The paradoxes

What is a paradox? For the purposes of this discussion we can regard it as a contradiction which flows, by apparently impeccable reasoning, from apparently true premises.[9] What the paradox shows, of course, is that appearances deceive: correct reasoning cannot lead from truth to contradiction.

As Russell himself emphasized, not every contradiction is a paradox. There is nothing paradoxical about the claim that there are round squares, or about the story of the village whose barber shaves all and only those who do not shave themselves (cf. *PLA* 261). In each case we can happily accept what the contradiction makes us accept: there are no round squares, there is no such village. In the case of paradox, however, we are not quite happy to give up any of the propositions or principles of inference from which the contradiction flows (or seems to flow).

What makes a contradiction a paradox has something to do with our expectations and instinctive beliefs. As these change, a paradox may diminish to a humble contradiction. For example, some would say that Zeno's paradox of Achilles and the tortoise is no paradox for us, since it depends on a premise that *we* are happy to reject: 'that any infinite succession of intervals of time has to add up to all eternity'.[10]

The most important paradox is that about non-self-membered classes, which is now generally known as Russell's paradox. Russell discovered it in 1901 in the course of examining Cantor's proof that there is no greatest number.[11] His early attempt at a solution, published in *PofM*, dissatisfied him, and it was not until 1908 that he published the supposedly improved solution I shall discuss: the ramified theory of types. Even this improved version he regarded, in 1919, as 'still inchoate, confused and obscure' (*IMP* 135). While he proposed some modifications in PM_2 (1925) it is unlikely that he can have regarded them as entirely satisfactory. None the less, he retained confidence in the general principle underlying the ramified theory, writing in 1959 that he had seen no argument against it which seemed to him cogent (*MPD* 83). Russell rightly regarded his paradox as a difficult problem for logicism, since it threatened the very foundations of logic. The paradox, and related ones, have stimulated

[9] This is too narrow for general use: some paradoxes merely *seem* to be contradictory, and some seem merely to be *false*.

[10] Quine, 'Ways of Paradox' 5. This gives an excellent account of the nature of paradox. Zeno's paradox is only a contradiction if we take it that 'Achilles overtakes the tortoise' flows, by apparently impeccable reasoning, from apparently true premises.

[11] For an account of the connection between Russell's paradox and Cantor's proof see *EA* 138–9. The proof itself is summarized in note 18 below.

some of the most important developments in mathematical logic in this century.[12]

The remainder of this section is devoted to stating and clarifying this paradox and some of the others which Russell, in *PM*, takes to be intimately connected with it.

(1) Russell's paradox: Some classes are not members of themselves. For example, the class of men is not a member of itself, for it is not itself a man. Some classes are members of themselves. For example, the class of non-men is a member of itself, for it is itself a non-man. Now consider the class of all and only those classes which are not members of themselves. If it is a member of itself then, since its members are *only* those classes which are not members of themselves, it is not a member of itself. But if it is not a member of itself then, since it is the class of *all* classes which are not members of themselves, it is a member of itself. In other words, it is a member of itself iff it is not a member of itself; and so, in classical logic, it is a member of itself and also not a member of itself.

So much for the contradiction. To have a paradox, there has to be some natural tendency to suppose that *there is* such a contradictory class. The harder it is to rid ourselves of the tendency, the deeper is the paradox. Russell at one point (*EA* 145) identified the culprit as our tendency to believe that every propositional function determines a class. Thus 'x is a man' determines the class of men, 'x is round and square' determines the class of just those things that are both round and square, that is the null class. A sentence like 'the class of men is a member of the class of men' seems to be false, and therefore significant; so its negation should be significant; so the open sentence '$x \notin x$' should be significant; so there should be a class which it determines. The Russell paradox is paradoxical to the extent that this reasoning seems cogent.

Ramsey proposed that the paradoxes Russell discussed could be divided into two categories: the logical paradoxes, whose central features are logical notions like class, relation, propositional function; and the semantic paradoxes, whose central features are semantic notions like truth, denotation, naming. Russell mentions three logical paradoxes: the class paradox just discussed, an essentially similar paradox concerning relations, and the Burali–Forti paradox concerning the greatest ordinal. I shall content myself with the Russell paradox as an example of a logical paradox,

[12] There were also less happy consequences. When Frege learnt of the contradiction in a letter from Russell, while his own second volume of the *Grundgesetze* was in press, he is said to have replied 'Arithmetic totters'. He made an unsuccessful attempt to eliminate the contradiction from the *Grundgesetze*; then his work seems to have come almost to a standstill for several years.

and turn now to the semantic paradoxes. It must be emphasized that Russell did not make the distinction between the logical and the semantic paradoxes, and indeed it is an important part of his position that there is no essential difference between the various kinds of paradox he discusses. This assumption is unwarranted, for systems can be constructed in which one can derive logical paradoxes but not semantic ones. An example is Frege's system in the *Grundgesetze*.

(2) The *Epimenides*:
The oldest contradiction of the kind in question is the *Epimenides*. Epimenides the Cretan said that all Cretans were liars, and all other statements made by Cretans were certainly lies. Was this a lie? (*PM* 60).

The formulation is somewhat loose (does someone lie if he sincerely says what is false?). We might tidy it up as follows. Let 'U' abbreviate this utterance by Epimenides:

All Cretan utterances occurring before t are false.

(The mention of time adds some plausibility.) Now the following appear to be consistent:

  (a) U is a Cretan utterance.
  (b) U occurs before t.
  (c) All Cretan utterances distinct from U and occurring before t are false.

These seem to be consistent, for surely we can easily imagine that Cretans utter only falsehoods for a certain period, and then one of them utters U. However, we seem to be able to derive a contradiction. For suppose that all Cretan utterances occurring before t are false. Then since U is a Cretan utterance (by (a)) and occurs before t (by (b)), U is false. But if U is false, then it is not the case that all Cretan utterances occurring before t are false. So if all Cretan utterances occurring before t are false, then it is not the case that all Cretan utterances occurring before t are false. Now suppose that it is not the case that all Cretan utterances occurring before t are false. Then some Cretan utterance occurring before t is not false. By (c) it cannot be other than U, which is therefore true (bivalence). Thus all Cretan utterances occurring before t are false. So if it is not the case that all Cretan utterances occurring before t are false, then all Cretan utterances occurring before t are false. So, by classical logic, all Cretan utterances occurring before t are false, and in addition some are not. It is worth remarking that the step I labelled 'bivalence' relies on the principle that if an utterance is not false it is true. So one might prefer to say that it is not the conjunction of (*a*) and (*b*) and (*c*) that the contradiction shows to be impossible, but rather the conjunction of these with the principle of bivalence.

(3) Berry's paradox: this is Russell's account of a paradox he attributes to G. G. Berry (*PM* 61):

> The number of syllables in the English names of finite integers tends to increase as the integers grow larger, and must gradually increase indefinitely, since only a finite number of names can be made with a given finite number of syllables. Hence the names of some integers must consist of at least nineteen syllables, and among these there must be a least. Hence 'the least integer not nameable in fewer than nineteen syllables' must denote a definite integer; in fact it denotes 111,777. But 'the least integer not nameable in fewer than nineteen syllables' is itself a name consisting of eighteen syllables; hence the least integer not nameable in fewer than nineteen syllables can be named in eighteen syllables, which is a contradiction.

Some clarificatory points may be of use. The expression 'nameable' might look modal, so that '*x* is nameable' would be true of an object iff it is logically possible that it be named. In this sense of 'nameable' we would have no reason to think that only finitely many numbers are nameable by expressions with less than nineteen syllables, and so there would be no paradox (cf. *ML* 79). (To show this, consider the fact that for every number, *n*, it is logically possible that it be John's favourite number, and thus 'named' by 'John's favourite number'.) Rather, '*x* is nameable' has to be understood as true of an object iff there is a name (genuine *name* or definite description) which denotes it. Then, since in any language there are finitely many names with fewer than nineteen syllables, only finitely many numbers are denoted by some name from this collection, and so one would think that there must be a greatest number thus denoted, and so a least number *not* thus denoted.

'Nameable' has to be understood as relative to some language. The first sentence of the quoted passage suggests that this language is to be English. The only condition the relevant language must satisfy is, as Russell implies, that there must be, for any number *n*, only a finite number of *n*-syllabic names in the language.

It is doubly misleading to claim that 'the least integer not nameable in fewer than nineteen syllables' denotes 111,777. For one thing, given that the relevant language is English, a larger number is denoted by 'the cost in pounds of World War II'. For another thing, the paradox itself shows that nothing is denoted by the expression 'the least integer not nameable in fewer than nineteen syllables'.

Once these points are cleared away, this paradox is quite convincing: that is, it is not easy to see where the reasoning apparently leading to the contradiction breaks down.

Russell mentions some other semantic paradoxes in his discussion in *PM*, but as they raise no new issues of principle I shall not expound them. However, it will be useful, for the sake of a later point, to have before us a paradox which Russell mentions in *PofM* (80, 97, 102), but which is nowadays generally attributed to Grelling.

(4) Grelling's paradox: an expression is said to be 'heterological' iff it is not truly ascribable to itself. Thus 'long' is heterological since it is not long, 'German' is heterological since it is not an expression of German; but 'short' and 'English' are not heterological, as the one is short and the other English. 'Heterological' is heterological iff it is not: for to say it is not heterological is to say it *is* truly ascribable to itself, which means it is heterological; and if it *is* heterological then it is not truly ascribable to itself, which means that it is not true that 'heterological' is heterological. The paradox lies in the fact that an apparently coherent definition leads to a contradiction.

What would 'solving' or 'resolving' the paradoxes consist in? At the formal level, we need a logical system which is consistent, and an essential feature of Russell's method of achieving consistency is his use of formation rules blocking the formation of sentences which, if admissible, would lead to inconsistency if the inference rules of the system were applied to them. At the philosophical level, we need an analysis of the tendencies which make the contradiction paradoxical, together with therapy to attenuate them. The 'vicious-circle principle', which Russell developed from a suggestion by Poincaré, is supposed to play this philosophical role.

Since some of the paradoxes among those first to command attention were concerned in one way or another with infinity, as for example the Burali–Forti (see *PM* 66), some philosophers, in particular at one time Poincaré, believed that the blame for the paradoxes should be laid at the door of the concept of infinity. This Russell rejected, citing the Epimenides (*EA* 197). He could as well have cited the class paradox. It is against this background that we must understand his insistence that the paradoxes showed that it was not so much mathematics as logic that needed reform (*MPD* 76).

He held that the reforms should be governed by the following constraints:

(*i*) They should deal with all the paradoxes. He held that his *PofM* theory is unsatisfactory in that there are some paradoxes (what *we* would call semantic paradoxes) which it does not block (*PofM* 527). Moreover, he maintained that the paradoxes are essentially similar in virtue of possessing 'a common characteristic, which we may describe as self-reference or reflexiveness' (*ML* 61).

(*ii*) The reforms should have 'a certain consonance with common sense' (*ML* 59).

(*iii*) Finally, they should be as conservative as possible; that is, they should preserve as much as possible of classical logic and mathematics (*EA* 145).

These requirements of adequacy are brought together in *MPD* 79–80.

In the next section I state the reforms Russell proposed, which consist in the restrictions on sentence-formation imposed by the ramified theory of types. In section 8 I consider whether they block the paradoxes. In section 9 I discuss the philosophical rationale: the vicious-circle principle. The final section concerns the Axiom of Reducibility, which Russell introduced to prevent the ramified theory from being excessively unconservative.

7 The ramified theory of types

Russell discovered the class paradox in 1901, and *PofM* contains a sketch of a theory of types designed to avoid it. This early theory did not satisfy him, one ground being that it failed to deal adequately with what we would now call the semantic paradoxes. Bringing these within the scope of the theory required the further assumption that 'propositions themselves are of various types' but 'this suggestion seems harsh and highly artificial' (*PofM* 528). In the end, Russell came to accept this suggestion, but its harsh and artificial appearance was supposedly softened by establishing the new theory on a different, and, Russell thought, more profound and adequate basis. This basis concerned the fundamental nature of propositions.

In 1906, Poincaré[13] suggested that the paradoxes were due to viciously circular definitions, and later in that year Russell published a paper ('Les Paradoxes de la Logique', *EA* 190–214) in which he accepted this vicious-circle principle as the 'fallacy' underlying all the paradoxes. This resulted in the ramified theory of types, first published in *ML* (1908).

Russell thought that the hierarchy of orders is essentially required to avoid semantic paradoxes. The hierarchy needed to avoid the logical paradoxes is the hierarchy not of orders but of types. Russell tried to extract the latter hierarchy from the vicious-circle principle by means of the doctrine that a function presupposes its values. This

[13] 'Les Mathématiques et la Logique', 307. Poincaré points out that a similar suggestion had earlier been made by Richard.

attempt to unify the logical and semantic paradoxes, by supposedly showing that both kinds flow from vicious circularity, is in my opinion unsuccessful. I discuss this issue further in section 9 below.

Mathematicians tend to understand by the 'ramified theory of types' a theory comprising formation rules, which determine the formulae of the theory, together with axioms and rules of proof, which determine the theorems of the theory. Thus a mathematician may regard the Axiom of Reducibility as belonging to the ramified theory of types. For our purposes, however, it is convenient to adopt a different usage. We are interested in the restrictions on formation imposed by the ramified theory, for it is these that are of the essence in blocking the paradoxes. It will therefore be convenient to refer to these restrictions as 'RT'.

As I have implied, RT involves two hierarchies: the hierarchy of orders, designed to block the semantic paradoxes, and the hierarchy of types, designed to block the logical paradoxes. It is generally agreed that RT can be analysed as the superimposition on the hierarchy of types of the hierarchy of orders.[14] It is therefore convenient to begin by considering the more basic hierarchy of types, which leads to what is sometimes called the 'simple theory of types'; the hierarchy of orders introduces the ramification. The formation restrictions imposed by this simple unramified theory may be referred to as 'ST'.

The basis of ST is the sorting of non-linguistic entities into types. The lowest type, type-0, consists of individuals, which Russell defines as whatever are neither propositions nor functions (properties) (*PM* 51). The higher types consist of properties. A type is defined in such a way that a property can apply significantly only to objects of a single type (cf. *ML* 75). Type-1 properties are those that apply significantly to individuals, like the property of being a man. Type-n properties are those that apply significantly to entities of type-$(n-1)$. For example, the property of being a desirable property in a man is a type-2 property, since it applies significantly to just type-1 properties. In general, the type of a property is one higher than the type of entities to which it may be significantly applied, or, as I shall put it, is one higher than the type of its arguments. (Here, and in what follows, I consider only monadic predicates and properties.)

This typing of non-linguistic entities induces a rule of significance at the linguistic level. If a predicate expresses a type-n property, it may be significantly concatenated with a term only if that term denotes a type-$(n-1)$ entity. Thus we have an indirect attribution of types to predicates, terms (a term, be it a variable or a name, has the type of the

---

[14] If Chihara's interpretation of Russell's RT is correct, this remark would require some qualification. See note 15 below.

entities or entity it ranges over or denotes) and to open sentences (an open sentence of type-n has its free variable of type-$(n-1)$). However, this indirect attribution of types to expressions must be treated with caution. Expressions *qua* objects all belong to a single type. In Russell's view, they are all classes of individuals, and so, by the no-class theory, they are properties of individuals, and thus entities of type-1. The indirect attribution of types to expressions is simply a way of expressing the rule of significance of ST: a predicate must be one type higher than any term to which it is applied. Types attach not to expressions *qua* objects but to expressions in use.

The type-hierarchy suffers from two kinds of vagueness. On the one hand, there is vagueness in the definition of an individual, and on the other hand there is vagueness concerning what properties significantly apply to what objects. (For example, Carnap at one time thought that the property of thinking about Vienna could not apply significantly to a stone. If he is right then ST yields at best only a necessary and not a sufficient condition for significance.) However, problems about the nature of individuals turn out to be of little moment, for, as Russell emphasizes (*PM* 161–2), it is only relative type that matters. In blocking the paradoxes, what matters is that properties are of higher type than their arguments. It does not matter to what absolute type the properties in question belong.

ST is close to the *PofM* theory, and, quite independently of RT, it suffices to block the Russell paradox. The essential point is that it rules as insignificant the application of a property to itself, and thus, in the presence of the no-class theory, rules as insignificant expressions of the form '$a \notin a$', and hence rules as insignificant the specification from which the paradox results, viz.:

$$x \in a \leftrightarrow x \notin x.$$

The next paragraph gives the details which establish this point.

'$a \notin a$' is meaningful only if '$a \in a$' is meaningful. A class variable, like 'a' in this context, abbreviates a class-abstract variable (cf. *PM* 190), so '$a \in a$' is meaningful only if some expression of the form '$\hat{z}(\psi z) \in \hat{z}(\psi z)$' is meaningful. Now let us modify *20·01 so as to eliminate the '!') which derives from RT: the result is '$f\{\hat{z}(\psi z)\} =_{df} (\exists \varphi)((\forall x)(\varphi x \leftrightarrow \psi x) \& f\{\varphi \hat{z}\})$'. Putting '$\hat{z}(\psi z) \in$' for '$f$' gives:

$$\hat{z}(\psi z) \in \hat{z}(\psi z) =_{df} (\exists \varphi)((\forall x)(\varphi x \leftrightarrow \psi x) \& \hat{z}(\psi z) \in \varphi \hat{z}).$$

Reapplying the modified *20·01 to the definiens, putting '$\in \varphi \hat{z}$' for 'f', yields:

$$=_{df} (\exists \varphi)((\forall x)(\varphi x \leftrightarrow \psi x) \& (\exists \chi)((\forall x)(\chi x \leftrightarrow \psi x) \& \chi \hat{z} \in \varphi \hat{z})).$$

Now let us modify *20·02 so as to eliminate the '!' which arises from

RT. The result is: '$x \in \varphi \hat{z} =_{df} \varphi x$'. Applying this to the definiens, and putting '$\chi \hat{z}$' for 'x' we have:

$$=_{df} (\exists \varphi)((\forall x)(\varphi x \leftrightarrow \psi x) \,\&\, (\exists \chi)((\forall x)(\chi x \leftrightarrow \varphi) \,\&\, \varphi(\chi \hat{z}))).$$

But this expression is illegitimate. Since 'φ' and 'χ' are coextensive, they are of the same type, and so '$\chi \hat{z}$' cannot occur in the argument-place of 'φ'. So the definiendum '$\hat{z}(\psi z) \in \hat{z}(\psi z)$', and thus '$a \in a$' and '$a \notin a$' are illegitimate. Hence the Russell paradox cannot be significantly formulated if one adheres to ST.

Frege's system in the *Grundgesetze* incorporates a hierarchy of levels which is in some ways similar to ST. Yet Frege's system is demonstrably inconsistent, since the existence of the paradoxical Russell class can be proved in it (cf. Hatcher 110). How does this situation arise? The answer is that Frege treats classes as genuine objects, and the hierarchy of levels does not induce a corresponding hierarchy of classes. If we add to Frege's system Russell's no-class theory, the paradox cannot be formulated within it. The reason is that Frege's hierarchy of levels forbids expressions of the form '$\varphi(\psi \hat{x})$' unless the level of 'φ' is greater by one than the level of '$\psi \hat{x}$', but this formation rule would be violated by expressions of the form '$\hat{z}(\varphi z) \in \hat{z}(\varphi z)$' if one regarded class abstracts as defined in the way Russell's theory stipulates.

To say this is not to say that Frege's system plus the no-class theory is consistent, for perhaps other contradictions are provable in it. However, adding the no-class theory seems to block other well-known ways of formulating provable contradictions in Frege-style theories, for example by the method involving chains of classes (see Copi 9).

Commentators are generally agreed that ST is entailed by RT: that is, that any sentence ruled as insignificant by ST is also so ruled by RT. However, there is room for disagreement about other aspects of the relationship between ST and RT, and in particular concerning how the types of ST interlock with the orders of RT. The possibility of disagreement stems partly from Russell's rather loose use of the terms 'type' and 'order' in *PM*, and also, and more importantly, from his very informal manner of presenting the formation restrictions. The clearest presentation would indicate types and orders by appropriate subscripts or superscripts on *PM*-expressions, and give precise formation rules in terms of these subscripts or superscripts. Russell does not adopt this course, at least partly because it would have introduced into his notation a considerable complication which would have been irrelevant for his practical purposes. Rather, he relies on the convention of 'systematic ambiguity', whereby type and order postscripts are suppressed, and a given formula is regarded as a representative of any formula like it in structure, however postscripts are supplied; it is well-formed provided that there is a way of supplying postscripts that accords with Russell's rather informally stated criteria. This device is powerful: it permits generalization over all the permissible order/type variants of a given formula. But Russell's use of it has the disadvantage that it enabled him to leave some details of his theory obscured. It is true that he frequently and essentially uses '!' as a symbol to indicate *relative* order, but this leaves certain questions unresolved.

None the less, the outline of RT is plain enough, and I shall start by presenting this. Then I shall offer a rather more speculative interpretation of the details.[15]

Consider the properties of a given type, let us say type-1. Is this a 'legitimate totality' in the sense in which Russell used this phrase in connection with the vicious-circle principle? He argued that it is not. For suppose it is. Among type-1 properties we would have $(\forall\varphi)\varphi\hat{x}$; that is, the property of having *every* type-1 property. Russell argued that this property 'involves' the totality of all type-1 properties, and

[15] This interpretation follows that given in Hatcher's *Foundations of Mathematics*, though greatly simplified by considering only monadic predicates and properties. Other accounts of RT can be found in the literature: for example, Copi, *The Theory of Logical Types*; and Chihara, *Ontology and the Vicious-Circle Principle*.

Copi suggests that Russell's RT divides each type into orders in accordance with the following principle: first-order properties of type-τ are those type-τ properties which are expressed by a predicate which is either quantifier-free or the domains of whose quantifiers do not include type-τ entities. Second-order properties of type-τ are those expressed by predicates involving quantification over first-order type-τ properties, but not over any higher-order properties of this type. In general, a type-τ property of order Ω is one whose predicate involves quantification over $(\Omega$-1)th-order properties of type-τ, and over no type-τ properties of order higher than Ω-1. (Cf. Copi 84–7.)

The accuracy of Copi's interpretation can be challenged on two counts. A relatively minor point is that Copi allows a first-order property in each type whereas, as we shall see, Russell defines 'first-order' in such a way that all first-order properties are of type-1. More importantly, Copi's definition of order within a type, τ, attends only to quantifiers ranging over type-τ entities. A higher-order quantifier ranging over a higher type of entity would not, apparently, affect the order of a predicate in which it occurred. This is inconsistent with Russell's idea of constructing types and orders from the bottom up: the intrusion of a quantifier ranging over type-τ + 1 entities in a predicate of type-τ ought to mark some further removal from the basis of the construction, yet such a quantifier has no such effect, on Copi's account.

Chihara has proposed an at least superficially distinct account in his *Ontology and the Vicious-Circle Principle* (19–23). Deciding whether Chihara's interpretation is significantly different from Hatcher's and, if so, whose is closest to Russell, would require a detailed study of the formal parts of *PM*, and this I have not been able to undertake. However, I am reasonably confident that even if the account of RT that I present here is not exactly true to *PM*, the error is not of the sort that will affect any of the philosophical issues discussed in this book.

thus that the vicious-circle principle entails that it cannot itself belong to that totality. In other words, there can be no such type-1 property as that of having every type-1 property; nor can such a property belong to any other type. Hence the corresponding predicate abstract is ill-formed. (Cf. *PM* 48–9; and, for the connection with the coherence of substitutional predicate quantifiers, pp. 284–90 above. For a discussion of the vicious-circle principle, see section 9 below.)

Russell's solution is to divide the properties within a type into various orders, following in effect the principle that we start with properties whose specification requires no quantification over properties, and then construct further properties in stages: but at any stage we are permitted to quantify only over properties which have already been constructed. Thus in type-1 we will start with those properties of individuals expressed by predicate abstracts which either contain no quantifiers, or else only quantifiers whose domain is individuals. These constitute the lowest order of properties within the type. The next stage will include all those properties expressed by a predicate abstract involving quantification over the lowest order. And so on.

Russell puts the idea this way:

(1) A function of the first order is one which involves no variables except individuals, whether as apparent variables or as arguments.
(2) A function of the $(n + 1)$th order is one which has at least one argument or apparent variable of order n, and contains no argument or apparent variable which is not either an individual or a first-order function or a second-order function . . . or a function of order n (*PM* 167; cf. 53).

So much for the outline. Now for the details. What order is the lowest order of type-2 property? We might be tempted to answer 'first-order', but this turns out to be plainly at variance with Russell's intentions, for first-order properties are so defined that they are all of type-1 (see the passage just quoted and also *PM* 51). The natural suggestion is that the order of a property must be at least as high as its type. So in type-n the lowest order property will be nth-order. A property cannot have as its argument range all the entities in the next type below for, according to Russell, this forms an illegitimate totality. One could restrict a property's argument range to a single order of entities in the type next below, but in fact Russell's formulations (e.g., in the passage just quoted) appear to allow that all the properties of a given type up to and including some definite order constitute an argument range (cf. Hatcher 129). The order of a property will be at least one higher than the highest order of entity in its argument range. There are thus two sources of high-order in a property: one is high-order in its arguments, and the other, already noted, is high-order in the entities in the domain of a quantifier in the predicate abstract which expresses the property.

In order to know how a predicate abstract expressing a property F can significantly occur there are three things we need to know about F: the order of F; the type of F (which of course settles the type of F's arguments); and the order of F's arguments. In a fully explicit notation, predicates, predicate abstracts and variables would contain a device which would indicate these three facts.

Such a device would be provided by Hatcher's notion of an *index*. An index is a sequence $< \tau, \Omega, \alpha >$ of non-negative integers such that $\Omega > \alpha > \tau - 2$. The first element specifies the type of a property, the second its order, and the third the order of its highest-order arguments. Variables will be superscripted with an index-expression. (In future I shall normally call an index-expression an index.) The index of a predicate abstract will be computed as follows: its type is given as one more than the type of its arguments, its order is given as one more than the highest-order bound variable it contains (remember that circumflexed variables are bound), and the final element is given by the order (i.e. the second element in the index) of the circumflexed variable. The formation rules will count as well-formed only those expressions which have indices which conform to these rules.

(In type-0 we may as well drop all save the first element of the index, since type-0 entities must be 0th-order, and there is no question about the third element of the index of a type-0 entity since such entities do not have arguments. Similarly, in type-1 one may as well suppress the last element of the index, since all arguments to type-1 entities are 0th-order.)

A *predicative property*, relative to an entity of type τ order Ω, is a property whose index is $< \tau + 1, \Omega + 1, \Omega >$. A predicative predicate abstract is one which expresses a predicative property. A predicative predicate variable is one ranging over properties which are predicative relative to all their arguments. Russell marked predicative predicate variables by postfixing an occurrence of '!'. The importance of predicativity, in the present sense, will be discussed shortly in connection with the Axiom of Reducibility.

Russell once said that the theory of descriptions was the first step on the road towards the resolution of the paradoxes (*MPD* 79). He never offers an account of the intervening steps, but it is illuminating to attempt a reconstruction, though this is of necessity somewhat speculative.

One result of applying the theory of descriptions (where this is taken to include the theory that some names are descriptions) is that certain syntactic names do not require bearers in order to be meaningful. In the present case, this would show at best that the *meaningfulness* of class names does not require the existence of classes. However, the *truth* of any sentence '*Fa*' containing a syntactic name '*a*' does require the existence of some corresponding object. So the mere discovery that class names are descriptions seems to have no bearing on the question of what must exist for class theoretic sentences to be true, and no bearing on the solution of the paradoxes.

The no-class theory treats class names as 'incomplete symbols', just as the theory of descriptions treats descriptions. This could show an ontological dependence: for example, it could show that the existence of classes is dependent on the existence of properties. However, this in itself appears not to be to the purpose of avoiding paradoxes.

Russell's position can be understood if we recall that his theory of descriptions is historically associated with his idea of there being entities which can only be described and not named. If classes were genuine entities, whose existence and nature owed nothing to human thought, it would be impossible, one might think, to accept that there could be any restrictions on how we specify them or that their existence could properly be derived from considerations about the logical systems we can frame. If, on the other hand, classes are not nameable (despite syntactic appearances to the contrary, which are dissolved by the theory of descriptions), then one is at once committed to an anti-realist view of them, in the light of which their nature is determined by our specificatory capabilities. The role of the theory of descriptions in pointing towards a solution to the paradoxes is to sustain the position that classes are not nameable, and thus to suggest an anti-realist view of classes in the light of which the formation restrictions of the kind proposed in RT would seem more plausible.

As I have said, ST alone suffices to block the Russell paradox. It remains to determine whether RT blocks the semantic paradoxes.

8   Does the ramified theory block the semantic paradoxes?

The Ramified Theory not only blocks the known logical and semantic paradoxes, but is demonstrably consistent (Copi 91).

The notion that Russell's orders were relevant to such paradoxes [sc. semantic ones] is not one that I know how to make plausible while maintaining a distinction between attributes and open sentences (Quine, *Set Theory* 384).

The truth is, as I shall argue in this section, that Copi overestimates and Quine underestimates the power of RT: it blocks some but not all of the paradoxes usually classified as semantic.

In arguing for the power of RT, Russell's procedure is informal: he uses informal analogues of the formation restrictions of RT in ordinary English, and claims that these prevent the expression in English of the paradoxes. I shall for the most part follow this informal approach.

Russell also draws on a further hierarchy, that of propositions. He gives the following rule for deriving it from the hierarchy of properties discussed in the last section: the order of a proposition is greater by one than that of the highest-order variable in the sentence which expresses it (*PM* 55). In practice he exploits only part of the structure of this hierarchy. When he discusses the paradoxes, he takes it that the lowest order of propositions is that involving no quantification over propositions, and that a proposition of order $n > 0$ is one involving quantification over propositions of order $n-1$ and involving no quantification over propositions of order greater than $n-1$.

Russell takes it that a consequence of this hierarchy is that 'true' and 'false' are systematically ambiguous. I discuss one of his detailed arguments for this position later in this section (p. 324 and note 16).

Let us see, in Russell's own words, how he applies this apparatus to the Epimenides.

> The word 'false' is ambiguous, and . . . , in order to make it unambiguous, we must specify the order of falsehood, or, what comes to the same thing, the order of the proposition to which falsehood is ascribed. We also saw that, if p is a proposition of the nth order, a proposition in which p occurs as an apparent variable is not of the nth order, but of a higher order. Hence the kind of truth or falsehood which can belong to the statement 'there is a proposition p which I am affirming and which has falsehood of the nth order' is truth or falsehood of a higher order than the nth. Hence the statement of Epimenides does not fall within its own scope, and therefore no contradiction emerges (*PM* 62).

My analysis of the Epimenides was given in terms of utterances, so let us suppose for the moment that these can be identified with propositions. Then, in order to obey the restrictions, U will have to be recast to something of the form:

U': All Cretan utterances occurring before t and of order not greater than Ω are false.

Likewise, (a) and (c) will have to be recast along these lines:

(a') U' is a Cretan utterance of order $\Omega + 1$.

(c') All Cretan utterances distinct from U' and occurring before t and of order not greater than Ω are false.

The first part of the argument for the contradiction now fails. We suppose that all Cretan utterances occurring before t and of order not greater than Ω are false. But since (by (a')) U' is of order $\Omega + 1$, this supposition fails to entail that U' is false. Russell's RT thus successfully blocks the Epimenides, if one can identify utterances with propositions.

However, it would seem that the Epimenides can be reconstructed in other ways, for example, in terms of sentence-types: U'' is the sentence-type of which a token occurs on the next line:

$(\forall s, p, t)(($ sentence-type (s) & Cretan (p) & $t < \alpha$ & tokens $(p, s, t)) \rightarrow$ $\sim$ true $(s, p, t))$.

Here 'true (ζ, ζ, θ)' expresses a relation between sentence-types, persons and times. (No doubt a fuller relativization is in general required, but this is inessential for present purposes.) The following appear to be consistent:

(a'') Cretan (Epimenides) & tokens (Epimenides, U'', w) & sentence-type (U'').

(b'') $w < \alpha$.

(c'') $(\forall s, p, t)(($ sentence-type (s) & Cretan (p) & $t < \alpha$ & tokens (p, s, t) & $(p \neq$ Epimenides v $w \neq t$ v $s \neq U'')) \rightarrow \sim$ true $(s, p, t))$.

However, suppose that $(\forall s, p, t)(($ sentence-type (s) & Cretan (p) & $t < \alpha$ & tokens $(p, s, t)) \rightarrow \sim$ true $(s, p, t))$. (Call this the Supposition.) Then by instantiation:

(sentence-type (U'') & Cretan (Epimenides) & $w < \alpha$ & tokens (Epimenides, U'', w)) $\rightarrow \sim$ true $(U''$, Epimenides, w).

(a'') and (b'') give the antecedents of the conditional, so by modus ponens: $\sim$ true $(U''$, Epimenides, w). In other words, U'', as tokened by Epimenides at w, is not true. Since in uttering U'' at w Epimenides states the Supposition, the falsity of U'' entails the falsity of the Supposition, which must therefore be rejected. Now suppose that the negation of the Supposition obtains, i.e. that $(\exists s, p, t)(($ sentence-type (s) & Cretan (p) & $t < \alpha$ & tokens (p, s, t) & true $(s, p, t))$. Together with (c'') this yields: true (Epimenides, U'', w). But this in turn yields the Supposition, since the Supposition is what Epimenides asserts by tokening U'' at w. Hence the negation of the Supposition, which we are currently assuming, must be rejected. Hence, in classical logic, the Supposition both obtains and does not.

322

When I described the hierarchy of properties required to set up RT, I stressed that the consequent ascription of indices to expressions attached to them in use, rather than as objects. Hence on the face of it there is no way to apply RT to block the present version of the Epimenides: for it seems that to quantify over a certain collection of sentences (as in U'' and (c'')) is not to use any of these sentences. Nor would it be satisfactory for Russell simply to stipulate that there is to be a hierarchy of sentence-types, as well as the hierarchies of properties and propositions (or simply to stipulate that sentence-types are propositions). For although this would have the desired result of making U'' of higher order than any of the sentence-types over which it quantifies, it would sever the connection between RT and its philosophical rationale. For this rests on taking an anti-realist view of the entities in the relevant hierarchy, and at first sight it is hard to see how this could sensibly be done in the case of sentence-types.

A defender of Russell might seek to turn this difficulty by identifying sentence-types with properties, and in this way trying to use the hierarchy of properties to block paradoxes like the Epimenides. (There is no hint of this line of argument in Russell's own discussions.) The first step might be to identify sentence-types with classes of equiform tokens, as Russell himself does in *IMT* (22). (This is not satisfactory as it stands, since distinct untokened sentence-types will be identified with the null class and thus with each other, but let us ignore this problem.) Now, by Russell's no-class theory, talk of classes is parsed into talk of properties. The properties in question in the case of sentence-types will all be properties of individuals (tokens), and so will all be of a single *type* (in the sense of RT). But the defender I have in mind claims that the relevant properties will not be all of the same *order*. For, it will be claimed, if a sentence-type s contains quantification over sentence-types a, b, c ..., then the property with which s is identified will involve quantification over the properties with which a, b, c ... are identified, so that the s-property will be of higher-order than any of the a-, b-, c- ... properties. Then names and variables for sentence-types will, by RT, have different orders. Thus the Epimenides will be blocked in essentially the way already discussed. If the variable 's' in the Supposition is of order Ω, then U'', since it contains 's', will be of order at least $\Omega + 1$, and thus will not be a legitimate replacement for 's' in the step of instantiation.

I have a number of doubts about the adequacy of this defence. For example, it might be suggested that sentence-types will be identified with such properties as that of consisting of an occurrence of '(' followed by an occurrence of '$\forall$', followed by an occurrence of ')' followed by an occurrence of '(' ... ; and this sort of property will not have a high order, even if the sentences which possess it contain high-order quantifiers. However, it may be that Russell can be defended further, along the suggested lines. I leave this issue open.

From the point of view of determining whether or not RT is adequate to block the semantic paradoxes, the issue has little importance. The reason is that we can easily reconstruct the Epimenides in terms of sentence-tokens rather than sentence-types. We need only read 'sentence-token' for 'sentence-type' in the account just given, and derelativize the truth-predicate. Sentence-tokens are individuals, disturbances in the air or particular marks on paper, so all are of lowest type and order, so there is no scope for the formation restrictions of RT. Nor could this difficulty be overcome by inventing a hierarchy of sentence-tokens. For a hierarchy of individuals, physical events or things, would be an absurdity within any framework at all like Russell's.

Various remarks need to be made about this state of affairs. First of all, current orthodoxy, deriving from Tarski, would seek to avoid the semantic paradoxes by the notion of a hierarchy of languages, arranged in such a way that no language contained a truth-predicate applying to its own sentences. This theory will avoid the construction of the Epimenides in terms of sentence-tokens, since the truth-predicate will have to be relativized to a language, and thus U'' cannot belong to the language the other Cretans speak. Now surely Russell's own hierarchy of truth and falsehood ought to secure just this result; and, if so, this shows that there is something wrong with my claim that RT does not block the sentence-token version of the Epimenides.

It is certainly correct that *if* Russell can be granted the hierarchy of truth and falsehood, he can block the sentence-token version of the Epimenides. But he thought to derive the hierarchy of truth and falsehood from the hierarchy of propositions.[16] If, however, we see truth as a predicate of sentence-tokens, there is no hierarchy from which Russell can derive the hierarchy of truth and falsehood, for there is no hierarchy of individuals. The present criticism of Russell's RT should thus be disjunctive: either it permits a semantic paradox, or else it consists of two quite disparate parts which Russell failed to distinguish: the restrictions on formation stated in the last section, together with a hierarchy of truth and falsehood.

In fact, since a criticism similar to the present one can be made

---

[16] The derivation is as follows (*PM* 41–2). For any propositional function, it is significant to assert all its values. Hence '$(\forall p)$(false (p))' is significant. Since, by the hierarchy of propositions, this cannot be quantification over all propositions, the significance range of 'false' must fall short of being all propositions. Equiform predicates applying to higher-order propositions must be semantically distinct. When sentence-tokens are thought of as truth-bearers, the analogous premise would be absurd, even if we accept the conclusion, for it would rule out such commonplaces as that all sentence-tokens are individuals.

about some of the other semantic paradoxes, Russell will have to append to RT not merely a hierarchy of truth and falsehood, but also a hierarchy of naming and denoting. Consider the Berry paradox. The key quantification here is in the definition of 'ζ is namable' as 'there is an English phrase which denotes ζ'. If we think here of phrase-types, then we have the possibility of the same sort of defence as the one just discussed. It will be claimed that phrase-types are properties, and so are compartmentalized into orders by RT. Then 'the least integer not namable in fewer than nineteen syllables' will be of higher-order than the order used to define 'namable', so that it will fail to show that there is a phrase-type *of the relevant order* which denotes the least integer not namable in fewer than nineteen syllables. Once again, there is no need for us to determine whether or not this defence is sound. For the inadequacy of RT to this paradox is sufficiently shown by the fact that it can be reconstructed in terms of phrase-tokens. Then it will be blocked neither by RT nor even, in default of further analysis, by RT in conjunction with the hierarchy of truth and falsehood. A hierarchy of denoting is needed.

Thus RT without the hierarchies of truth, falsehood and denoting is inadequate to block the paradoxes. On the other hand, once we have the hierarchies of truth, falsehood and denoting, etc., there seems to be no need for the hierarchies of properties which characterized RT, if our only thought is to block the semantic paradoxes.

Not only is RT too permissive, it can also be argued that it is too restrictive, particularly concerning its ban on regarding such sentences as 'Everything A says is false' as meaningful. Such a sentence may be uttered in circumstances in which no paradox arises. Alternatively, it may be uttered in unfavourable circumstances, which lead to paradox, for example, if one of the things A said was that everything the utterer of the sentence just mentioned says is true. So it looks as if an adequate theory should not restrict the formation of every sentence which could lead to paradox, for the paradoxes do not show that when an utterance of such a sentence does not lead to paradox the sentence is none the less meaningless. Rather, one might look for a theory which would have as a consequence that nothing is said by a meaningful sentence if it is uttered under circumstances which threaten paradox. (Cf. Kripke, 'Outline of a Theory of Truth'.)

9 The vicious-circle principle

It is important to observe that the vicious-circle principle is not itself the solution of the vicious-circle paradoxes, but merely the result which a theory must yield if it is to afford a solution of them.

It is necessary, that is to say, to construct a theory of expressions containing apparent variables which will yield the vicious-circle principle as an outcome. It is for this reason that we need a reconstruction of logical first principles, and cannot rest content with the mere fact that the paradoxes are due to vicious circles (*EA* 205).

By the time of *PM* this insistence on arguments for the vicious-circle principle (VCP) independent of its power to block the paradoxes is greatly attenuated. There, Russell contents himself with the remark that, in addition to blocking the paradoxes, the VCP also 'has a certain consonance with common sense which makes it inherently credible' (*PM* 37). The 'consonance' later suggested appears to be located in the same place as the 'reconstruction' earlier promised: the theory of quantification. The connection is this: the VCP proscribes certain totalities as illegitimate, and the paradoxes supposedly flow from attempts to quantify over these illegitimate totalities.

The plan of this section is as follows: (*i*) I shall start by giving an exposition of the VCP, and I shall suggest that in reality there are two distinguishable principles; (*ii*) the first of these, proscribing certain kinds of *totality*, is, I shall argue, open to a number of criticisms; (*iii*) the second principle, proscribing certain kinds of *definition*, may, if suitably restricted, be regarded as the expression of a kind of constructivist programme in mathematics; (*iv*) finally, I shall consider the connections between the VCP and, on the one hand, the paradoxes, and, on the other hand, the theory of quantification.

(*i*) Gödel has suggested that we can distinguish three versions of the VCP in Russell's writings ('Russell's Mathematical Logic' 135). Thus:

VCP I: (*a*) Whatever involves *all* of a collection must not be one of the collection (*PM* 37; *ML* 63); (*b*) Whatever involves an apparent variable must not be among the possible values of that variable (*EA* 198; *ML* 75).

VCP II: (*a*) If, provided a collection had a total, it would have members only definable in terms of that total, then the said collection has no total (*PM* 37; *ML* 63); (*b*) No totality can contain members defined in terms of itself (*ML* 75).

VCP III: Given any set of objects such that, if we suppose the set to have a total, it will contain members which presuppose this total, then such a set cannot have a total. By saying that a set has 'no total', we mean, primarily, that no significant statement can be made about 'all its members' (*PM* 37).

The basis of Gödel's tripartite division is the different relation between the entities and the totalities from which they are excluded: entities may *involve* (VCP I), be *definable only in terms of* (VCP II) or *presuppose* (VCP III) the relevant totalities. However, I can find no corresponding clear differentiation in Russell: he seems to use these three expressions more or less indifferently.

On the other hand, one can, I think, detect in the quoted formulations, as also in Russell's discussions, *two* distinct principles: one concerned quite generally with totalities and quantification over them, the other concerned more specifically with certain kinds of definition. The more general principle, expressed by both VCP I and VCP III, apparently blocks quantification over certain collections under all circumstances. The narrower principle, expressed by VCP II, restricts the block to the special circumstance in which one is attempting to provide a definition. It is obvious from the outset that the narrower principle is weaker than the wider one, and so, in particular, that the former does not entail the latter. What may be reprehensible or viciously circular in a definition may be quite acceptable in other contexts.

(*ii*) Considering first the wider principle, one of the collections which Russell takes to be illegitimate under all circumstances is that of all properties, and this leads to the proscription of unrestricted predicate quantification. It is not entirely obvious how this proscription is extracted from the VCP. For example, a proposition to the effect that $(\forall\varphi)$ (. . . φ . . .) is not itself a property. So it does not matter that, since it involves *all* of the collection of properties, it is not among the collection.

The required connection is as follows. Russell does successfully show that the VCP ensures that there is no such property as that of having every property, for such a property would both involve, and also be among, a certain collection, which is what the VCP declares impossible (cf. *PM* 49). Now if we allow that there is unrestricted predicate quantification, there would be a proposition of the form $(\forall\varphi)(\ldots a \ldots \varphi \ldots)$. But it follows from this that there would be a property $(\forall\varphi)(\ldots \hat{x} \ldots \varphi \ldots)$, in violation of the VCP. Hence the VCP rules out unrestricted predicate quantification.

A further illegitimate totality is that of all propositions. This raises no new issues of principle.

One might accept some hierarchy of properties without accepting RT. For example, Russell's hierarchy is finite in the sense that only finite numbers index orders, whereas there seems nothing in the VCP to rule out transfinite orders. (However, transfinite orders *are* ruled out if ramification is seen as stemming not just from the VCP but from the coherence of substitutional predicate quantification.)

Even if one accepts the proscription of unrestricted predicate quantification which flows from the wider version of the VCP, other of its consequences, or apparent consequences, are clearly unacceptable. In some sense, the tallest man in the regiment 'involves' all the men in the regiment, but this does not prove that he is not a member of the regiment (cf. Ramsey 41). Likewise, the tallest man in the regiment in some sense 'presupposes' the regiment, but this does not mean that the regiment has 'no total' or that we cannot quantify over all its members. Thus, in default of further elucidation and restriction of the notions of involvement and presupposition, the VCP is plainly false. It is not hard to guess how these notions ought to be restricted, if my earlier suggestions are accepted. An entity will involve a certain collection if there is quantification over this collection in the canonical specification of the entity (cf. pages 285–6 above). However, it cannot be said that any such elucidation is to be found explicitly in Russell's writings.

There are two further criticisms to be made. One is that in presenting and discussing the VCP Russell sometimes gives the impression that he thinks that all forms of self-reference are to be proscribed. This is suggested in, for example, *EA* (196 *n*. 3), where he associates the VCP with a remark of Occam's, and in *PM* (61) where he claims that the common characteristic of the paradoxes is 'self-reference or reflexiveness'. But it is certainly a mistake to suppose that all forms of self-reference are illegitimate, as is strikingly shown, in a formal way, by Gödel's work: his incompleteness proof essentially involves self-referential sentences.

Secondly, there is much in Russell's discussion of the VCP to suggest that corresponding to every quantifier there must be a *set* or *class* of entities over which it ranges (see especially VCP III). This is what Russell sometimes relies on to justify the move from 'there is no set of all the Xs' to '"all Xs" is insignificant'. The underlying assumption, though shared by those who suppose that if there is a coherent semantic account of a language there is a coherent model-theoretic account, stands in need of justification. On a naïve reading, Cantor's result that, since every set is less numerous than its power set, there is no set having everything as a member, is stated by using a quantifier ranging over absolutely everything, and thus by one to which no set corresponds. The naïve view may be mistaken; but if this is so it should be proved and not assumed. (Like Russell, I make no distinction between 'class' and 'set' (cf. above, page xii). It may well be that this distinction must be made for an adequate account of the difficulty under discussion.)

(*iii*) Like VCP I and VCP III, VCP II, overtly concerned with definition rather than with totalities or quantification in general, can easily be interpreted so as to make it obviously false. The tallest man in the regiment is a counter-example to one reading of VCP II(*b*), and the electron now closest to the centre of mass of the solar system is a counter-example to the same reading of VCP II(*a*). The reading involves taking 'define' as 'characterize', and, in the second counter-example, taking the modal qualification as relative to our current human powers. However, if we abandon VCP II(*b*), and strengthen our interpretation of the modal qualification so that it has the import that the entities in question are those that can *in principle* only be defined in the relevant way, then we have in effect a restriction of the VCP to those things we view anti-realistically. An entity we view realistically is one for which we could in principle introduce a name. An entity we view anti-realistically is one for which we think this does not hold, so that our way of specifying the entity forms part of its essence. If the VCP is taken as thus restricted, it is surely correct: for an entity fit to be construed anti-realistically is one that can enter our thought and talk only through a definition, and that definition cannot without circularity quantify over the entity defined, for this would be to presuppose that it had already been introduced by some other means. What is problematical is not whether VCP II is true of all entities properly construed in the anti-realistic fashion, but whether there are any such entities.

We have already seen that a case can be made out for the claim that properties fall into this category. But what of classes? On Russell's no-class theory, there is no further question about classes, once the question about properties has been settled. But this situation puts a great deal of pressure on the no-class theory; for on the reality of classes opinion is deeply divided.

Russell's position about the nature of classes can be seen as closely allied with what is now often called 'constructivism'. This is the position that the right procedure in mathematics is to allow oneself a denumerable infinity of initial entities (Russell's individuals), but permit classes only to the extent that they can be constructed in a step-by-step fashion. In general, the warrant for the existence of a non-initial entity is that it can be defined in terms of entities already constructed. So if X is to be defined in terms of all the Ys it must not, on this view, and as the VCP II insists, be numbered among the Ys. Russell's construction is somewhat more indirect, since the classes are in effect constructed by constructing properties, but the same principles apply.

The point can be put another way. Let us say that something is *impredicative* if it involves quantification over a domain to which it belongs. (The expression 'impredicative' must be carefully distinguished from the expression 'non-predicative'. The latter is the contradictory of 'predicative' in the sense in which this occurs in RT; a definition occurs on page 319 above. Non-predicative properties are consistent with RT, though the Axiom of Reducibility deprives them of much interest. According to Russell, there could not be impredicative properties.) The notion of *involvement* could do with some refinement. We could rely on our earlier discussion, and say that an entity, x, involves quantification over a domain to which it belongs if the canonical specification of x contains a quantifier ranging over a collection of objects which includes x. For our present purposes, however, there is no need to rely on this idea. It will be enough to say that a class is impredicative if it cannot be specified by the primitives of our system except by a definition involving quantification over a domain to which it belongs. In the presence of the no-class theory, VCP II can be seen as entailing that there are no impredicative classes, in virtue of its consequence that there are no impredicative properties. But this consequence can well be challenged.

Indeed, the tradition of classical class theory, from Cantor on, freely admits impredicative classes, and though steps must be taken to avoid the Russell paradox, there are well-known systems of impredicative class theory in which no inconsistency can be found, despite extensive investigations. This shows that the threat of paradox alone is insufficient to motivate the denial of impredicative entities, and more generally that justification is required for the denial. As Gödel points out (136), if classes exist independently of our activities, there is no more absurdity in supposing that we can only specify some of them impredicatively than there is in supposing that there are some soldiers and some electrons we can specify only in this way.

Although a constructivist attitude is deeply embedded in Russell's philosophy, I have not discovered the sorts of argument about the relationship between reality and knowledge which could be used to support it. I shall refrain from embarking on this very difficult, though important, issue, and will instead mention a well-known difficulty into which Russell was led by his constructivist ban on impredicative classes. This is that the ban made it impossible to recapture certain standard results in analysis without introducing the unwarranted Axiom of Reducibility, which in effect undermines the very constructivism we have been discussing. This will be discussed in the next section.

However, it should not be supposed that the ban on impredicative classes, or adherence to a suitable version of the VCP, inevitably makes analysis impossible. Recent work by Feferman shows that it is possible to recapture the standard results in analysis in a system which avoids impredicative classes.[17]

(*iv*) Does the VCP isolate the common essence of the paradoxes? The fact that impredicative specifications occur in systems which, so far as is known, are consistent, for example in classical set theory, already shows that the VCP does not identify a feature which always leads to paradox. The fact that there appear to be paradoxes not involving quantification suggests that not all paradoxes have the feature isolated by the VCP. For example, 'This sentence is false', used self-referentially, or the version of the Grelling based on the following definitional schema

$$\text{Het}(`\varphi') =_{\text{df}} \sim \varphi(`\varphi')$$

lead to paradox but, at least on the surface, do not involve quantification. Appearances may be deceptive: demonstratives might be analysed by the theory of descriptions, and quotations might be analysed in a way which introduces quantification (cf. Copi 89ff.). But these further analyses have to be provided and argued for, and they are not to be found in Russell.

More importantly, how does the VCP even begin to look as if it puts its finger on the source of the Russell paradox? For in Russell's analysis that arises in effect through allowing a function to be argument to itself, and on this point the VCP seems at first sight to have nothing to·say.

None the less, Russell tries to extract the self-inapplicability of a function from the VCP via the premise that 'a function is not well-defined unless all its values are already well-defined' (*PM* 39). (I shall leave 'function' ambiguous between 'open sentence' and 'property', though on occasion I offer variant readings in brackets.) A 'value' of a function results from it by replacing the variables (filling the gaps) by names (objects) to yield a sentence (proposition). Thus, according to Russell, ' "φx" *ambiguously denotes* φa, φb, φc, etc., *where* φa, φb, φc, etc., *are the various values of* "φx" ' (*PM* 39). The upshot is supposed to be that ' "φx" only has a well-defined meaning . . . if the objects φa, φb, φc, etc., are well-defined' (*PM* 39). But if 'φx' occurred as an argument in one of its values, this would be impossible. Hence a function can be meaningful only if it cannot occur as argument to itself. Putting it in terms of the VCP, a function denotes some one of the totality of its values: 'hence this totality cannot contain any

---

[17] Feferman's work is a contribution to what is called 'predicative' analysis. There is the gravest risk of terminological confusion: in Feferman's usage 'predicative' means not what I, following Russell, have meant, but what I would express by 'non-impredicative'. See also above, page 330.

members which involve the function, since, if it did, it would contain members involving the totality, which, by the vicious-circle principle, no totality can do' (*PM* 39).

Suppose that one could understand an expression denoting a function only if one already understood every value of the function. Then Russell's case is made. For if a function's values included '$\varphi(\varphi\hat{x})$', and one could understand '$\varphi\hat{x}$' only if one had already come to understand every value of 'φx', then one could understand '$\varphi\hat{x}$' only if one already understood '$\varphi\hat{x}$', which is another way of saying that one could not come to understand '$\varphi\hat{x}$'. But Russell himself quite rightly denies the premise on which this argument is based:

> A function can be apprehended without its being necessary to apprehend its values severally and individually. If this were not the case, no function could be apprehended at all, since the number of values (true and false) of a function is necessarily infinite and there are necessarily possible arguments with which we are unacquainted (*PM* 39–40).

He goes on to offer what could be regarded as a weaker version of the rejected premise:

> What is necessary is not that the values should be given individually and extensionally, but that the totality of the values should be given intensionally, so that, concerning any assigned object, it is at least theoretically determinate whether or not the said object is a value of the function (*PM* 40).

But this weaker version, so far as I can understand it, will not support the argument. There is nothing *indeterminate* about the stipulation that any result of putting an expression fit to occupy name position in place of 'x' yields a value of 'φx', and that '$\varphi\hat{x}$' occupies name position. The stipulation may lead to paradox, or make it impossible to give a coherent semantic account; but that is another matter, and not the source of Russell's present argument.

Because of his carelessness about use and mention, it is worth getting a possible confusion out of the way. Since an open sentence (predicate) cannot occupy name position, there is no question of treating as sentences such expressions as '$\varphi(\varphi x)$' (respectively '$\varphi(\varphi\xi)$'). But this is for a trivial grammatical reason, and has nothing to do with the recurrence of 'φ'.

Once this is set aside, it is quite unclear, apart from the threat of paradox, why an open sentence (property) should not be ascribed to itself. At least there is no vicious circularity, for we could master the predicate in straightforward applications, and then extend this mastery to self-application. In other words, self-application is plainly not an application thanks to which alone we can define, or come to master, an open sentence. If there is something wrong with such sentences as '"x is an open sentence" is an open sentence' or '($\hat{x}$ is not a man) is not a man' it is not that the self-application makes them incomprehensible. On the contrary, we think we know enough about the meaning of these sentences to pronounce both of them true. If we are mistaken in all this, it is because we have unwittingly subscribed to a principle which leads to paradox. But that is another matter. Russell was supposedly applying the VCP to yield the banishment of self-application. Thus this part of his argument is wholly unconvincing.

I conclude this section by summarizing its main claims. The VCP is best seen as advocating constructivism concerning properties, propositions and, given the no-class theory, classes. Concerning properties and propositions this claim seems to me very plausible, though it requires elaborate argument which it does not receive from Russell. In the case of classes, the claim must have a more programmatic aspect, in view of the existence of, and as far as is known consistency of, impredicative class theory and analysis. Even were the non-existence of impredicative classes, properties and propositions granted, the VCP is still insufficient to yield the precise nature of the hierarchy of orders (since it does not justify the exclusion of transfinite orders); it comes nowhere near to justifying the hierarchy of types (in view of the failure of the argument from the VCP to the non-self-applicability of properties); and it does not isolate the single common feature of the paradoxes, for there is no such feature.

10 The Axiom of Reducibility

Russell introduced the Axiom of Reducibility because without it substantial mathematical results – 'a great mass of reasoning' (*PM* 56) – appeared to be incapable of proof, or even formulation, within RT.

One example which Russell gives of this problem is that one wants to define an inductive number as one possessing *every* hereditary property of 0 (cf. page 305 above). However, this definition is illegitimate in RT in view of the unrestricted quantification over properties. Nor is there an easy remedy, for if we insert a restriction to even a very high order there would still be the possibility that some yet higher-order property is possessed by 0 and is hereditary for + 1 and yet is lacked by some entity which, on this modified definition, is an inductive number. In short, it seems that however we restrict the order of the relevant properties we shall not have a definition answering to our purposes.

There is a further example of the undue restrictiveness of RT in

333

connection with the least upper bound (LUB) theorem. This asserts that every collection a of real numbers which has an upper bound has an LUB: that is, a number than which no member of a is greater, but which is not greater than any other number than which no member of a is greater. When real numbers are developed, as in *PM*, as classes of rationals, an LUB of a class a of reals is identified with a set of rationals each of which belongs to a member of a. Since there is quantification over the members of a in the specification of the LUB it must be of at least as high order as a, and this prevents it being a member either of a or of the complement of a. The result is that even though the existence of an LUB is provable, it cannot serve the purposes for which it is required in analysis.

Cantor's proof that every class, a, is less numerous than its power class, Pa (i.e. the class of all its sub-classes), serves as a further example of the difficulties caused by the restrictiveness of RT.[18] This is a proof which one would wish to preserve. But in RT the sub-class β which supposedly provides a counter-example to the similarity of a with Pa cannot belong to Pa: for the specification of β involves quantifying over the domain Pa, and thus its order is higher than that of any member of Pa.

Russell had a further cause for dissatisfaction with RT: it does not allow the definition of the identity of a and b in terms of their possessing all the same properties, in view of the illegitimate unrestricted quantification over properties.

All these difficulties are supposedly resolved by the Axiom of Reducibility, which may be symbolically expressed (*PM* 56):

$$(\forall\varphi)(\exists\psi)(\forall x)(\varphi x \leftrightarrow \psi! x).$$

This purports to say that for every property there is a coextensive predicative property, where a property is predicative iff it has the lowest order consistent with its type (cf. page 319 above). However, this is, on the face of it, doubly illegitimate, for it involves quantification over properties which is restricted neither to type nor order: a quantification of just the sort supposedly proscribed by the VCP.

Russell was aware of this difficulty, and tried to circumvent it by means of the claim that 'We can speak of *any* property of x, but not of

[18] Suppose there is a one-one correlation R between a and Pa. Consider the sub-class β of a having as members just those members of a which do not belong to their R-correlate in Pa. If β has an R-correlate, x, in a, then, since the members of β are *only* those things not belonging to their R-correlate, x does not belong to β; but if x does not belong to β then, since the members of β are *all* those things not belonging to their R-correlate, x belongs to β. So the supposition that β has an R-correlate in a must be rejected, so there is no one-one correlation between a and Pa. Since Pa is obviously at least as numerous as a, it follows that it must be more numerous.

all properties' (*ML* 68; the claim is not made in *PM*). This is nothing but confusion. For 'any', so far as one can determine from Russell's discussion, is used to mark an occurrence of a universal quantifier having wide scope, and so its unrestricted use must be as illegitimate as that of 'all' (cf. Bostock 30–1). Rather, one does best to regard the so-called Axiom as in reality an axiom schema, which yields an infinity of genuine axioms by the imposition of indices on the variables of predicate quantification. Thus each genuine axiom will have the type and order restrictions RT requires. (This schematic interpretation is suggested by Russell's remarks in *PM* 55.)

Before attempting an assessment of the Axiom, I shall consider some of its applications. In the case of mathematical induction, it is supposed to have the consequence that the scruples we felt about the adequacy of the definition of an inductive number, once a restriction is placed on the order of the hereditary properties, can be swept away; and not by selecting some very high order of hereditary property, but rather the lowest order consistent with the type of numbers. Applied to the LUB theorem, the Axiom means that the LUB does after all lie within the union of the bounded set of reals with its complement. For the property which determines the LUB has a coextensive one of low enough order to be of the same order as that of the property specifying the original bounded set. Applied to Cantor's proof, the Axiom means that the supposedly counter-exemplary sub-class β or α, though specified by a higher order property than that specifying any of the members of $P\alpha$, could have been specified by a property of low enough order for β to belong to $P\alpha$. In the case of identity, the Axiom assures us of the adequacy of the definition in terms of predicative properties:

$$x = y =_{\mathrm{df}} (\forall \varphi)(\varphi! x \rightarrow \varphi! y) \;(^*13\cdot01).$$

For any instance of 'φx & $\sim\varphi y$', at whatever order, will reduce to a predicative instance.

One of Russell's arguments in favour of the Axiom is that it is less strong than the assumption of the existence of classes (*PM* 58). The reason he gives is that the Axiom is entailed by the existence of classes. For if classes exist, then for any property $\varphi\hat{x}$ there is a class α of just those things having $\varphi\hat{x}$, and so there is a predicative property coextensive with $\varphi\hat{x}$; viz.: $\hat{x}$ belongs to α.

This argument is illuminating for its presupposition that any genuine entity can be named, where a name must be (at least) a simple and undefined expression. Without this presupposition, Russell's claim would be a gross *non sequitur*: for if the definition of 'α', as it occurs in 'x belongs to α', involved predicate quantification, we would have no right to assume that this predicate abstract is

335

predicative. We have already seen that we can distinguish a realist from a constructivist approach to properties on precisely this point. A constructivist will assert, and a realist will deny, that how we can specify properties enters into their identity. The same test can be used to distinguish constructivism from realism about classes. The realist will assert that how we can specify them has no bearing on their nature: in principle, each could be specified in a way uniform with the 'specification' of every other kind of thing, that is, by a name.

The Axiom of Reducibility runs sharply counter to the view which animated RT, and comes close to reintroducing a realist theory of classes. For, first, the Axiom asserts the existence of a property independently of whether or not we can specify it, which runs counter to the idea that we are to construct properties from the bottom up. And, second, the Axiom has it that any class which can be specified at all can be specified predicatively, which means that the whole hierarchy of non-predicative properties is irrelevant to mathematics. For classes, there will remain the hierarchy of types, but the Axiom in effect suppresses the hierarchy of orders, which in turn means that the ban on impredicative specification, though officially retained, is idle. The effect of the ban is that when we try in RT to construct an impredicative specification we end up with something at a higher order than the one we were aiming at. The Axiom assures us that there is a coextensive predicate at the order originally intended. Hence, so far as the question of what extensions there are is concerned, RT in the presence of the Axiom is no more restrictive than realism and the acceptance of impredicative classes.

Russell held that the Axiom is weaker than the assumption of classes. He gives no explicit argument for this view (cf. *PM* 58), but one may surmise that his thought is as follows: to 'assume' classes is not merely to accept that there are such things, but is also to take a realist view of their nature. However, the Axiom does not impose such a view on us. On the contrary, in the presence of the no-class theory, anti-realism about properties will leak through to classes, since the existence of the latter depends on the existence of the former. The argument may have some appeal, but it should not be allowed to obscure the measure of agreement between Russell and one who allows impredicative classes, and is thus committed to realism. Where the impredicativist sees a class, Russell must allow that there is some property with the corresponding extension. In the presence of the Axiom, Russell's anti-realism concerning classes is of an attenuated kind.

He never thought that the Axiom was self-evident, but in *PM* he held that there was none the less strong inductive evidence for it: 'the reasonings which it permits and the results to which it leads are all such as appear valid' (*PM* 59). Such ground is dangerous for a logicist, for it distracts attention from the key point that if logicism is to succeed the Axiom has to be a *logical* truth. No doubt all sorts of distinctively mathematical as opposed to logical propositions could be justified by the sort of argument just mentioned. But in the case of the Axiom, the proper premise would be that it leads only to *logical* truths, and this is plainly unavailable to Russell on pain of circularity.

In *IMP* (193) Russell states categorically that the Axiom is not a necessary truth, and that its inclusion in a logicist foundation was a mistake. He eliminates it in PM_2, in which the theory of types is simplified (in effect to ST) on lines suggested by Ramsey. The result, however, is a substantial loss to analysis: 'it seems that the theory of infinite Dedekindian and well-ordered series largely collapses, so that irrationals, and real numbers generally, can no longer be adequately dealt with. Also Cantor's proof that $2^n > n$ breaks down unless n is finite. Perhaps some further axiom, less objectionable than the Axiom of Reducibility, might give these results, but we have not succeeded in finding such an axiom' (PM_2 *xiv*). So Russell eliminates the Axiom only at the price of abandoning logicism.

Wittgenstein (*Tractatus* 6.1232–3), Ramsey (*Foundations* 57) and other writers have agreed with Russell in maintaining that the Axiom is not a necessary truth, but they do not give arguments for this assertion, and I cannot share their confidence in it. I think it is plausible to maintain that properties are necessary existents, so that assertions of the existence of properties are necessarily true, if true, and necessarily false otherwise. If this is right, the non-necessity of the Axiom entails its falsehood. (However, cf. Ramsey 57.) But is it non-necessary? What reason is there for thinking that it is metaphysically possible that new extensions should be introduced as one climbs the hierarchy of orders within a type? I do not know how to answer this question, so I shall content myself with some more modest comments.

(*i*) The *truth* of the Axiom does not touch the anti-realist view of properties which underpins RT. (It is not as if the Axiom claimed that a property which exists at any order *exists* at the predicative order.) However, to *assert* the Axiom squares ill with the anti-realist view, for one thereby asserts the existence of properties, without having the warrant that constructing them would provide.

(*ii*) I surmise that if there were a decisive refutation of impredicative class theory, the refutation could be extended to the Axiom. This is in virtue of the extent of agreement between the impredicativist and the defender of the Axiom. However, no such refutation seems to be in sight.

(*iii*) If the Axiom is true, and thus, on my view, necessarily true, it remains an open question whether or not it is a logical truth. One might seek to show that it is not, by selecting a domain of interpretation consisting of just one property, and that a non-predicative one. I can imagine the following reply on Russell's behalf: this would show as much about the logical truth of the Axiom as the selection of an interpretation in which '=' is assigned to the greater than relation would show about the logical truth of the law of identity; to hold the interpretation of the quantifiers constant is to interpret them over the hierarchy of orders, just as to hold the interpretation of '=' constant is to interpret is as identity. However, I shall not investigate this issue further.

(*iv*) The presence of the Axiom thwarts Russell's aim of *establishing* logicism by the system of *PM* (cf. *MPD* 74). For this aim involves *establishing* that the Axiom is a logical truth, and not only did Russell not do this, he came to think that it could not be done.

If one wished to draw together some of the main points of this chapter, one could do worse than reflect on two Axioms: of Reducibility and of Infinity. The Axiom of Reducibility must be understood against the background of the paradoxes and RT. It is a partial retraction of a metaphysical view (anti-realism about classes) in response to technical difficulties in analysis. Russell's Axiom of Infinity serves as a reminder that, in his system, even finite arithmetic requires an ontology which goes beyond that with which logic can be credited. The Axiom of Reducibility shows that Russell's brand of logicism has not been established; the Axiom of Infinity shows that it cannot be.

Bibliography*

(Entries in square brackets indicate editions to which page numbers in the text refer, where these differ from the edition first cited.)

Ayer, A. J., *Russell and Moore: The Analytical Heritage*, London, 1971.
Ayer, A. J., *Russell*, Fontana Modern Masters Series, London, 1972.
Benacerraf, Paul, 'What Numbers Could Not Be', *Philosophical Review*, 74, 1965.
Blackburn, Simon and Code, Alan, 'The Power of Russell's Criticism of Frege: "On Denoting" pp. 48–50', *Analysis*, 37, 1978.
Bogen, James, *Wittgenstein's Philosophy of Language*, London, 1972.
Boolos, George, 'On Second-Order Logic', *Journal of Philosophy*, 72, 1975.
Bostock, David, *Logic and Arithmetic: Natural Numbers*, Oxford, 1974.
Bouwsma, O. K., 'Descartes' Evil Genius', *Philosophical Review*, 58, 1949.
Bradley, F. H., *Appearance and Reality*, London, 1893 [second edition 1897].
Burge, Tyler, 'Reference and Proper Names', *Journal of Philosophy*, 70, 1973.
Carroll, Lewis, *Through the Looking-Glass, and What Alice Found There*, London, 1872.
Chihara, Charles S., *Ontology and the Vicious-Circle Principle*, Ithaca and London, 1973.
Copi, Irving M., *The Theory of Logical Types*, London, 1971.
Cresswell, M. J., *Logics and Languages*, London, 1973.
Davidson, Donald, 'Truth and Meaning', *Synthese*, 17, 1967.
Davidson, Donald, 'Action and Reaction', *Inquiry*, 13, 1970.
Davidson, Donald, 'In Defence of Convention T', in H. Leblanc, ed., *Truth, Syntax and Modality*, Amsterdam, 1973.
Davidson, Donald, 'The Method of Truth in Metaphysics', in Peter A. French, Theodore E. Uehling, Jr, and Howard K. Wettstein, eds, *Midwest Studies in Philosophy, Volume II: Studies in the Philosophy of Language*, Morris, USA, 1977.

---

* Only works cited are listed. For more comprehensive bibliographies see Schilpp (*op. cit.*) and Harry Ruja, 'A Selective, Classified Bertrand Russell Bibliography', in D. F. Pears, ed., *Bertrand Russell: A Collection of Critical Essays*, New York, 1972.

Davies, Martin K., 'Weak Necessity and Truth Theories', *Journal of Philosophical Logic*, 9, 1978.

De Long, Howard, *A Profile of Mathematical Logic*, Reading, Mass., USA, 1970.

Donnellan, Keith S., 'Reference and Definite Descriptions', *Philosophical Review*, 78, 1968.

Dummett, Michael, *Frege: Philosophy of Language*, London, 1973.

Eliot, T. S., 'Mr Apollinax', in *Collected Poems*, London, 1963.

Evans, Gareth, 'The Causal Theory of Names', *Aristotelian Society Supplementary Volume*, 47, 1973.

Evans, Gareth, 'Identity and Predication', *Journal of Philosophy*, 72, 1975.

Evans, Gareth, 'Semantic Structure and Logical Form', in Evans and McDowell, *op. cit.*

Evans Gareth, 'Pronouns, Quantifiers, and Relative Clauses', *Canadian Journal of Philosophy*, 7, 1977.

Evans, Gareth and McDowell, John (eds), *Truth and Meaning: Essays in Semantics*, Oxford, 1976.

Frege, Gottlob, *Begriffsschrift, eine der arithmetischen nachgebildete Formelsprache des reinen Denkens*, Halle, 1879 [translated by Terrell Ward Bynum in *Conceptual Notation and Related Articles*, Oxford, 1972].

Frege, Gottlob, *Die Grundlagen der Arithmetik. Eine logisch-mathematische Untersuchung über den Begriff der Zahl*, Breslau, 1884.

Frege, Gottlob, 'Über Begriff und Gegenstand', *Vierteljahrsschrift für wissenschaftliche Philosophie*, 16, 1892 ['On Concept and Object', in Peter Geach and Max Black, trans., *Translations from the Philosophical Writings of Gottlob Frege*, Oxford, 1966].

Frege, Gottlob, 'Über Sinn und Bedeutung', *Zeitschrift für Philosophie und philosophische Kritik*, 1, 1892 ['On Sense and Reference' in *ibid.*].

Frege, Gottlob, *Grundgesetze der Arithmetik*, 2 vols, Jena, 1893–1903.

Geach, Peter, 'A Program for Syntax', in Donald Davidson and Gilbert Harman, eds, *Semantics of Natural Language*, Dordrecht, 1972.

Gödel, Kurt, 'Russell's Mathematical Logic', in Schilpp (*q.v.*).

Goodman, Nelson, *Fact, Fiction and Forecast*, Indianapolis, USA, 1955 [second edition 1965].

Goodman, Nelson and Leonard, H., 'The Calculus of Individuals and Its Uses', *Journal of Symbolic Logic*, 5, 1940.

Grice, H. P., 'Meaning', *Philosophical Review*, 66, 1957.

Hardy, G. H., *Bertrand Russell and Trinity*, Cambridge, 1970.

Hatcher, W. S., *Foundations of Mathematics*, Philadelphia and London, 1968.

Henkin, Leon, 'Completeness in the Theory of Types', *Journal of Symbolic Logic*, 15, 1950.

Hornsby, Jennifer, 'Singular Terms in Contexts of Propositional Attitude', *Mind*, 86, 1977.

Hume, David, *A Treatise of Human Nature*, London, 1738.

Hume, David, *Enquiry Concerning Human Understanding*, London, 1748.

Kripke, Saul, 'Naming and Necessity', 1970, in Donald Davidson and Gilbert Harman, eds, *Semantics of Natural Language*, Dordrecht, 1972.

Kripke, Saul, 'Outline of a Theory of Truth', *Journal of Philosophy*, 72, 1975.

Kripke, Saul, 'Is There a Problem about Substitutional Quantification?', in Evans and McDowell, *op. cit.*

Kripke, Saul, 'Speaker's Reference and Semantic Reference', in Peter A. French, Theodore E. Uehling, Jr, and Howard K. Wettstein, eds, *Midwest Studies in Philosophy, Volume II: Studies in the Philosophy of Language*, Morris, USA, 1977.

Marsh, R. C. (ed.), *Logic and Knowledge*, London, 1956.

McDowell, John, 'On the Sense and Reference of a Proper Name', *Mind*, 86, 1977.

Moore, G. E., 'External and Internal Relations', 1919, in his *Philosophical Studies*, London and New York, 1922.

Nerlich, G., 'Presupposition and Entailment', *American Philosophical Quarterly*, 2, 1965.

Peacocke, C. A. B., 'Proper Names, Reference and Rigid Designation', in Simon Blackburn, ed., *Meaning, Reference and Necessity: New Studies in Semantics*, Cambridge, 1975.

Peacocke, C. A. B., 'What is a Logical Constant?', *Journal of Philosophy*, 73, 1976.

Pears, David F., *Bertrand Russell and the British Tradition in Philosophy*, London, 1967 [1968].

Plantinga, Alvin, *The Nature of Necessity*, Oxford, 1974.

Poincaré, H., 'Les Mathématiques et la Logique', *Revue de Métaphysique et de Morale*, 13–14, 1906.

Popper, Karl R., *The Logic of Scientific Discovery*, Vienna, 1934 (English language edition 1959 [1968]).

Quine, W. O., 'Two Dogmas of Empiricism' (1951), in his *From a Logical Point of View*, Cambridge, Mass. 1953.

Quine, W. O., 'Variables Explained Away', *Proceedings of the American Philosophical Society*, 103, 1960.

Quine, W. O., *Set Theory and Its Logic*, Cambridge, USA, 1963 [§§ 34–5 reprinted in E. D. Klemke, ed., *Essays on Bertrand Russell*, Chicago and London, 1971].

Quine, W. O., 'Ways of Paradox', in his *Ways of Paradox and Other Essays*, New York, 1966.

Quine, W. O., *Word and Object*, Cambridge, Mass., 1960.

Quine, W. O., *Philosophy of Logic*, Englewood Cliffs, N.J., 1970.

Ramsey, F. P., *The Foundations of Mathematics*, R. B. Braithwaite, ed., London and New York, 1931.

Robb, A. A., *A Theory of Time and Space*, London, 1913.

Russell, Bertrand:

German Social Democracy, London, New York, Bombay, 1896.

'On the Relations of Number and Quantity', *Mind*, 6, 1896.

An Essay on the Foundations of Geometry, Cambridge, 1897.

A Critical Exposition of the Philosophy of Leibniz: With an Appendix of Leading Passages, Cambridge, 1900 (*Leibniz*).

The Principles of Mathematics, London, 1903, second edn 1937 [1956] (*PofM*).

'On Denoting', *Mind*, 14, 1905 [in R. C. Marsh, *op. cit.*] (*OD*).

'Mathematical Logic as Based on the Theory of Types', *American Journal of Mathematics*, 30, 1908 [in R. C. Marsh, *op. cit.*] (*ML*).

Principia Mathematica, with Alfred North Whitehead, Cambridge, 1910–13 (*PM*), second edition 1925 [1950] (*PM₂*).

Philosophical Essays, London, New York, Bombay and Calcutta, 1910 (*PE*).

'Knowledge by Acquaintance and Knowledge by Description', *Proceedings of the Aristotelian Society*, 11, 1910–11 [in Russell's *Mysticism and Logic* (*q.v.*)] (*KAKD*).

The Problems of Philosophy, London, 1912 [Oxford Paperbacks, 1968] (*PP*).

'On the Notion of Cause', *Proceedings of the Aristotelian Society*, 13, 1912–13 [in Russell's *Mysticism and Logic* (*q.v.*)].

Our Knowledge of the External World as a Field for Scientific Method in Philosophy, Chicago and London, 1914, revised 1926 [1949] (*OKEW*).

'On the Nature of Acquaintance', *Monist*, 24, 1914 [in R. C. Marsh, *op. cit.*] (*NA*).

'The Relation of Sense-Data to Physics', *Scientia*, 4, 1914 [in Russell's *Mysticism and Logic* (*q.v.*)] (*RSP*).

'The Ultimate Constituents of Matter', *Monist*, 25, 1915 [in Russell's *Mysticism and Logic* (*q.v.*)] (*UCM*).

Principles of Social Reconstruction, London, 1916.

Mysticism and Logic, New York, Bombay, Calcutta and Madras, 1918 [paperback edition, London, 1963].

Roads to Freedom: Socialism, Anarchism and Syndicalism, London, 1918.

'The Philosophy of Logical Atomism', lectures delivered in London in 1918, *Monist*, 28, 1918 and 29, 1919 [in R. C. Marsh, *op. cit.*] (*PLA*).

Introduction to Mathematical Philosophy, London and New York, 1919 [1967] (*IMP*).

'On Propositions: What They Are and How They Mean', *Proceedings of the Aristotelian Society*, Supplementary Volume 2, 1919 [in R. C. Marsh, *op. cit.*] (*OP*).

The Analysis of Mind, London, 1921 [1971] (*Mind*).

Introduction to Wittgenstein's *Tractatus* (*q.v.*).

'Logical Atomism', in *Contemporary British Philosophy: Personal Statements*, First Series, London and New York, 1924 [in R. C. Marsh, *op. cit.*] (*LA*).

'Mind and Matter', *Nation and Athenaeum*, 37, 1925 [in Russell's *Portraits from Memory* (*q.v.*)].

The Analysis of Matter, London, 1927 [1959] (*Matter*).

An Outline of Philosophy, London, 1927.

Marriage and Morals, London and New York, 1929.

The Conquest of Happiness, London and New York, 1930.

An Inquiry into Meaning and Truth, London, 1940 (paperback edition, 1962 [1967]) (*IMT*).

'My Mental Development' and 'Reply to Criticisms' in P. A. Schilpp, ed., *The Philosophy of Bertrand Russell* (*q.v.*) (Schilpp).

A History of Western Philosophy, London, 1945, second edition, 1961.

'Whitehead and *Principia Mathematica*', *Mind*, 57 (1948).

Human Knowledge: Its Scope and Limits, London, 1948 (*HK*).

'Is Mathematics Purely Linguistic?', posthumously published in *EA* (*q.v.*).

Human Society in Ethics and Politics, London, 1954.

Common Sense and Nuclear Warfare, London, 1959.

Portraits From Memory, London, 1958 [Readers Union Edition].

'The Cult of "Common Usage"', in his *Portraits From Memory* (*q.v.*).

My Philosophical Development, London, 1959 [1969] (*MPD*).

Has Man a Future?, London, 1961.

War Crimes in Vietnam, London, 1967.

The Autobiography of Bertrand Russell, 3 vols, London, 1967–9 (*A*).

Essays in Analysis (1904–57), Douglas Lackey, ed., London, 1973 (*EA*).

Sainsbury, R. M., 'Semantics by Proxy', *Analysis*, 37, 1977.

Salmon, W. C., 'Russell on Scientific Inference *or* Will the Real Inductivist Please Stand Up?' in George Nakhnikian, ed., *Bertrand Russell's Philosophy*, London, 1974.

Schiffer, Stephen R., *Meaning*, Oxford, 1972.

Schilpp, P. A. (ed.), *The Philosophy of Bertrand Russell* (The Library of Living Philosophers), New York, 1944 [third edition, 1951].

Searle, John, 'Proper Names', *Mind*, lxvii, 1958 [in P. F. Strawson, ed., *Philosophical Logic*, Oxford, 1967].

Searle, John, 'Russell's Objections to Frege's Theory of Sense and Reference', *Analysis*, 18, 1958.

Skyrms, Brian, *Choice and Chance: An Introduction to Inductive Logic*, Encino, USA, 1975.

Stich, Stephen P., 'What Every Speaker Knows', *Philosophical Review*, 80, 1971.

Strawson, P. F., 'On Referring', *Mind*, lix, 1950 (in Irving M. Copi and James A. Gould, eds, *Introduction to Logical Theory*, London, 1952 [Paperback edn, 1967]).

Strawson, P. F., *Individuals: An Essay in Descriptive Metaphysics*, London, 1959.

Strawson, P. F., 'Is Existence Never a Predicate?', *Critica*, 1, 1967.

Strawson, P. F., *Subject and Predicate in Logic and Grammar*, London, 1974.

Strawson, P. F., 'Positions for Quantifiers', in Milton K. Munitz and Peter K. Unger, eds, *Semantics and Philosophy*, New York, 1974.

Watling, John, *Bertrand Russell*, Edinburgh, 1970.

Williams, Michael, *Groundless Belief*, Oxford, 1977.

Wittgenstein, Ludwig, *Tractatus Logico-Philosophicus*, 1921, translated by D. F. Pears and B. F. McGuinness, London, 1961.

Wittgenstein, Ludwig, *Philosophical Investigations*, Oxford, 1953.

Wittgenstein, Ludwig, *Philosophische Bemerkungen*, Frankfurt, 1964.

Index

A, xiii, 1, 3, 5, 274
acquaintance, principle of, 13, 20,
26–41, 44, 57–8, 76, 82, 83, 86, 87,
142, 143, 191, 195, 240; *see also*
knowledge; sense-data
ambiguity, 135; *see also* scope
analysis, philosophical, 14, 16ff., 27ff.,
218, 229, 235; *see also* unanalysable
anti-realism, 108, 117, 285, 286, 320,
329, 336
a priori knowledge, *see* knowledge
aspect, 244; *see also* sensibilia
atomism, logical, *see* construction; logic;
simple
Ayer, A. J., 48, 76, 99, 202, 221, 239, 248

belief: relational, 63–4; Russell's
analysis of, 12, 64, 141, 149, 156,
224–8; singular, 30–1, 60, 63–6
Benacerraf, Paul, 300
bivalence, 108, 117–19, 310–11
Blackburn, Simon, 106
Bogen, James, 50
Boolos, George, 276–7
Bostock, David, 301–2, 307, 335
Bouwsma, O. K., 190–1
Bradley, F. H., 2, 229, 232, 233–4
Burge, Tyler, 61

Cantor, Georg, 4, 12, 274, 328, 330, 334
Carroll, Lewis, 139
causal theory of names, 38
Chihara, Charles S., 314, 317
circumflexion, xii, 15, 23, 279ff.
class: class abstract, 296; class

membership ('∈'), xii, 296; impure,
306; manufactured, 167–8, 170, 176;
no-class theory, 293, 296, 298, 306,
316, 320, 329; v. set, xii
Code, Alan, 106
compresence, 269ff.
concepts (as meaning-relata), 17ff.
constituent, 26ff., 104, 145, 149, 275; *see
also* meaning-relatum
construction: contrasted with inference:
200–11; impure translational, 239–40;
logical, 6, 13–14, 25–6, 36, 47, 53, 162,
192, 200ff., 210–11, 218, 225–6,
236–71; pure translational, 240;
substitutional, 237; *see also* number
context, 114–16, 119–20, 127
continuity: sensible, 246ff.; spatio-
temporal, 251ff.
Copi, Irving M., 316, 317, 320–1, 331
Cresswell, M. J., 42

Davidson, Donald, 42, 149–53
Davies, Martin K., x, 80
Dedekind, J. W. R., 12
De Long, Howard, 273
denotation (contrasted with meaning in
Frege's theory), 100, 104–6, 117–18
denoting phrases, 17–20; *see also*
descriptions
Descartes, René, 162, 163, 181, 189–91
descriptions: attributive v. referential,
113, 122–6; entity invoking use of,
113, 116, 120, 121, 122–3, 125,
126–33; primary v. secondary
occurrences of, 67–8, 97; Russell's

345